Marcus, Aliza

Blood and belief: the PKK and the
Kurdish fight for independence

Blood and Belief

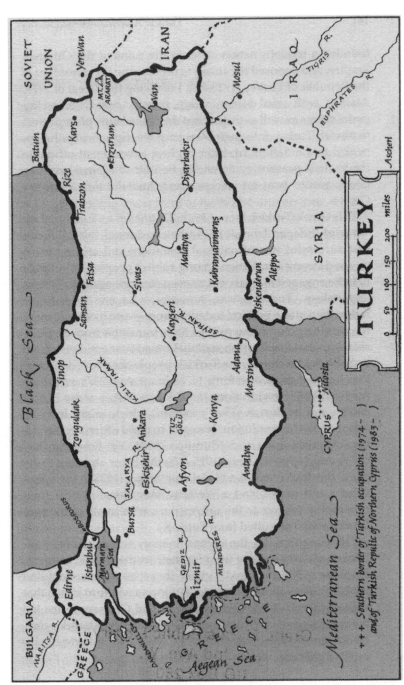

TURKEY

miles
0   50   100 150 200

+ + + Southern border of Turkish occupation (1974–)
and of Turkish Republic of Northern Cyprus (1983–)

BULGARIA

GREECE

SOVIET UNION

IRAN

IRAQ

SYRIA

Black Sea

Mediterranean Sea

Aegean Sea

Marmara Sea

CYPRUS

Nicosia

GREECE

MARITSA R.

Edirne

İstanbul

Bursa

İzmir

GEDIZ R.

MENDERES R.

BOSPORUS

DARDANELLES

SAKARYA R.

Eskişehir

Ankara

Afyon

Antalya

Konya

TUZ GÖLÜ

KIZIL IRMAK

Zonguldak

Sinop

Samsun

Fatsa

Sivas

Kayseri

SEYHAN R.

Adana

Mersin

İskenderun

Aleppo

Kahramanmaraş

Malatya

Diyarbakır

Erzurum

MT. ARARAT

Van

Trabzon

Rize

Batum

Kars

Yerevan

Mosul

TIGRIS R.

EUPHRATES R.

Aschen

Aliza Marcus

Blood and Belief

The PKK and the Kurdish
Fight for Independence

New York University Press • *New York and London*

NEW YORK UNIVERSITY PRESS
New York and London
www.nyupress.org

Frontispiece: Map from *Turkey: America's Forgotten Ally* by Dankwart A. Rustow (Council on Foreign Relations Press, 1987).

Library of Congress Cataloging-in-Publication Data
Marcus, Aliza.
Blood and belief : the PKK and the Kurdish fight for independence /
Aliza Marcus.
p. cm.
Includes bibliographical references and index.
ISBN-13: 978-0-8147-5711-6 (cloth : alk. paper)
ISBN-10: 0-8147-5711-1 (cloth : alk. paper)
1. Partiya Karkerên Kurdistanê—History. 2. Kurds—Turkey—
History—Autonomy and independence movements. 3. Turkey—
Ethnic relations.   I. Title.
DR435.K87M37 2007
956.6'703—dc22
2007007891

New York University Press books are printed on acid-free paper,
and their binding materials are chosen for strength and durability.

Manufactured in the United States of America
10 9 8 7 6 5 4 3 2 1

Contents

IV   Ocalan's Capture and After

A Note to Readers

This book is based on extensive interviews with former members of the Turkish Kurdish rebel group the PKK. These interviews enabled me to reconstruct the history of the PKK, track its guerrilla war, and explore the rise of a more radical, Kurdish nationalist sentiment in Turkey. At the same time, speaking with these former rebels and party officials gave me real insight into the group's internal functioning and what motivated so many young Kurdish men and women to join the PKK—a group denounced by the United States, Turkey, and much of Europe as a terrorist group. Along the way, I believe I have managed to explain not just the group's attraction for so many Kurds, but also what has kept people fighting despite hardships and misgivings and, finally, the capture of PKK leader Abdullah Ocalan.

There are some who will complain that this book places too much stock in information provided by former PKK members. They will argue this information is suspect, because people who have taken part in an illegal, violent movement cannot be trusted. In response, three things must be noted. First, I believe that in order to really understand the PKK—or any such movement, for that matter—it is necessary to talk to those people who actually were part of it. (For a variety of reasons, but mainly because current PKK members rarely speak freely, I limited my interviews to former members.) Second, information used was multiple-sourced. This was done by cross-referencing interviews —former rebels, for example, often passed through the same training camps, took part in similar attacks, and attended the same meetings— and referring to published Turkish and foreign sources to back up and confirm, whenever possible, dates and events. Third, while interviews with ex-PKK members form the core of this book and give it structure, they were not the sole source of information. This book incorporates information from a variety of sources, including interviews with well-known Kurdish opponents of the PKK, independent Turkish and Kurdish activists, and foreign sources with knowledge or former

connections to the group. In total, I spoke with or formally interviewed close to 100 people. In addition, I relied on my own, extensive
reporting about the PKK and the Kurdish conflict, carried out between
1989 and 1996. As the reader will discover, the sources utilized in this
book are varied and many.

There are not many in-depth, published studies of the PKK and
apart from this, none that extensively incorporate first-hand interviews with former participants. But a handful of works proved a very
useful guide both to the Kurdish conflict and to the larger Turkish
and international context. These included U.S. experts Henri J. Barkey
and Graham E. Fuller's *Turkey's Kurdish Question*; Turkish journalist
Mehmet Ali Birand's *Apo ve PKK*; former PKK member Selahattin
Celik's *Agri Dagini Tasimak*; Turkish journalist Ismet Imset's *the PKK*;
British expert David McDowall's *A Modern History of the Kurds*; and
Turkish academic Nihat Ali Ozcan's *PKK [Kurdistan Isci Partisi]*. Citing these works in no way implies their endorsement of my book,
nor does it imply my agreement with all they wrote, but it does acknowledge the debt of ideas I owe to those who tackled this subject
before me.

This book, obviously, could not have been written without the
willingness of so many former PKK members to speak with me. The
interviews usually took upward of 12 hours or more—split up over a
number of days—and in some cases, included follow-up meetings,
emails, or phone calls. Making contact with former PKK members is
not always easy—apart from everything else, they frequently change
their phone numbers—and I specifically have to thank former militant
Selahattin Celik, who generously opened his memories and his phone
book to me. Celik's willingness to discuss in detail his experiences,
coupled with his ability to review, with impressive objectivity, PKK
activities and decisions, was invaluable to my work.

In addition, Murat Dagdelen, a former political operative, gave
me access to his private writings and archives; founding member
Huseyin Topgider patiently put up with the some half dozen meetings
it took to cover his more than 20 years in the PKK; Sukru Gulmus,
who runs the PKK opposition website www.nasname.com, frequently
suggested new contacts; Selim Curukkaya, an early PKK dissident,
provided important insight into the PKK's functioning; Ayhan Ciftci,
Zeki Ozturk, Neval, and the dozens of others I interviewed all answered my questions with much patience and honesty. Not only were

they always willing to answer just one more question, but they and their families also opened their homes to me, making it easier for me to do this research as I traveled around Europe.

Likewise, Hatice Yasar, from the Ala Rizgari group, gave me a whirlwind tour of Kurdish history and of Paris; Kemal Burkay, founder of the Kurdistan Socialist Party, was generous with his time; Kendal Nezan, director of the Paris-based Kurdish Institute, has been a helpful contact and gracious host over the years; and independent Kurdish politician Serafettin Elci has always been ready to answer questions.

The MacArthur Foundation, through an 18-month research and writing grant, made it possible for me to start this project. A number of individuals, some friends, some professional contacts, provided other, no less important, support. Jim Ron's willingness to debate my ideas helped me better formulate my theses, and he was a good friend and staunch believer in this project; Gulistan Gurbey's expertise in Turkey's relations with Europe and Iraq was invaluable; Aram Nigogosian always kept me abreast of new articles on the PKK and reviewed some translations; Robert Olsen, an academic expert on the Kurds, read many chapters and made important comments; Omer Erzeren, with whom I took my first reporting trip to southeast Turkey in 1989, provided valuable comment on certain chapters; Zeynel Abidin Kizilyaprak, an independent Kurdish journalist from Turkey, helped me organize my thoughts on the larger political Kurdish framework and tracked down some hard-to-find information; and Faruk Bildirici and Namik Durukan were invaluable reporting partners in Iraq in 1995 and good friends.

I also availed myself of the Paris-based Kurdish Institute's library and relied on the Berlin-based Kurdish Institute's library, which contains extensive back issues of Kurdish newspapers and books related to the PKK. And my research would have been that much harder without the Berlin Staatsbibliothek's excellent collection of Turkish newspapers.

Over the years, Yavuz Onen and Mehmet Ali Birand were important contacts for the exchange of ideas; Veli Yilmaz lived too short after his release from prison, but I valued the few talks we did have; and the late Emil Galip Sandalci was an important influence. In addition, I would like to thank the following people: Wafa Amr, Emma Camatoy, Mitchell Cohen, Belinda Cooper, Caroline Fetscher, Suzy Goldenberg,

Andrej Gustincic, Corry Guttstadt, Agnes Heller, Ertugrul Kurkcu, Ziva Little, Jessica Lutz, Shanna Marcus, Nadire Mater, Judith Matloff, Anya Schiffrin, Hannes Stein, Liane Thompson, Nealy Troll, and Sahika Yuksel. There are others in Turkey I would like to mention, but the sensitivity of the subject addressed by my book makes me hesitate to publicize their names.

Finally, my editor at NYU Press, Ilene Kalish, showed an incredibly deft hand in editing my first, much-too-long draft; John Lister gave me important encouragement, help, and more; Sharon Moshavi provided invaluable support—both as a close friend and expert editor.

Stylistic Note

In order to make it less cumbersome for those who are unfamiliar with the Turkish alphabet, I decided to rely on the Western spelling of Turkish names and words. Turkish readers, I hope, will forgive me. Conversely, I did not translate Turkish-language works that are referenced in the footnotes and bibliography. This would have made the book even longer and would have been of marginal use to non-Turkish readers. When it came to translating Turkish words used in my text, I relied on common usage and also took care to ensure that translated statements (especially those made by Ocalan) were understandable to the reader. Finally, readers also should not read too much into the occasional use of the word Kurdistan. The word is used to denote the region where Kurds have long lived, and not to make a political statement about the territory in question.

Acronyms

ANAP (Anavatan Partisi) Motherland Party. A Turkish political party.

ARGK (Kurdistan Halk Kurtulus Ordusu) People's Liberation Army of Kurdistan. The PKK's military wing. In 2000, the military wing was renamed Halk Savunma Gucleri (People's Defense Forces).

CHP (Cumhuriyet Halk Partisi) Republican People's Party. A Turkish political party.

DDKD (Devrimci Demokratik Kultur Dernegi) Revolutionary Democratic Culture Association. An illegal Kurdish group active in the 1970s.

DDKO (Devrimci Dogu Kultur Ocaklari) Revolutionary Eastern Cultural Hearths. A legal Kurdish club active in Turkey in the late 1960s.

DEHAP (Demokratik Halk Partisi) Democratic People's Party. A legal Kurdish political party formed in 1997 and merged into DTP in 2005.

DEP (Demokrasi Partisi) Democracy Party. A legal Kurdish political party formed in May 1993 and closed down by a Turkish court in June 1994.

DSP (Demokratik Sol Partisi) Democratic Left Party. A Turkish political party.

DTP (Demokratik Toplum Partisi) Democratic Society Party. A legal Kurdish political party founded in November 2005.

DYP (Dogru Yol Partisi) True Path Party. A Turkish political party.

ERNK (Eniya Rizgariya Netewa Kurdistan) National Liberation Front of Kurdistan. The PKK's nonmilitary wing.

HADEP (Halkin Demokrasi Partisi) People's Democracy Party. A legal Kurdish political party formed in May 1994 and closed down by a Turkish court in March 2003.

HEP (Halkin Emek Partisi) People's Labor Party. A legal Kurdish political party formed in June 1990 and closed down by a Turkish court in July 1993.

KADEK (Kongreya Azadi Demokrasiya) Congress for Freedom and Democracy in Kurdistan (the name the PKK adopted in April 2002).

KDP (Kurdistan Democratic Party [Iraq]) The Iraqi Kurdish party headed by Massoud Barzani.

KONGRA-GEL (Kongra Gele Kurdistan) Kurdistan People's Congress. The name that KADEK/PKK adopted in October 2003, before returning to the name PKK in April 2005.

KKK (Koma Komalen Kurdistan) Kurdistan Confederation. An umbrella group for the PKK's military and political affiliates, formed after Ocalan's capture.

KUK (Kurdistan Ulusal Kurtulusculari) Kurdistan National Liberators. An illegal Kurdish group active in the late 1970s.

MGK (Milli Guvenlik Kurulu) National Security Council. Turkey's National Security Council.

MHP (Milliyetci Hareket Partisi) Nationalist Action Party. A Turkish political party.

PCDK (Kurdistan Democratic Solution Party). An Iraq-based pro-PKK Kurdish party.

PJAK (Kurdistan Free Life Party) An Iranian Kurdish pro-PKK party.

PKK (Partiya Karkeren Kurdistan) Kurdistan Workers' Party.

PSK (Kurdistan Sosyalist Partisi) Kurdistan Socialist Party of Turkey. An illegal Kurdish party formed in the 1970s.

PUK (Patriotic Union of Kurdistan [Iraq]) The political party founded by Jalal Talabani.

PWD (Partiya Welatpareza Demokratik) Patriotic Democratic Party. A party formed in 2004 by PKK militants who had split off from the group, including Abdullah Ocalan's brother Osman.

RP (Refah Partisi) Welfare Party. A defunct Turkish political party.

SHP (Sosyal Demokrati Halkci Partisi) Social Democratic Populist Party. A Turkish political party.

TAK (Teyrebazen Azadiya Kurdistan) Kurdistan Freedom Falcons. An urban militant wing of the PKK formed in 2004. Although it claims to be independent of the PKK, it pledges loyalty to Abdullah Ocalan.

TKDP (Turkiye-Kurdistani Demokrat Partisi) Kurdistan Democratic Party of Turkey. An illegal Kurdish group formed in the mid-1960s and active in the 1970s.

Introduction

ONE CHILLY FALL night in 1978, a small group of university drop-outs and their friends gathered behind blacked-out windows in Turkey's southeast to plan a war for an independent Kurdish state. Driven by their revolutionary zeal and moral certitude, the young men and women did not see any serious barriers to their success. But outsiders might have been forgiven for thinking otherwise. Turkey's military had hundreds of thousands of experienced soldiers. A NATO member, its government was a close ally of the United States and its armed forces recently had showed their fortitude in the swift occupation of northern Cyprus. It was no wonder that those who tracked radical groups dismissed the newly founded Kurdistan Workers' Party (PKK) as nothing more than thrill-seekers or brigands.

Within a few years these pronouncements would be proven very wrong, as the PKK swept to dominance and radicalized the Kurdish national movement in Turkey. The small group of armed men and women grew into a tightly organized guerrilla force of some 15,000, with a 50,000-plus civilian militia in Turkey and tens of thousands of active backers in Europe. The war inside Turkey would leave close to 40,000 dead, result in human rights abuses on both sides, and draw in neighboring states Iran, Iraq, and Syria, which all sought to use the PKK for their own purposes.

Turkey's capture in 1999 of PKK leader Abdullah Ocalan, coupled with his subsequent decision to suspend the separatist war, was hailed as a great victory for Turkey and in the initial euphoria it was easy to believe the rebel group had collapsed. But the end of the war did not mean the end of the PKK nor the end of Turkey's Kurdish problem. The PKK, which for more than a decade had been the dominant political organization of Turkish Kurds, maintained its controlling power and influence. And Turkey, by its unwillingness to seriously address Kurdish demands, despite the new peace, kept the Kurdish problem alive.

1

In 2004, the PKK regrouped its forces and called off its lopsided ceasefire. By 2006, clashes again were rising and so was the death toll on both sides. The rebels had many reasons for returning to battle: it was a response to Ankara's political inaction; it was a way to ensure that the PKK remained relevant and in control; and finally, there was Iraq to consider. The U.S.-led invasion of Iraq in 2003 had given Iraqi Kurds an unprecedented chance to rule themselves—and they grabbed it. While the rest of Iraq stumbled toward civil war, Iraqi Kurds, who comprise about five million of the country's 26 million-strong population, withdrew into their relatively homogeneous enclave in the north. With grudging approval from the United States, which was loathe to oppose its one real ally in Iraq, the Kurds laid claim to autonomy and received formal backing for this in Iraq's new constitution late in 2005. Iraqi Kurdistan, as it is now known, has its own parliament, its own flag, its own army, and its own investment laws to regulate oil resources, making it look very much like the independent state that Kurds in Iraq, like many of those in Turkey, had long hoped for. And the PKK, once viewed as the dominant Kurdish group in the region, suddenly was afraid of slipping behind.

If there is one thing that all the countries in the region agree on—and the United States, too—it is that an independent Kurdistan is a bad idea. An Iraqi Kurdish state would splinter Iraq, leaving other ethnic and religious groups free to wage a violent battle for control of the rest of the country and its rich oil reserves. Turkey, Iran, and Syria, all of which border on Iraq, have other concerns: They face their own nationalist Kurdish movements, some of them armed. A Kurdish state in northern Iraq would embolden Kurdish activists everywhere.

The repercussions of the Iraqi Kurdish ministate—even one that is not officially independent, not yet—are rippling across the region. And no more so than in Turkey, where Kurds number some 15 million, making up about 20 percent of Turkey's 70 million population. PKK supporters are again taking to the streets with posters of Ocalan and leaving for the tough mountains on the Turkish-Iraqi border, where the rebels have their mobile camps. This time, the war may be even bloodier. A new urban militant wing, the Kurdistan Freedom Falcons (TAK), targets Western cities and tourism resorts. Its attacks are more frequent and professional than those staged in the 1990s. For the first time, there is a real danger of civil violence between Kurds and Turks in the country's urbanized, Western centers.

Things are growing more tense in other countries where Kurdish minorities have long been discriminated against or oppressed. In Syria, where Kurds make up about 10 percent of Syria's 18 million population, violent clashes have broken out between the security forces (and Syrian Arab crowds) and Kurds living there. The Syrian Kurds once gave their loyalty to the PKK, but this ended when Ocalan was kicked out and the group's activities shut down. Now, bereft of active representation and without much hope for democratic change, Syrian Kurds have turned more vocal. They may not want their own state—at least not yet—but they do want political rights and ethnic-based rights. These are demands that threaten the very foundation of the Arab nationalist, authoritarian Syrian state.

The situation is not that different in Iran, where Kurds make up some 7 percent of Iran's 68 million people. Kurdish activism in Iran surged following the overthrow of Saddam Hussein, as Kurds held noisy demonstrations in favor of the political gains made by their ethnic kin in Iraq. The PKK used to ignore Iranian Kurds—part of its deal for getting Iranian backing in the 1990s—but Tehran cut the support when Ocalan was captured. Now, the PKK is actively wooing Iranian Kurdish support. And Iranian Kurds, whose demands for political freedoms have long been ignored by the Islamic regime, are listening. A PKK-affiliated party for Iranian Kurds—PJAK, or the Party for Free Life in Kurdistan—is based alongside the PKK in the Kandil Mountains in northern Iraq. Its armed forces have become an effective irritant to Iranian troops, which in mid-2006 began carrying out brief armed incursions and shelling the mountain range to drive out the rebels.

The U.S. struggle to stabilize Iraq and bring democracy to the region is forcing the international community to pay attention. The Kurds are the world's largest stateless people and nearly half live in Turkey, making the battle there a crucial part of the larger Kurdish problem throughout the region. Understanding the PKK—and the demands of Kurds in Turkey—is key to understanding the challenges the United States faces in formulating stable policies in this troubled part of the world. The crisis in Iraq and tensions over potential Kurdish separatist interests there underscore that the region's some 28 million Kurds will long remain a source of instability for the governments that rule them and the Western powers that try to influence events there.

■

When I first traveled in 1989 to the remote mountain region of Sirnak, center of the PKK fighting in southeast Turkey, few foreign reporters had written in any detail about the Kurdish conflict in Turkey. It was just a year since Iraqi President Saddam Hussein gassed his own Kurdish population in the village of Halabja, but even that had not sparked much interest in the bitter battle underway across the border. The main reason was that when Kurds weren't being killed by the thousands—as happened in Halabja—the West didn't care. The Kurdish conflict seemed as remote as the region where they lived, a treacherous terrain intersected by the borders of Turkey, Iran, Iraq, and Syria. And the Kurds themselves were difficult to understand. Divided by borders, dialects, tribal loyalties, and blood feuds, it was easy to dismiss their uprisings as the machinations of gun-toting brigands suspicious of the central authority.

I remember the ride over a rutted dirt-packed road to get to the village of stone and mud houses, where a small gravestone marked the spot of a young PKK rebel, a girl. Her name was Zayide and she had been killed in a battle with the Turkish military. The people told me that when the army tried to bury her in a hidden spot outside of the village, their bulldozers could not break the ground. Three times they tried and three times they failed. The people took this as a sign that Allah was protecting the girl—and the PKK's struggle—and the military finally turned the body over to the girl's family for burial. Her small grave had become a shrine of sorts, where women especially came to pray for help in finding husbands and for fertility. Seeing this, I resolved to learn more about this group that, despite its brutality against its own members and bloody attacks on Kurdish civilians, managed to claim the loyalty of the majority of Kurds in Turkey and many in Europe. Over the next seven years, I traversed southeast Turkey and northern Iraq in search of stories, sometimes working as a freelancer and later as a staff reporter for Reuters news agency.

In 1995, in my second year as an Istanbul-based correspondent for Reuters, the Istanbul state security opened a case against me. The charge was "inciting" racial hatred and the crime was an article that described how the Turkish military was forcing Kurdish civilians out of their villages to deny the rebels support. The article had been used by a Kurdish newspaper in Turkey—the newspaper, like many others in Turkey, subscribed to the Reuters news service—which made it possible for the court to charge me. No-one ever suggested the article was false, just that it would have been better had it not appeared. I was acquitted, but Turkish authorities insisted I stop working in Turkey and Reuters subsequently transferred me to the their Middle East / Africa desk in Nicosia. I returned to Turkey many times, sometimes for work, other times to see friends, but to avoid problems with the authorities I avoided reporting on the Kurdish conflict in the southeast.

The idea for this book came to me after Ocalan was captured, when PKK rebels began to split from the group in frustration with Ocalan's new, more compliant stance and his call for the rebels to disarm. For the first time, well-known militants, often dispirited and coming to grips with their own past, were willing to talk. For the first time, it was possible to get detailed information directly from those who had been inside the group, without relying on Turkish army statements or statements by PKK militants in Turkish custody. Despite concerns I had about returning to this subject, I could not give up the chance to get the inside details about the PKK, a group about which I had written many articles, yet almost always based on information from civilian supporters and Turkish opponents.

I hope this book will make the Kurdish war in Turkey and the Kurdish conflict throughout the region more understandable. And along the way, help explain what causes a 16-year-old girl named Zayide to leave her family and friends and join a rebel war that, as she must have realized, was likely to lead to her death in a year or two.

Washington, DC, December 2006

Prologue

Imagining a State

ON A CRISP fall day in 1978, Huseyin Topgider boarded a bus in the Turkish city of Elazig for the three-hour trip to Diyarbakir, the unofficial capital of Turkey's Kurdish region. It was late afternoon and like most of the male passengers, Topgider smoked one cigarette after another as the bus drove over the winding roads that cut through the rugged terrain. But unlike the others, Topgider, a slightly built Kurdish man in his mid-twenties, kept to himself during the ride. Now and then he offered his neighbor a cigarette, or commiserated when someone spoke of the political anarchy gripping the country. For the most part, though, he was quiet—and watchful.

In Diyarbakir, Topgider clambered off the bus to the cries of young boys hawking cigarettes, glasses of tea, and home-made sandwiches. He quickly made his way down narrow streets, heading directly to a small restaurant just within the city's old black basalt walls. At a table in the back were two other men who had taken the same bus. During the trip, they had pretended not to know each other. It was safer that way.

A fourth man soon joined their table. They drank tea, exchanged a few words, paid the bill, and left. The sky was darkening and the sidewalks were crowded with peddlers trying to sell one last item before closing up their makeshift stands. The men made their way through the old part of town to a minibus parked on a small, side street. A few other men were already waiting. As the bus pulled away someone said, "If we're stopped along the way, remember, we're going to a wedding." The men nodded. They did not need to be told twice.

The minibus headed toward the main road going east out of the city. Diyarbakir was a noisy, crowded place of some 375,000, the largest city in Turkey's Kurdish region and a magnet for those trying to escape the desolate poverty and conservative life of the surrounding villages. Migrants crammed drab, concrete apartment blocks, searching for a chance to work. Students vied for places in the local university, hoping for a better way to succeed. But it was the late 1970s and Turkey was in a state of crisis—economic and political—and nothing was easy. The angry graffiti daubed on buildings and the smudged manifestos passed from hand to hand testified to the growing frustrations.

The bus jostled its way on the pot-holed roads, fighting for space with rattling cars belching black smoke and heavily laden trucks carting animals and goods to the outlying villages. The squat city buildings gave way to a flat stretch of land broken up by dusty gas stations and tired storefronts advertising car parts and repairs. Children in torn sweaters and plastic shoes played listlessly in the dirt. Now and then traffic slowed for a farmer on a donkey, the animal swaying heavily underneath the load.

Soon the bus turned up a narrow, two-lane road that headed north. The land became rougher, overshadowed by mountains that stretched into darkness. The villages here were almost invisible, either nestled in mountain crevices or else dark smudges along the side of the road. Electricity and running water had yet to reach these small settlements, although more than half the region's people lived in villages like these. Had it been daytime, it would have been possible to see the crude dirt roads that cut through the fields into the mountains. During most of the year, villagers made their way to town by walking for hours to the main road and then hitching a ride with a passing vehicle. When snow fell the trip was nearly impossible.

It took the men about three hours to reach their destination, a cinderblock house just out of sight of a small tea house by the side of the road. Topgider quietly greeted the teenage boy squatting by the side of the house, a cigarette in one hand, a rifle in the other. Those attending the meeting had agreed to come unarmed. This sharp-eyed son of the house's owner would be their only protection throughout the next few days.

Over the next few hours, more minibuses pulled up in front of the tea house that abutted the road, letting out people who quickly walked to the house. So many unrelated people in one place, a few under police suspicion, if not already wanted, could easily have raised questions among passers-by. But those who planned the meeting had done a good job. They knew that the chances of anyone noticing the unusual late-night activity was slight. In the climate of violence that had gripped Turkey for the past two years, people avoided being out on the roads after dark, when it was too easy to be shot for reading the wrong newspaper, belonging to the wrong trade union, or for just being in the wrong place.

Late that night, newspapers were taped up over the windows to keep out prying eyes and thin blankets were laid on the floor as makeshift beds. Topgider found it hard to fall asleep. He wasn't nervous, he was impatient. Although everyone was already there, the meeting was not set to start until the morning.

"I knew how the meeting would conclude," he recalled more than 20 years later, his hair now graying and his allegiance over, "and I knew the main thing was the work that would follow. What mattered was that to really become a mass political strength, a strength of the people, we had to become a professional organization. In that period if someone had a typewriter and a magazine then they had a party. So just to announce a party was not important, what was important was who was wearing the uniform."

Most of the two dozen people gathered in the Fis village in southeast Turkey the night of November 25, 1978 had spent the past two years working on a new political party. Now, after countless meetings and speeches, they were going to formally approve the program for the party. Not a political party that would field candidates in parliamentary elections. This was going to be an illegal party that would take up arms against the Turkish state. They planned to launch a war for an independent Kurdish state in Turkey's southeastern region. The new Kurdish state would be a model for those fighting to free the remaining parts of what they called Kurdistan, a region covering the shared border areas of Iraq, Iran, Turkey, and Syria. They planned for nothing less than freedom for all Kurds in the region.

Topgider, who studied to be a teacher before dropping out to devote himself to revolution, saw little reason to believe that anything but armed struggle would bring Kurdish independence. Turkey's Kurds were not recognized by the state as Kurds. Turkish officials stubbornly insisted that Kurds were actually Turks and that their language was a corrupted form of Turkish. Decades of nonviolent pressure had wrested little if anything from the central authorities in terms of Kurdish cultural or political rights. Those who tried to promote their ethnic identity ended up in prison on trumped up charges of trying to overthrow the state. Turkish television and radio barred the use of the Kurdish language in broadcasts, while Kurdish-language education was banned outright. Kurdish names were forbidden and Kurdish village names had been changed to Turkish ones. Kurdish history did not appear in the history books and the country's Kurdish region was dotted with the slogan reminding inhabitants that "Happy is He Who Calls Himself a Turk."

Looking across Turkey's borders to the other parts of the geographical region known as Kurdistan only underscored to Topgider the need for a new, strong movement to fight on behalf of their people. In Iran, Shah Reza Pahlevi's dictatorial regime kept tight control over all political activity, but especially that by Kurds. Yet Iran did not deny their very existence. Iraq's Kurdish minority had long been fighting an on-again, off-again war for autonomy and they were just starting to regroup after their latest, most bitter defeat in 1975. Although Baghdad brutally attacked Kurdish fighters and their families, it was the most lenient country when it came to permitting the Kurds cultural rights, but this did little to dispel demands for Kurdish autonomy in Iraq. The Kurds in Syria faced severe restrictions even though they were the most quiescent of the region. Damascus had stripped some Kurds of their citizenship, barred them from forming their own political parties, and marginalized them economically.[1]

None of the countries where the Kurds lived were true democracies and attempts to work within the political system for broader rights or autonomy had always failed. Either activists themselves gave up because there was no space for them to operate or else they were forced to give up because of arrest or exile. Governments simply were afraid that once they started giving in to Kurdish demands, Kurds (and other minority groups) would demand independence. Kurdish attempts to fight for what they wanted had been equally unsuccessful. The states were just too powerful and the Kurds too divided to make a successful stand.

Nonetheless, countries in the region did use Kurdish rebel groups for their own ends, be it to pressure a neighboring country or weaken the Kurdish movement as a whole. Iran intermittently gave weapons and safe haven to Iraqi Kurdish fighters in order to pressure Baghdad. In return, Iraqi Kurdish rebels agreed to limit the activities of Iranian Kurdish rebels seeking refuge in Iraq. Syria allowed an Iraqi Kurdish group to operate out of Damascus in the hopes of weakening the Iraqi regime. Iraq once backed one Iraqi Kurdish faction to offset Iranian support for another faction. Turkey, which arguably imposed the harshest restrictions on its Kurdish minority, briefly allowed one Iraqi Kurdish rebel force to set up bases in order to make it easier for the group to attack a rival Iraqi Kurdish force. The situation throughout the region was so dire, and relations among Kurdish groups so fraught with backstabbing, that former Iraqi President Saddam Hussein later happily noted that Kurdish organizations would never be able to achieve anything since they were hopelessly divided against each other and subservient to foreign powers.[2]

Topgider and the others at the meeting called by Abdullah Ocalan, a thin, tall university drop-out with a mesmerizing vision of an independent Kurdish state, were certain that this time, things would be different.

PART I

Ocalan, Kurds, and the PKK's Start

Right: Abdullah Ocalan, leader of the PKK. Photo by Chris Kutschera, 1993.

Below: Accused PKK members stand trial in a Diyarbakir courtroom. After the 1980 military coup, the large number of PKK detainees led authorities to hold group trials. Photo by Chris Kutschera, 1981.

Left: In November 1983, leading PKK militants gathered in their makeshift camp in Lolan, northern Iraq, to celebrate the fifth anniversary of the founding of the PKK. Behind them are pictures of PKK members who had been jailed in Diyarbakir prison inside Turkey and killed themselves the year before to protest prison conditions. Among those attending the meeting: On the far left is Duran (Abbas) Kalkan, currently a senior PKK official, and third from the left is Selahattin Celik. The other men are unidentified. Photo provided by Selahattin Celik.

1

The Origins of the PKK, 1949–1976

ABDULLAH OCALAN WAS born in a typical farming village in Sanliurfa, a province just on the edge of the Kurdish region.[1] He often said he did not know for sure the exact year of his birth. His parents registered it as 1949, but as sometimes was the case among rural people in Turkey, the registration might have been delayed a year or two due to disinterest in such official matters or to give young Abdullah a better chance once he was conscripted in the army. The area where he grew up was populated by Kurds, Turks, and Armenians and the different peoples mixed easily, going to school together, doing business, and among the Muslim villages at least, also intermarrying. Ocalan's grandmother on his mother's side, in fact, was a Turk, and he once claimed that his mother was as well.[2] Still, for all the intermingling, Ocalan did not learn Turkish until he entered elementary school.

Life in this region was marked by grueling poverty for most everyone but the landlords. In Ocalan's village of Omerli, men and women worked the harsh land, harvesting what they could and in summer supplementing the meager income by picking cotton in the fields of the wealthy landowners. It was a tough life with little money for anything but the basics and little hope that things would get better. Later on, Ocalan's supporters would make much of the fact that he came from as depressed surroundings as his followers, unlike many of the earlier leading Kurdish figures, who often were linked to large tribal or wealthy landowning families.

The seemingly inescapable cycle of poverty of such villages was captured more than 30 years after Ocalan's birth in an article in the French newspaper *Le Monde,* which looked at life in one typical Kurdish village in the Mardin province near the Syrian border: "Each family had a few chickens and possibly five or six goats. The agha [local landlord] would visit occasionally to reaffirm his authority and assign work. This consisted mainly of labor on the cotton plantations of the Mesopotamian plain two hundred metres below. All except the very old or very young would descend to the plain daily, to work an eleven-hour day. For this the rates of pay were US$1 for a child, $1.50 for a woman, and $2 for a man. Villagers reckoned they had a 30 percent mortality rate among the children."[3]

Ocalan, the oldest of seven children, grew up in an environment dominated by disappointment and violence. "Ever since I was conscious, in my family there was always fighting," he once said. "There was an overwhelming unhappiness."[4] One psychological profile of him attempted to understand his later militant nationalism in terms of his simultaneous desire for respect from his father and latent anger at his parents.[5] Although the reasoning is speculative, Ocalan often did refer to his childhood experiences in interviews and speeches to explain how he learned the importance of revenge and the uses of violence.

Ocalan's father was not only poorer than most others in the village, but he also apparently was weak-willed and felt humiliated by both the villagers and his own wife. "Not even his relatives took him seriously, and he was hurt by them. It was as if he did not exist, he was gone,"[6] Ocalan said in one wide-ranging interview in the early 1990s.

Ocalan's mother, in comparison, was a tough, angry woman who held nothing back, publicly humiliating her husband for being unable to support his family. Both parents pushed their first-born to be aggressive. Once when Ocalan was beaten badly by some other boys and he ran crying home to his mother, she threw him out of the house, warning him not to return until he had exacted revenge. Ocalan always claimed this went against his shy nature, but he quickly developed a reputation for being a wild, bold child. "Even though it was forced on me this first time, my tendency for action [toward taking revenge] had started. I began to be an attacker; I cracked the heads of many children,"[7] he recalled.

One of his major disappointments as a child was the marriage of his favorite sister, Havva, to a man from another village. Love did not play a role in such marriages and the bride-to-be rarely had any say. Havva herself was essentially "sold" for a few sacks of wheat and an unspecified amount of money. Ocalan later explained he saw such marriages as a type of death for women, and former PKK ideologue and scribe Mehmet Can Yuce cited Havva's marriage as a major influence on Ocalan's theories on the need to liberate women from the repressive roles inherent in traditional Kurdish male-female relations.

"I recall having a sense of regret," noted Ocalan, referring back to that period when his sister was married. "[I was thinking that] if I were a revolutionary, then I would not let this happen. They would not be able to take her away."[8]

Like many small settlements, Omerli did not have its own elementary school. Kurds saw this as an attempt to keep them ignorant, but it was to Ankara's advantage to offer schooling—and with it Turkish language and nationalism—to hasten assimilation. The truth was probably more benign. There were so many villages and even smaller hamlets that it would have been difficult to find enough money and personnel to set up schools everywhere. Instead, like many rural children, Ocalan had to trek an hour each way to attend school in a neighboring village. He was a good student and he absorbed the lessons of Turkish history and nationalism so well that he hoped to become a professional Turkish army officer. This was not an uncommon dream for a Kurdish boy schooled in the heroics of Turkey's founder and top general, Mustafa Kemal Ataturk. But Ocalan failed the exam for military high school and instead registered at a vocational high school in Ankara that trained students to work in the state's land registry offices.

Ocalan's arrival in Ankara in 1966 coincided with the quiet growth of a defiant Kurdish identity in the big cities. Teenagers purposefully smoked "Bitlis" cigarettes, whose name referred to the city where the tobacco was grown in the southeast.[9] In that Kurdish region, meanwhile, frustrated students and workers were soon staging mass meetings calling for democratic rights and protesting oppression of their identity. It was impossible for Ocalan not to notice. "These meetings affected me, even if it was just in a small way,"[10] he later explained.

In this, he was not much different from other young Kurdish men and women who began to explore their identity while in high school or university. Some fell under the sway of a teacher or youth leader who was a secret Kurdish nationalist, others came to see the contradiction between their personal lives—in which they were raised in a Kurdish-speaking village, listening to Kurdish radio emanating from across the borders—and the public ideology that insisted that Kurds were actually Turks. Like Ocalan, many were simply swept up in the leftist movements and Kurdish radicalism that burgeoned in the late 1960s.

When Ocalan graduated vocational school in 1969, he found work in the Diyarbakir government office responsible for measuring land for title deeds in the Kurdish region. After one year, Ocalan transferred to an office in Istanbul. The end of the 1960s were a period of great political upheaval in Turkey and Ocalan, like many other young men and women, was unclear where to turn. Not yet a Kurdish nationalist, he was beginning to recognize that there was a Kurdish problem and that something needed to be done about it. After reading a book entitled *The Alphabet of Socialism*, he decided that he was a socialist.[11]

But Ocalan was unsure how to combine his developing Kurdish political identity with his socialist ideals. In Istanbul, he started to follow the actions of the radical student-led movement, which believed Turkey needed to free itself from U.S. domination and capitalist servitude. It was hard to remain apart from the campus fervor even if, like Ocalan, one was actually not a student but instead a low-level state employee working in an office that handled title deeds.

History

The fact that Ocalan was nearly 20 years old before he started to think about his Kurdish identity in any political way was hardly unusual for a Kurdish man or woman growing up in Turkey during this period.[12] Shortly after the Turkish republic was formed in 1923, Kurdish nationalists rebelled against the state's authority. The uprisings were harshly put down and a host of laws were enacted to wipe out Kurdish history and identity. Kurdish village names were changed to Turkish ones, the word Kurdistan—until then used to denote a geographical region—was expunged from books and the language itself was essentially banned.

Turkey's repression of Kurdish ethnic identity was so complete and Kurdish fear and exhaustion so high after the failed rebellions that a British diplomat traveling through the Kurdish region in 1956 noted: "I did not catch the faintest breath of Kurdish nationalism which the most casual observer in Iraq cannot fail to notice."[13]

But Turkey could not close itself off from Kurdish nationalist activities in other countries nor from domestic shifts that encouraged a new, liberal approach to civil and political rights. These factors helped spark change in Kurdish views of themselves, their demands, and the best methods to reach their goals.

In 1960, the Turkish military staged a coup to halt what was seen as Prime Minister Adnan Menderes's increasingly autocratic rule. Ironically, the coup, which had the backing of the educated elite, ushered in the most liberal period the people had known. A group of academics was invited to draw up a new constitution. The resulting document enshrined broad freedoms to form associations, publish, organize trade unions, and call strikes—all limited since the founding of the republic.[14]

This expansion of Turkey's democracy coincided with the rise of a more educated and cosmopolitan Kurdish population. The first generation born after the Kurdish rebellions had come of age, and they did not carry with them the same fears and memories of the army's harsh put-down of the uprisings that helped silence their parents. More Kurds were attending university, where they were exposed both to new ideas and other Kurdish youth. At the same time, Kurdish peasants seeking a way out of economic hardship were moving to the cities, where they were more likely to hear grumbling about economic inequality between Kurds and Turks and whispers of a new Kurdish political agitation at home and in Iraq.

A legal socialist party, the Turkish Workers Party (TIP), was founded in 1961. Not surprisingly, it gained strong support among Kurds, who were attracted to its message of social and economic equality and justice. But in a sign of just how sensitive the Kurdish issue remained, the party did not tackle the issue for almost a decade. Some Kurdish activists tried to test the new liberal atmosphere directly but they were disappointed. The state moved quickly to shut down cultural magazines and Kurdish-language newspapers, charging the editors and writers with communism or separatism.[15] It seemed the liberalization of Turkey only went so far.

But soon, as Turkey always feared, the Iraqi Kurdish struggle spilled over the border. After the Iraqi monarchy was overthrown in 1958, the new Iraqi government had invited Iraqi Kurdish leader Mulla Mustafa Barzani home from exile in the Soviet Union. Barzani was a famed fighter and nationalist figure who led a revolt in Iraq in the early 1940s and helped defend the 1946 Kurdish Republic of

Mahabad in Iran. Never mind that the revolt failed and the Soviet-backed Mahabad republic did not even last a year: Barzani was the closest Kurds had to a real hero and his return to Iraq reinvigorated Kurdish nationalists everywhere. But within three years, Barzani's relations with Baghdad collapsed over Kurdish demands for autonomy and he launched a new rebellion.

This uprising caught the imagination of Turkish Kurds; in 1965, some Kurds formed the underground Kurdistan Democratic Party of Turkey (TKDP). This was the first nationalist Kurdish party inside Turkey since the state crushed the last of the rebellions in 1938.[16] It called for a Kurdish federation within Turkey's borders and, in theory at least, supported armed action to reach its goal. Ideologically, the party was close to Barzani's party, but the difficulties of Kurdish unity immediately showed. A letter sent by the Turkish party offering to assist Barzani went unanswered. Members took it as a sign that Barzani was unwilling to cross swords with Turkey.

"But despite this," insisted Serafettin Elci, a Kurdish lawyer who was sympathetic to the party, "the TKDP saw helping the Barzani movement as a national responsibility."[17]

The party also was not very popular with Kurds even inside Turkey. Kurdish youth were attracted to the leftist ideas promoted by TIP and spreading through the universities. The TKDP, however, reflected the same traditional, conservative approach that Barzani held and the Turkish Kurdish party's general secretary, Faik Bucak, was from a wealthy, landowning family in southeast Turkey. The murder of Bucak in 1966—he was killed in a blood feud, but many Kurds believe state forces were behind it—also weakened the party's ability to function effectively and garner support.

Kurds who wanted to take a closer look at their own situation remained bereft of outlets. The Turkish left, which was growing stronger, was vocally opposed to many of the state's policies, but on the Kurdish issue it was relatively silent. Kurds hoping to work through the left were dissatisfied yet there was nowhere else to turn.

"At that time we didn't think of having a separate organization," explained Kemal Burkay, a thoughtful Kurdish activist who started with the socialist party TIP. "The goal of making changes in Turkey, of winning democracy, of winning Kurdish rights was tied to the struggle of the two peoples working together. In time we understood that the Turkish left did not have a real Kurdish program."

Kurds Strike Out on Their Own

At the end of the decade, just as the student-led left began its turn to violence, Kurdish students and intellectuals formed their own organization. The Revolutionary Eastern Cultural Hearths (DDKO), which substituted the word "eastern" for the word "Kurdish" to avoid being shut down by the state, wanted to address social and cultural issues of concern to Kurds. The group blended the Marxism so popular at the time with a Kurdishness, thus marking a new step in development of a Kurdish political identity in Turkey.

Despite the organization's attempt to bypass bans on Kurdish activism, the state was suspicious. In October 1970, the group's leaders were arrested and charged with trying to establish a separate state. Although some members may have dreamed of an independent Kurdistan, other Kurds saw it as too timid in its veiled calls for Kurdish cultural rights. Still, the state's message to the first legal Kurdish group was telling: Political liberalization aside, bans on Kurdish activism would not be eased.

But even if the state's policy was stagnant, the politicization of Kurdish ethnic identity was not. By now Kurds were very active in the socialist TIP and at the Fourth Congress at the end of October 1970, delegates voted in favor of resolutions that reflected their nationalist interests and frustrations.[18] The resolutions started off with the simple yet controversial statement acknowledging the existence of Kurds in eastern Turkey. They then went on to condemn Turkey for imposing a policy of "repression, terror and assimilation"[19] against the Kurds.

Kurds were not the only ones unhappy with the pace of reform. Toward the end of the 1960s, the socialist movements sweeping across Europe took hold in Turkey. University students adapted the models and theories to their own situation and held large and rowdy demonstrations to vent their criticisms and demands. The focus was on Turkey's close ties to the United States, the dangers of capitalism and imperialism, and the need for radical change. U.S. intervention in Vietnam—and the guerrilla resistance—helped strengthen the anti-American feelings.

Gradually, leftist views hardened and spread. Student leaders went to Palestinian guerrilla camps in Lebanon for armed training. Trade unions became more radical in their demands. Universities had played an important part in demanding the end to the Menderes government and this boosted the student-led movement's belief that its role was to change society. The radical thinking was aided by what was seen as a shrinking space for democratic, legal activism. A 1968 election law aimed at limiting the growth of the socialist party TIP gave credence to the argument that nothing could be gained by working through the legal, political system.[20]

Early in 1970, the Turkish left spawned two armed groups, each espousing slightly different theories of violent socialist revolution. The groups turned to robbing banks to finance their activities and kidnappings to publicize their goals. Such actions underscored the government's loss of control. The militants made plans to take their struggles to the mountains, from where they would lead the revolution.

The combination of outspoken Kurdish organizations and violent leftist movements—along with attacks by armed rightists—plunged the country into a political chaos that was exacerbated by large-scale workers strikes. The growing urban violence threatened Turkey's domestic stability and potentially threatened Turkey's role as a valued NATO member and trusted U.S. ally. The Turkish military, which saw itself as the final guarantor of the country's secular democracy, was concerned. On March 12, 1971, the armed forces staged their second coup in a decade.[21] This time, the goal was to wipe out the encroaching radicalism and rewrite the liberal 1961 constitution and laws so that such violence could not emerge again. The day of the coup, officials from the socialist TIP party were charged with communist propaganda and supporting Kurdish separatism.

The military, worried about the difficulties of getting involved directly in running the country, instead oversaw establishment of a technocrat government. The new government's main task was to rewrite the constitution to limit those freedoms blamed for the spread of the radical groups. Martial law was imposed and political life came to a halt. Youth groups were shut down, trade union meetings banned, and authorities given broad powers to suspend publications. The remnants of the Kurdish cultural DDKO group closed down and TIP was banned. Many Kurdish and leftist activists who did not flee to Europe were detained and imprisoned.

At the time of the coup, Ocalan was a 21-year-old clerk in the state's land registry office in Istanbul. He had spent most of the previous year preparing for the university entrance exams and working hard to earn enough money to live on. Occasionally, he had gone to meetings of the Kurdish cultural clubs known as DDKO, but neither the Kurdish group nor the speeches of Turkish leftists roused him much.[22] He thought the Kurdish group ignored important political questions about the future of the Kurds, while the Turkish left refused to even see a Kurdish national question. Still, the political upheaval made him reconsider his own plans for his future: He had hoped to study law at Istanbul University, but he was growing more interested in other things, such as issues of politics and national identity.

Shortly after the coup, Ocalan decided to make a change. He quit his job in Istanbul and moved to Ankara, where he enrolled in the prestigious political science department of Ankara University.

"On one side there were the revolutionary movements, on the other side socialism and Kurdishness," explained Ocalan once. "A lot of questions had accumulated. I was going to find the answer to these in political science."[23]

The Prisoner

Abdullah Ocalan's real political education began in March 1972, a year into the new, military-backed government's rule. Armed Turkish leftists, hoping to force the government to free three compatriots sentenced to hang for treason, kidnapped three foreign NATO radar technicians. Police tracked the 11 hostage-takers to their safe house in Kizildere, a village not far from Ankara, and all but one of them (including the three hostages) died in the ensuing firefight. Students in Ankara, angered by the killing of the leftist militants, staged a protest. Ocalan, by then a university student, joined in.

The authorities had little tolerance for such actions and demonstrators, among them Ocalan, were detained. It was the first time Ocalan had been picked up, and he apparently comported himself well, giving back as good as he got during questioning.

"I didn't know him then, but after we were detained we were brought to a building for questioning," said Ibrahim Aydin, then a 22-year-old university student who had joined the protest. "One of the guards said the captain was coming and Abdullah Ocalan must have shown some sort of reaction because the captain came and took him out."

The two men were sent to Ankara's Mamak Military Prison, the center of the formerly vibrant student-led leftist movement. It was here that many arrested leaders of the movement were being held—including the three young men whose pending execution sparked the botched kidnapping attempt—as well as many of their supporters and sympathizers. Aydin and Ocalan were assigned to a cell of some 70 young men, many of them current or former university students who had taken up the banner of the radical left. These were not necessarily the most radical of those involved, but almost all were linked with Dev-Genc (Federation of Revolutionary Youth), the mass student organization out of which the armed leftist groups of the period had been born.

By chance, Aydin was given a bunk next to Ocalan. Aydin, a compact man studying to be a physical education teacher, was a supporter of Dev-Genc. He was a Kurd and he knew it—his mother's relatives had been killed by Turkish soldiers during the Dersim (Tunceli) uprising of the late 1930s—but like many in this period he had not yet developed a political Kurdish identity. He thought the Turkish left's promised revolution would solve his problems. "We didn't have a serious Kurdish feeling at the time, it was a natural thing, that's all," said Aydin, now living in exile in Sweden.

Aydin and Ocalan quickly struck up a camaraderie, as much because they were bunkmates as Kurds, and passed the time talking. Ocalan talked of the leftist movement in Turkey, its strategies and mistakes. It was easy to get books in the prison and Ocalan read a great deal, especially books on socialist issues, Marxist-Leninism, and Russian classics. To Aydin, it seemed that Ocalan always had something to say about politics and leftist theories.

But when it came to making his views more widely known, Ocalan was oddly quiet. The Dev-Genc people in the cell held regular debates to discuss issues of revolution and society, but Ocalan hardly ever took part. One reason might have been that for the others in the cell, Ocalan was a political novice, something he himself must have known. After all, the others had been linked not just with the main student movement in Turkey, but also with armed groups that promised revolution. In fact, some had been readying to start their armed struggle in earnest when the coup was staged and the mass arrests began. Ocalan, meanwhile, had been working for a state office.

But while Ocalan might not have spoken much to the others, he certainly listened to what they were saying. For the first time, he was exposed to the inner-workings of leftist groups and he saw how important it was to have a group to put forward one's political demands. He met leading members of the left, people who were adamant that only armed struggle would change Turkey. And there was one other thing Ocalan noticed: there was no discussion of the Kurdish problem.

In October 1972, about seven months after his arrest, Ocalan was released. He was a changed man: "For me, prison was a school on advancing the political struggle."[24]

Being arrested for joining a peaceful demonstration convinced Ocalan there was little room to act in Turkey's democracy; what he heard from the other prisoners made him think that armed revolution was the only answer. At the same time, his awareness of a Kurdish problem had begun to coalesce into a basic Kurdish nationalism and he started to think about forming his own group.

As Ocalan later explained: "This was my transition to becoming a professional revolutionary."[25]

Politics as Usual

The first national elections after the coup were scheduled for October 1973 and in January of the next year, newly elected Prime Minister Bulent Ecevit took office.[26] Within a few months he declared a general amnesty for those convicted of political crimes. But if the military hoped the two-and-a-half years of quasi-military rule would wipe out the vestiges of political violence, it was wrong. Almost immediately, leftists released from prison or returned from exile regrouped into both old and new organizations. If anything, members were even more numerous and more radical than before.

Kurdish activists who had been imprisoned or forced to flee the country when the military took over returned to political activism with a more definite agenda. Like their Turkish compatriots, those who had spent the intervening years in Europe were exposed to the German Baader-Meinhof gang, the Palestinian Black September movement, and other violent liberation organizations. In the free atmosphere of Europe, they also could easily read revolutionary tracts, attend lectures by leftist and nationalist intellectuals, and debate the merits of various strains of liberation theories. Those who were imprisoned inside Turkey during this period had the opportunity to meet with and exchange ideas with other Kurdish radicals, lay the groundwork for new organizations, and educate others in their philosophies.

By now many Kurdish activists, similar to Ocalan, had decided they needed their own groups. The Turkish left had proven a disappointment. Although leftist groups might pay lip service to the Kurdish problem, it was never at the top of their agenda. The more Kurds pushed for discussion of the Kurdish problem and possible solutions, the more the Turkish left grew intransigent. There was a natural tension within the socialist ideology between promoting nationalism and believing that socialism would solve all problems. Beyond this, there was also the underlying Turkish nationalism—so strong in the educational system—that even the radical left could not easily shake. The issue of a Kurdish state was not something the left wanted to tackle.

"The Turkish left was heavily influenced by Turkish ideology and could not openly come up with a Kurdish solution," said Burkay, the soft-spoken Kurdish lawyer, sometime poet, and former socialist party member who fled to Europe after the coup and returned when the amnesty took hold. Once back in Turkey, he worked on forming his own party. "We wanted to put issues openly in front of the Kurdish people and we figured in the end, we could only do it with our own party."

Besides, Kurds no longer needed Turkish intellectuals and activists to explain to them what the agenda was or how to make revolution. Not only had the activism of the late 1960s and early 1970s sparked a violent political awakening in Kurds, but also the state's own assimilationist policies had in some cases awakened exactly what it was trying to wipe out.

Ankara hoped that offering educational opportunities to Kurds would hasten their assimilation by teaching them the Turkish language and history as if it were their own. In 1961, special regional boarding schools were established to remove Kurdish children from their home environment and educate them in a wholly Turkish one.[27] But this had the unintended effect of boosting Kurdish identity. Young men, who before would have had no choice but to drop out of school and work in the family fields or hawk wares in a dusty town, were offered spots in regional boarding schools. Here they could receive an education through high school and could even qualify for university.

Instead of remaining locked in their small village or town, with little exposure to what was happening in the rest of the country, let alone the world, they were thrust into a new environment of ideas, debates, and other Kurdish students.

"The goal of [these schools] was to turn the children into Turks, but because of that there was a reaction," said Ramazan Ulek, a Kurdish boy from a poor family in the southeast who was educated in such schools. "Before, none of us had left our villages and suddenly we had a chance to see the world and how it worked."

Ocalan, the Activist

When Ibrahim Aydin was reintroduced to Ocalan in 1973, about a year after they shared a cell together in Mamak prison, Ocalan seemed a different man. The quiet prisoner had turned into an outspoken radical who insisted that Kurds needed to launch an armed struggle to free themselves from Turkish colonization. Ocalan and four friends who would later form the nucleus of the PKK rented an apartment in the Bahcelievler district of Ankara, where every night a dozen or so people would cram into the dingy rooms and debate the Kurdish issue.

Aydin, who stayed in the house while waiting to be assigned a job as a physical education teacher, was still affiliated with the Turkish left but increasingly unhappy there. His leftist comrades made disparaging comments about Kurds and he himself was thinking more about his own Kurdish identity. Talking to Ocalan focused him on the Kurdish problem. The political science university student had a very insistent manner and what he had to say about Kurdish history and socialist revolution seemed to make sense. Ocalan, always well-read, had turned into an effective debater with the ability to make his arguments appear to be the only logical line of reasoning. Like many others who fell under Ocalan's influence in the 1970s, Aydin saw him as someone who was always thinking and planning ahead. For a young hothead like Aydin, Ocalan's ideas were irresistible.

"We were all students," said Aydin, now a middle-aged father of three marveling over the audacity of youth, "and we had no guns, we couldn't even find enough food, but we were going to fight for the Kurds."

That same year—the spring of 1973—Ocalan called together a few of his university friends for a secret meeting to discuss how to approach the Kurdish problem.[28] They agreed they first needed to research the problem and lay out potential solutions. Given the lack of materials on Kurdish history and past rebellions, it made sense to compile their own histories and analysis to explain what they wanted and why they were more credible than others.

"We could call this a research group," Ocalan later explained. "We didn't plan for any future serious actions."[29]

Following the return to full civilian rule in 1974, Ocalan joined the Ankara Democratic Higher Education Association (ADYOD), a new student organization that promoted socialism.[30] He wanted to use this organization as a legal front for his planned illegal activities. By now he and his friends were convinced Kurds needed an independent organization to fight for their national rights, although they also believed that Turkish and Kurdish socialists could find common cause and jointly carry out the revolution. Ocalan hoped to forge the necessary links through ADYOD.

Ocalan's ideas did not get much support from Turkish leftists in the student organization. They maintained that their soon-to-be revolution was all that was needed to free both Kurds and Turks. It is also possible that the leftists were not as impressed with Ocalan and his plans as he was. In any case, ADYOD quickly fell afoul of Turkish laws barring communist propaganda and in 1975 it shut down.

The negative reaction of the Turkish leftists to his ideas helped convince Ocalan that there was no point in continuing to look for a Turkish partner. The legal troubles ADYOD faced also helped convince Ocalan to abandon the idea of creating a legal front for his nascent organization. He thought that legal associations or cultural clubs drew too much police attention, making it hard to maintain the secrecy he felt was crucial for success. Ocalan also believed that such legal fronts encouraged lengthy debates and discussions among members, slowing down the process of staging revolution.

Soon, Ocalan's new organization took shape. In 1975, at a meeting in the Dikmen suburb of Ankara, Ocalan and about 15 others decided to give up on university completely and focus on forming a Marxist-Leninist group that would fight for an independent Kurdish state.[31] They wanted to take their ideas and struggle directly to the people in the Kurdish southeast, and they made plans to get people's attention and support: These activities, more spontaneous than well-planned, included attacking right-wing extremist groups that defended Turkish nationalism, debating (and sometimes fighting) militant leftists who did not see the need for Kurdish nationalism, and holding noisy demonstrations and marches to focus attention on their own seriousness.

The nascent group also decided that they would not publish a newspaper or magazine that, in any case, the poor could not afford and the illiterate could not understand. Instead, they would count on their one-on-one meetings with Kurds in the southeast to foster the support they wanted. This decision, coming as it did at a time when both Kurdish and Turkish radical groups believed they needed at least some sort of legal front to spread their arguments, was an unusual one. But it was an important one. Rather than spending time raising money to rent offices, buy printing machines, or deal with the court cases invariably opened against such radical magazines, Ocalan and his backers could focus on the revolution they promised.

"Turkey's democracy had a secret face, it was a false democracy," said Selahattin Celik, who was studying engineering at Hacettepe University in Ankara when friends introduced him to Ocalan. "To get rid of [Turkey's rule] you couldn't use legal ways or democracy. We thought the only way to win was through armed struggle. We hadn't lived democracy so we never learned anything about democracy."

Although he still had little to show for all his efforts, Ocalan was so sure of himself and his plans that he tried to recruit the top people from other organizations. In January 1976, a former chairman of Revolutionary Democratic Culture Association (DDKD), which was established in 1975 as a pro-Soviet separatist Kurdish group, agreed to attend one of Ocalan's Ankara meetings. After he listened to the speakers, he made clear to Ocalan that he would never join such an organization.

"If the Turks hear what you are saying, in three months they will destroy you,"[32] Ocalan recalled the man telling him.

All Alone

Ocalan was unable to get support from any of the established Kurdish activists. These men—except for Hatice Yasar of the Rizgari group, all the leading activists were men—not only saw themselves as leaders in their own right, but also generally regarded Ocalan with suspicion. Apart from the seven months Ocalan spent in prison for joining a demonstration, the former university student did not have any discernable experience as a revolutionary. His plans, meanwhile, called for immediate revolution, while other activists were still debating the proper time, method, and underlying ideology. Although Ocalan, despite his inexperience, believed that he was ready to lead the first successful Kurdish uprising in history, more established Kurdish activists were hardly convinced. Many saw him less as a revolutionary than as an overly violent, somewhat uneducated, and rather immature person.

While there is no question that such criticisms were rooted in very real concerns Kurdish activists had about Ocalan's plan for winning Kurdish independence, part of Ocalan's problem in gaining acceptance was that he came out of nowhere. For all the leftist revolutionary fervor, Kurdish society was incredibly traditional, and one's tribal or family affiliation, profession, or at least activist background were important to one's credibility.

Ocalan's family did not hail from any of the well-known, nationalistic tribes or families and he was a university drop-out without a profession. Other activists had long histories either with the socialist party TIP, which had been closed after the military coup, or else they had worked in the since-closed Revolutionary Eastern Cultural Hearths (DDKO) or were lawyers or publishers or came from prominent families. The parties they established had definite links to or roots in other leftist, Turkish Kurdish, or Iraqi Kurdish organizations.[33]

Ocalan was not just a newcomer to the field, but he was one without an identifiable past. Except for a rather unmemorable stint in DDKO—Ocalan claimed to have been a well-known speaker at meetings, but others do not recall him—Ocalan was a nobody. While this meant Ocalan could operate free of former debts or links to other groups, leaders, or ideas, it also made him an easy target of derision for more established activists.

Kemal Burkay, some 10 years Ocalan's senior, was one of the more prominent activists who dismissed Ocalan from the outset. Since returning to Turkey after the amnesty, Burkay had followed through with his plan to start up a new socialist Kurdish party. The party championed independence but, unusual for that period, it relied on nonviolent methods. His Kurdistan Socialist Party (often called Ozgurluk Yolu after the group's newspaper, or PSK after its Kurdish initials) attracted many of the luminaries of the former socialist party TIP and would grow into one of the largest Kurdish groups of the late 1970s.

When Burkay heard about Ocalan's emerging group around 1976, he was suspicious of its promises and plans. He didn't know any of the group's members, was uncomfortable with Ocalan's violent verbal criticisms of anyone he viewed as a rival—Ocalan referred to them as "collaborators," "opportunists," and, worse still for the Marxists, "petit-bourgeois"—and Burkay thought Ocalan was wrong to so forcefully push armed struggle when the people, as Burkay believed, were not ready to take this step.

"Our party's view was very definite on this [armed struggle]," Burkay, a tall, almost delicate-looking man, told me when I met him in his party's headquarters outside Cologne. The rooms were lined with bookcases containing the many magazines, newspapers, history books, speeches, and novels published by the organization's legal, European office Komkar. There was a stack of bound copies of the monthly newspaper Burkay published in Turkey in the 1970s. "Kurds have staged rebellions many times and never succeeded, so we believed that Kurdish society first needed a political organization before staging a rebellion."

Another well-known Kurdish activist at the time, Ahmet Zeki Okcuoglu, was busy with Kawa, a publishing house that was soon to spawn an underground organization of the same name. He had run into Ocalan a few times. "He was very unimpressive," mused Okcuoglu years later as we sat in a café in Berlin, where he fled to avoid a prison sentence in Turkey. "I spoke with him a little bit and felt he knew nothing about Kurdish history."

But to a growing number of young Kurds, Ocalan's plan for revolution was attractive. Ibrahim Aydin, Ocalan's old prison cell-mate, finally decided to join the nascent group even though he had just received his first job as a physical education teacher. Ocalan insisted that Aydin not resign from his job.

"He said there was no reason why I couldn't do both, and even use my job to help the new organization," Aydin recalled.

The education ministry assigned Aydin to work in a Turkish town near the western coast. Almost immediately, Aydin started lobbying for a position in the Kurdish region. Soon he was reassigned to a school in the southeast, a region that Turkish teachers usually shunned. There he started to speak to students and fellow teachers about this so-far unnamed organization that was going to liberate the Kurds from Turkish control.

2

Abdullah Ocalan, Leader, 1975–1980

IN MARCH 1975, the Kurdish nationalist movement suffered its biggest blow since the collapse in 1946 of the Mahabad republic in Iran's Kurdish region.[1] Iraqi Kurdish leader Mulla Mustafa Barzani, whose military prowess and nationalist fervor had driven a nearly 15-year-old on-again, off-again armed struggle with Baghdad for Kurdish autonomy in Iraq's north, was forced to admit total and final defeat. On March 6, Tehran and Baghdad had settled their long-standing border disputes during an OPEC meeting in Algiers. As part of the Algiers accord, the Kurds, so ably used and armed by Iran and its ally the United States to pressure Iraq, were to be abandoned.[2] Within hours, Iran pulled out its fighters—who had been fighting alongside the Iraqi Kurds—and the United States halted its assistance, leaving Barzani at the mercy of the better-equipped and trained Iraqi troops. Once again, the Kurds found themselves abandoned to the exigencies of larger political stakes. Barzani was forced to admit defeat and in return he was given two choices: seek asylum in Iran, which agreed to take in hundreds of thousands of Iraqi Kurds fleeing certain Iraqi retribution, or accept an offer of asylum from the Soviet Union, where he had lived in exile in the 1950s.

Such choices were not new for Barzani, but now he was an old man who had spent almost all of his 72 years fighting one country or another. He did not know it yet but he was sick with cancer and had only four years to live. He also was facing serious opposition within the Iraqi Kurdish movement from Jalal Talabani, a much younger rival who had long challenged Barzani's dominance. Under these pressures, Barzani gave up and left the remains of his party to his sons Idris and Massoud. Apart from a few months in Iran, Barzani spent the remainder of his life in exile in the United States, where he died in 1979.

Barzani's ignominious battlefield defeat was a shock to many in the developing Kurdish political movement in Turkey. It forced some groups to reevaluate their own plans and allegiances, while others decided that they would have to be even more decisive if they were going to accomplish anything. Although not everyone supported Barzani, he had been an important rallying symbol for Kurdish separatists. His disappearance from the stage opened the way for someone else to take his place.

For Ocalan, Barzani's defeat was a symbol of all that was wrong with the Kurdish national movement—except for his own organization. The fiery young man argued that the elderly Barzani's fatal flaw was that he always remained part of feudal Kurdish society and that he relied on the United States and its lackey Iran for support. Worse still, Barzani had called for autonomy instead of demanding independence. Ocalan used the collapse of Barzani's movement as proof that to be successful one needed to be independent of all major powers, be it the United States or the Soviet Union. The defeat was also a sign that one had to stand against the tribal leaders and large landowners that controlled so much of Kurdish society. In Ocalan's eyes, Barzani represented the "primitive" ideology that had held Kurds back for so many decades.[3]

Ocalan did not stop his attacks with Barzani. In speech after speech to his supporters and in any other platform he could find, he argued that the previous Kurdish uprisings in Turkey failed because they were neither sufficiently socialist nor truly national liberation struggles. He also blamed the relatively well-off of Kurdish society—its landowning and professional classes—for working hand-in-hand with the oppressive Turkish state to further their own interests at the expense of the others. The large landowners especially were as guilty as the state itself for stripping the Kurds of their right to an independent state.

But Ocalan saved his greatest criticism for those he saw as his rivals. The other new Turkish Kurdish groups—such as Kawa, Ozgurluk Yolu, DDKD, and the reformed TKDP—were rejected as "collaborators" and "revisionists." Their demands for an independent Kurdish state were dismissed as false fronts, their promises of armed struggle were called fantasies, and their leftist ideologies were rejected as being some variant of feudal or bourgeois thinking. He made it clear that these groups were a disgrace to the Kurdish national movement, their leaders in essence traitors who had capitulated to the forces of capitalism or to the demands of China, the Soviet Union, the United States, or Turkey.

Ocalan's attacks on his rivals were not always very logical nor necessarily truthful, but they resonated among twenty-something Kurds eager for an independent state. Frustrated by their history of failed uprisings and forced assimilation, these people were open to an ideology that purported to explain why no separatist Kurdish group had yet to be successful. Ocalan's absolute dismissal of the luminaries of the Kurdish nationalist movement—from Barzani in Iraq to Kemal Burkay in Turkey—answered the question of why the Kurds always lost. The reason was that these leaders were not true Kurdish revolutionaries. It was a simple and attractive explanation. While rivals accused Ocalan of hate-mongering, some Kurds saw in his stance a certain independence that made them think he could be the one to lead them to their own state.

The Followers

Despite legal limits on leftist political activity in the 1970s and the state's attempt at absolute repression of Kurdish identity, radicals of all persuasions found that they could organize with little interference. Authorities at first ignored the growing activism, thinking that as long as people were just talking there was little to worry about. In part this was hubris. Security officials believed the 1971 military coup, coupled with the new, more restrictive legislation, had wiped out the vestiges of the radical '68 movement. Later on, as the political atmosphere grew more heated in the latter half of the 1970s, the problem was that officials often were overwhelmed by the violent and nonviolent political agitation.

The Kurdistan Revolutionaries, as Ocalan's supporters began to call themselves around 1975, recruited aggressively. Members of Ocalan's "inner circle"—or the Ankara group—were assigned regions where they were responsible for promoting the new group's line. Recruitment methods, whether in the southeast or in Ankara, focused on one-on-one debates to win people over. Supporters thought nothing of sitting with someone for 24 hours straight to argue for the new group; one early recruit remembers visiting a friend almost every day for a year until the young man pledged his support.

"When we said we were working then, it meant working to change a person's thinking," said Mehmet Can Yuce, who spent 20 years in prison for his unapologetic role in the PKK. "We wouldn't get bored no matter how long this took because giving our views and getting them accepted was very important for us."

Sometimes this meant actually convincing someone that first he was a Kurd, second that Kurds had a right to their own state, and third that only the Kurdistan Revolutionaries could do this. Other times this required simply promoting the group's developing ideology to already-committed Kurdish nationalists. The fact that followers promised armed struggle—other groups were still debating the how, when, and why of taking up arms—gave their message a clarity that was proving attractive.

"We said it was necessary not just to say that we wanted armed revolution and then go home and discuss it," said Selim Curukkaya, who traveled throughout the southeast recruiting as a 21-year-old student at the Tunceli Teachers School in 1975. "We wanted to know how we can get guns and we discussed this and then we went out and got them. Our thing was that we actually did what we said we would."

In Ankara, where Ocalan and his friends were still registered as students (and receiving government subsidies that they used for their clandestine activities), they worked to made inroads among the other Kurdish university students, the very people Ankara assumed had been assimilated into forgetting—or at least ignoring—their Kurdish roots.

"At the end of 1975 or in early 1976 some friends introduced me to Ocalan in Ankara," recalled Selahattin Celik, then an engineering student in his mid-twenties. "We had all heard of him, that he was smart, that he created a sort of psychological environment when he spoke. For example, you bring him tea, he wouldn't be the one to bring you tea."

By his own account, Celik, a short, wiry man now in his late forties, was an easy target for Ocalan, who promised to wage a real war for an independent Kurdistan. Celik had always been sympathetic to Kurdish nationalism—his father was an admirer of Mulla Mustafa Barzani—and Ocalan's focused arguments drew the engineering student in. Almost without thinking, he started to operate with the group, joining their protests, attending their meetings.

"This sort of politicization didn't necessarily have a real ideological base," said Celik, sitting in his small Cologne apartment, which he shares with two computers and a wall of books. "Maybe you had a friend who took you along to a meeting, maybe you remembered when the soldiers came to your village and you were afraid, these things leave marks on a person. Also, as a child, from the day you were old enough to understand things, you realized something was different. The language you spoke was different, these sorts of things."

The early recruits were often university and teacher's school students or drop-outs. Their origins were rooted in the poor, mainly landless villagers that comprised the overwhelming majority of Kurdish society, families with close to a dozen children, illiterate mothers, and a tough life based on small-scale farming and animal husbandry. Going to school usually entailed boarding with relatives far from home, or vying for one of the coveted spots in the state-run regional boarding schools. What distinguished people like Celik, Curukkaya, and other recruits from the rest of Kurdish society was that they had options.

Some supporters, like Curukkaya, had good job prospects, while others, like Celik, actually had well-paying jobs. While it is true, as is often claimed, that the PKK attracted the "lumpen" of Kurdish society, what is missed is that many of the early supporters were actually those who had lifted themselves out of their poverty-stricken, uneducated "lumpen" surroundings. These were young men—and a few young women—who could have gone on to have much better lives than their parents could ever have imagined. In fact, these Kurds in their twenties, with their good Turkish and higher educations, were the people who were supposed to assimilate into Turkish society and culture. At least that was Ankara's plan. But despite Ankara's best efforts, it was proving impossible to stamp out Kurdish identity and, by association, Kurdish nationalism.

Taking the Show on the Road

On the eve of the 1977 new year, about 20 people from Ocalan's "inner circle" gathered in the central Dikimevi suburb of Ankara for a two-day, two-night meeting in which they started laying out the group's official party program.[4] The holiday was specifically chosen because a police raid seemed less likely then, but if it did occur they could claim they were celebrating the new year. They also evaluated recruitment to date—they had gathered together some 250 to 300 members over the past two years—and planned for Ocalan to hold a series of clandestine talks to core supporters in the Kurdish southeast.

The Dikimevi meeting marked the start of the preparatory work to set up a proper, professional (albeit illegal) organization with an official ideology. Shortly afterward, Ocalan embarked on a six-week trip through the remote mountain villages and dusty cities of the southeast. For many of his supporters, this was the first time they were meeting the man they viewed as their leader and they were not disappointed.

"Listening to him speak helped make certain things clear in my mind," said Yuce, who years later published a breathless hagiography of Ocalan and the PKK's founding. "He was able to explain some theories and plans in a way that made the group's ideology seem even more compelling."

As a speaker, Ocalan tended to be longwinded and his analyses —of the history of colonialism, the evils of imperialism, and the theories of his ideological heroes Marx, Engels, and Stalin—could be convoluted. But Ocalan also simplified the future of the Kurdish struggle. For Ocalan, there were no tortured debates on whether Kurdish society had reached the necessary level of ideological development for launching armed struggle or questioning whether the society's economic status was appropriate for communist warfare or whether Mao's "Three Worlds" theory should be adopted. Instead, there was the problem—Turkey's colonization of the Kurdish region coupled with imperialism and capitalism. And the solution—armed struggle and socialism.

At this time there were nine or more illegal Kurdish organizations operating in Turkey (the number kept on rising through the end of the decade because of ideological divisions that split groups). They all supported an independent Kurdish state, at least in theory, and most believed that Kurdistan was divided among four countries (Iran, Iraq, Syria, and Turkey), although at least one thought that the division also included a sliver of the Soviet Union. They also all promoted some sort of socialist model for their hoped-for Kurdish state. It was in the details, however, where sharp differences among the groups arose.

Some backed a Maoist model, while others preferred the Stalinist or another radical left variation. Their underlying ideology was reflected in their political sentiments: some were pro-Soviet, others pro-

Mao, one was both anti-Soviet and anti-Maoist and believed in a Chinese-styled revolution and supported Albania, leaving it seemingly confused. Yet beyond ideology, they were unanimous in believing that armed struggle was necessary to liberate what they called northern Kurdistan. Only Burkay's Kurdistan Socialist Party did not support armed struggle. Even then, in theory he was not opposed, but he believed that the conditions in Turkey were not ripe for a successful fight.[5]

In this crowded atmosphere, it was not always easy for a Kurdish nationalist to choose whom to follow. But Ocalan's rhetoric implied the sort of commitment to armed struggle that was lacking in other groups. Ocalan and his followers theorized that the severe clampdown on Kurds following the failed rebellions in the 1920s and 1930s made people extremely fearful of joining any uprising. In order to offset this, what was needed was an aggressive approach that proved they were both committed and capable. Once people saw that the group was serious about armed rebellion, they would support the fight.

"If a people embraces its own tradition, uses its own language and makes its culture come alive, this too is a rebellion," said Ocalan in his 1977 speech in Elazig, a speech that was the basis for the group's first published pamphlet on its ideology. "But the highest form of rebellion is armed rebellion."[6]

The aggressiveness of Ocalan's approach was the nascent group's primary strength. Ocalan differentiated himself from his rivals not only by insisting the uprising had to start right away, but also by promoting violence to the exclusion of any other avenue for change. This focus on fighting had a certain logic given the political conditions. Turkey's democratic system had never functioned very well nor very democratically, so it was not difficult for Kurdish nationalists to reject any attempt to work through the legal system.

The political chaos that engulfed Turkey in the late 1970s did give de facto breathing room to illegal leftist and Kurdish groups. Nonetheless, activities such as writing about the Kurds, or calling for a Kurdish state, remained absolutely banned. Kurdish activists had little recourse but to break the law if they wanted to promote their ideas, even if only in a magazine. After awhile, younger Kurds especially began to ask themselves why they should risk prison for a magazine article, when a gun seemed so much more effective.

"The PKK understood well the psychology of the Kurdish people," said Huseyin Topgider, who split from the TKDP in 1978 to join Ocalan. "They understood that the people are weak, so they need guns. The other groups kept seeing these things as something in the future, and their approach was that first you think, argue and develop a consciousness and then organize. But in that period in Turkey you needed to be armed to accomplish anything."

The Action

Despite Ocalan's vociferous call to war, at the outset the Kurdistan Revolutionaries were more interested in attacking their leftist and Kurdish rivals than the state.[7] Throughout the Kurdish region, Ocalan's followers increasingly took an unforgiving view toward other groups and armed clashes followed. The fighting could be sparked by a debate gone out of hand, accusations of rigged voting for a union, or a misconstrued statement. Mainly, it was enough that a rival group was active in the same town where the Kurdistan Revolutionaries wanted to gain a foothold.

Ocalan's speeches—some of which were taped and distributed—made clear his lack of respect for rival groups. And while he may not have ordered all attacks, he did not condemn them when they occurred. At the same time, the still loose organization of the Kurdistan Revolutionaries made it easy for followers to take matters in their own hands, and the idea of setting themselves up as the sole force seemed logical.

Ocalan's supporters shared a Leninist-inspired outlook that saw rival groups as impediments to the one-party rule they believed necessary for a successful revolution. While other Kurdish groups tried to prepare peoples' consciousness for the revolution by holding meetings, Ocalan's followers tried to clear the field so they could start the revolution. This included targeting the rightist groups that promoted a militant Turkish nationalism, the leftist groups that opposed Kurdish nationalism, and the Kurdish groups that refused to make way for Ocalan's group. Fighting might take place with fists or with guns, but the goal was to stake claim over what little territory they could control, such as who had the right to hold court in a certain coffeehouse, speak in a certain school, or "patrol" in a certain neighborhood.

"In this period in the whole leftist movement, Turkish and Kurdish, everyone's view was that the only right view is my own view," said Mehmet Can Yuce, himself marked for assassination by his former comrades after he split from the PKK in 1999. "You believed that views apart from your own were wrong, that such views were helping the bourgeois. And when you don't see the others as legitimate, then you don't see them as having the right to live."

Fighting among Kurdish rebel groups striving for the same goal was commonplace throughout the region. Ocalan and his backers only had to look across the border into northern Iraq. Relations among Kurdish activists had quickly deteriorated after Baghdad's triumph over KDP chief Mulla Mustafa Barzani in March 1975.[8] His long-time rival Jalal Talabani took opportunity of the power vacuum to form the more socialist-oriented Patriotic Union of Kurdistan (PUK). But Barzani's successors, including his sons Idris and Massoud and high-level official Sami Abdul-Rahman, were not pleased with this threat to their power base. The KDP officially reformed in 1976 and clashes broke out between the two groups.

Talabani suffered three deadly attacks on his men before he had the chance for revenge. In April 1978, he planned a raid on KDP bases, but his letter of instruction fell into Abdul-Rahman's hands. The KDP laid a trap for the PUK forces just as they crossed the mountains into Turkey to pick up smuggled weapons. A large number of PUK fighters were killed and Talabani's two top men were executed on orders from Abdul-Rahman. The attack was one reason for the mistrust, hatred, and pitched battles that continued between the two groups through the late 1990s.

As Ocalan's group grew more confident—and as security forces were overwhelmed by the increased armed activism from all sides—clashes with rivals became more organized, more deliberate, and more deadly. Ocalan's fighters, who often took the offensive in the clashes with other Kurdish groups, lost more men, and also lost what little goodwill it still had among its rivals. Opponents of Ocalan said the unceasing aggressiveness proved he was more a menace than a nationalist. Supporters of Ocalan used the attacks to show that they were serious about liberating Kurdistan and would let nothing stand in their way.

"We believed in socialism and it was a Stalin type of socialism we believed in," stated Selim Curukkaya, in the matter-of-fact manner that former PKK members use to explain why they spent the late 1970s fighting other Kurds instead of the Turkish state. "The 1920s were our model, how the Russian Communist Party forbade all other parties and got rid of the cliques. We saw this as all positive and we wanted to do the same."

Love

Abdullah Ocalan married in 1978. The bride was a 25-year-old university student named Kesire Yildirim, one of the first women to support the nascent Kurdish group. Yildirim, dark-haired and serious, came from a middle-class Kurdish family, very different from Ocalan's village upbringing.[9] Her father was said to be a regional member of the mainstream Republican People's Party (CHP)—the party founded by Ataturk—and he raised his family in the relatively large town of Karakocan on the edges of the Kurdish region. Yildirim, the oldest child in the family, was encouraged to study. She attended teacher's school in Elazig and then won a place in Ankara University's journalism school, where she subsequently met Ocalan.

PKK supporters viewed marriage as a bourgeois undertaking that weakened people's commitment to the fight. "From the beginning there was a rule against marrying, or maybe not a rule, but it was an idea, a way of thinking," said Selahattin Celik. "Love was something for the small bourgeois, something unnecessary." Nonetheless, a number of the PKK's first members were married—some, like Ocalan, married other supporters—but the pressures of the illegal life made it hard to maintain a traditional relationship.

Ocalan himself seemed to have mixed feelings about getting married, telling some people that he did so only to make it easier for Yildirim to work in the Kurdish region, where an unmarried, young woman could not travel alone. Years later, after Yildirim split from the PKK, Ocalan offered other rationalizations for why they had married —mainly, he claimed he wanted to save her from her family's links to the state—but he also hinted that he truly was attracted to Kesire, described by former acquaintances as a cultured, pretty, and intelligent woman.

"I didn't consider it very likely that the relationship would succeed," he explained after they split. "But I also was dragged along by the desire for love, emotion and marriage."[10]

Some of Ocalan's supporters were uncomfortable with the relationship. Quite apart from the belief that both marriage and sexual relations were an unnecessary diversion from the revolutionary struggle, they were suspicious of Yildirim's background. Her relatives were said to have teamed up with the Turkish state during the Kurdish rebellions of the late 1920s and 1930s, and her father was involved in mainstream politics. In his retelling of the PKK's founding, Yuce noted that other militants were convinced that with such a family, Yildirim had to be working for the state: "A policeman's child is a policeman, an agent's child is an agent."[11]

It probably did not help that Yildirim, whose family was better-off than many in the group, appeared to want the normal trappings of married life. "The house that [she] arranged looked more like that of a petit-bourgeois than that of a revolutionary militant,"[12] complained Yuce.

Ocalan and Yildirim, both strong-willed and intelligent, also fought a lot. Ocalan later said that another man—a more traditional Kurdish man—would have beaten or divorced a wife who argued. In Ocalan's case, he claimed that he instead learned to be patient, calm, and above all, careful. "I didn't throw her out of the house. Just the opposite, sometimes I fled the house."[13] Some of Ocalan's supporters, angry at how their leader was being treated—and at the disrespect shown to a Kurdish husband—briefly considered assassinating Yildirim, but abandoned the plan because of concern that Ocalan would not approve. Still, Ocalan used this as proof of his ability to withstand anything—even a wife his friends wanted to kill.

Ocalan's marriage soon unraveled. By the mid-1980s, the two were estranged and Ocalan reportedly had taken up with another woman. In 1988, Yildirim, by then working for the PKK in Athens, tried to stage a coup against her husband but failed. She went underground and it is widely rumored that Ocalan bought her silence in exchange for a financial stipend and a promise that she would not be killed.

Still, the PKK leader never forgot her betrayal. Her life—and their marriage—was turned into a rhetorical device, something that Ocalan used to underscore the constant dangers he and the PKK faced and the need to be ever-vigilant against traitors. He also used it to buttress his views on marriage and sexual relationships, both later banned for PKK militants. He insisted that his experiences with Yildirim underscored the anti-revolutionary dangers of traditional, Kurdish marriages—although he and Yildirim did not have a very traditional marriage—and pointed to the need for women to be able to act independent and free from male pressure. The connection to his wife was not always exact, but for Ocalan, the conclusion was always more important than the factual details that preceded it.

"If a woman tries to pressure me, then I am forced to learn what being a woman means," he told Turkish writer Yalcin Kucuk in 1992. "In this sense, Kesire was one of my biggest teachers, but a very harsh teacher."[14]

A Fortuitous Death

On the evening of May 19, 1978, a Kurdish militant named Halil Cavgun was shot dead in the rough Kurdish town of Hilvan.[15] Cavgun was a member of the Kurdistan Revolutionaries and his murderer someone from the landowning tribe known as the Suleymanlar. There are different versions of what led up to the attack, but tension between leftist Kurdish groups trying to gain a foothold in the town and the Suleymanlar tribe, which essentially controlled the town and surrounding villages, had been mounting for weeks. The Suleymanlar saw these leftists as a threat to the existing order, while the Kurdistan Revolutionaries viewed oppressive, landowning tribes like the Suleymanlar as much the enemy as the state itself.

By their own admission, Ocalan's men initially failed to get support for a revenge attack. In fact, apart from two or three families, nobody wanted anything to do with them. The local people, poor and landless, were understandably hesitant to take a stand against a relatively wealthy tribe that controlled the municipality and counted the police among its allies. Killing someone from the tribe could set off a blood feud that could engulf anyone (and his relatives) linked to the Kurdistan Revolutionaries.

But for Ocalan, the killing of Cavgun demanded a response in kind. This was the second murder of a high-level member in just over a year and the group's reputation was at stake. Ocalan had promised his supporters an uprising against the state, but until then fighting had been mainly with rival groups, the Turkish left- or right-wing sympathizers. Retaliating against the Suleymanlar would make clear the Kurdistan Revolutionaries' opposition to those wealthy landowners who oppressed the local people and, just as importantly, collaborated with the state against Kurdish nationalists. Such an attack would also underscore the group's commitment to armed struggle. Two of the group's top men were sent to the region to prepare an attack.

The Kurdistan Revolutionaries struck back two months later, killing the tribe's leader Mehmet Baysal. In the battles that raged over the next few months between the two groups, the Kurdish nationalists gradually gained wide support in the town. Their cause—attacking a tribe that worked hand-in-hand with the ultra-right-wing MHP political party—was a sympathetic one to many. But it was only when the Kurdish leftists proved their willingness to stick out the fight, despite the high cost to their own men, that people showed support. Other Kurdish separatist groups were just as opposed as Ocalan was to the state and the state-allied wealthy landlords, but few took concrete action. Increasingly, it appeared that only Ocalan and his followers were willing to fight.

"After years of oppression suddenly there was a group to stand against that and it was like we could finally take revenge," said Ramazan Ulek, who was from a village not far from Hilvan. He was a university student in 1977 when he grew close to Ocalan's group, which he believed to be the group most likely to carry out the revolution it promised. "In my village, for example, everyone had a relative who had been beaten by the soldiers and the PKK was a stand against that. The PKK was also against the aghas [wealthy landowners] who would steal everything, even gold off a woman's neck. After years of being repressed, suddenly there was something and everyone ran to the PKK."

The Hilvan fight marked the start of a new offensive posture by the Kurdish group. The group began to target the large tribal leaders who dominated the region's economy and worked with the state. A few months later, on July 30, 1979, the group staged a daring assassination attempt against a Kurdish parliamentarian and head of the powerful Bucak tribe. Mehmet Celal Bucak was a member of the Justice Party, which had forged a governing alliance with the ultra-right-wing Nationalist Action Party (MHP) in the 1970s. Bucak himself had a reputation for cruelly treating those who lived in "his" villages. In a sign of the divisions even within tribes, one of Bucak's relatives had been the founder of the TKDP Kurdish party tied to Barzani's movement across the border.

The willingness of Ocalan's followers to go after such a high-profile target was a clear sign of the aggressive approach that was so attractive to their supporters. The fact that Bucak was only wounded did not diminish the boldness of the plan and the backing they gained from it.

"Attacking Bucak was like attacking the state since the state supported the wealthy landowners," said Celik, who by then had graduated from university, worked a year as an engineer, and quit to be a full-time revolutionary. "A lot of fighting broke out after Bucak was attacked and many people died. But Apo believed that if a big fight broke out, then support for the PKK would grow," added Celik, referring to the PKK leader by his nickname, a common diminutive of Ocalan's first name, Abdullah. "According to Apo, even if 100 people were to die, still, their children would become PKK supporters [to take revenge]."

The Party

Assassinating Bucak was supposed to be the public announcement of the founding of the PKK, known in Kurdish as *Partiya Karkeren Kurdistan* (and in English as the Kurdistan Workers' Party).[16] The party actually was formed eight months earlier on November 28, 1978, during the clandestine meeting at Fis village outside Diyarbakir, but the group had decided to delay making a statement until they could do so with fanfare. Although they failed to kill Bucak, the assassination attempt received wide notice and leaflets laying out their goals were scattered throughout the region. The leaflet included an overview of Kurdish history and called for a national revolution to overthrow the Turkish state:

> Forward to an independent, united, democratic Kurdistan!
> Down with imperialism and colonialism!
> Long live independence and proletariat internationalism!
> Long live the PKK (Kurdistan Workers' Party)![17]

The distinction between the new party and the old group was mainly an operational one. Following the founding meeting, held in the Fis village outside of Diyarbakir, supporters were expected to turn "professional." Previously, Ocalan's supporters acted on their own initiative, although always within the confines of the general nationalist, leftist ideology and goals. The Fis meeting sought to replace this independent approach with a more structured, controlled framework. A three-person central committee (initially comprised of Ocalan, Sahin Donmez, and Cemil Bayik) was set up. Next in the governing structure were five-person Regional Preparations Committees, which were established throughout the Kurdish area and were supposed to decide the local actions.[18] In conjunction with these changes supporters, who were now de facto members of the new organization, often dropped out of school or quit their jobs in order to devote themselves to the PKK. Some members were sent to their home regions to assist in recruitment or to work on taking over trade unions and educational associations from rival organizations. Armed clashes were often part of these operations.

But despite this attempt at control, activities were almost as chaotic as before. Members continued to make their own decisions without checking with their local regional committee. Part of the reason was that Turkey was growing more chaotic and it was not always practical to consult before acting. In addition, the PKK's base of support was among eager—some would say hotheaded—Kurdish young men, who joined precisely because they did not want to wait to start the armed struggle.

"As general secretary of a committee you might even say no to a planned attack, and it would still happen," recalled Huseyin Topgider, who was named general secretary for the Malatya-Elazig area. "The youth were like that. For example, people on their own would decide to go and stage a robbery to get money, or steal guns or something sensationalist like attacking someone who was an agent of the state."

Meanwhile, the proclamation of the organization was supposed to mark a new step on the road to Kurdish liberation, but within a few months the PKK found itself hemmed in on all sides. The gains it made in the previous year were slowly being eroded, not least of all because of its own aggressiveness. Its violent attitude toward rival groups made it hard for supporters to work freely: other Kurdish groups tried to block them from taking part in public meetings, saying PKK members were coming armed to make trouble. One rival Kurdish group briefly found common cause with the police to run PKK militants out of the town of Dogubayazit.[19] In Hilvan, the Suleymanlar tribe renewed their attacks on the PKK, kidnapping and killing six villagers.[20]

The renewal of clashes in the Hilvan area quickly spiraled out of the PKK's control, as villagers and PKK sympathizers sought revenge against one another. Soon, serious armed clashes would break out with the well-armed rival Kurdistan National Liberators (KUK) in the Mardin area, sapping energy and people. Meanwhile, in the spring of 1979, central committee member Sahin Donmez was arrested.

Donmez was not very well liked among his comrades, but he was a hard-worker and had been rewarded with a top position. His organizational work for the PKK took him throughout the region and in May, shortly after he arrived in Elazig province, he was captured by police. Ocalan received word of the arrest when he was in Diyarbakir. He quickly left for the nearby city of Mardin, correctly assuming that Donmez knew the addresses of the PKK's safe houses in Diyarbakir. As police swept through PKK hideouts in the region, picking up activists, it became clear that Donmez was holding little back. "We immediately understood that our end was coming,"[21] Ocalan said.

The arrest of Donmez helped convince Ocalan that he should leave Turkey for a safer place. The rumor was that a military coup was in the works. Already, the security forces were taking up more positions throughout the region, although they continued to complain to their commanders that it was impossible to function because of the prevalence of armed Kurdish militants. A report from one branch of the security forces just a month before Donmez's arrest said: "Only a brave officer will go into a village with less than twenty people to catch an outlaw."[22] But the pressure, like the arrests, was mounting.

Perhaps nothing underscored this as much as Ocalan's inability to find a safe place to stay after fleeing Diyarbakir. Even those areas where the PKK presence had been strongest were now practically off-limits. The combination of pressure from rival groups, police searches, and the overall difficulty of maintaining hold of an area month after month had taken its toll on the PKK's strength. Ocalan grew more worried.

I was looking for a house in Urfa. We were going to stay for a few days. . . . Even the spouses of some of our sympathizers had started to see us as a burden and they would come up with all sorts of reasons to get us out of the door. Like "yesterday the police came here." You say "really?" . . . and you look for another place; but it is hard to find.[23]

In July of the same year, Ocalan secretly fled across the border into Syria and in a sign of just how loosely organized the PKK was at the time, some PKK members did not realize Ocalan was gone until the following year. By then, hundreds of Turkish and Kurdish activists had begun to flee the country, either to escape imminent arrest or else because they were certain that a coup was in the planning. In the summer of 1980, just a few months before the military coup, Ocalan sent word to the militants that they should try to get out of Turkey and join him in Syria.

Turkey in Collapse

One reason that the PKK was able to operate seemingly unchecked throughout the latter half of the 1970s was that all of Turkey was spiraling out of control.[24] Following the return to democracy in 1974, the government's hold over the country gradually grew weaker and weaker. The country's coalition governments—there were four between 1975 and 1980—could barely function, one of which lasted less than six months before falling on a vote of confidence. Even when the coalition government managed to hold together, deep ideological divisions and old suspicions within the coalitions and the Assembly made it hard to agree on necessary laws and then get them passed.

The political uncertainty was worsened by the country's contracting economy amid a recession in Europe. By 1979, inflation had jumped to 90 percent. Import restrictions to save foreign currency reserves led to an oil shortage that forced daily power cuts. Businesses could no longer import needed raw materials and production dwindled. Light bulbs, medicine, and even toilet paper became unavailable. Unemployment, meanwhile, continued to rise. And universities could take only 20 percent of each year's high school graduates, leaving those who could not find work easy fodder for recruitment by the extreme right and left.

Political violence also jumped in the second half of the 1970s. The paramilitary Grey Wolves grew stronger when the political party with which it was affiliated, the ultra-right-wing Nationalist Action Party (MHP), was included in two of the coalition governments. The Grey Wolves fought with the radical left-wing groups, and later on the Islamists joined in on the side of the right-wing extremists. The leftists were more fragmented than the right—there were some 40, illegal left-wing groups professing armed revolution—and they fought against the Grey Wolves and among themselves.

Extremist groups battled it out on the street and university campuses became no-go areas except for members of the various armed groups that controlled different sections. People began to fear leaving their homes. In 1976, there were 104 political murders; in 1977, the number rose to 230, and by mid-1979, some 20 people were being killed a day. Targets grew more indiscriminate. Few people were arrested for these murders, and when they were they found it easy to escape.

Despite imposition of martial law in some provinces starting in 1978, the military claimed it did not have the necessary power nor political backing to halt the violence. The police, meanwhile, were themselves riven by ideological divisions, leading to allegations that some officers conspired with the extremist right. In Istanbul, a large-scale May 1 workers rally in 1977 was first disrupted by Maoists, and then by shots from the nearby rooftops. In the ensuing panic—worsened when police barricaded streets through which people could have escaped—nearly 40 people were either trampled or shot to death. There was reason to believe that the killings were helped by sympathizers within the security forces. This bloody incident was followed by attacks on minority Alawite communities by the Grey Wolves, including the Kahramanmaras massacre in 1978, which only ended when the army was sent in.

The armed forces began discussing the possibility of a takeover as early as 1978. But within a year, as the political, economic, and social situations all worsened, discussions took on the concrete questions of exactly when and how a coup would be carried out.

At four A.M. on September 12, 1980, Turkish state radio began broadcasting military marches as an announcer read a statement from

General Chief of Staff Kenan Evren declaring the military takeover. Soldiers fanned out to the houses of the top politicians to arrest them. Parliament was abolished and martial law was imposed throughout the country.

Over the next three years, tens of thousands of leftists, Kurds, and rightists would pass through the courts and prisons, torture of detainees would become routine, and all democratic opposition would be muzzled. The constitution would be rewritten yet again, the philosophy of the country's founder Ataturk would be promoted anew, and the universities would be restructured to stop them from ever turning into political arenas again. Yet when the country returned to democratic rule in 1984, the PKK was just gearing up for its first flamboyant attack.

3

The Flight to Survive, 1980–1982

IBRAHIM AYDIN WAS on guard duty in the mountains abutting Kiziltepe, a Kurdish city-town not far from the border with Syria, when the military coup was announced.[1] Aydin, who heard the news on his portable radio, woke the others. Aydin's team of about a dozen PKK militants was responsible for maintaining ties between the militants inside Turkey and the PKK leader. They helped couriers cross the border, found safe houses around Kiziltepe, and arranged meetings to announce plans and tactics. The coup, they agreed that day, did not change their responsibilities or goals. If anything, it only emphasized the need to quicken their fight against the state.

But two weeks later a courier arrived from Syria, carrying the message that everyone should flee. Ocalan decided it was too dangerous to keep his forces inside Turkey. By then, most militants were in agreement: the military's massive arrests had cut avenues for action and forced them even further underground. Leaving Turkey seemed the only answer. Aydin began preparing his escape. The nearby Syrian border usually was easy to cross. The smugglers who regularly plied the route had cleared paths through the mined no-man's land and the Turkish border guards were overstretched.

"We crossed very easily," recounted Aydin. "We had help from a village nearby and we stayed in the village until night. The [Turkish] soldiers were right there, they even went to the house next to the one where we were staying to drink tea and watch TV, but they didn't notice us."

Aydin ended up at the Syrian border city of Qamishli, a dusty, depressed looking place of some 100,000 people just south of the border. Most of the people in Qamishli were Kurds; in fact many had fled from Turkey after the unsuccessful uprisings that started in the 1920s.[2] Not only were they interested in what was happening in Turkey, but also in neighboring Iraq, where the late Mullah Mustafa Barzani's fight had captured their imagination and support. The PKK was not particularly popular in Qamishli—people usually sympathized with the Syrian offshoot of Barzani's party or the Turkish offshoot KUK, which had been very active in the area—but locals were sufficiently nationalistic to welcome any fleeing Kurdish militant, even if some were encouraged to move on quickly.

Aydin stayed a few days in Qamishli before traveling down to the Syrian capital of Damascus, where he saw Ocalan for the first time in more than a year. The PKK leader expressed relief at the number of militants able to flee.

"He told me, 'We've been saved,'" Aydin said. "At that point he wanted everyone to leave Turkey and said we must make preparations [for the rebel war] from outside. He was very definite about this."

Ocalan's apparent optimism about what the PKK could now do masked the unpleasant fact that the military regime's crackdown had succeeded in halting the extremist violence. Thousands of people were arrested after the coup, among them more than one thousand suspected PKK supporters.[3] As arrests continued into the next year, the PKK soon gained the dubious honor of being the Kurdish organization with the most militants in prison. Although the large number of imprisoned PKK supporters indicated the group was more popular than rivals wanted to admit, this was little consolation to those who had failed to flee in time. The group was hemorrhaging men and women, including some of its most capable and charismatic.

"The PKK was falling apart," said Sari Baran, who set out with eight others for Syria shortly after the coup. Unlike Aydin, Baran's trip started from a mountain encampment far from the border and took a harrowing 20 days. During the day, they hid in the mountains, and at night they navigated unfamiliar terrain, relying on villagers to provide food and clothing. Guides who knew the area were enlisted to help, but some showed up days late and others never appeared. "There were a lot of military operations and the pressure on the villagers was high." The journey, he added flatly, "was not easy . . . some people were killed along the way."

PKK rebels were not the only ones trying to reach Syria. This Arab country had long been a haven for Turkish leftist extremists—Damascus, which had numerous disputes with Ankara, operated on the principle that its enemy's enemy was its friend—and militants from both Turkish and Kurdish groups were fleeing there. Some saw it only as a way-station until they could get the right passports and visas for Europe, others planned to stay in Syria or move on to Lebanon or Iraq, three countries where they, like the PKK, had the chance to get the weapons and training for the revolution they promised their followers.

"When we fled to Syria we all thought it would be so easy," explained former PKK militant Selahattin Celik, who went into hiding shortly after the coup and arrived in Syria about a month later, crossing near Qamishli like so many others. "We thought we would spend a few months in Syria and then go back in [Turkey] and start something like the Vietnam war, push out the army. . . . [T]hat's what we talked about, how we would soon go back and fight."

Ocalan Finds the PKK a New Home

Selahattin Celik stayed two weeks in the border town Qamishli until he got word to Ocalan that he had arrived. Then he took a bus to Damascus, where Ocalan had arranged for PKK militants to stay at different apartments throughout the city. Some were the apartments of Syrian Kurds in the Palestinian or Kurdish quarters of Damascus, others apparently had been rented by Ocalan or else by his new Palestinian contacts. "Already then Apo was sort of a big man," noted Celik, who soon was tapped to help oversee PKK training in Palestinian military bases in Lebanon.

Ocalan had been out of Turkey for just over a year, and during this period he had worked hard to secure his position in the tumultuous political landscape.[4] Like those who fled after the coup, Ocalan arrived on foot, crossing the lightly guarded border with the help of a local smuggler. His immediate goal was to save himself; his long-term plan was to arrange for PKK fighters to get training from the Palestinian militant groups in Syria and Lebanon. The Palestinians were well known for assisting foreign revolutionaries, including some Turkish leftists for brief periods in the early 1970s. But Ocalan had few, if any, contacts in Syria, and he failed to secure an introduction to the Palestinian factions that kept political bureaus in the Syrian capital.

After a short time in Damascus, Ocalan gave up and made his way to Beirut. Lebanon had just come out of a year-long civil war and much of the country was divided between Palestinian and Christian militias. Syrian troops, who moved into Lebanon in 1976 to force an end to the fighting, directly controlled the Bekaa Valley in Lebanon's eastern region and exerted effective control over much of the rest of the country. Ocalan found a place to stay in the Lebanese capital and made contact with Kurds living there. A large part of the Kurdish community in Lebanon originally came from Turkey—they had immigrated decades earlier to escape the failed Kurdish uprisings and the poverty—and there always were new arrivals looking for work in the construction industry.[5]

"There were Turkish and Kurdish families there," Ocalan explained. "I used the name Ali . . . and in this way six months, maybe a year, passed."[6]

In late 1979 or early 1980, Ocalan succeeded in getting a meeting in Beirut with Nayif Hawatmah's Syrian-backed Democratic Front for the Liberation of Palestine (DFLP). This meeting, probably arranged by Kurds that Ocalan met in Beirut, led to a second, more serious meeting in Damascus with Abu Laila (Qais Abdul-Karim), a member of the Palestinian group's political leadership. Abu Laila had known quite a few leftist revolutionaries from Turkey—many came seeking some sort of assistance, he explained—and what they said about Ocalan was not very flattering.

"The other factions accused him of using terrorist methods and dealing with his opponents in the party by killing people and things like that," recalled Abu Laila, who spoke with me in Ramallah in the Palestinian-administered part of the West Bank. "Of course, he didn't admit this [to us] but he was very militant in his ideological positions. He gave me a long lecture about revisionism and how important it is to get rid of the revisionists in order to make war against the enemy."

Between Ocalan's penchant for lecturing and the time it took for the translations, the midnight meeting lasted until nearly dawn. Abu Laila laughed. "It was one of the most difficult and strenuous meetings of my life." But the Palestinian official was impressed with Ocalan. "We had met other Turkish Kurds and they didn't seem to be very reliable. This man [Ocalan] seemed to be serious. He didn't want [military or financial] assistance . . . he only wanted to send volunteers . . . to be trained for the future."

The Democratic Front initially agreed to take in a small number of PKK militants and train them in the basics of guerrilla warfare. The offer was not unusual. At various times, the DFLP trained Nicaraguan

Sandinistas, Iranian leftists, Greek Communists, and even the odd Saudi. "We accept the Marxist-Leninist groups because we are Marxist-Leninist," explained Mamdoh Nofal, a former military commander of the Democratic Front, which was one of the largest Palestinian groups inside the umbrella PLO organization. "We are revolutionaries and we support the revolutionary movement."

The DFLP likely also had more concrete reasons for helping. Giving shelter to other leftist revolutionaries allowed the DFLP to promote the image of an important, international revolutionary movement, one to be reckoned with both by its allies and other members of the umbrella Palestine Liberation Organization. And it helped them pad their numbers at a time of rising tension with Israel. Although the DFLP did not plan to involve the Kurds in the fight against Israel—for one thing, Nofal noted, the PKK militants were too inexperienced—it was understood that the Kurds would defend the base if attacked by Israel. But PKK militants made clear they did not want to mix battles.

"They had their own interests and we didn't interfere," said Nofal.

A handful of PKK militants crossed into Syria for training in the first half of 1980; after the military coup militants arrived in large numbers. They were dispersed among a number of DFLP camps in Lebanon, including the Helwe camp, which was on the edge of the Syrian-controlled Bekaa Valley, not far from the Lebanese village al-Hilwah. Syria had occupied the Lebanese Bekaa Valley in 1976 to protect its own border, and Syrian heavy artillery ringed the nearby hills.

When PKK militants started training at Helwe in 1980, the DFLP-run camp could hold perhaps 100 people.[7] The main building was used for political training and discussions and three or four smaller ones included sleeping quarters, a kitchen, and toilet facilities. Military training discussions were held in the big hall, but the surrounding hills were the actual training grounds, a scaled-down version of the Kurdish region where the PKK planned to fight. Palestinians and Kurds usually did their military training together but separated for political classes.

"The [military] courses depended on them," said Nofal. "Some courses were only training in explosives, which needs only 10 days or two weeks to learn. Some courses took two months, for example, for staff officers, they took courses in military, topography, explosives, artillery and guerrilla fighting."

The Palestinians were experienced fighters and they trained the PKK in the mainstays of guerrilla war. "In general, we had no experience as guerrilla fighters and the Palestinians did, and their instruction was useful and seemed correct," recalled Baran.

Nor did the Palestinian trainers ignore the other ways that groups could wage battle, such as with propaganda and with a motivated and organized civilian population. In what turned out to be popular tools for the PKK, the Palestinians educated them on the usefulness of a "civil militia" to collect information about troop movements and arrange food and shelter and setting up general committees, such as for women and students, in order to expand control and support.

Between 1980 and 1982, about 300 PKK militants arrived for training. The DFLP camps could no longer hold all the arrivals and Nofal complained to Ocalan that the training was starting to cost the Palestinian group too much money. The DFLP not only covered the basic expenses of militants in its camps, but also paid a monthly allowance —variously said to be $15, $100, and $300 per person—to help cover other expenses.

"I noticed that they had started to bring large numbers to our camps and we said we can't accept all your members to stay long periods of time because it costs a lot," explained Nofal, who said he suggested the PKK train on its own in the Bekaa or move people to apartments in Damascus, where Ocalan often stayed.

Ocalan, in the meantime, successfully established similar training arrangements with other Palestinian organizations. This allowed the PKK to spread its people among the different Palestinian factions, including Yasir Arafat's Fatah, George Habash's Popular Front for the Liberation of Palestine, Samir Ghosheh's Palestinian Popular Struggle Front, and the Lebanese Communist Party. The Kurdish militants were useful. They helped build fortifications and, in case of an Israeli attack, they could be pushed to the frontline to defend.

"These people turned out to be really serious, real fighters, real soldiers," Abu Laila said. "It was clear he [Ocalan] really had some popular base in Kurdistan and that his men were much more disciplined and united than the other groups. We thought that this group [the PKK] was the most serious group in Turkish Kurdistan. This is why we kept them [in the camps]."

PKK militants viewed the situation with a certain rationality. "We all wore the uniform of whatever place we were staying in, but we had agreements that the PKK would not get involved in fights among Palestinian groups or between the Palestinians and Lebanon," explained Celik. Not only did splitting up their people relieve the burden on any one Palestinian group, but it also allowed the PKK to hedge its bets, just in case Syria turned on Hawatmah or Arafat suddenly was thrown out of Lebanon.

"What did we gain by fleeing to Syria?" asked Celik, pausing for a moment. "In reality, we were finished as an organization after 1980. We had no strength in Europe, in Turkey we were in prison. But in Syria we could gather ourselves together. The minute we got money we used it to send people to Europe [to work in the Kurdish community there]. From the Palestinians we learned things. We learned about making demonstrations for martyrs, about ceremonies. We did a lot of reading on a people's war, we also had armed training. They gave us clothing, cigarettes. We owe the Palestinians something."

The Syrian Connection

Militants fleeing across the border may have tried to keep their arrival secret, but the Syrian intelligence services were vigilant.[8]

"When they came to Syria they had to use secret names, and we were meeting them and hiding them in our houses," recalled Kamiran Hajo, then a Kurdish high school student living in the border town Qamishli. "We thought nobody knew anything. But that was stupid."

While some Turkish Kurds believed they arrived undetected—and certainly, some people did, although they likely did not remain so for long—others quickly discovered that they were under surveillance. A militant from the Kurdish group Rizgari was visited by someone from the intelligence services the day after he turned up.

"How did the Syrians know we were in the country?" said a former member named Kamuran, who now lives in France. "The minute we crossed the border and got to someone's house, the Kurd in the house would go straight to the intelligence services and tell them he had a guest, if not he could face trouble."

The question of whether or not to remain in Syria, an authoritarian-ruled country that repressed its own Kurds, frequently was discussed. "We debated whether we should allow ourselves to be under Syrian control," said Kamuran. "Because apart from the Turkish military regime, Turkey was a much better state than Syria. Syria was a dictatorship, or worse, a tyranny."

Some groups looked for alternatives to Syria, either because they did not like the idea of relying on Damascus or, more commonly, because they wanted to base their forces in Kurdistan itself, be it the Turkish or Iraqi part. But regardless of whether or not they wanted to work out of Syria, almost every group kept representatives in the capital and the top people came there for meetings.

"There was a contradiction [in relying on Syria], but there were a lot of contradictions in the Middle East," noted former PKK militant Ibrahim Aydin.

Syria's support for Kurdish groups was, at least initially, more tacit than overt. In practice this meant that Damascus did not block the flow of illegal refugees from Turkey, did not make trouble for Kurdish militants setting up house in Syria, and did not impede traffic back and forth to Lebanon. It was not, however, that Syria was uninterested in the new arrivals. For starters, Syria had its own domestic Kurdish population to worry about and wanted to ensure that Syrian Kurds were not encouraged to stand against the state. The PKK was well aware of the limits, despite its official rhetoric that saw an independent Kurdistan stretching over part of Syria.

"It was always clear we wouldn't take any action that was against Syria," said Celik. "There was no decision. We just knew that we couldn't do anything proper . . . that's it."

Palestinian groups that offered to train Kurdish militants also paid attention to Syria's interests. Syria was an important backer of the Palestinians in their fight against Israel, and it exerted de facto control over much of Lebanon. Syria's views had to be considered by all Palestinian groups operating between Lebanon and Syria, but especially for those that based their political headquarters in the Syrian capital. "Without Syria's approval, no Palestinian organization would have helped Turkish or Kurdish organizations," noted Mesut Akyol, a pseudonym for a Turkish leftist who traveled in and out of Syria in this period. "Syria's approval was a condition."

One reason for Syria's feigned disinterest was that the government wanted to pretend these militants, fugitives from Turkish justice, were not there. The identity cards the Kurdish and Turkish opposition groups received—from Palestinian groups, Iraqi Kurdish and other opposition groups, the Syrian Communist Party, and, sometimes, the

Syrian *mukhabarat*—allowed Damascus to deny their presence and to deflect, at least officially, Ankara's wrath.

"We all took Arab names," recounted Kamuran, whose identity card, provided by the Syrian intelligence services, identified him as an Iraqi Kurd. "Syria said we had to take these identity cards so that when Turkey asked for us to be sent back, the Syrians could say that we weren't in the country."

Syria had a number of outstanding disputes with Turkey that made it willing to tolerate, if not encourage, these militant groups.[9] For starters, Damascus still claimed ownership of the former Syrian province Alexandretta, which was absorbed by Turkey after a plebiscite in 1939 that Syria never recognized. Much to Turkey's discomfort, Syrian maps still showed the province, since renamed the Hatay, as part of its own country. Assad also was concerned about Turkey's ongoing large GAP dams project, designed to harness the waters of the Tigris and Euphrates for domestic agricultural and electrical purposes. Because the two rivers originated in Turkey—the Tigris delineates part of the border with Syria before flowing into Iraq, while the Euphrates flows across Syria and then into Iraq—the dams project would give Ankara a great deal of control over the flow of water to the more arid Syria. Finally, Syria believed that Turkey gave shelter to members of the Muslim Brothers, the militant opposition force that had launched an all-out attack on the Syrian government just around the time Ocalan and other renegades began to cross into Syria.[10]

But Damascus had few options when it came to pressuring Turkey, which was nearly five times the size of Syria in terms of both land mass and population. Turkey was a long-standing member of NATO and a prized U.S. ally. Turkey's border with the far-western flank of the Soviet Union ensured that in Cold War terms, at least, it could not be abandoned by the West. Assad understood that militarily, at least, he had little chance of standing against Turkey. His best chance for affecting Turkish policies was to find a group whose actions matched Syria's interests.

Looking for proxies to use in its various regional conflicts was nothing new for Damascus. In fact, Syria had long relied on foreign militant groups to promote its political and military objectives.[11] The Palestinian organizations that Syria supported, for example, were useful because their attacks against Israel furthered Assad's desire to weaken the Jewish state. They also helped secure Assad's foothold in

Lebanon and could be used against other Arab states if necessary. All this could be accomplished without Syria having to get directly involved and face the risk of direct retaliation.

Likewise, Syria was engaged in a bitter rivalry with Iraq for leadership of the region. The Iraqi Kurds, dispirited by the collapse of their fight against Baghdad in 1975, proved to be willing partners for the Syrians.[12] Iraqi Kurdish leader Jalal Talabani initially took refuge in Syria and Talabani announced his new PUK organization in a statement issued in Damascus. Likewise, the Kurdistan Socialist Party, which broke away from Talabani's PUK in 1979, also kept an office in Syria, as did the Iraqi Communist Party, which was allied with the Kurds.

Syria's generosity toward Kurdish groups from Turkey and Iraq was not indicative of how it treated its own Kurds.[13] Damascus had always been afraid that Syrian Kurds might demand independence or otherwise threaten the regime's stability. In the 1960s, some 120,000 Syrian Kurds were stripped of their citizenship, forcing them to live in a sort of grey zone where they could not own property, were banned from certain professions, could not own cars, and could not get passports to leave the country. Syria also banned Kurdish political parties and put limits, similar to its neighbor Turkey, on Kurdish-language publications and education. Syria's Kurdish minority chafed under these restrictions, but they had few options under the brutal, authoritarian system that Assad led.

But especially in Qamishli, the Syrian Kurdish town that bordered Turkey and Iraq, the exploits of the PKK and other groups were followed with growing interest. The in-fighting among the some dozen small, ineffectual Syrian Kurdish groups had left many people disenchanted with their own leadership. With Mulla Mustafa Barzani's fight over, the loyalty of Syrian Kurds appeared up for grabs.

Ocalan Reaches Out

Ocalan had always seen himself as leading the Kurdish national movement in Turkey and now that he was based in Damascus, he had time to survey what remained of the competition.[14] Most radical organizations were scrambling to get reestablished, the bulk of their cadre in prison, their surviving leadership unsure of what to do next.

The promises of liberation of both Turkish and Kurdish leftists had ended in disaster, with military rule and repression much worse than any of them had ever experienced.

"Everyone was in shock," Metin Kahraman, a musician sympathetic to the left, said 25 years later. "I was crushed. Because the revolution was going to happen soon. When 12 September happened, maybe for one, two years, in isolated places there was some resistance. But it was clear these wouldn't accomplish anything. Before everything else, exhaustion developed."[15]

Ocalan was not surprised at the swift collapse of so many once-popular groups. In his mind, at least, this merely confirmed his leadership capabilities. As he explained a few years later, he saw his decision to flee Turkey in 1979 as a fortuitous one, allowing him to save not just himself, but his organization, and giving him a head start when it came to competing with the Turkish revolutionary movement after the 1980 coup in Turkey.

"The others could only get out two years after me, after they had already lost their organization," he later said. "Because I got out before Sept. 12, I could both save hundreds of my comrades and get them trained."[16]

The PKK leader decided it was time to make a peace overture to his rivals in the Turkish and Kurdish left and he asked them to consider a common front against the military regime. Whether this was a ruse to help him gain credibility, an attempt to absorb one-time rivals into his own organization, or a real attempt to jettison old ways and work with others was something with which these militants had to grapple. In long letters that he sent to leading Turkish leftists in Europe, Ocalan laid out his new reasoning and aims. He did sound sincere.

"In his letter, Apo referred to the Turkish national liberation movement," Mesut Akyol, one of the founders of the Turkish leftist Devrimci-Yol group (commonly called Dev-Yol, or Revolutionary Path), wrote in a political autobiography years later. The Turkish War of Independence, noted Akyol, "was won as a result of a coalition between Turks and Kurds. Apo was saying, 'Why can't we do the same thing that our bourgeois and feudal ancestors accomplished?'"[17]

Dev-Yol, which before 1980 was the largest militant leftist group in Turkey, had been decimated by the coup. Most of its members were in prison, others had died in detention or were killed trying to flee.

Akyol, who had fled abroad in 1977 to escape an eight-year prison term for making "communism and Kurdish propaganda," now became de facto leader of the once-powerful movement. Ocalan's message appeared to address the very issue—lack of unity—that the Turkish left now believed was to blame for their massive, collective failure.

"I found Ocalan's suggestion very attractive," wrote Akyol. "When I mentioned Apo's messages about getting in touch, my friends told me, 'he sends similar messages to us as well. Why don't you listen to him and figure out what he is saying.'"[18]

In the spring of 1981, Akyol flew to Damascus to talk with Ocalan. The PKK leader took Akyol to the Helwe training camp to see the setup. There was no ignoring that the man Akyol and his friends once dismissed as a "little crazy" for his dream of making armed revolution in the Kurdish region had come a long way. Akyol, for one, returned to Europe convinced that Ocalan truly wanted to work with other groups and was serious about renouncing violence against his former rivals.

Over the next few months, the two men discussed the details of how an alliance could function. Their working supposition was that only armed revolution could force the military regime to give up power. Such a struggle had to be carried out by Turks and Kurds fighting in partnership.

"Apo had a saying, 'Apo will spark rebellion in Turkey from below [Kurdistan] and we will do it from above [the cities],'" Akyol recalled. But many inside Dev-Yol remained deeply suspicious of the PKK and questioned whether Ocalan really was ready to abandon the attacks on rivals that previously seemed to define the group's strategy. Akyol, shuttling around Europe to discuss with other Turkish leftists the proposed front, warned Ocalan that he needed to repudiate the PKK's previous attacks and confirm, in writing, that there would be no such actions in the future. "This was a basic condition of ours," explained Akyol.

Ocalan also was trying to woo the Kurdish opposition and he sent out messages that he wanted to meet with the other Kurdish leaders. Ocalan's attempt to make peace with his rivals was supported by PUK leader Jalal Talabani, who since had relocated to an armed camp just inside the Iranian border with Iraq but continued to come back and forth to Syria.

"I mediated," Talabani told Turkish journalist Mehmet Ali Birand. "I worked to overcome their differences in views, if nothing else, to stop the in-fighting."[19]

Talabani, joined by the Iraqi Communist Party and various Syrian Kurdish parties, pushed Kemal Burkay to talk to Ocalan. Burkay was the leader of the Kurdistan Socialist Party, one of the more influential Turkish Kurdish groups, and a rapprochement between him and Ocalan could ease the way for other groups to do the same. Burkay lived in Europe—like Ocalan, he had the foresight to leave Turkey before the coup—and he frequently visited Syria, where his group kept some representatives. But Burkay, a fierce critic of the PKK's attacks on rival Kurdish groups, initially balked at the idea. The PKK had murdered an activist from Burkay's party in the Turkish Kurdish city Dogubeyazit in March 1979, and Burkay did not believe that Ocalan could be trusted.

"These other groups said, 'the PKK made some mistakes, but now they accept this,'" recalled Burkay, "They [the other groups] did not like what I said. They figured, they [the PKK] are Kurds too, and each group is accusing the other of something" so it was meaningless to take any accusation seriously. "They said 'now Apo is not in Turkey, let's try to change the group.'"

Somewhat reluctantly, Burkay agreed to talk with Ocalan. The two men met at the house in the Syrian capital where representatives of Burkay's party stayed. The last time Ocalan and Burkay had met was maybe three or four years earlier in the Turkish capital Ankara. Ocalan, then an excited young man trying to form his own group, had turned up at Burkay's law office with a friend, hoping the seasoned Kurdish activist could adjudicate an argument over whether or not Kurdistan was a colony. Burkay had written a book arguing just that, and Ocalan left pleased to discover he had been right. This time, Ocalan came to Burkay on something closer to equal footing.

"We sat and talked," recalled Burkay, "and he did a self-criticism, and he said, 'we have changed.'" There were about five people at the meeting, including Talabani. "I said to [Ocalan], 'these were not mistakes, you killed our people, you chose your methods, was this a mistake? You tried to make us look like the enemies of our own people. If this was all a mistake, make a statement to your people, say that we are not the enemy, that it is time for all of us to work together," Burkay recounted, his frustration with Ocalan still clear more than 20 years later. Other Kurdish organizations, Burkay said, called on Ocalan to do the same thing. If Ocalan did this, the other Kurdish groups would sit down and talk with him seriously about the possibility of working together.

Shortly thereafter, the PKK held its 1st Conference, the largest gathering of PKK militants since the party's founding. Some 80 people attended the July 15–26 meeting at Helwe camp in 1981. The discussions focused on what needed to be done to ensure the group could remain viable and restart its battle inside Turkey. A decision was taken to boost organizational operations among Kurds in Europe and begin planning for the war they wanted to launch inside Turkey. And, as demanded by Akyol, Burkay, and others, Ocalan made a critique of his past "mistakes," which referred primarily to the group's physical and verbal attacks on leftist and Kurdish rivals.

The critique, coupled with the promise of a written statement, was sufficient for Dev-Yol. The following year, the United Revolutionary Front Against Fascism (FKBD-C) was announced, a grouping of PKK, Dev-Yol, and about five other small leftist parties.[20] The PKK and Dev-Yol formed a European Committee—Birlik Komitesi (Bir-Kom)—which became an important center for Turkish leftist opposition to the military junta. In Syria, the two groups established a General Staff to plan for their military struggle. Dev-Yol, separately, started to send people to Syria and Lebanon for training with Arafat's Fatah.

But Ocalan's attempts to draw in Kurdish parties failed. Burkay and other Kurdish leaders, who had borne the brunt of Ocalan's violence before the coup, were not convinced that Ocalan had truly changed. Some Kurdish activists complained to Akyol that the new alliance gave Ocalan legitimacy that he did not deserve. And Hatice (Haco) Yasar, one of the leaders of Ala Rizgari, warned Akyol he was making a mistake.

"Haco said, 'don't believe this guy, he will never change, the PKK needs blood.'"

The PKK in Europe

The PKK always had a handful of members in Europe, but in mid-1981, five senior militants were sent there to expand operations.[21] It was remarkably easy for people without valid passports, some on the run from the Turkish authorities, to travel. One popular method was to get the passport of a friend or relative, change the picture, apply for a visa in Damascus and get on a plane. "With money, you could do everything in Syria," remarked Ibrahim Aydin, who himself flew to Germany from Syria in this period.

Europe was then home to some two million so-called guestworkers from Turkey, more than half of whom lived in Germany, and as such was seen by militant groups as a good place to try and win new supporters and financial donations. Europe also was an attractive place for activists forced into exile, and tens of thousands came after the takeover in Turkey.[22]

"Leftists would swear at Europe, calling it imperialist, but when it came time to take refuge somewhere, everyone preferred Europe," said Mesut Akyol, who himself chose to apply for asylum in Germany when he fled Turkey via Syria in 1977. "Because they knew that the democracy there would protect them. The second factor was the presence of so many [Turkish] workers."

The PKK's initial organizational work took place in Germany, gradually spreading to other countries, starting with Holland, Sweden, and France. "At first, the PKK was more active among the refugees, those coming from the rural areas," said Selman Arslan, then a PKK activist in Europe. "It made more sense to organize among the newly arrived, those who were not yet organized, instead of trying to go after the others."

The centers for PKK activity were cultural clubs that doubled as cafes, reading rooms, debating centers, and social welfare offices. "The idea was to educate people [about the PKK], and also to help them with their problems and have folk songs and things like that," said Arslan, who opened the Frankfurt Workers and Culture Association in 1981.

The plight of the political prisoners in Turkey and the military repression fueled the agenda of the militant groups now active in Europe. The fact that the Turkish military regime shut down civic organizations, trade unions, and political parties, fired state workers suspected of leftist sympathies, closed down newspapers, and wrote a new constitution that limited more than it allowed, only seemed to underscore leftist claims that Turkey was a fascist state that would not change without revolution. The mass arrests of opposition figures, the military trials, the reports of torture and deaths in custody, the state executions and extrajudicial executions, the torture and humiliation of Kurdish prisoners forced to chant Turkish nationalist slogans and recite Ataturk's speeches, provided rallying points for demonstrations and recruitment.

Like the other groups active in Europe, the PKK used these to promote its own political agenda. But the group gained extra respect and support because its imprisoned militants led—the PKK always said—the resistance inside Diyarbakir Military Prison, the most brutal jail in Turkey at the time. In truth, other members of other Kurdish groups also tried to stand up to the ill-treatment, but the PKK, whose militants were the majority in the prison, arguably was the most vocal and best-organized Kurdish group to do so.[23]

"Every night the sound of men screaming under torture was heard," wrote Mehdi Zana, mayor of Diyarbakir on the eve of the coup. Zana, who was not a PKK sympathizer, was arrested 12 days later. He ended up in the Diyarbakir Military Prison. "Hearing these screams, the screams of howling animals, we suffered as much as if we were receiving the blows ourselves."[24] Prisoners were sodomized with batons, dunked into vats filled with excrement, left in rat-infested cells, terrorized by a dog, given water mixed with detergent to drink, and forced to lie in the snow in their underwear.

"In order not to undergo . . . torture, the prisoners submitted," wrote Zana. "So they were forced to shout, 'I am proud to be Turkish' or 'A Turk is worth the whole universe.'"[25]

The night of March 21, 1982—the Kurdish new year—PKK prisoner Mazlum Dogan hanged himself in protest. On May 18, four other PKK prisoners burned themselves to death. On July 14, 1982, PKK prisoners led a "death fast" to demand an end to abuses and by September, four of the group's senior cadre had died. Reports of the mistreatment of Kurdish prisoners inside Turkey, coupled with the resistance shown by PKK prisoners, helped boost the group's name.

"This gained a lot of sympathy [for the PKK] here and in Turkey," recounted Arslan.

The PKK also was helped by the focus of its message. Its supporters in Europe continued to stress that the goal was armed struggle to liberate Kurdistan. Other Kurdish groups either said it was not the right time for revolution or else were engaged in internal debates on the issue.

"We were more believable, more devoted," said Arslan, who

himself comes across as very earnest and believable. "We insisted on the need for there to be force against Turkey, saying that without that we would never get our rights." With a military dictatorship in power in Turkey, the "idea that you could get such rights through peaceful means seemed impossible," he added.

Building a Base in Northern Iraq

Massoud Barzani took over as leader of the Iraqi Kurdistan Democratic Party in November 1979, a few months after the death of his father, Mulla Mustafa Barzani.[26] Massoud Barzani—then 33 years old and a peshmerga fighter for more than half his life—inherited an organization riven by political splits and weakened by military defeat. The collapse of the Kurds' fight against Baghdad four years earlier—when Iran pulled its support after striking a diplomatic deal with Iraq—had left the KDP in disarray, with some high-level members breaking off to form their own political parties. One of the main new opposition parties, the Patriotic Union of Kurdistan, was skirmishing with the KDP in the mountains of northern Iraq. Meanwhile, Iraq had enacted the very Autonomy Law that sparked the 1974–1975 war with the Kurds, simultaneously razing an estimated 1400 villages and forcibly relocating at least 600,000 people. Although the Iraqi Kurds, now newly divided among competing parties, had renewed their armed struggle against Baghdad, the fight was hobbled by the memory of their defeat and the armed rivalry among themselves.

The fall of the Iranian Shah's regime in 1979 and Iraq's invasion of Iran in 1980 gave the Iraqi Kurdish parties an old card to play: once again, they were useful to the larger regional powers. The KDP forged close ties with the Iranian Islamic regime, which needed assistance to put down a rebellion by Iranian Kurds hoping to wrest autonomy from the new government. On the other side, Talabani's PUK become an ally of the Iranian Kurdish KDP, with which it shared a leftist outlook, helping Iranian Kurdish rebels in their attack on the city Mahabad. And simultaneously, the two Iraqi Kurdish groups fought with each other.

By 1982, the war with Iran had turned against Saddam Hussein, and he was forced to relocate the bulk of his forces to the country's south to better stave off Iranian advances. Although Saddam Hussein believed the Iraqi Kurdish parties were too divided to make an effective stand against his rule, he did boost the Kurdish pro-government forces to help secure the area. But the mountainous border area was near impossible to control even under the best of circumstances, and this military shift gave the Iraqi Kurdish parties the chance to expand their hold. Barzani's party, in particular, extended its control from the Iranian border along the Turkish border region, an area called Behdinan, and villagers started to return to their homes under protection of Barzani's armed force. Talabani's fighters were stronger in the Sorani-speaking Suleymania area, which was south of the KDP-controlled border area. The two rivals agreed that their fighters could now travel throughout the region unmolested, but clashes started up less than a year later in April 1983.

Ocalan had little interest in the intra-Kurdish clashes in Iraq, but he was interested in setting his people up in northern Iraq. A few PKK militants had gone to Iran right before the start of the Iran-Iraq war, where they settled into KDP camps near the Turkish border. Such small-scale mixing was not uncommon, and Iraqi Kurdish fighters—perhaps because for so long they were the most powerful and most active—frequently hosted people from Turkish Kurdish groups. But the PKK was looking for more than just a temporary resting spot. It needed free passage through northern Iraq in order to stage attacks inside Turkey—and withdraw, if necessary—and it needed bases, however crude. The Israeli invasion of Lebanon in the summer of 1982 had made the situation in the Bekaa unstable. And Syria, while a good place for taking refuge, was not appropriate for launching attacks. The terrain between Turkey and Syria was too flat, and anyway, Damascus did not want PKK militants fighting from its territory. That would be too much of a provocation to Turkey.

Ocalan's realization that he needed access to northern Iraq—specifically, that part controlled by Barzani's KDP—in order to reach Turkey forced him to reconsider his previously derogatory stance toward the Barzani family. Ocalan's vicious criticisms of Mulla Mustafa Barzani had been rendered moot by the KDP chieftain's death and, in any case, Ocalan was usually careful to put practicalities ahead of ideologies. Sometime in 1982, Ocalan reached a deal with Massoud Barzani to allow the PKK to use the border territory controlled by Barzani's fighters. Under the agreement, which was formalized and made public a year later, the Iraqi Kurdish group gave Ocalan's militants space to build camps in northern Iraq and agreed not to stop them from crossing into Turkey from KDP-controlled land.

"Ocalan developed good relations with Barzani at the end of 1981 or during 1982 . . . and the conclusion of these talks was that the PKK received permission to settle in northern Iraq," said Akyol, who frequently met with Ocalan in their capacity as leading members of the FKBD-C alliance. "After one of the talks, Ocalan himself told me that from the PKK perspective, this was a historical turning point."

The agreement was crucial to the PKK's plan to launch war inside Turkey and as important, if not more so, than its ties with Syria. Without the agreement, the PKK would have faced the impossible task of trying to launch and run a guerrilla war from inside hostile Turkish territory. What Barzani realized from the deal was more amorphous. In the years since Mulla Mustafa Barzani retreated into exile, the KDP had lost support. It was no longer the sole Iraqi Kurdish party and its willingness to attack Iranian Kurdish forces at the behest of Tehran had hurt its image. The KDP had also lost its former allies in the Turkish Kurdish national movement, if only because most of these groups no longer were active, and it faced armed threats from the PUK. The agreement with Ocalan reaffirmed—in however a limited way—the pan-Kurdish appeal of the KDP.

"For us, it is always a source of pride that in regions that we have liberated with the cost of our blood, we have opened the area as a fortress for every Kurdish fighter," Barzani told an interviewer years later. "We signed the alliance with the PKK with this logic and for these reasons."[27]

The PKK did not waste any time in taking advantage of the new agreement. It built its main camp in Lolan, a clutch of valleys and mountains on the edge of the area known as the *ucgen,* or triangle, the stretch of territory that straddles the Iranian, Turkish, and Iraqi borders. Lolan always had been an important base for KDP fighters, and its proximity to the Turkish border made it perfect for the PKK. PKK militants who had been staying with various Iraqi Kurdish groups were called to the new, central camp or dispersed in smaller, mountain outposts along the Turkish border. Some flew from Damascus to Tehran and then crossed the border on foot into Iraq; others walked across the sharp intersection of the Syrian-Turkish-Iraqi border, cutting briefly into Turkey before entering Iraq, and continued on foot from there.

"We had to walk through the mountains to get there, it was a very hard journey," said Celik. "It was cold and snowy." The situation in the crudely constructed camps in Lolan was not any better. "In Lebanon, you could eat meat everyday, you had cigarettes, clothing," he said. "But in the Iraqi camps in the mountains there was nothing. We ate *bulgur* [boiled, pounded wheat] and soup. We got covered in lice." The rough conditions were perfect for training for the rigors of guerrilla war. In Lebanon they learned how to make bombs and throw grenades, but in northern Iraq they would learn how to survive in the mountains as a guerrilla force.

Exit, Most Others

Ocalan's claim that he was going to launch a guerrilla war gradually became something of a joke among his Kurdish rivals who passed through Damascus.[28] It had been three years since the military coup, and the PKK had yet to begin its promised war. Although the group was sending fighters into Iraq, many of those who then crossed into Turkey were captured or killed; some used the opportunity to flee the group.

"He was telling his cadre that 'next summer we will start,'" said Akyol, "and then it was the summer of 1982 and the armed struggle hadn't started, and so he would say it's been postponed until 1983 . . . and this became a joke for people, but for him it was serious. He had a fixed program and he had in his mind a certain time to start the armed struggle."

Kemal Burkay, perhaps Ocalan's fiercest and most influential Kurdish critic, issued an updated and expanded version of his pre-1980 critique of the PKK. The book, published in March 1983, was an intelligent yet patronizing analysis of the PKK's actions and statements to date. Burkay concluded that the PKK was a failed movement of failures—"uneducated people with a low level of consciousness"[29]—and that once people were properly educated, they would abandon Ocalan.

But claims that the PKK had failed were perhaps as much a reflection on the PKK's actions to date as they were on the state of the other Kurdish organizations. Ocalan was not the only one who promised to liberate the Kurdish region, and his rivals had not been any more successful. Ala Rizgari, for example, which sent about 150 militants to northern Iraq in 1980, was beset by ideological divisions and they abandoned their camps in early 1983.[30]

"Every state [in the region] had its own Kurdish problem, and whatever happens in one part of Kurdistan affects the other part of Kurdistan, so whenever one government helps a Kurdish group, it is to control it and to take the support is self-destructive," said Yasar, a lively, chain-smoking woman who still talks fiercely of the need for an independent Kurdish state. "We understood that such relations were ultimately self-defeating." Ala Rizgari's withdrawal took its militants on a four-month secret trek through Turkey to Syria, from where they left for Europe.

Other groups also were starting to reconsider being based in Syria, and between 1982–1984, most closed up and transferred their operations and people to Europe. "We decided we had been defeated by Turkey," said Kamuran, a Rizgari member. "We decided not to stay. We didn't have any militants."

Likewise, DDKD, which had been training with Yasir Arafat's Fatah, decided to move its people out of Syria. "We had a community there for about two years, but no-one really wanted to have relations with Syria," explained Vehbi Aydin, who had fled to Syria from Turkey in 1981 to avoid arrest and now lives in Paris. Besides, the group's plans for guerrilla war had not worked out. "We sent some unarmed people back into Turkey and some were arrested," said Aydin. "Our thinking was to raise the consciousness of the people first and then do the armed struggle."

At the same time, militants within Dev-Yol, Ocalan's leftist Turkish partner, were reconsidering their alliance with the PKK. There were disturbing indications that the PKK had started to revert to its old, violent ways. Some PKK members were missing, and it was rumored they had been arrested by their own organization. Burkay's KOMKAR association in Europe contacted Akyol and gave him a list of forcibly detained PKK militants.

"The PKK started to arrest some of its own people and no one knew what would happen to them," Akyol explained in his political autobiography. "I wrote a harsh letter to Abdullah Ocalan. I told him that he should immediately release the individuals . . . and that he was acting in contradiction with the agreements we made . . . [Otherwise] we would publicly denounce the PKK."[31]

But Ocalan ignored Akyol's threats. Dev-Yol was no longer the same strong, politically committed organization it was when it allied itself with the PKK. "[Our demands] did not have much influence on Apo because we [Dev-Yol] were no longer a strong political organization," Akyol wrote. "We were on the verge of splitting apart."[32]

Dev-Yol members were in the midst of a bitter internal discussion about the group's Leninist-styled organizational structures and its revolutionary aims. Akyol led the faction that believed they had to re-evaluate their methods and goals. The debate was sparked by a number of factors—the influence of living in democratic Europe, complaints by Turkish sympathizers in Europe that their needs were being ignored, and a growing sense of being out-of-touch with what was happening in Turkey. And in the process, plans for armed struggle began to seem unrealistic to some inside Dev-Yol, including Akyol.

"I can say that our romantic and childish movement was soon hit hard by the bitter realities of life," wrote Akyol in his political autobiography. "[W]e did not have the kind of organization that could actualize our dreams. I soon realized that we were living in a dream world."[33]

In parts, the discussion taking place inside Dev-Yol mirrored that taking place in other militant organizations. The main question these groups faced was whether armed struggle was still practical or even possible. The truth was, for all the impassioned rhetoric, no group had been able to do anything inside Turkey, let alone develop a base of support. The violence fostered before the coup by the leftist, rightist, and Kurdish militant organizations had terrorized the country, and for the most part, people in Turkey were happy with the enforced peace.

"The majority of the population supported the junta and, our movement, which used to control whole cities," wrote Akyol, "had lost all its public support."[34] Later, in one of our many phone calls, Akyol patiently tried to explain the change in his thinking. "I became more and more aware . . . that what we were doing in Syria and Germany was childish. There was no organization in Turkey, no mass support, nothing, just some crazy guys playing revolution outside."

There were other problems as well, mainly related to relations between Damascus and the foreign militant groups it hosted. The Israeli invasion of Lebanon in 1982, and the concurrent attacks on Syrian positions, dealt a physical and psychological blow to Syria and put Syrian President Assad on the defensive. Simultaneously, a rift between

Palestinian leader Yasir Arafat and Assad—over the PLO chief's political maneuverings with other Arab countries and Syria's attempt to influence him—and Syria's conflicts with other Arab countries deepened Assad's concerns about ensuring he had a say in where the region was headed.

The Syrian president sought to exert more control over Palestinian groups and, it turned out, he wanted something similar when it came to the Turkish and Kurdish groups based on his territory. Syrian authorities suddenly refused to recognize the Palestinian identity cards held by at least some foreign organizations, like Dev-Yol, and demanded they accept identity cards issued by the intelligence services, known as the *mukhabarat*. The PKK and its partner, Dev-Yol, also were asked to produce a list of members in Syria and Germany.

"This was a huge debate and it was the turning point for us," Akyol explained. "The Syrian demand meant that we would no longer be able to fight for democracy in Turkey, not if we are a pawn of the Syrians. This was our thinking. We felt very strongly about this." But Akyol was unable to convince Ocalan that giving in to the Syrians was a dangerous step.

"I discussed this with him and he's not a stupid guy," Akyol continued. "I told him, if you stay longer, you will be a pawn among the states in the region. He replied, 'of course I know this, but I need time. I know they want to use me, but I will use them as well.'"

Around the end of 1983, Dev-Yol began pulling its people out of Syria rather than accept the new demands. "The Syrian authorities understood we were cold to their suggestions," recalled Akyol, "and they didn't create any problems when we left." Dev-Yol's decision was an obvious blow to its revolutionary plans, but those plans anyway seemed less real now. The group was splintering over this very issue, with Akyol leading the faction that had decided to abandon both the dream of armed struggle and the centralist internal structures formed to promote it. The alliance with the PKK ground to an end.

"Since the PKK was organizing a long-term armed struggle, Ocalan interpreted my taking a step 'back' as betrayal,"[35] Akyol wrote in his essay.

The departure of Dev-Yol militants from Syria, the splintering of the group, and the collapse of the alliance—although formally, the FKBD-C Front continued, only marginal groups remained—marked the end of the experiment in Turkish-Kurdish revolution-making. To a large extent, it also marked the end of the more than 20-year experiment in radical Turkish revolution-making. With the decision of Dev-Yol, almost the whole of the Turkish left had abandoned its plans for armed struggle, or if not abandoned, then suspended them indefinitely. With their ideologies under review and their chief ideologists either dead, scattered among Turkish prisons, or eking out a refugee life in Europe, the future of the radical left was uncertain.

"It was not so clear where we were going, the only thing we knew was that we must leave Syria and that we must work through the next period of time," said Akyol, who later returned to his academic studies and now teaches in a Western university. "If necessary, yes, we would return to armed struggle, maybe 90 years later, but for now, there was no possibility of this."

4

On the Road to War, 1982–1984

THE FORMER PKK militant best known as Sari Baran, a tall, gangly man with deep-set eyes, was sent to northern Iraq late in 1982 as part of the gradual shift of PKK militants in Syria to makeshift bases closer to the Turkish border. The winter months are brutal in the mountains of Kurdistan, and it is near-impossible to move through the treacherous terrain, but by March areas start to turn passable. It was then, in 1983, that Baran and two other men slipped across the border from northern Iraq into Turkey, and began a six-month trek to map out that part of the Turkish Kurdish region that stretched from Hakkari to Tunceli. Another team was sent to explore the southeastern Turkey's Diyarbakir to Sirnak region. The teams were tasked with collecting the detailed information—about the people and physical layout of the region—that would allow the PKK to finally start its war.

"We stayed in the mountains, moving from mountain to mountain," said Baran, who joined the PKK in 1978 after splitting off from another Kurdish party. "The goal was to learn the geography, figure out where the guerrillas could hide, find out the views of the people to the [PKK] struggle and learn where the Turkish soldiers were based."

More than half the people of northern Kurdistan, as the PKK called it, lived in rural settlements, some of them small villages that had neither electricity nor paved roads.[1] The remoteness of many villages made it easier for Baran's team to evade Turkish authorities. Turkish military outposts were closer to the big cities or main roads, not deep in the mountains where the PKK militants hid themselves. When the military did hear of rebel activity, its raids were large, noisy affairs, and Baran's team found it easy to melt away.

"In some places, the people we ran across would later inform on us, but of course, by then we had left the area," said Baran. "In such a landscape, it was very easy for three people to hide."

The mandate was very clear: collect information and return safely to northern Iraq. To minimize the risk of being captured by Turkish troops, it was agreed in advance they would avoid action that might draw the attention of the military. This meant not engaging Turkish soldiers in firefights unless forced, and refraining from any of the retaliatory attacks PKK militants liked to stage on Kurds accused of working for state forces.

"We carried guns . . . but we didn't clash with anyone," explained Baran. "Our aim was to get information." Baran's team, for example, would not stay overnight in a village house, and even when they came to a village to make propaganda, they only approached Kurds living on the perimeter of the settlement. "That way, if there was a problem, you could leave immediately," explained Baran. "Also, you didn't want neighbors to see you going into a house because the next day that person might go and inform on the family to the police."

In the Kurdish region, it was not uncommon for those on the run —leftists, Kurdish nationalists, people accused of various common crimes—to take to the mountains to avoid arrest and villagers often assumed the three men also were fugitives. Baran said villagers sometimes were sympathetic, even willing to give information about which villages were pro-state and which were known as Kurdish nationalists, but they were not very interested in what he had to say about the PKK's planned fight:

> People were under a lot of pressure and demoralized. They were listening to us, but not really. They assumed we were Kurdish students, students who had suffered in Turkey and that's why we were hiding. When they looked at us, they saw their own children, they saw us as people forced to go to the mountains. They figured if the state catches us we will die, so they were feeling a little sorry for us and they felt they had to help us, give us food. But then they wanted us to leave and not come back.

Now and then, however, Baran's team did run across people, sometimes shepherds grazing their flocks in the mountains, who wanted to know more. Baran, like others in the PKK, was careful to tailor his propaganda to his audience. "If we met someone who was interested we would talk about Marxism-Leninism, otherwise, we would speak of the national struggle. That's what people were interested in. Either they really weren't able to understand anything about socialism, or else they opposed socialism because they saw it as anti-Islamic."

Some young men they spoke with wanted to join, but the team refused to take anybody with them. "That wasn't out goal," said Baran, sitting in his sparsely decorated apartment on the outskirts of Stockholm, where he applied for asylum in the late 1990s. "But we would try to make arrangements for these people to go to Iraq and join the PKK there."

Kurds, especially those in remote villages, relied on the radio and word of mouth for their information—literacy ranged from a low of 31.6 percent in Hakkari province to a high of 60.6 percent in Tunceli province[2]—and whatever their misgivings about hosting the three men, the arrival of Baran's team was a chance to catch up with the news.

"Sometimes they would ask what was happening in south Kurdistan. They wanted to know what we wanted and what was the chance of the PKK winning." Baran sensed that the PKK's first fight—the fight to win support in the region—would not be simple. The repression that followed the coup had made people afraid and hopeless. But at the same time, anger at the state—for the mass arrests, the torture, and the threats—had created an environment receptive to revenge attacks.

"People were ready, there was a leaning in favor of armed struggle," said Baran. "But because of the failed Kurdish revolts, there was a certain hopelessness. We understand that if we started the armed struggle, and gave the image that we are growing and strong, then we could win the support of the people."

The things Baran noticed—a certain helplessness coupled with a definite anger—were noted by other groups as well.[3] That same year, a 29-year-old member of Rizgari, newly arrived from Syria, also crisscrossed the region to gauge support for Rizgari and its plan to reestablish itself and work toward armed struggle.

"Everyone was just waiting for the organizations outside Turkey to do something, there was an expectation [that something would happen]," said Seymus Ozzengin, a voluble man captured by Turkish forces about a year after he secretly entered Turkey from Syria. It seemed to him that "whoever would start the armed struggle would get the support" of the people.

But at that point, no group was in any position to act, he recalled. Even his own. "There was no group doing systematic work, there was a base [of support for Kurdish groups] but no organizational activity."

PKK militants active in that period saw it differently. Despite the small numbers of rebels who were able to operate inside Turkey, the group saw itself as both active and growing. Everywhere Baran went, he stressed to people he met that the PKK was preparing for a long battle.

"The guerrillas have left, but they will return and will start the struggle. This message we were able to give."

War

By early 1984, the PKK was ready. The survey teams had returned safely from Turkey, bringing information about troop locations and nationalist sentiments. Dozens of militants were firmly ensconced inside Turkey, where they worked to set up a civilian militia. A handful of attacks on alleged Kurdish collaborators had—so the PKK believed —gained the group valuable sympathy in the region. In Damascus, Ocalan called some top militants together to discuss the situation. Sometime in the spring or early summer of 1984, the PKK leader issued the final order: It was time to fight.

The PKK militants working on the plan's final details usually met in an abandoned Iraqi Kurdish village called Mivroz on the Turkish-Iraqi border, due south of the Turkish town Yuksekova. "It was a more secret place [than Lolan],"[4] recalled Celik, one of the three main organizers. They picked three provinces inside Turkey for the first strike, looking for areas where people were sympathetic to Kurdish nationalism and where the terrain was rough enough to favor guerrilla fighting. Three armed units of between 10 and 30 people were formed, each responsible for a different target. Rebels began to cross into Turkey to scout out specific targets within the agreed-upon provinces. They wanted sites central enough so that the attacks would be noticed, yet located in areas that allowed the attackers to escape capture. Targets on the border were ignored because clashes there might either be blamed on smugglers or dismissed by both Kurds and the state as not a serious challenge.

"Our goal really wasn't to kill a lot of soldiers," explained Baran. "The attack was more to gain people's support and get them to join us. At the same time, we wanted to stage an attack that would give people trust [in the PKK's abilities]."

Once targets were chosen, a handful of people did the final reconnaissance inside Turkey.

"We would go into the cities [where the attacks were planned] and look around, look at the security set-ups, watch how they changed the guards, how the soldiers moved around," said Baran, deputy military commander in the March 21 Semdinli Unit which, like the other two units, was named for dates on which PKK members in Diyarbakir prison had staged suicide protests.

Rebels also studied entry and exit routes, prepared weapons depots, and identified hiding places. Shortly before the planned attacks, the units regrouped in the mountains overlooking their respective target sites.

"Our information was that the state didn't expect anything, the state felt it had a lot of strength," Baran, a small smile on his lips, noted.

On August 15, the Semdinli and Eruh teams struck.[5] "We were all waiting for such an action," shrugged Baran, a bit surprised at being asked how he felt that night. "This is what we had been preparing for."

In Eruh, a town of 4,000 people surrounded by mountains, about 30 rebels swept into the city around 7:30 P.M. One team opened fire on the military barracks, killing one guard. This team then took up position in front of the barracks to ensure no soldiers tried to stage a counterattack, while another team occupied the mosque, using the mosque's loudspeakers to announce their presence. Some rebels headed for the town's main street, where they distributed leaflets and explained to the men in the storefront coffee shops that this was the start of a Kurdish liberation war. When it became clear there was no immediate threat of a counterattack—the soldiers stationed in the town were so unprepared for such an assault that no-one left the barracks—the rebels raided a military building for weapons. The weapons were loaded on a state water administration truck, which the PKK drove out of town.

Two hours later in Semdinli, a town of 2,000 also set amid high mountains, the second PKK unit struck. Using the same tactics as in Eruh, eight of the 18 militants took up positions outside the gendarmerie barracks and an officer's club—firing warning shots to ensure nobody left—while the other 10 went to the city square.

"Our unit guarded the road so that [if the paramilitary rural police left the barracks] they couldn't enter the city," said Baran. "But the soldiers were unable to function, they didn't leave their station."

In the city square, the rebels, Baran among them, read out a prepared statement on the formation of the HRK (Hezen Rizgariya Kurdistan—Kurdistan Liberation Unit) modeled after the North Vietnamese rebel units that fought U.S. forces. Those who gathered to listen were more curious than frightened.

"The people were surprised, they wanted to know what was happening," said Baran. "They could hear the shots. We explained that the war is starting. Not just here, but in other places as well."

The Kurds of the southeast knew about Kurdish wars—in Turkey and in neighboring Iran and Iraq—and they knew these uprisings had always failed. To counter this, PKK militants knew they had to project a show of strength, courage, and readiness to maintain a long battle against the Turkish army.

"The goal wasn't to kill soldiers, but instead to break the link between the soldiers and the people and to read the announcement [announcing the founding of the HRK armed units]," explained Baran. "We wanted to make an attack that would give people the trust in us." The former military commander hunched forward in his chair, intent on making his point. "Was it a success? Did we achieve our goals?" he asked rhetorically. "We believed we had."

PKK militants withdrew to prearranged hiding spots in the mountains, stymieing the military's efforts to track them. "The Turkish army started looking for us, but they couldn't do anything," recalled Baran, who withdrew with his team in the difficult terrain overlooking Semdinli. "We knew the region very well."

Rebels were worried that the more remote mountain villages might not have heard of the attacks—or if they had, that the news came from Turkish state radio and did not explain the PKK's aims. So they traveled among the small population settlements, bringing news of their fight.

"We would go to a village, gather everyone together and tell them what was happening. We told them [the fight] was necessary, that there was no other way except with arms," Baran said. Like those who had gathered in the Semdinli town square on August 15, villagers were interested but decidedly wary. "They would ask questions like,

'Is the fighting only here or will it spread elsewhere? What's your strength?' recalled Baran. There was one other thing villagers wanted to know. "They asked, 'What will the state do?'"

In early October, the PKK struck again, killing three soldiers while Turkish President Kenan Evren toured the area in a show of strength. A Turkish newspaper, quoting an angry President Evren, shouted, "The snake must be killed while its head is small."[6] A few days later, the PKK killed eight soldiers in Cukurca, near the Iraqi border. Then an army captain was ambushed and killed. The resurgence of armed attacks shocked the army and impressed local people. The PKK's propaganda war was working.

"These sorts of attacks built up trust in the people," said Baran, who operated in the Semdinli area, where most of the ambushes occurred. "There were thousands of soldiers, but nothing happened to us." Some young men, emboldened by the attacks, decided to join up with the rebels. "If we were 18 in the first attack," said Baran, referring to the number of people in his team that staged the Semdinli attack, "then by the end of 1984 we were 50. [Our unit] could have been even bigger, but some people were sent to North Iraq, or else we kept them more like local militia."

Around October 1984, Celik left the PKK's Mivroz camp, went to Tehran, and flew to Damascus to meet with Ocalan. In Damascus, he found the PKK leader in a good mood. "I saw that his self-image had really gone up," recalled Celik.

Ocalan prepared about six hours of taped speeches for Celik to bring back to the militants in the mountains. The speeches contained Ocalan's instructions for what he wanted the militants to accomplish the next year. The PKK's successes in attacking the Turkish army convinced Ocalan that in a few months, when the snows melted and fighting could begin again, the PKK should widen its area of operations.[7] In order to help organize local people inside Turkey, the Central Committee formed the ERNK (Kurdistan National Liberation Front). Members of this front, which at the outset was not fully distinguishable from the HRK armed units, started to infiltrate into Turkey in the spring of 1985. Ocalan expected that under the guidance of the ERNK, local uprisings against the state would begin in the summer of 1985. But when the new year broke, the situation inside Turkey and inside the PKK had changed and Ocalan suddenly was on the defensive.

Turkey Caught by Surprise

The PKK's attacks on Eruh and Semdinli caught Ankara by surprise.[8] Just eight months earlier, the military regime had transferred power to a civilian government elected in democratic—if somewhat restricted —elections. Martial law, which had ruled the country since the 1980 military coup, was in the process of being lifted. Although the military should have known about Ocalan's intention to wage war—this plan was stated every month in the party's *Serxwebun* newspaper, published in Germany—those at the top clearly misjudged the PKK's ability to carry out its threats.

"It was an unexpected event," admitted Lieutenant General Kaya Yazgan three years later. He had been in charge of the Seventh Army Corps in the southeast at the time of the attacks. "Up until that point we didn't know Apo. His name was known, but he was not someone who was focused on. And besides, PKK militants were seen more as bandits." Yazgan complained that even after the attacks, the newly installed civilian government did not take this new threat seriously. "The politicians in Ankara did not believe that this event was the first sign of a big start. It was being evaluated as the remnants of what took place before Sept. 12 [the military coup]."[9]

In retrospect, it was not surprising that the PKK's first strike caught the political and military establishment unaware. The military rulers who ran the country from 1980–1983 had been ruthless in their methods and targets, but they were successful. Political violence dropped by more than 90 percent, the economy stabilized, and the generals stuck to their promise to give up power. Nearly a year after the military stepped down, there was little reason to think political violence would break out anew.

The generals not only had punished those it blamed for the instability of the late 1970s, but also changed laws they believed had allowed the mayhem. To this end, the National Security Council, the ruling body after the coup, restructured Turkey's legal, political, and ideological systems. The constitution was rewritten to limit explicitly freedoms of expression, movement, association, and even scientific research. In almost all cases, the deciding factor for restricting activity was protecting the security and unity of the state. These two vaguely worded concepts could be interpreted by the authorities as needed and, in these years, were applied to halt a broad range of activities deemed to be critical of the military's actions.

"We have to sacrifice some personal rights for the security of the community,"[10] General Chief of Staff Kenan Evren, leader of the coup, explained in his memoirs.

The generals blamed political parties and the parties' inability to work together for the stalemated parliament of the previous decade, and they systematically worked to destroy the old parties and restrict new ones. Former political party leaders were barred from politics for ten years, and the old parliamentarians were banned for five years from forming new political parties or holding executive posts in parties. The parties that had existed before the coup were dissolved. The relevant law governing the activities of political parties was rewritten to bar parties from forming youth or women's branches or opening offices in villages. University students and professors and civil servants were banned from joining political parties. The goal was to depoliticize the youth especially, in hopes of avoiding the radicalization of the 1970s.

The generals' attempt to remake Turkish society did not stop with new laws and regulations. In the run-up to national elections in November 1983 for a new, civilian government, the National Security Council retained the right to veto who could found a political party and who could stand for parliament. In total, some 700 candidates were barred from running and, of the 15 new political parties that tried to stand in elections, only three were permitted. Of those three, only one was truly independent of the military and its ideology. In a rebuke to the generals' attempt to totally restructure and guide Turkish society, it was the independent Motherland Party, headed by economic technocrat Turgut Ozal, that won the elections.

But the generals took steps to ensure their voice would be heard even after returning the country to civilian rule. The 1982 constitution named Evren president for seven years, giving him expanded powers that expired when he left office. The National Security Council added four civilian members after the transition but was dominated by its five military members (the president, in this case coup leader Evren, was the fifth civilian member). The revamped NSC officially was an advisory body, but in practice it was the deciding body on issues of national security. The constitution stated that its pronouncements had to be given "priority" by the government and, in this period, they were.

In Turkey's reestablished democracy, Kurdish activists—whether in exile, in prison, or free in Turkey—saw no reason to believe there was room for them to operate. There also was no reason to think that even their basic, ethnic identity would be recognized. The new constitution the military rulers prepared stated that every citizen of Turkey was a Turk, another named the state language as Turkish, and another said that this article could never be changed. Under the law governing political parties, it was not allowed to claim that minorities existed in Turkey, nor was it permitted to "protect [or] develop non-Turkish cultures and languages."[11]

In fact, Kurdish could not be taught or used at all under the military regime's special law 2932, which specifically banned all uses of the Kurdish language without actually mentioning the word Kurdish. Such a fearful approach to anything Kurdish was not new, what was new was the maze of constitutional articles and legal additions that sought to forestall even minimal cultural expressions of ethnic identity.

If something was to blame for the military and political establishment's surprise when the PKK attacked, perhaps it was that the generals had done too good a job remaking Turkey. Kurds never officially existed inside Turkey, but in the 1960s and 1970s, they slowly had organized groups, published magazines and books, and elected local officials with nationalist bents. All this was destroyed in the 1980 coup.

In the new Turkey the generals fashioned, Kurdish cultural, linguistic, and political identity was eradicated by law. The simplest expressions of cultural identity—giving children Kurdish names, singing Kurdish songs, and certainly, speaking Kurdish in state offices—was seen as a separatist act. Kurds as Kurds ceased to exist in the official, public realm, to the point that a Turkish journalist visiting a Kurdish village two months after the PKK's attack was only able to write that the people there spoke Turkish with great difficulty. But of the language they did, in fact, speak—Kurdish—there was no mention.[12] The ban on Kurdish-related activities was so complete that the ruling powers could be forgiven for having forgotten that there was, in fact, a Kurdish problem in Turkey.

PART II

The PKK Consolidates Power

Right: Cetin (Semir) Gungor, shown here in an undated photo taken in Tunceli when he was probably in his late teens, abandoned plans to be a schoolteacher in favor of joining the PKK in the 1970s. He later fled Turkey and ended up working in Europe to help organize support for the PKK. After raising some doubts about the PKK's direction and Ocalan's leadership, he was forced out of the group. In 1985, he was assassinated in Sweden. Photo provided by Muslum Arslan.

Below: PKK rebels carry the body of PKK group commander Necim (Cuma) Celik, who was killed in a clash with Turkish soldiers in January 1992. Photo provided by Selahattin Celik, the older brother of Necim.

5

Loyalty and Violence, 1985–1990

TWO YEARS BEFORE the PKK launched its war, Cetin Gungor, a high-ranking member of the group's European committee, began to argue for internal reform.[1] Gungor, by all accounts a hardworking, intelligent, and committed PKK militant, had come to think the group was too authoritarian and he especially was uncomfortable with the way PKK members voted: They wrote their names on their so-called secret ballots. Gungor's concerns had developed during the year he spent working for the PKK in Europe—he was sent there in 1981 to build up a local support network among Kurdish refugees—and he hoped to spark a discussion on these things during the PKK's 2nd Congress in August 1982. But Gungor, who returned from Germany for the meeting, held in an abandoned Palestinian encampment near Syria's border with Jordan, did not get very far. Ocalan was openly hostile and stifled any discussion with some jokes about Gungor's new, European ways. In any case, most of the others at the congress had little interest in what Gungor was saying.

"We were all focused on starting the war, and we couldn't understand why he was raising what seemed like unrelated issues," said S., a former PKK member who has since built up a successful life in construction in Germany. "It seemed like he had lost some of his nationalist focus."

Gungor, better known by his PKK code-name Semir, refused to abandon his concerns. When he returned to Germany following the congress, he continued to discuss the need for reform. Apart from his still-vague concerns about the PKK's authoritarian structure, Semir believed the PKK needed to rethink its European activities, which at the time were directed toward collecting money and cadre for the planned war. He thought that PKK activists in Europe should instead try to strengthen the local Kurdish community by educating and assisting people with their daily problems. He also argued that the PKK, in order to be more effective, needed to expand its relations beyond marginal left groups to include more mainstream political parties and nongovernmental organizations. To do so, he made clear, would require a stronger, more independent European committee, one that had the freedom to make its own analyses and act upon them. Unsaid, but certainly not unnoticed, was that Ocalan's authority over the European operations would be limited.

"Semir was not a dogmatic person," explained Selman Arslan, a former PKK militant who worked closely with Semir in Europe. "For him, everything could be debated, talked about, [decisions] did not have to come from the top down. . . . He wanted people to use their own experiences, their own autonomy, to make decisions."

Ocalan always was concerned about challenges to his authority and to the unity of the PKK under his authority and he began to see in Semir a problem. At first, he sought to reduce Semir's influence and power within the European committee. A whispered campaign of complaints emanated from Damascus, as PKK members known to be close to Ocalan flew to Europe and raised questions about Semir's capabilities. They hinted at cracks in Semir's commitment to the PKK and its revolutionary principles and presided over meetings in which they criticized the PKK's local operations.

"One by one they would go to different people and try to convince them that Semir was making mistakes, they said the European committee had not reached its goals," explained Arslan. "Today, when I look back, I see that the point of all this was to get rid of him."

Semir, who had given up on plans to be a teacher to join up with Ocalan around 1975, believed in the PKK and its goal of an independent Kurdish state. He also was smart, inquisitive, and somewhat stubborn. Despite the growing pressure from Ocalan's emissaries, Semir continued his work and refused to back down from his ideas, making clear that he believed the PKK needed to moderate its internal, Leninist-like governing structure. Semir was smart enough to avoid directly questioning Ocalan's position as leader of the PKK, but he did ask whether Ocalan should be relied on to decide every action and solve every problem.

"The party's activities cannot be carried out solely with the individual efforts of the extraordinary cadre, which brings us to the phrase 'Comrade Ali will solve it,'" he wrote in a letter to others in the European committee, referring to Ocalan by his code-name. "It is necessary not to live in this fantasy world."[2]

Yet, it was unclear whose view reflected the reality in which the PKK operated. Semir had lived for nearly three years in Europe, where he had been exposed to real democracies, democratic institutions, and free debate. He also had worked closely with the PKK's Turkish leftist partner Dev-Yol, which had started to rethink its Leninist posture and the belief that democracy should follow the revolution, rather than coming first. All this affected and shaped his thinking and convinced him the PKK needed to change.

But Ocalan lived in a different world. He was based in Damascus, a dictatorship, and beyond Syria's borders were other dictatorships or highly imperfect democracies. In these countries there was no free debate and those in power did not like to share it. And when Ocalan looked at Dev-Yol—whose alliance with the PKK was unraveling—he saw a group that barely functioned anymore, largely because its members could no longer agree on goals or methods. In Ocalan's mind, it was Semir who lived in a fantasy world.

"Inside the PKK, there is only one way of analyzing things," Ocalan said years later, in one of his many speeches denigrating Semir. "Since the PKK was founded, its mistakes, weaknesses and successes were analyzed at the congresses and conferences." Claiming that Semir's critiques of the PKK's activities were illegitimate because he issued them in Europe, instead of during the 2nd Congress (where he had been forced to abandon his critique under pressure), Ocalan hinted that Semir had other, more devious plans. "It is clear Semir did not act in order to strengthen the PKK."[3]

Semir's ability to operate grew more limited. He insisted he was still the general coordinator of the European Committee, but Ocalan's emissaries claimed otherwise. Semir, unable to carry out his responsibilities and increasingly at odds with the others in the European operations, announced that he needed time to rethink his involvement.

"The party's internal dogmatism turned out to be stronger than me. That's why leaving the ranks [for now] is an honorable and necessary decision," wrote Semir, in an open letter to his comrades in Europe dated May 10, 1983. "I know that you are not in a position now to understand me. Maybe the time will come when you will."

It was not easy for Semir to abandon the group. Part of the reason was ideological—whatever his criticisms of Ocalan and of the group's activities, he supported the PKK as a whole. And part of the reason, almost certainly, was that it was not easy to give up on a group that had given his life direction—and directed it—for some seven years. A few months later, Semir agreed to meet PKK activists at an apartment in Cologne, Germany, hoping for some sort of reconciliation. Following two days of what Semir believed were positive talks, the others unexpectedly turned on him. They accused him of having links to Sahin Donmez, the well-known PKK member turned informer in 1979, and told him he could not leave the apartment until they had investigated this. When Semir tried to leave, they stuck a guard in the apartment and locked him inside. That night, he pushed his way out, only to be tracked down by four men roaming the city in taxis and forced back to the apartment. Semir was stripped of his money and his identity card. "[This was] something I never guessed could happen nor expected," Semir angrily wrote later in an open letter to the PKK dated October 19, 1983.

Semir's unexpected absence worried his friends and their attempts to find him raised the tension in the apartment. Both the PKK guards and Semir grew more nervous about what might happen. "I was told that if this [kidnapping] was made public within the revolutionary community my life would be in danger," Semir recounted in the same letter. A week later, Semir again escaped, but this time, he hid himself well. In the October 19 letter he wrote after his flight, he announced he was severing all relations and promised to fight against what he termed the group's dangerous ideology.

"I now understand better how dangerous is the danger of the PKK's dogmatism and how right I was to rebel against this damned logic," continued Semir, who still saw himself as committed to Kurdish revolution, but not in the way the PKK was planning. "I am obliged to continue to work for revolution. Don't block me," he warned. "It won't do either of us any good if you force us to be enemies."

Semir's announcement that he would keep up his work was interpreted by the PKK as a direct challenge and by Ocalan as a personal threat. The PKK had never tolerated splits—the tone was set in 1977, when PKK militants murdered two activists from the Gaziantep area who announced they were splitting off to form their own group—and Semir had announced himself as a rival. Early in 1984, the group's internal newspaper, *Serxwebun*, named Semir a traitor. In the PKK's vocabulary, this meant he was marked for death.

It did not matter that Semir, more an intellectual than a fighter, did not pose a real danger to the PKK's developing dominance. Most of his friends and associates in the PKK had cut contact with him. His chances of working with another group were limited. Not only were the other groups weak, but also Semir's call for internal democracy did not match their own approach. Meanwhile the increasingly harsh tone of his leaflets, in which he wrote that Ocalan was psychotic, the group fascist, and its struggle doomed to failure, was backfiring. Even PKK militants who thought Ocalan had blown up the threat from Semir to protect his own leadership grew uncomfortable with Semir's attacks.

"I really didn't think he was an agent, but I didn't think what he was doing was good for the PKK," recounted Arslan. "All I saw was that on one side, there was this organization fighting for a Kurdish state, and someone fighting against it wasn't going to help the struggle."

Semir relied on friends in the Turkish left to keep him safe, but PKK operatives were searching for him. "He would find a place to stay and then the PKK would raid it," said S., a friend of Semir's from the Turkish left in Hamburg. In 1984 or early 1985, Semir applied for and received political asylum in Sweden, where it so happened that some other dissident PKK members lived.

"His initial decision was not to be very active in politics, instead he wrote some pamphlets in which he tried to develop his ideas of democracy," recalled Mesut Akyol, the former Dev-Yol leader who sheltered Semir after he fled PKK detention in Cologne. "Then he decided to go public, and this was the signing of his death sentence." Akyol paused. "We're so much older now and things look different to us, but Semir was at that age and at that period in his life when he really believed in democracy and in certain ideas and he was willing to risk his life for this."

One November evening in 1985, Semir and two other former PKK members joined a meeting of Kurdish activists in Stockholm. It was one of Semir's first public appearances. During the break, a young man walked up behind Semir and shot him dead. The assailant, caught as he tried to flee through a window, was a Kurd who insisted the killing had to do with a personal dispute. But Semir's former comrades in the PKK had little doubt why he was killed. The PKK itself issued a leaflet in which it hailed the murderer as a patriot: "This agent-provocateur [Semir] . . . has been brought to justice by our people."[4] Ocalan avoided taking personal responsibility, but he later made clear that people like Semir—PKK members who abandoned the group and publicly criticized it—should expect to be hunted down.

"Semir was going to be killed wherever he was,"[5] Ocalan stated.

The murder of Semir marked Ocalan's public victory over the first, open challenge to his authority. But Semir was not the only victim of Ocalan's drive to ensure that neither his rule nor the group's unity was challenged. Between 1983 and 1985, Ocalan ordered or encouraged the murder of at least 11 high-level former or current PKK members, including Semir.[6] Some managed to flee and hide themselves, but most were gunned down either in Europe or in northern Iraq in the PKK's Lolan Valley camp. Nearly all these people had worked with Semir in the group's growing European operations, and even if they did not speak out in favor of Semir, that contact was enough to condemn them. Others simply did not seem sufficiently loyal to Ocalan's leadership. Ocalan did not always order the murders himself, but he created an atmosphere in which it was clear certain people had to be killed.

"It was rule that traitors were killed," said one PKK militant, shrugging his shoulders. "Who would question the killing of someone who had been named a traitor?"

Ibrahim Aydin, who met Ocalan when they were both imprisoned in Ankara in 1972, had backed Ocalan in the dispute with Semir. After returning from Germany and working in Syria, Aydin was sent to Lolan camp in northern Iraq around the end of 1984. Aydin was devoted to the PKK's struggle and accepted orders without question. But he noticed that he was being treated suspiciously by the others. Around May 1985, Aydin overheard a conversation that made him realize that he was in danger of being named a traitor and killed. The next morning, on the pretext of gathering firewood, Aydin fled Lolan and took refuge with Massoud Barzani's Iraqi Kurdish forces who were based just inside the Iranian border.

"I made a definite decision that I would not go over to the side of the enemy [Turkey], I would not give myself up," Aydin said in a midnight interview after he had closed up the pizza parlor he runs off a desolate stretch of highway in Sweden. "But I also would not allow myself to be killed by the PKK."

A woman only known by her code-name Evin was not as fortunate. Evin was executed in a PKK camp in Lebanon in 1985 with Ocalan's approval. She had worked with Semir in Europe but sided with Ocalan in the dispute. "The idea was simply to get rid of anyone who was involved in any way," said a militant who was in Lebanon at the time. Saime Askin, who defended Semir after she came to Damascus from Germany at Ocalan's request in 1983, also was killed. First, Ocalan ordered her to Lolan camp in northern Iraq. "She was the sort of woman who debated, who argued," said one PKK militant who saw Askin in Lolan. "In general, people saw a dangerous potential in her." In late 1984 or the first half of 1985, she was executed by the PKK. Suphi Karakus, known by his code-name Sores, also worked with Semir and later was sent to Lolan Valley. He was killed in late 1984.

At least three PKK members who had worked in Europe with Semir and quit the group about a year after he did were murdered in Europe in 1984: Zulfu Gok, Enver Ata, and Murat Bayrakli.[7] "Poor Murat," said one PKK militant, "there was no reason to kill him, but who knows, Ocalan maybe saw some threat somehow." As for Ata, although eulogized as a hero by the handful of other PKK militants who had joined up with Semir, he hardly seemed a threat to either Ocalan or the PKK. "Enver never spoke out," mused a chain-smoking woman who used to be in Dev-Yol and knew Enver. "Why they killed him I don't know." And Gok kept such a low-profile that it is hard even to find mention of him in PKK materials.

Ocalan simultaneously worked to isolate and kill others who had raised similar but separate concerns about the PKK's methods and plans. Central Committee Resul (Davut) Altinok was detained by the PKK in 1982, subsequently transferred to Lolan camp, and late in 1984 he was executed.

"The order came directly from Ocalan," explained the militant who received the order. "Ocalan said, 'There is no more reason for him to be left alive.'"

Cemile Kaytan, better known by her code-name Seher, was luckier. She also quit the group in 1983, sharing Semir's displeasure with how things were working. She had accompanied Semir to the rented hall the night he was killed—but managed to hide herself in Europe and start a new life. Baki Karer, another former central committee member, also managed to survive, but just barely. He was detained in 1982 and sent to Lolan, but thanks to an inattentive guard he managed to escape. His guard fled later as well. Karer subsequently received refuge in Sweden and joined forces with Semir to denounce the PKK's practices and its leader. When Semir was killed, Karer was in the same hall. "I feel regret that I took part in this bloody organization," he told a Turkish newspaper shortly after Semir was murdered. "These years will stay as a black stain on my life."[8]

These murders set the pace for what would come over the next few years. As the PKK fought to establish itself inside Turkey, Ocalan continued to fight against real and potential critics inside the organization. To Ocalan, dissent was a danger to his authority and control over the PKK. Many PKK members simply viewed dissenters as a danger to the group's plans.

"The thinking inside the PKK was that we were doing something that was holy, sacred. In that atmosphere, how could someone go and criticize you?" explained a former PKK member. Ocalan may have been the driving force behind these murders, but many in the PKK agreed with what he was doing. "Ocalan laid out the path, and the rest of us followed."

This unforgiving view toward dissent helped the PKK avoid the ideological splits that fatally weakened other Kurdish organizations. But it also strengthened the already dictatorial powers of Ocalan and quickly became a tool he and senior PKK militants freely used to dispose of those who displeased them, who seemed untrustworthy, or who simply were a burden on the battlefield.

Former PKK members based in northern Iraq in the mid-1980s say that another six or eight experienced PKK members—possibly more, but nobody knows for sure—were summarily killed between 1984 and 1985 because they were viewed as a possible threat or a burden. One woman, for example, apparently suffered a nervous breakdown after she was jailed and tortured in Turkey. When she was released, she rejoined the PKK, but her colleagues in Lolan, either because they suspected she was an agent or because they did not know what to do with her, shot her.[9] But even 20 years later, the exact names and events of those killed in the remote mountains of northern Iraq are shrouded by fears and old loyalties.

The PKK's critics argued the murders were a sign the group was weakening. In fact, the opposite was true. It was only after the PKK successfully launched its August 1984 attack against Turkey that Ocalan ordered the executions in Lolan camp.

"He knew now nobody would pay attention or even care," said one PKK militant active at the time. "After all, the war had started."

Back to Turkey

Selahattin Celik, who returned to northern Iraq late in 1984 after his meeting with Ocalan, planned to enter Turkey early in the new year but this proved impossible.[10] The winter was severe, making it hard to cross the snow-covered mountains, and many PKK militants who managed to cross the Iraqi border were gunned down by Turkish patrols. Celik and the other senior militants preparing for the next phase of their battle had not expected this.

"We sent a group and it was caught," said Celik in a phone conversation in Germany, in the midst of another harsh winter. "We sent another group and the people were either killed or captured. Another eight people who were sent died in a clash. The Turkish soldiers had set themselves up well."

Turkish generals, surprised at the PKK's initial attacks, had spent the intervening months building a strategy. Five divisions were shifted to the southeast, the number of gendarmerie (rural police) were increased and police were ordered to take a more active role in hunting down insurgents. In addition, military installations were boosted and security officials established outposts near mountain villages, on which the PKK relied for food, information, and new recruits.

"In 1985, for the first time, we started to establish ourselves in the region," General Mustafa Necdet Urug, then Turkey's top military commander, and Land Forces Commander General Mustafa Necdet Oztorun explained to Turkish journalist Mehmet Ali Birand. "We stacked up soldiers in the region and we combed through it."[11]

Kurdish rebels operating inside Turkey—there were about 200—immediately noticed the change. Armed PKK units traveling from one part of the area under their command to another found their routes blocked by Turkish soldiers. Militants who clashed with the soldiers used to be able to count on the troops withdrawing by nightfall; now, the soldiers stayed and fought, sometimes for days, draining the PKK's strength and supplies.

"They kept sending in more soldiers so the clashes would continue . . . and every time we had losses," recalled Baran. "We were limited in our ability to enter villages . . . we couldn't make our propaganda very easily, which hurt our ties to the people." The reduced access also cut into their food supplies. "Sometimes you could eat for two days and on the third day there was not enough bread."

By the middle of the year, PKK rebels faced a new danger: Kurdish villagers armed and paid by the state to fight the guerrillas. The Turkish state had established a civilian militia in the early years of the republic to help secure the new borders, but in the 1960s the idea was deemed undemocratic and the relevant law repealed. Following the PKK's August attack, this force was renewed, after the Turkish president noted that there simply was no other way to ensure the security of these remote settlements, which lacked electricity, telephones, and paved roads. The village guards received a monthly salary of 35,000 lira (about $70), a grand enough sum that by the end of 1985, some 13,000 men were enrolled. The village guards were not just a new threat to the PKK, but made some militants uncomfortable.

"I didn't want to fight them, they were Kurds too," said former PKK rebel S., who had been operating in the Van-Hakkari region since 1984. "I was paralyzed."

The PKK's struggle was not even a year old, but it seemed the state had gained the advantage. Some rebels grew disenchanted and gave themselves up, citing the new "Repentance Law" that vaguely promised a lesser sentence to those who turned themselves in and provided useful information about the group's activities. "Things turned against us," Celik said. "The news we were getting from Turkey was not positive. People were betraying us, they were giving themselves up. They were appearing on television and retracting what they had done." Celik estimated that some 90 rebels and local supporters died in fighting with the Turkish army.

Yet the number of people joining the PKK rose. A former PKK rebel noted that, "Whenever a gun exploded, wherever an attack took place, right afterward there would be new recruits."[12] Equally important, the rebels in the field maintained their fight, even as they lost specific battles. "The state couldn't push us out and when people saw this, they again grew responsive to us," said Baran. "In the end the military was unsuccessful because we were able to hang on to the areas where we were."

Friends of the PKK

Iran, Iraq, and Syria were experienced in using their neighbors' Kurds as proxies in battles with their own Kurdish groups and in their disputes with each other. Now, a Turkish Kurdish group had emerged that appeared strong enough to be of use. Syria was the first to take advantage of this, while Iraq initially failed and Iran's relations only started to develop at the end of the 1980s.

Syria always had the closest relations with the PKK and around 1985 Damascus expanded ties.[13] The PKK was allowed to take full control of the Helwe training camp in the Syrian-controlled Bekaa Valley, where PKK militants trained with Palestinian guerrillas before the 1982 Israeli invasion of Lebanon pushed both the Palestinians and PKK militants further north. At the same time, contact between Syria and Ocalan became more frequent. Although Damascus relied on its intelligence services and local intermediaries to carry out dialogue with foreign militant groups, President Hafez al-Assad's younger brother Cemil Assad took a particular interest in the PKK and visited its Helwe camp. Apart from a seat in the People's Assembly, Cemil Assad had no official position in the Syrian government, but he essentially controlled the port city of Latakia, and PKK militants believed he was responsible for organizing Arabs living in Turkey's Hatay region, the former Syrian province that Syria still claimed.

Syria hoped that its relations with the PKK would force Ankara to make concessions on the myriad of issues that bedeviled their bilateral relations, and in 1987, the Syrian approach appeared to be working. Turkey's Prime Minister Turgut Ozal made an unprecedented trip to Damascus to press for a security cooperation protocol. Although Syria officially denied that Ocalan was in Damascus, it agreed to bar attacks on Turkey from its territory and to exchange security information with Turkey. In return, Ozal tried to address Assad's concerns about Turkey's vast dams projects along the Tigris and Euphrates rivers, promising to guarantee that a set amount of water flowed downstream into Syria.

Syria's success in using the PKK as a tool of its foreign policy only reinforced its interest in maintaining close ties to the Kurdish rebels. Although, as promised in the new security protocol, Damascus did warn the PKK not to cross from Syria into Turkey, it is unclear how long this stayed in effect. And when Kurdish rebels could not cross the Syrian border into Turkey, they took a plane to Tehran or else crossed the Syrian-Iraqi border. More important, Syria took no steps to limit PKK training, recruitment, or organizational work. Nor did it try and hamper Ocalan's activities.

"If Syria wanted to, could it stop you?" asked Turkish journalist Mehmet Ali Birand in 1988, in what was the first Turkish interview with the PKK leader. "Certainly," replied Ocalan. "With a special order it could stop us."[14]

Damascus was wary of its own Kurdish minority and it continued to make clear to the PKK that it could not agitate on behalf of Syrian Kurds. However, Damascus began encouraging the PKK to recruit members from among the Syrian Kurdish population, hoping this would redirect local Kurdish attention away from fighting for change inside Syria. The PKK already was fairly well known among Syrian Kurds. In his first few years in Syria, Ocalan gave speeches to Syrian Kurds, and PKK militants often traveled around the Syrian Kurdish villages to make propaganda and collect money.

Syrian Kurds, especially university students, were excited by the PKK and its promise of an independent Kurdish state, even if it was going to be a Turkish Kurdish state. Syrian Kurdish political parties barely were active—between the in-fighting and the state pressure, they had little chance to put together a viable program—while the PKK actually was fighting.

"People were fed up with the Syrian Kurdish groups because they never did anything, all they did was talk, that's it, just talk," said Akif Hasan, a slight, dark-haired man with a fluent, if somewhat stilted English. "The PKK was very different from the Syrian groups, it seemed to be disciplined, intellectual and more socialist. The PKK was like a ray of sun, of hope."

Syrian Kurds generally saw no contradiction in their supporting a Turkish Kurdish party. They often had relatives on the Turkish side, and the brisk smuggling trade between helped maintain family ties and encouraged political links.

"Turkish Kurdistan was the biggest part and it was always in our imagination," said Kamiran Hajo, a Kurdish activist from Syria who initially was interested in the PKK. "We thought that we had to support Turkish Kurdistan because we failed [to make a state] in Iraqi Kurdistan."

Besides, the PKK's program envisioned a greater Kurdistan that would unite Kurds from Turkey, Iraq, Iran and Syria. The group's focus was on liberating the Kurdish region inside Turkey's borders, but after that was done the other Kurdish regions were expected to wage their own war with the guidance of the new Turkish Kurdish state.

"We students were convinced that this time, something would happen," said Hasan. When Hasan joined in 1985, there were just a few Syrian Kurds inside the PKK. Within a year the number had increased to about 45 and the year after that it tripled to about 130. And this number reflected only the active members trained at Helwe. In the Syrian Kurdish villages along the border, there were many more willing to help out with food, money, and shelter.

Iraqi Friends of the PKK

Syria's foe, Iraq, was not oblivious to the PKK. Iraqi security services apparently were eager to make contact with the Turkish Kurdish rebels. Baghdad did not want to use the PKK against Turkey—at the time, Iraq exported some of its oil via a pipeline that ran through Turkey—but instead wondered whether they could encourage the Turkish Kurds to fight against Massoud Barzani's Iraqi Kurdish rebels. Iraq had been at war with Iran since 1980 and despite U.S. assistance to Iraqi President Saddam Hussein to ensure that the Iranian Islamic regime did not win the war, Saddam was worried about the situation in the Kurdish northern part of the country. His main concern was Barzani, who received weapons and financial assistance from Iran and whose men sometimes fought alongside Iranian forces in assaults on Iraqi forces in the north. PKK fighters were located on Barzani-controlled territory and they had some conflicts with the KDP—two things that made them of possible interest to Baghdad.[15]

Selman Arslan, a PKK member who returned to Damascus from Europe in 1985 and then continued onward to northern Iraq, was captured by Iraqi soldiers as he crossed the Turkish-Iraqi border, sometime around April 1986. After an initial interrogation, he was transferred down south to Baghdad. In the capital, he was blindfolded and driven to what he believes was a military interrogation center, quite possibly part of the notorious Abu Ghraib prison.

Prisoners in Iraq held for political reasons rarely escaped horrible torture but Arslan was lucky. It seemed the Iraqi security services actually wanted to keep him alive. They apparently were interested in making contact with the PKK and now that they had one of the militants—and one with direct dealings with Ocalan—they were not going to waste the opportunity by chancing his death through torture, at least not immediately.

"I could hear people screaming, I knew they were being tortured," recalled Arslan, who now lives in Germany. "One night someone was put in the cell with me, he was a Syrian. He told me it was a very bad place. I was hit once or twice before I admitted I was with the PKK, and I was given a little electric shock, but otherwise nothing."

Over the next few weeks, Arslan was questioned extensively about the PKK.

> Based on what they asked me, they were not interested in using the PKK against Turkey, nor did they ask me whether the PKK would fight against Talabani. [Instead] they asked me a lot of questions about relations between the PKK and Barzani's KDP. They wanted to know if the PKK would fight against the KDP. I said I didn't think the PKK would fight the KDP, but if it was necessary they wouldn't avoid fighting. Then they asked if they gave the PKK weapons, would the PKK accept the weapons? And would they then fight against the KDP? I said that the PKK wouldn't say no to the weapons, but I still didn't think they would fight against the KDP. But in general, I did think that if the PKK had the chance, it would want to establish relations with Baghdad.

Months passed. Arslan grew depressed and begged them to release him. But the Iraqi security officers did not know what to do with him. They did not seem interested in handing him over to Turkey, yet releasing him did not appear to be a priority. Arslan believed that one reason was that the Iraqis were considering how to use him to pass on their interest to Ocalan. But they did not know how to ensure he would. Finally, some nine months after his capture, the Iraqi security forces, perhaps giving up on the idea, handed Arslan a faked Turkish passport and put him on a plane to Belgrade, accompanied by an Iraqi diplomat. After the two swept through passport control, the Iraqi diplomat took the Turkish passport back. Arslan, in Belgrade with no money and no identity papers, soon was detained by Yugoslav authorities.

By the time Arslan was free again and back in contact with the PKK, the Iraqis had taken the offensive against their domestic Kurdish rebels and needed no help from the outside. Besides, the PKK was suspicious of Arslan's long absence, and the PKK members who subsequently interrogated him were more interested in whether he might be an Iraqi agent (or a German agent, or a Turkish agent, or an agent of Barzani's) than in any messages he might be carrying.

Not until the end of the 1980s, when the Iraqi military had reestablished control over parts of its border with Turkey, did Baghdad have direct contacts with the PKK. The cooperation was established and maintained on the level of local military commanders. Iraqi military officials in camps on the border agreed to ignore PKK rebels in exchange for information on Barzani's KDP rebel forces.[16]

"Generally, the situation was that Baghdad closed its eyes to us," said Azman, a former PKK rebel who operated in the region in the late 1980s. "There was no real help, which wasn't because the PKK wouldn't take the help, but because Saddam didn't want to give it."

This unofficial sort of contact continued until the 1991 Gulf War, after which Iraq's forces were pushed out completely from northern Iraq and the balance of power changed dramatically.

Iraqi Kurds

Massoud Barzani once told a Turkish Kurdish visitor that Ocalan was going to save the Kurdish people, but after the PKK started its war, the Iraqi Kurdish leader began to view the PKK more as a liability than an asset.[17] The Turkish military was aware the PKK had established military camps along the Iraqi-Turkish border and Ankara pressured Barzani to kick out the rebels from his territory. Barzani was concerned about possible Turkish retaliation—in 1983, a Turkish incursion, supposedly directed against PKK rebels, instead destroyed Barzani's bases. Barzani's brother Idris asked the PKK to relocate their bases and not stage attacks near the border.

"He made clear they were getting pressure from Turkey," said Selahattin Celik, who attended the October 1984 meeting at the KDP's Iranian camp in Razhan. The PKK refused Barzani's request, arguing it needed its bases near where it crossed into Turkey, but gradually they did make some changes to reduce the chances that Turkey would retaliate against the Iraqi Kurdish fighters and villagers near the border.

Ankara was uninterested in the PKK's cosmetic changes. In October 1984, the Turkish foreign minister, accompanied by a large number of military officials, came to Baghdad to discuss the situation.[18] Both Turkey and Iraq were opposed to Kurdish independence in any part of the region and Turkey had little difficulty negotiating an agreement that allowed its military to conduct raids on PKK encampments in northern Iraq.

Baghdad had two reasons for agreeing, despite its long-time suspicions that Ankara sought to reclaim control of the non-Arab (and now oil-rich) Iraqi northern provinces previously under Ottoman control. One, Iraq needed to maintain good relations with Turkey because of the oil it sent through Turkey and other commercial links. Two, it no doubt hoped any Turkish cross-border operations would also target the PKK's Iraqi Kurdish partner, Barzani's KDP, with which Baghdad was at war. Nonetheless, Iraq remained sufficiently wary of Turkey that it refused to allow Turkish troops to push further than five kilometers into Iraqi territory. Ankara's displeasure with this limit probably was offset by the knowledge that, given Iraq's lack of control over its own border region, it was unlikely anyone would be around to measure just how far Turkish troops went.

Both Talabani and Barzani were uncomfortable with this agreement. Barzani, who controlled territory up to the Turkish border, would suffer the most in any cross-border operation and partly because of this, the Iraqi Kurdish leader's relations with Ocalan worsened. Barzani's fears that he would be targeted in any Turkish raid soon were realized. On August 15, 1986, the second anniversary of the start of the PKK's fight, the Turkish air force bombed northern Iraq, killing an estimated 100 Iraqi Kurdish civilians and KDP fighters. The Turkish military continued smaller operations in the next year, and then in March 1987, another big, cross-border bombing raid wounded many Iraqi Kurds and destroyed dozens of houses.[19] Two months later, Barzani formally abandoned the protocol he signed with the PKK.

Perhaps mindful of the PKK's growing popularity in the region, Barzani insisted he did not see the Turkish Kurdish group as an enemy. "We have nothing to say about the PKK's attacks on the [Republic of Turkey]," Barzani stated. "But after all that has happened, it is absolutely impossible for the PKK to stay in the areas under our control."[20]

Notwithstanding Barzani's demand that the PKK leave its mountain camps, the formal end of the alliance had little effect on the PKK or its operations in north Iraq. The alliance had allowed the PKK to establish itself militarily inside northern Iraq, and now they were so well entrenched that it was impossible to dislodge them without an all-out armed assault—and even this was not certain to work. And in any case, Ocalan had long since started to lose interest in the alliance. Earlier on, the PKK leader had renewed his criticisms of Barzani, whom he accused of carrying out a "primitive" struggle because his goal was autonomy and not independence.

"I saw Massoud Barzani a few times and he complained that using such language was shameful," said S., a PKK militant active in the region then. "He insisted that the situation of the Iraqi Kurds was not like that of the Turkish Kurds, and that for them to demand independence was very difficult."

At the same time, Barzani long had been uncomfortable with the PKK's armed aggression against some other groups in northern Iraq. In April 1985, PKK rebels attacked militants from the Iraqi Communist Party, claiming the communist group backed a Turkish Kurdish group with which the PKK fought, among other things. However, the Iraqi Communist Party had its own alliance with Barzani's rebel group and Barzani interpreted the PKK's attack as an attack on his own party. After that, the protocol between the two parties all but formally ended.

Hidden behind the PKK's attack on the Communist Party—and Barzani's angry response—was a conflict between Barzani and Ocalan's leadership methods. While Ocalan was a fiery leftist who had made himself chairman of the PKK, Barzani was a traditional tribal leader who inherited his position when his father died. Barzani could be ruthless toward his enemies, including other Kurds, but he did not need to worry about internal claims on his leadership, as Ocalan did. Nor did Barzani believe in using internal execution as a means of controlling his fighters, a method more common, anyway, to extreme leftist groups. The PKK's violent attacks on the Communist Party and its angry, verbal attacks on Barzani were sparked, at least in part, by the willingness of both Iraqi groups to give sanctuary to PKK militants who had fled. Barzani, who had not quite realized Ocalan's unwavering antagonism to PKK members who quit the group, once even tried to negotiate the safe return of one PKK militant who feared execution.

"Massoud Barzani sent news to [PKK senior militant] Cemil Bayik and they met, and then Massoud told me I should go back to the PKK," said Ibrahim Aydin, who was turned over to Barzani's forces by Iranian Pasdaran after he was caught crossing the border into Iran when he fled the PKK. "But I refused, saying he didn't know the PKK like I did."

The problem was, no matter how much the other Kurdish leaders disliked Ocalan's methods or mistrusted his promises, it was impossible to ignore the PKK.

"They are not strong, but they are the most popular of the Kurdish groups," Jalal Talabani said in the late 1980s, in a somewhat convoluted attempt to explain the PKK's growth, despite all the criticisms. "In order to be strong one needs a strong organization, a strong leader and well-armed fighters. From that perspective they are not strong, but what they do have is support."[21]

6

The Struggle to Succeed, 1985–1990

SELAHATTIN CELIK FINALLY made it back into Turkey around the middle of 1985, crossing the mountains that led from northern Iraq to the Sirnak area of southeast Turkey. "We were about 30 or 50 people and it had to be done carefully, but Turkish soldiers couldn't control the whole mountain range on the border," he recalled. Once, during an earlier foray into Turkey, Celik had met up with his father and brother in their old village. This time, it was impossible to consider such a meeting. The Turkish military's offensive had dealt a blow to the relatively inexperienced guerrilla units. It was difficult for PKK fighters to traverse the region and armed clashes were frequent and fierce.

"[PKK commander] Mahsum Korkmaz staged an attack in the Sirnak area in September and the Turkish soldiers retaliated with a big operation, wounding two of our people. By chance I wasn't hit," Celik recalled.

Late that year, Celik walked back into northern Iraq, crossed the border into Iran and went to Tehran, where he boarded a plane to Damascus using a faked Turkish passport. In Damascus, he briefly met with Ocalan before going on to Helwe camp.

"Ocalan was criticizing different people, but I didn't pay any attention," said Celik. "I was focused on what we needed to do to build up the rebel war."

The PKK was preparing for its 3rd Congress, scheduled for the end of October 1986, when delegates would evaluate the group's activities and plan the next phase of the war.[1] Already, militants had started to gather in Helwe camp to write up the reports that would form the basis for the meeting. Celik joined the group working on a big analysis of the PKK's armed battle to date. Six months into his assignment, he was arrested by the PKK.

"I was arrested in the evening," began Celik, somewhat reluctantly. "It was the summer, the weather was nice in Helwe. Someone I knew well, Halil Kaya, came to my room and said, 'We have to put you in prison until a report is written.' He took my gun—I always carried a pistol—and put me in a room alone."

The PKK's internal prison was located in one of the only two-story buildings in the camp. The ground floor was used for people accused of being agents or saboteurs, at that time mainly Kurdish workers in Lebanon, while the upper floor held PKK members accused of more generally mismanaging their duties and obstructing the group's struggle.

"I stayed there for a few months." Celik shifted uncomfortably in his chair. "It wasn't like I was locked up. I could walk around, go to the library. There was a guard for the room where you were kept, but there was no need for a guard, because what would you do? But it was to threaten you. To show the others that you were responsible for certain failings."

Ocalan was displeased the rebels had not reached the military goals he had set, despite the group's slow, if somewhat fitful, gains. His hopes for liberated zones and mass uprisings were far from being realized. Instead, PKK guerrillas inside Turkey still were working on proving themselves as a fighting force. Turkish soldiers also had managed to wipe out large numbers of rebels, including fabled commander Korkmaz, killed in March 1986. To the militants doing the fighting, it seemed that at least part of the fault lay in Ocalan's unrealistic analysis of the PKK's strength and capabilities. To the PKK leader, however, those implementing his instructions were to blame.

"What was the obstacle before us?" thundered Ocalan in a speech prepared for the congress. "Was I the obstacle? Never!"[2]

In truth, the senior commanders organizing the fight had made mistakes. Their initial decision to create armed groups that consisted of about three to five people each led to many problems for the guerrillas. These groups were too small to stand up to any concerted Turkish attack and it was easy for the soldiers to wipe them out. It was not until about mid-1985 that Celik and other senior commanders combined the units, creating more of a proper guerrilla force. Given their inexperience and small numbers, such errors hardly were surprising.

But Ocalan was unwilling to accept any responsibility for strategic or tactical errors. Ocalan always had expressed a forceful and unwavering belief in the PKK's ability to succeed—part of his charisma—and he insisted his fighters were not being aggressive enough, particularly in recruiting new supporters. At the same time, the military mistakes were almost a boon for Ocalan. The PKK leader saw an opportunity to undermine the more senior commanders, thereby minimizing the possibility that any of them later could challenge his authority.

"Ocalan staged a coup at the third congress," Mehmet Can Yuce, a former PKK prison leader, wrote years later, "and took all the power in his hands."[3]

Ocalan used simple but effective measures. Along with Celik, a number of other senior people were detained, disarmed, and forced to make humiliating statements at the congress. Their lack of protest seemingly proved Ocalan's right to take such action and reinforced his authority.

"Those of us who had been in the mountains organizing the war didn't think about—or couldn't think about—how to realize a political gain from our newfound importance," Celik, a slightly bitter tone in his voice, explained. "It didn't occur to us that we could use this to take over the organization. We didn't even think of it. We were busy in the mountains. But Apo thought differently, he thought of this possibility and he wanted to take away any chance of this happening."

The five-day congress opened on October 25. In theory, congresses were supposed to be the forum where members freely debated and discussed issues. In practice this had never happened. The PKK's founding congress, held in 1978 inside Turkey, was by necessity a hurried affair. At the 2nd Congress, held in 1982 in Syria, Cetin (Semir) Gungor's attempt to question Ocalan's decision-making was successfully undercut by Ocalan, who then forced Semir out of the PKK and encouraged, if not outright ordered, his murder. By the 3rd Congress, it was clear that not only was real debate not allowed, but also that any analysis had to conform to Ocalan's views, and to assure this he freely rewrote reports to incorporate his interpretation of what had happened and who was to blame.

Celik's turn came toward the end of the congress.

"It was a good thing Apo wasn't there, had I seen him we would have killed each other," Celik simply said. He sat on a chair on a slightly raised wooden platform, facing some 80 people sitting on wooden benches and stools. "They ask you questions," said Celik. "They accuse your father of being an agent, or say that you tried to poison someone, or that you didn't follow Apo's orders."

He stopped and lit a cigarette. "It was very difficult for me. It was the first time I had been accused of such things. It really was very difficult. They wanted to destroy my individuality. They don't even give you the chance to speak. If you speak, it means you are against the party." Celik shook his head. "I had to accept certain things. I also wrote a report that was published in the PKK's newspaper. So I suppose you could say that Ocalan won."

Ocalan similarly targeted many other PKK members who had risen to positions of responsibility and respect, going after almost everyone who had a leading role in the PKK's historic August 1984 attack. Duran (Abas) Kalkan, who had overall political responsibility for the Semdinli attack and had been named Ocalan's deputy after the second congress, was arrested. Ali (Terzi Cemal) Omurcan, commander of the failed Catak raid in August 1984, was arrested after the congress. Ocalan's wife, Kesire (Fatma) Yildirim, who had taken part in the final vote approving the start of the war, also was arrested. Yildirim was an outspoken woman with an independent streak, two things that clashed with Ocalan's growing fixation on ensuring his authority: Plus, there were credible rumors Ocalan had taken up with another woman and Yildirim had found out.

Those who escaped Ocalan's wrath either were dead—like Korkmaz, commander of the August 1984 Eruh raid, and Abdullah Ekinci, commander of the August 1984 Semdinli attack—or were unable to make it to the congress. One former PKK guerrilla laughingly suggested that the only reason Ocalan didn't go after every well-known person in the PKK was simply that he needed to keep some people around him to keep the group going.

But if Ocalan relied on public humiliation and arrests to protect his dictatorial authority, he also offered forgiveness as a means to tie people even tighter to his leadership. After the congress, the disgraced militants were offered new positions of responsibility. While one or two turned down specific jobs, they all agreed to take on new responsibilities. (Ocalan's wife, for example, went to Athens to organize for the PKK and Celik went to Germany.) Now, Ocalan had asserted himself not only as the man who could destroy someone's position in the PKK, but also as the one who could forgive and bring a person back into the group and into respectability.

"People weren't afraid of death, they were afraid of being called a traitor," said Celik. Apart from that, it was hard to leave the one group fighting for a Kurdish state, even if that group had just smeared your name and reputation in front of its membership. "How could you come out against what was being done, even if it was being done to you?" asked Celik. "To come out against the PKK? It was a good organization, an important one, you just couldn't imagine speaking out."

Those who joined the PKK in the 1970s, when the group was more loosely organized and Ocalan's authority haphazardly applied, could see that Ocalan was consolidating his power. But either they did not care or saw no chance to challenge him. However, those who joined the group later did not necessarily see what was happening. These new recruits, who came mainly from Europe, entered a ready-made organization in which Ocalan was supreme and his leadership was not open to question.

The period that encompassed the 3rd Congress marked the near conclusion of Ocalan's struggle to take control over every aspect of the PKK. But Ocalan was not content with ruling only the PKK. Having asserted his dominance over the party and its members, he sought to apply his authority to Kurdish civilians in the southeast. At Ocalan's behest, the 3rd Congress approved a number of controversial decisions. Lead among them was forced military conscription, according to which Kurdish young men of military age had to join the PKK or risk being kidnapped. Those attending the congress also accepted a law on forced taxation of civilians in the region. Both laws supposedly would help assert the PKK's control in the region, but at the outset at least, the laws turned some Kurds against the PKK, encouraging them to join the state-sponsored Kurdish militia as a means to protect their families and their livelihoods.

The PKK in Prison

Kurds arrested inside Turkey for supporting the PKK often were held in Diyarbakir Military Prison, a military-controlled prison completed in 1980.[4] This complex of squat buildings, barbed wire, and guard towers was once located on the city's periphery. But later, as Diyarbakir grew to accommodate villagers looking for economic opportunities—and also, those fleeing the war—the city swelled around the prison walls. The prison generally held about 2,000 people, most of them picked up for alleged ties to the PKK. Among them was a core group of a few hundred PKK members arrested in the months preceding or immediately following the military coup. These prisoners included some of the most committed militants, many of whom faced the death penalty for their activities. Although they had no contact with the guerrillas who were infiltrating into Turkey—and certainly none with Ocalan in Damascus—they continued to see themselves as active members of the PKK and tried to maintain an organized political presence inside the prison.

Diyarbakir Prison, also known as Prison No. 5, was renowned for its brutal conditions and severe torture of prisoners. But in 1984, conditions inside the prison eased, largely because of Turkey's return to democratic rule, renewed European pressure on the country's oft-criticized human rights record, and a January 1984 protest in which two prisoners died in a "death fast," two hanged themselves, and one was beaten to death.[5] For the most part, torture ceased, living conditions were somewhat improved, they could get books and newspapers, and for the first time, prisoners were allowed into the courtyard for fresh air and exercise. A lawyer who represented prisoners in Diyarbakir said that when conditions changed, "prisoners thought they were living in heaven."[6]

Like most prisons in Turkey, the cells in Diyarbakir Prison were large, crowded dormitories. Prisoners were crammed into rooms that held anywhere from 40 to more than 100 people, sleeping on narrow double or triple bunk beds and eating food that was brought to the cell door. This dormitory-like system was a boon for PKK prisoners, making it easier for them to organize themselves, maintain control over their cadre, and even expand their support base.

"The PKK prisoners were very active and focused," recalled Recep Marasli, a Rizgari member imprisoned in Diyarbakir for most of the 1980s.

PKK members in prison applied the same rigor to their activities that they had before they were arrested. They formed a central committee to run their own affairs, and each cell had a local committee for day-to-day affairs. They also began holding regular meetings and conducting study groups.

"Every day, one person would teach PKK history or, especially in the evenings, PKK people would be split into groups, where they would discuss things like Kurdish history, the history of the PKK or the international politics and power struggles," explained Rafik, the pseudonym of a Kurdish law student turned PKK activist, who was arrested around the 1980 coup.

The start of the PKK's armed struggle raised prisoners' spirits. "People who took part in the early attacks were captured and in prison they explained what was happening," said Rafik. "Villagers [accused of helping the militants] also were sent to prison, and they would tell us about the PKK, how it would come to their village, how it was organizing."

The war, coupled with the PKK's strong, organized activities inside the prison, helped boost the group's reputation. Relatives of imprisoned PKK members were impressed by their unwavering commitment to Kurdish independence and their activism, even inside the prison, and this view was relayed to friends and neighbors. At the same time, the security forces heavy-handed approach to fighting the insurgency—which included near-random arrests of people after a rebel attack—helped spread the PKK's message. Villagers whose only contact to the PKK might have been providing them with food at gunpoint were imprisoned with experienced, committed, Kurdish nationalists. Although they usually were held in different cells, they could communicate between the cells and spoke with the PKK prisoners during the exercise periods.

"The PKK was able to build up a real base of support from this," explained Marasli.

PKK prisoners searched for ways to establish ties with their party. "We wanted information, we wanted to know what the party was doing or thinking," said Mehmet Can Yuce, a member of the PKK prisoners' central committee. But it was difficult to make contact. Prisoners had limited opportunities to speak to those outside the prison. Letters were read and censored and the regularly scheduled visiting days—which until the late 1980s were limited to close relatives—were held under the supervision of prison guards with prisoners and visitors separated by a tightly knit mesh wire. Sometimes, on holidays, prisoners were allowed so-called open visits, in which they and their relatives could freely mix in one room. To pass a message to the guerrillas, prisoners needed family members willing to somehow sneak out a message unnoticed.

"In 1987 we built a tunnel and we wanted to get a message to the PKK about this, to arrange for them to meet us on the day we escaped," recounted Yuce. "We wrote up a small note like this"—he held up a tiny square of paper the size of a matchbook—"wrapped it in plastic so it wouldn't get wet. During an open visit, one of the prisoners, Mehmet Sener, stuck it in his mouth and when he kissed [the visitor] he did it on the mouth and transferred the note to her mouth." Yuce laughed. "You know, we Kurds don't kiss hello on the mouth, but he had to do it. Anyway, he told her to send the note to the mountains."

The note never made it. It took another three tries or so to contact a rebel unit in the mountains. But the escape plan failed. The tunnel ended not, as the prisoners planned, far outside the prison walls, but instead in front of a prison guard booth.

"We heard the PKK had sent one person to that place and he was arrested," said Yuce.

Prisoners rarely received information about what was happening inside the PKK and when they did, such as reports about the 3rd Congress or the killing of PKK traitors, they had little reason to mistrust the reports. Besides, they also believed in a strong party and opposed action that might split the PKK, as had happened to other Kurdish and leftist groups. "We wanted a group that protected its power and organization," admitted Yuce. "The issue was not whether one criticized or did not criticize, the important thing was the struggle, the principles, the sacrifices people had made for the struggle. This was what was important. Are you with them or against them?"

Taking Aim

One June evening in 1987, PKK rebels partly encircled a small village of about 60 people in Mardin province.[7] It was after dinner time and Pinarcik's eight members of the state-financed village guard system already were in their guard positions. Later, one guard recalled that PKK rebels shouted at them to surrender, but the men apparently did not pay much attention.

It was not the first time PKK rebels had come to Pinarcik village, which was nestled between two hilltops, about 10 miles from the nearest main Mardin-Omerli road. Once or twice before rebels had turned up on the village outskirts, firing off a few warning shots and leaving notes that warned the men to quit the state-financed militia. This time, however, the rebels fired directly on the village. The guards fought back, but they were outnumbered nearly four-to-one and, as one man later complained, hobbled by a lack of sufficient ammunition. Thirty rebels then descended upon the village and continued the shoot-out with the village guards. The firefight lasted more than two hours. At the end, 16 children and six women lay dead—shot by the PKK rebels —along with eight men. Turkish columnist Mehmet Ali Birand, who had distinguished himself for his attempts to write openly about the country's Kurdish issue, called it a crime of "historical"[8] proportions.

The Pinarcik massacre—as it was called by the Turkish media— was the PKK's most brutal attack on villagers since the state-sponsored militia had been formed. The rebels' goal was to force Kurdish villagers to quit the guard system, which not only was supposed to keep the PKK from the villages but also sometimes helped Turkish soldiers operating in the unfamiliar mountain terrain. "In order to [strengthen our presence], collaborationists will be completely wiped out,"[9] warned the PKK's *Serxwebun* party newspaper, making clear that Kurds who worked with the state were viewed the same as enemy Turkish soldiers.

The existence of these guards, who received a monthly salary, not only threatened to impede the PKK's growth in the region, but also undermined the PKK's claim to be the main force in the region. Village guards, like members of rival Kurdish groups, were seen as traitors to the PKK's cause. To make this clear, the PKK often hanged the guards in trees, their mouths stuffed with money.

But the attacks on village guards were haphazard, with little or no attempt to avoid killing women and children. Sometimes, as in Pinarcik, the rebels appeared intent on killing as many people as they could, regardless of whether they were armed guards or their unarmed wives and children. Many assaults were staged in a manner that seemed designed to hit civilians as well: the houses of village guards were firebombed late at night, minibuses carrying people back and forth to the villages linked to the militia were shot up. In the first two months of 1987, PKK rebels killed 35 Kurdish villagers, of whom at least seven were children. Ocalan did not publicly condemn these sorts of killings and PKK officials tried to rationalize them. A few days after the attack on Pinarcik, a PKK spokesman in Brussels dismissed the killing of civilians as something unavoidable. "In every struggle people die," he said. "[But] we do not support the killing of civilians."[10]

Even after it became clear that women and children made up a large proportion of villagers killed, PKK rebels in Mardin province, where most of the attacks occurred, did not change their tactics. In fact, a few days after the raid on Pinarcik, PKK rebels visited a nearby village and warned people, "If you don't want us to repeat the Pinarcik massacre, don't betray."[11]

These attacks galvanized Turkish public opinion against the PKK —and raised the group's profile—but militants discovered that local Kurds frequently ignored or overlooked these abuses. Reaction to the killings—if one measures it in relation to the PKK's continued growth in 1987 and 1988—was muted. The reasons varied. Sometimes people barely heard the news. Small mountain villages did not always have electricity for televisions or telephones, and certainly did not get newspaper delivery service. Often, Kurds dismissed the reports as Turkish lies designed to smear the PKK's reputation.

"The state lied so often, and these lies were reflected in the newspapers and television, that when they said something true I didn't believe them," said Nejdet Buldan, who later became mayor of Yuksekova, a city near the Iranian and Iraqi borders.

It also was clear that some Kurds saw the killing of civilians as an unfortunate but unavoidable aspect of the PKK's legitimate fight. It helped that these killings were not so foreign to the rural Kurdish areas. Blood feuds, which still broke out in the region, demanded revenge for death or serious dishonor. This revenge did not have to be exacted from the person who carried out the initial attack, but could be visited on almost any member of the tribe.[12] Women and children were not necessarily exempt from attack. "The PKK," wrote one Turkish expert, "has exploited this crooked tradition to its best."[13]

Perhaps equally important, the PKK's attacks were not directed at random civilians, but instead directed at villages that had accepted money and weapons from the state. For example, just a week after the attack on Pinarcik, PKK rebels raided three Mardin province villages that had not joined the state militia. Rebels simply gathered the people in the center of the village and forced them to listen to speeches extolling the Kurdish fight. Nobody was killed. The message was clear. Villagers who did not ally themselves with the state would be safe—at least from PKK attack.

The brutal attacks on those who joined the state's guard system were part of a broad change in tactics that followed the 1986 3rd

Congress, when the PKK decided it needed to directly and decisively show its authority in the region. Targeting village guards was just one change. PKK rebels also kidnapped young men—sometimes picking up dozens at a time—and demanded that they join the Kurdish fight.

The PKK's so-called military conscription law was an attempt to mimic the power of the Turkish state, which had its own compulsory conscription, and also boost the rebels' forces, estimated at anywhere from a few hundred to more than 1,000. In their zeal to enforce conscription, some rebels took everyone they could.

"One day I was looking through the binoculars and I saw a big group coming towards us, there were these women in their village dresses, which were all different colors and billowing around them," said Huseyin Topgider, at the time a fighter in what the Kurds called Botan, a central and fairly pro-PKK region of the southeast.

"I asked a friend who they were and he said, 'Oh, that's Dr. Kendal's new unit!'" Topgider laughed. "A guerrilla group went to a village and took a group of young women, but these were all married women and they refused to change their clothes or take guns. We ended up sending them back to their village."

The policy was controversial even inside the PKK. Some commanders thought it counterproductive to force people to fight, especially since young men started to hide themselves at night to avoid being kidnapped, and they tried to avoid implementing the law.

"The people [who made the decision] at the congress didn't really know fighting," complained Sari Baran, who commanded a main force of 40 to 50 fighters in the Cukurca-Hakkari area. "I knew the military conscription law would cause people to turn against us. You would take people, and then the village would react, then the people you took would run away, and then you had to kill them."

The PKK also directly sought to weaken the state's influence and authority in the region. Civilians who worked on public works projects, like paving roads or cutting down trees, were warned to give up their jobs and their machinery was torched and burned. The PKK also warned teachers to leave the region. In 1988, they killed five teachers, all of whom worked in Mardin province, where the Pinarcik massacre had taken place.[14] They burned some schools and health clinics in different areas. In 1989, they killed four more teachers and continued to burn schools and clinics.

PKK supporters argued the teachers were either agents or soldiers and that the schools and clinics were used as military barracks. In fact, soldiers sometimes did turn these buildings into temporary guard stations, and in 1989, the state prepared a program with the defense ministry to send soldier-teachers to the region because of the problems getting teachers to accept assignments there. Such tactics on the part of the state only helped convince the PKK and its supporters that the rebel attacks were justified, even if most of the teachers killed were just teachers.

The PKK's new, more aggressive tactics had mixed success. For example, the first year that the militants targeted village guards, new applications dropped and the number of guards declined by about two-thirds, to some 6,000 armed men.[15] But in response, the state boosted assistance to the guards, increasing salaries, distributing wireless radios, and even giving them parkas, which helped gain new members and made them a more committed force. The attacks on village guards also helped turn their relatives into enemies of the PKK, further isolating a segment of the Kurdish population from the PKK.

"The state tried to turn Kurd against Kurd," said Topgider, "and we shouldn't have fallen into their trap."

The PKK, however, showed a tactical versatility that, like its ideological versatility, played an important role in its ability to garner support. Ocalan soon realized the negative effect the attacks on civilians had on the PKK's image, especially abroad, and in 1988, he publicly claimed that he opposed such killings and blamed them on what he said were the mistakes of some rebels.[16] In 1990, participants at the PKK's 4th Congress expressed their opposition to attacks on civilians (although not on the guards themselves) and for at least three years, these sorts of killings declined. In 1991, the PKK announced a limited amnesty for village guards who quit the militia. Although continued mistrust of the rebels, financial incentives from the state, and strong state pressure stopped many guards from accepting the PKK offer, the fact the rebels made such a peace offering (now and then repeated later on) helped win the group more respect from Kurds in general.

Similarly, forced conscription did not win the PKK real support; if anything, it made new enemies. Many of those kidnapped sought to flee and when they did, they needed to prove to the security forces that they had not joined the PKK willingly.[17] To do so, they often gave up valuable information about PKK positions and plans. Forced conscription also endangered gains the PKK realized from its attacks on village guards.

"These [kidnappings] encouraged villagers to join the village guards because people wanted to get weapons to protect their children," explained former rebel commander Selahattin Celik.

The PKK soon reviewed the forced military conscription as well. In 1990, at the 2nd national conference in Lebanon, participants agreed to suspend the military conscription law, a decision that was reaffirmed at the 4th Congress a few months later, participants said. It helped that at this point, the PKK was sufficiently popular that forced conscription no longer seemed necessary.

The PKK's willingness to take into account the demands and criticisms of the people it wanted to represent was an important factor in the group's growing popularity. The fact that some people still were forced to join the rebels—and sometimes, women and children still were killed in attacks—was not as critical. What seemed to matter was the PKK's public attempt to respect the wishes of its support base. And, of course, what mattered was its fight.

In towns and villages on the edge of the Cudi Mountains, the rough mountain range where the PKK had set up mobile camps, stories started to spread of the rebels' commitment to Kurdistan, their honesty and their respect of their people: Four Kurds who raped a woman had been captured and executed by the PKK; a man who stole money from the rebels was ordered to pay it back with interest, but the PKK only charged him the official interest rate. The moral of these stories was clear: the rebels were exacting, but fair, and those who did not cross the PKK would not face problems.

The PKK often said the initial phase of its war was a propaganda battle, in which rebels tried to gain the trust and respect of the people and prove that they could stand up to the state. By the end of the 1980s, the PKK appeared to be winning this battle.

Ocalan Reaches Out

Abdullah Ocalan, like other Kurdish leaders in the region, had few qualms about establishing relations with countries that repressed their own Kurdish populations.[18] He viewed such ties as necessary to enable the PKK to wage its fight and as the PKK's war spread across eastern Turkey, he and his military commanders sought ways to make contact with Iran and Iraq, both of which bordered Turkey's Kurdish region. The Iraqi Kurdish leader Massoud Barzani had excellent relations with the Iranian government, and for awhile, PKK rebels used Barzani's contacts in order to travel across Iranian territory.

But in 1986 or 1987, as the alliance between the PKK and Barzani unraveled, Ocalan attempted to establish direct ties with Tehran. His younger bother Osman, who other PKK members said previously was involved in recruiting support and money for the PKK among Kurdish workers in Libya, was sent to Iran to build contacts. By 1987, the PKK had received permission to use Iranian territory, and group houses were arranged for militants in Urumiye, Maku, and probably other towns in western Iran, not far from the Turkish border.

The new arrangement was very useful to the PKK. The risk of a Turkish military strike was much lower than in northern Iraq, where Baghdad neither had sufficient control nor particularly cared enough to protest the occasional Turkish bombing raid against PKK camps. But Iran was fully in control of its Kurdish region, suspicious of Turkey's Western ties, and much less likely to ignore military actions that infringed on its territorial sovereignty. As a result, the PKK was able to use its camps in Iran as secure meeting spots for senior commanders, places to hold political training for new recruits, and centers to treat wounded rebels. Depending on where a rebel unit was based inside Turkey, it might be easier to reach northern Iraq by cutting across Iran. And because militants now had a direct route to eastern Turkey via Iran—before, they had to make a long and dangerous trip that began at the Iraqi border, walking north through a huge section of southeastern Turkey—the PKK was able to expand operations there.

Iranian security officials—one PKK member identified them as being from the Pasdaran or Revolutionary Guards—gave at least some PKK militants special passes or identity cards to ease their travel through the country. No doubt, this also was a way to keep track of PKK movements. By the late 1980s, the relationship was sufficiently open that PKK militants who crossed from Turkey into Iran often went to the nearest military outpost and announced their presence. Sometimes, the intelligence services then picked them up in jeeps or open trucks and drove them to their camps, which really were houses or apartments. Later on, PKK rebels established direct ties with Iranian Kurds—it is unclear if this was done with the intervention or knowledge of the security services—who might drive the rebels from one town to another.

The Iranian regime, which had fought hard to break its own Kurdish resistance in the early 1980s, was not in favor of an independent Kurdish state, neither in its own country nor anywhere else. But Tehran saw the benefit in assisting rebels fighting its neighbors, especially when it had ongoing conflicts with them. The Iran-Iraq war gave Tehran good cause to back Iraqi Kurdish fighters in the 1980s, and Tehran's irritations with Ankara sparked interest in a similar arrangement with the Turkish Kurdish rebels.

Iran and Turkey were both Muslim countries, but they had very different approaches to religion: Iran was an Islamic theocracy, Turkey was firmly secular. They also were in different geopolitical camps: Turkey was a NATO member and hosted U.S. military bases, Iran was convinced that the United States sought to overthrow the Islamic government. Iran did not like that its political opponents were allowed to resettle in Turkey, nor was it comfortable with Turkey's military incursions into northern Iraq. Apart from the problems this caused for Iran's Iraqi Kurdish allies, Tehran probably did not want Ankara setting up a permanent presence in northern Iraq, giving it stronger influence in the region and along that stretch of the Iranian-Iraqi border.[19] Ankara might not be an immediate threat to Iran, but it probably appeared prudent to use whatever tools available to ensure this remained the case.

In return for allowing the PKK to set up camps on its territory, Tehran demanded and received information about Turkish and U.S. military installations. This information was gathered primarily from recruits who crossed into Iran to join the PKK. The new arrivals were questioned by senior PKK militants and this information, also useful to the PKK, was passed on to the Iranian intelligence contacts. It can be assumed that experienced militants who crossed back and forth also provided similar information.

At the same time, Osman Ocalan, who ran the PKK's operations in Iran, was expected to provide the names, code-names, and other relevant information about new recruits who came via Iran. The Iranians may have wanted this information so they could run their own checks to ensure these new recruits did not pose any threat to the Islamic republic. Tehran warned the PKK against doing any propaganda work within the Iranian Kurdish community or assisting the Iranian Kurdish KDP party. The PKK also was barred from staging attacks on Turkey from positions on or near the Iranian border. Iran, which constantly denied it was assisting the PKK, wanted to maintain this fiction and reduce the chance of Turkish armed retaliation.

Meanwhile, in the convoluted alliances of the Kurdish region, the PKK finally made contact with Baghdad. The March 1988 Iraqi chemical attack on Halabja and the ongoing military offensive against Iraqi Kurdish militants—coupled with the Iran-Iraq ceasefire—had strengthened the Iraqi army's hold over northern Iraq. The border area, however, was hard to control for any army, and Baghdad was concerned that Iraqi Kurdish militants might reinfiltrate from the newly established refugee camps inside Turkey. Baghdad hoped that by encouraging the PKK to settle on the border, it could block the build-up of Iraqi Kurdish forces.

"In 1988 many of Kurds in that region either were killed or expelled," the Iraqi Kurdish leader Barzani said a few years later. "At that time Saddam Hussein gave permission for PKK military bases."[20]

It is unclear how much permission the PKK actually needed to maintain or expand camps in the formidable mountains along the border, but the new ties certainly eased things for the rebels. In exchange, the Iraqi military wanted the PKK to provide information about Turkish and Iraqi Kurdish troops movements. Some of the PKK's bases were in the same general area as Iraqi military outposts, and commanders from both sides started to meet.

"It was about the trading of information," said senior PKK militant Azman. "They closed their eyes to us and in return, the PKK gave them information."

In the winter, when some Iraqi military outposts shut down because of the severe snow, PKK militants would move in and use the buildings for shelter. Ocalan's enthusiasm for ties with Iraq did not seem matched by Iraqi officials and the relationship was fairly informal, certainly more so than the PKK's relations with Iran. "There wasn't much the PKK could provide Iraq," noted Azman.

In between building these new relationships, Ocalan wooed Jalal Talabani.[21] The Iraqi Kurdish leader finally had made peace in 1986 with his long-term rival, Massoud Barzani, and he also had established ties to Iran. Similar to Barzani, Talabani's party now received weapons and financing from Tehran, having promised to halt support for the Iranian Kurdish rebels.[22] Ocalan's alliance with Barzani officially was still in force, but in practice, it had collapsed and the PKK leader wanted to secure alternate ties in northern Iraq to ensure access. Given Talabani's good relations with Tehran, the PKK may have also hoped that an alliance would help secure their presence in Iran, which at the time was still being negotiated.

In 1986, just around the time Barzani demanded PKK militants leave KDP-controlled territory, Ocalan sent a letter to Talabani suggesting the two groups work together. The PUK leader had always championed the idea of alliances among Kurdish groups and he saw an opportunity to act as a moderating influence on the PKK, whose bloody attacks inside Turkey threatened the reputation of all Kurdish fighters. In October 1987, five months after Barzani formally ended his ties to the PKK, Talabani met with a PKK delegation in north Iraq. He demanded that the PKK first end its attacks on civilians, condemn terrorism in general, and stop its verbal and physical attacks against rival Kurdish groups. By January, the two sides had worked out their differences, and an agreement was finalized in May 1988.

Similar to Ocalan's former agreement with Barzani, it was more of a mutual support pact than any plan to merge the groups or fights. The agreement stressed the importance of each group's separate fight, the need to end their disagreements, and the need to focus on the national question of a Kurdish state. Talabani explained, "We accepted [this agreement] because it was important for the Kurdish movement."[23]

But the protocol was finalized two months after the Iraqi chemical attack on Halabja, by which time there was little Talabani could offer the PKK. The Iraqi army's assault on northern Iraq forced Kurdish fighters and civilians out of much of the region, leaving the PKK freer to operate there. Ocalan, realizing the shifting power in the region, had started to work on setting up a separate deal with Baghdad. Soon, the PKK leader resumed his verbal attacks on Talabani, accusing him of trying to undermine the PKK by making overtures to the United States and Turkey. Ocalan angrily cancelled the agreement in 1989, criticizing him for, among other things, being willing to settle for Kurdish autonomy instead of demanding independence. It seemed more likely that Ocalan simply decided he no longer needed Talabani. Talabani, ever the statesman, appeared more disappointed than angry at Ocalan's turnaround.

"If the PKK were to liberate all of Kurdistan and reach independence, then all of us would recognize him as our chairman," Talabani told an interviewer that same year. "But he won't be able to do anything. When we were his age . . . we said the same things. But later on, we understood what could [and could not] be done."[24]

The Limits of Turkish Politics

Early in 1988, a Kurdish parliamentarian from the left-of-center Social Democratic Populist Party (SHP) took to the podium and called on his fellow politicians to end the Kurdish taboo.

"The Kurdish problem must be taken up in all its angles, and this problem must be debated in details and realistic solutions must be proposed," said Eren, who had not told his party of his planned remarks. "Until now, the proper approach to this problem has not been shown, and the existence of Kurds constantly is being denied."[25]

Eren had not even finished speaking when pandemonium broke out. Deputies from the governing right-of-center Motherland Party tried to drown him out by banging on their tables—one man stood up and started yelling—while another spat at Eren and at the other Social Democratic deputies. The interior minister insisted on reciting aloud from the constitution (presumably to remind Eren that, as the constitution stated, everyone in Turkey was a Turk) and, a day later, former coup leader and current president, Kenan Evren, simply said: "If it is as I heard, this is something that I cannot sanction."[26]

But the former military regime's efforts to remake Turkey's political scene were starting to unravel, giving room to both the old and a new generation of Turkish and Kurdish politicians.[27] The ban on pre-1980 political party leaders taking part in active politics had been lifted by a public referendum in September 1987, and national elections two months later returned some of the old guard and their supporters to parliament. Although Prime Minister Turgut Ozal's Motherland Party retained its majority, the Social Democratic Party, which in 1983 had been barred from standing in the elections, entered parliament as the second largest party.

Kurds always had been more attracted to left-wing parties and the Social Democratic parliamentarians included a handful of politically conscious Kurds, some of whom had been detained or jailed in the

1970s or early 1980s for Kurdish activism. Ozal, the technocrat-turned-politician, suddenly faced a more lively and more savvy opposition and he struggled to maintain his focus on liberalizing the economy in the face of attempts by some deputies to push for change in restrictive laws passed by the military regime. Soon, Kurdish deputies, specifically those in the Social Democratic Party, tried to force a discussion on the unrest in the southeast and limits on Kurdish identity.

"Giving this speech had been my goal in entering parliament," said Eren, who was 37 years old and a lawyer by training when he got a slot on the party's list. "I couldn't change society [as a lawyer] and decided to go into politics because that way, I could be more effective."

Eren was not completely surprised by the parliament's reaction. It was one reason he kept his plan a secret. "They could have tried to block me," he noted. Still, he had hoped his speech would spark more than outrage.

"I was someone who knew the region well, I knew the PKK's organizations and methods and I knew Turkey well," explained Eren, sitting in his cramped law office on the edge of an upscale part of Istanbul. "I thought that the fighting was going to harm both Kurds and Turks and I wanted to prevent this, I thought this needed to be solved through democratic means. I thought that if the other parliamentarians would take up the issue then we could prevent [the war] from getting bigger."

Instead, the opposite happened. "After this, I had a lot of problems in parliament, they wouldn't let me speak anymore. I was isolated by my party."

One popular newspaper columnist accused Eren of working together, however unwittingly, with the terrorists trying to divide Turkey. "Moreover, in Turkey there does not exist a 'Kurdish minority,'" wrote Oktay Eksi. "What does exist are some Turks who accept or think that they came from an ethnic group known as Kurds."[28]

Nearly a year later, another Kurdish deputy, Ibrahim Aksoy, was suspended from the party for giving a speech to European parliamentarians in which he criticized Turkey's policies toward the Kurds. Only his parliamentary immunity saved him from being tried for the crime of "separatism." Turgut Ozal, who had since moved into the presidency, warned that "those who want to divide our country are being nourished from the outside."[29]

The Turkish political establishment's inability—or refusal—to allow discussion of the Kurdish issue was to be expected. This approach was rooted in the country's long-standing and popularly accepted Kemalist ideology that denied the existence of Kurds, or at least insisted that identifying people as such was irrelevant and counterproductive and therefore needed to be avoided. In addition, Turkey was fresh out of a military coup. And although the military had withdrawn from politics, it regularly exercised its views through the National Security Council (MGK), which frequently took up the Kurdish issue under the rubric of terrorism. Politicians had reason to be wary of challenging the military's approach to the Kurdish issue. Three coups between 1960 and 1980 were a clear enough example of what happened when the armed forces believed that the country was threatened from within.

But new approaches were being pushed from outside the country as well. In October 1989, the Kurdish Institute in Paris, whose soft-spoken chairman, Kendal Nezan, had fled Turkey in 1971 and trained in France as a physicist, held what was called the first-ever international Kurdish conference.[30] Nezan was well known and well liked and the conference was cosponsored by a human rights group headed by Danielle Mitterrand, wife of the French president. A slew of Kurdish activists, political party representatives, and politicians, along with foreign experts, were invited to speak on the plight of Kurds in general and those from Iraq in particular.

Iraq and Iran had agreed to a ceasefire in August 1988, but in the meantime, Iraqi forces had opened a full-scale attack on Iraqi Kurdish civilians and fighters alike. Chemical attacks—the first big one, against Halabja, followed the town's capture by Iranian and Iraqi Kurdish forces working together—were accompanied by mass round-ups and executions of civilians, including sometimes women and children, and wholescale razing of villages and towns. In total, an estimated 200,000 people were killed and 1.5 million forced out of their homes in what Iraq dubbed the Anfal campaign. Hundreds of thousands of Iraqi Kurds had since fled the country, with some 60,000 in Turkey and the remainder in Iran. Nezan hoped the conference would devise a plan for assisting Iraqi Kurds and draw attention to the problems Kurds faced throughout the region.

Among those invited were about 30 parliamentarians from Turkey, of whom seven Kurdish deputies from the Social Democrats, plus the now-independent deputy Ibrahim Aksoy, accepted.[31] The party chairman, Erdal Inonu, who also was invited, at first appeared unsure what to do. But then he barred party members from going, complaining that their presence at such a meeting would open up the party to criticism from the Turkish public. The deputies refused to heed Inonu's ban, and upon return from the conference—which Turkish newspapers followed closely—were called before the party's discipline committee. Four weeks later they were kicked out of the party for what was described as taking part in political activities contrary to the party's fundamental principles.

Eren, who attended the conference, summed up the party's reasons: "It was," he said, "a Kemalist party."

The decision by the Social Democrats sparked an angry reaction from Kurdish members throughout the country and 12 provincial chairmen from the southeast resigned. It was not only Kurds who were upset. Some Turkish members of the Social Democrats, mainly those who came from its more leftist wing, protested the decision and around one dozen parliamentarians, some Turks, some Kurds, soon submitted their resignations. Over the next few months, these newly independent deputies, joined by other disgruntled party members, discussed how they could retain an influence in the political sphere. It seemed clear to them that in order to address certain problems facing Turkey—above all, democratization of the country and the Kurdish problem—a new political party was needed.

The Limits of Turks and Kurds in Politics

Turkish leftists interested in a new party accepted the need for a different approach toward the Kurds, but expected the party to focus on all issues facing Turkey, from the economy to the environment.[32] However, the idea of a new party had been sparked by the expulsion of Kurdish deputies, and Kurds saw in this an opportunity to build a party that would address their problems and interests. The mass resignations in the Kurdish region created a ready and experienced political cadre that knew what it wanted. And for Kurds who neither supported the PKK nor believed in armed struggle, this democratic development finally offered them a chance to push their national or cultural identity in a nonviolent, nonextremist way.

As work progressed on the new party, some Turkish supporters felt uncomfortable with the increasing focus on the Kurdish issue, and gradually, main Turkish backers dropped out. Aydin Guven Gurkan, who had been an important member of the Social Democratic Party and was expected to be the new party's general secretary, apparently was worried that the party's composition was too narrow. He suggested that more time be taken to try to expand the party's support base. But there was little interest and soon Gurkan quit the working group.

"Every day, another Turkish leftist left the party," recalled Mahmut Kilinc, who had resigned as SHP provincial chairman in Adiyaman after the Paris Conference. "They saw that the new party was splitting from the classic type of party and becoming a Kurdish mass party. Every day, the numbers of Turks got less and less and one day, we were pretty much all Kurds in the party."

The People's Labor Party (HEP) officially was founded on June 7, 1990. In keeping with the professed desire to be a party for all of Turkey, HEP's chairman was supposed to be a Turk and the general secretary a Kurd. The party, officially at least, was not a Kurdish party. Turkey's political parties law banned formation of parties that defended what usually was called regionalism or racism (as in, discriminating among people by claiming Kurds existed and needed special rights), or that threatened national unity by promoting other languages or cultures. But this was the first, legal Kurdish party in the country's history, regardless of the linguistic tricks employed to avoid being identified as such.

It was not immediately clear how popular the party would be. By 1990, the PKK had grown bigger and there were some Kurds, particularly younger men and women, who did not believe that the political system would ever be receptive to Kurdish demands or a legal Kurdish struggle. Initially, the PKK's approach to the new party combined scorn with disinterest. Militants fighting the Turkish state thought the party was a waste of time, unnecessary, and, ultimately, a tool of the state because it was part of the state structure.

"We didn't take it seriously," said Sari Baran, a commander from the Hakkari region. "We thought that only armed struggle made sense."

Some of HEP's early supporters tried to make clear that they were not forming a party to challenge the PKK. This approach was the most logical given the realities of both the war and the Kurdish region. Taking an active stand against the PKK would only have hurt the party in its attempt to woo average Kurds, a growing number of whom had either helped PKK rebels in some small way or had relatives in the rebel ranks.

Certainly, there were many inside HEP who neither liked Ocalan nor believed that armed struggle was the best way to realize Kurdish goals. Nonetheless, even the PKK's critics had to admit the fight reflected real grievances and desires and they understood what drove people to choose armed struggle. The Kurds who had come together to try legal politics simply hoped that the two parties—one, the PKK, engaged in an illegal struggle, the other, HEP, working in the legal, political field—could leave each other alone.

Turkey

In the late 1980s, Turkish officials realized there was a serious problem developing in the Kurdish region, but they continued to blame economic underdevelopment and outside forces for fomenting the PKK's violence. While there was truth to these claims, support for the PKK was rooted in people's frustrated Kurdish nationalism. Ankara's refusal to see the PKK as an indigenous problem, one that was based in and sustained by a variety of state policies, made it difficult for the authorities to take realistic steps to counter the rebels' growing popularity.

"Those [Kurds] who are tired of waiting [for help from the state] become more sympathetic to the PKK,"[33] noted *Milliyet* newspaper columnist Mehmet Ali Birand, the iconoclastic journalist who approached the issue with a degree of impartiality unusual at the time. Instead, the state expanded its repressive hold on the region. Martial law was replaced in the southeast by emergency rule, a quasi-martial law system presided over by a specially appointed regional governor.[34] In a clear sign the government felt it was losing the propaganda battle, the government issued a special decree in April 1990, giving the regional governor the power to ban any Turkish publications that misrepresented events in the emergency rule region—at least misrepresented them according to the government's view. The regional governor also could shut down offending printing presses anywhere in the country, order people into internal exile, and evacuate villages without prior notice.[35] Decree 413, slightly modified over the next few months because of protests by the Social Democrats, reinforced Kurdish views that the state still hoped to repress and deny Kurdish identity out of existence. The PKK's argument that only violence would win Kurds their rights appeared ever-more attractive.

7

The Deluge, 1988–1991

ZEKI OZTURK, LATER known as Azman, was a lawyer before he joined the PKK. He picked law school partly because of pressure from his grandfather, a former government parliamentarian put on trial after the 1960 military coup, and because of an American television program whose name he never managed to remember. But when he started practicing in 1985, two years after the military regime gave up power, he was disappointed.

"What I encountered was very different [than I imagined]," said Azman, as he is better known. "On the one side, there were laws, but no real freedoms. And on the other side, every day new laws were being made that limited the activities of the press, organizations, meetings, and even Turkish political parties. There was no pride in being a lawyer."

After about a year working in Ankara, Azman relocated to the resort city Antalya on the Mediterranean coast. There was a fairly large Kurdish community in Antalya—maybe because of all the work to be found in the tourism industry—and Azman and his friends often debated the PKK's fight. Most of them, like Azman, were beginning to feel a certain respect toward the PKK. As a high school student in Turkey in the late 1970s, Azman was interested in Kemal Burkay's nonviolent Kurdistan Socialist Party. But legal activism had not accomplished much.

"Burkay's party supported political reforms, but in that period an unarmed struggle did not seem possible," explained Azman, who still speaks in the highly educated language of a lawyer. "In that period there was no democratic opening in Turkey," he insisted. "Yet there was a resistance [the PKK's fight] and this had an influence on people, despite other concerns they might have had with the PKK."

Azman's more radical thinking was shaped, in part, by PKK civilian activists (usually called *milis*), who were sent to western Turkey starting in 1986. Their job was to recruit for the rebel group—and to make sure people knew what was going on in the southeast. In the southeast, gaining Kurdish attention was not difficult: The sound of gunfire was heard in city centers, increased military patrols buttressed PKK claims that Kurdistan was occupied, and Kurds might run into rebels or their active sympathizers during visits to relatives in villages.

But in Turkey's western provinces, where millions of Kurds migrated over the decades in search of economic opportunities or simply to escape the tensions of the remote Kurdish region, the PKK needed to do more to reach people.[1] Both the rebel group and its war were that much further away, and information was limited to Turkish news reports, which rarely veered off the government's line. However, the bans on Kurdish identity and the problems faced by democratic activists were the same. Panel discussions on human rights abuses were broken up by police, torture of detainees was common, and the small, mainly leftist publications that covered the Kurdish issues faced legal difficulties. The courts did not offer much recourse. Azman knew a prosecutor who tried to complain about legal mistakes in a case against PKK members. "They just laughed at him and told him to approve the decision, saying, 'There's no law here.'"

By 1988, PKK militants and their civilian *milis* activists were well established in the local, activist Kurdish communities in western Turkey. "In Antalya we had one acquaintance, he was a villager, someone who didn't know much about the world, but he was the representative of an illegal organization and this sparked a certain interest among some of us," recalled Azman.

Azman seriously began to consider joining the rebel fight. "I had some questions about some of their actions, their treatment of rival groups, but when I debated this with myself . . . I saw I could stay passive, I could become a state bureaucrat, or I could join the PKK. It was as if there was no alternative. In fact, there was nothing else."

In 1988, Azman abandoned his law practice and joined the guerrillas. "People chose armed struggle as a last resort, it wasn't the first choice. In Europe or the United States, it seems like a strange choice, but for someone from the Middle East, the conditions are different, the evaluations different. There was no democratic opening in Turkey."

The PKK's war also began to have a certain attraction for people who had tried and failed to make revolution through other Kurdish groups.

"After I left prison in 1987, I saw that the only group left was the PKK, all the others had exploded, finished," said Ahmet H., a university drop-out arrested in 1979 for membership in Denge Kawa. "Denge Kawa didn't exist anymore, Kawa [the original group] had been finished off and I started to believe that Apo's [Ocalan's] way was correct."

Ahmet H. was 34 years old when he was released from prison in the mid-1980s. He moved down to the western resort town of Fethiye, where he hoped to find work in a restaurant owned by a Kurdish acquaintance. Soon, he met some of the PKK operatives sent to the Aegean region in 1986 to coordinate operations.

"They would come to us, to our home, have a meeting," explained Ahmet H., who began to assist the PKK in 1988. "I looked at the guerrilla struggle with excitement," he said, "and there was a desire for revenge [against the state] that helped drew me and others closer to the PKK. Besides, all the other groups were finished."

The PKK's shift toward urban centers in western Turkey helped it also gain the attention of Kurdish university students. In the 1970s, university students (and teachers-in-training) had formed the group's core, but when the rebel war started in the rural parts of the southeast, it was Kurds in the villages who were drawn in. At first, Kurdish students in the 1980s were more intent on assessing general, nationalist issues than asking whether or not they should support the PKK.

"When I arrived in Istanbul University in 1986, there was no PKK organization in Istanbul, and state pressure was still heavy," explained Ayhan Ciftci, who grew up in an assimilated, economically stable family. "We students would discuss what we should do and we did general research about Kurdish issues."

Political events in the region had caused Kurdish students—and other Kurds—to look anew at how they were treated by the Turkish state. In neighboring Bulgaria, the state had embarked on a drive to forcibly assimilate its ethnic Turkish minority. Ankara's strong protestations in 1989 were like a slap in the face to Kurds who faced similar restrictions in Turkey. Iraq's 1988 chemical attack on Iraqi Kurds in Halabja and the world's relative silence were signs that Kurds could not rely on others to protect them. Kurdish parties who still argued for peaceful resistance to Turkish policies had problems getting student support.

"This was not an argument that appealed to many youth," noted Ciftci. "There was nothing wrong with what they were saying, but I didn't think it would bring us closer to building Kurdistan. They were saying let's wait, conditions aren't right yet to take action, and meanwhile, the state wanted to kill us, to quickly assimilate us."

At the time, one of the PKK's main recruiters in Istanbul was a man named E. He utilized old acquaintances in the city to make contact with students, focusing on those who turned up at the small, hasty protests that PKK sympathizers and other activists sometimes held. E. worked to draw people in by asking them to take on small tasks, like holding a bag for a few days, or letting someone stay at their apartment for a few nights. Those who seemed interested in the PKK and its battle were urged to make a decision on whether or not they wanted to take part. Ciftci explained what it was like:

> You are young, you want to do something. You couldn't write articles, you didn't have a newspaper and you couldn't hold demonstrations. My name was known [by police] and I was detained more often, even before there was some sort of demonstration, even if I had no involvement at all. A lot of students had started to join then and I had come to a certain place where either I would join or I would have to cut ties.

For a politically minded, Kurdish university student, one eager to take action and unable to see how legal work would do anything but land him in prison, the choice seemed obvious. Ciftci shrugged. "One day a friend of mine said he was joining . . . then he told me V. [in charge of coordinating new PKK recruits] wanted to meet with me. I went to see him. When the proposal came for me to join, I said yes."

The Aftermath

Ocalan and his military commanders were unprepared for these relatively better-educated, more worldly recruits who burst into the PKK at the end of the 1980s. Many were students or professionals, and they were used to questioning and debating ideas, especially their incipient Kurdish nationalism. It was not always easy for them to adapt to the strict military atmosphere inside the PKK, nor did they expect such intolerance toward debate or free discussion. Some found the mountain conditions too rough and wanted to leave. Others were surprised and disillusioned by the political training lessons, which demanded a blind acceptance of Ocalan's analysis of Kurdish society, history, and its future.

"The students came with information about the world and they were seen as suspicious," said a militant who joined in this period. "It was the first time so many people joined and there wasn't a proper readiness for this. Everyone was viewed as a [potential] agent."

In 1989, Ocalan issued a directive to his commanders, warning them that some recruits actually might be Turkish agents sent to destabilize the organization. "He said to take care, that there could be agents among them," said the same militant.

Because of this fear—one militant called it a paranoia—at least 24, perhaps closer to 50 or 100, new recruits were executed in 1989 and 1990 on suspicion of being real or potential traitors. The killings took place wherever PKK militants gathered: in the rudimentary camps inside Turkey, in the semipermanent bases along the Iraqi border, and in the Mahsum Korkmaz Academy (as the Helwe camp was now known) in the Bekaa Valley.[2]

In one incident in 1989, about a dozen students from a university in the western city Eskisehir were executed by the PKK soon after they joined the rebels in the mountains in southeast Turkey.[3] The students apparently had been introduced to the PKK by a former Ankara University student named Mehmet, who arranged to take the new recruits into the Cudi Mountains in southeastern Turkey to join different armed units. One version has it that one student was the daughter of a policeman, and this was enough to damn her and all those who came with her. Whatever the reason, each student was executed within a few days of joining his or her new armed unit. By the time the PKK guide, Mehmet, ended up in the PKK camp in Cukurca, near the Iraqi border, only he and one other man, someone named Hayri from Diyarbakir, were still alive.

It was in this camp that Mehmet, newly arrived, told the whole story to a former schoolmate turned rebel, who then told it to me when we met in his apartment in Germany. "The PKK directors weren't ready for such university students," explained the man, once a highly placed PKK militant. "This was normal, these internal executions, sometimes they were almost tragic-comic.

"In the fall of 1989," continued this commander, "I was at a PKK conference in Botan. Afterward, some executions were ordered for certain people who, it was said, were agents and had been sent by the state. One of these people was a man named Karasu and a group took him and killed him. The next day, someone saw Karasu. They went to the group and said that Karasu had not been killed. But the group insisted they had done it. It turned out they had mixed up the name and taken the wrong person." He shrugged. "The value of a person was very low. Everyone knew about these things, but by this point, the thinking was, 'How do I protect myself?' You didn't want to get involved."

These sorts of killings—as opposed to the targeted killings of PKK dissidents—had started a few years earlier in the Mahsum Korkmaz Academy in the Bekaa Valley, where the sudden surge in recruits from Europe in 1986 and 1987 made Ocalan fearful of attempts to destabilize the PKK and his control. According to one former PKK member who observed some of the killings, Ocalan ordered—or tacitly approved—the execution of an estimated 20 or so new recruits. The reasons were never clear. Some recruits had asked to be sent home, others fell under suspicion because of idle comments or because of some vaguely suspicious behavior. Another two dozen or more Kurdish workers in Lebanon, similarly accused of trying to undermine the group or otherwise marked out for punishment, also were murdered, said two former PKK members there at the time.

"Maybe these killings were a way of teaching a lesson, or as a deterrent," said an eyewitness. "Some people believed, some people were used. Either way, how could you say anything? Where could you go?"

The Bekaa executions reached their apex in 1989, when university students began to flood to the camp. Ocalan ordered the academy's coordinator to investigate new recruits and identify those deliberately sent to destabilize and destroy the PKK.

Ipek, then a 27-year-old female militant at the camp, described a chaotic, fearful atmosphere: "Groups of people came from universities, cities. . . . Many were stamped with being an agent. You would look around, and the next day, these people would be gone."[4] The camp's administration employed harsh methods to get people to admit to being agents, including torture. Former PKK commander Selahattin Celik dryly noted in his history of the PKK that, "As the number of agents who were discovered increased, so did the number of graves."[5]

Those who had taken part in what might be termed a hysteria in the Bekaa—or simply watched it unfold—later applied the same approach in the mountains of southeast Turkey and northern Iraq. "Everyone became suspicious of everyone else, and in this environment of chaos, people would get afraid," said a former rebel commander. "People got used to these things," he added. "At first it looks special, after that, it's just something that happens."

However, Ocalan soon realized that such rampant executions posed a danger to morale and party discipline, and the presence of so many alleged agents made the party look weak. Early in 1990, the accidental shooting death of childhood friend Hasan Bindal—killed by the academy's director, Sahin Balic, during military exercises—gave Ocalan the opportunity to shift blame for the executions at the Academy on Balic.[6] Ocalan claimed that the shooting was a deliberate attack on his leadership. Balic was put on trial, found guilty, and executed by a firing squad.

Ocalan then accused Balic of having been behind all the executions at the Academy—while he certainly had been in charge, it was Ocalan who named him coordinator, ordered him to investigate new recruits, and quietly watched what followed—and used this as a way to put a brake on the killings. In total, at least a dozen new recruits were murdered in this period in the Bekaa for being alleged agents, while many others were accused but not executed.

That same year, Ocalan ordered an investigation into the killings in Turkey as well and publicly blamed a variety of people, including Cemil (Hogir) Isik, a regional commander who since had fled the PKK, for these killings and the murders of civilians inside Turkey. A committee was established to gather information on who was killed and at the 4th Congress later that year, many of them were named as martyrs in the fight against Turkey. "It was not that the killings had been so much," said one commander, "but it had reached a level that Ocalan tried to solve it to a certain extent."

Simultaneously, the PKK's military command tried to control executions in the field by ordering that trials first be held. The impact of this was minimal. These trials were brief, one-day affairs, in which even the defendant did not always have the energy to contest the charges.

"The defendant would say something, but the atmosphere was such that nobody would deny the indictment, not even the defendant," said one man, describing a trial he witnessed in 1991. If the sentence was death, the execution was carried out the same day, usually in front of everyone there. "One execution was carried out by a team of six to seven people with Kalashnikovs, then one person went up and shot the man in the head. I remember that a female guerrilla fainted."

Despite these measures, the number of internal executions did not really decline, although those targeted no longer were mainly new recruits. Militants still might be taken away and simply shot, without a trial, or without Ocalan first being informed. One popular method to get rid of someone was for a commander to arrange for the person to lead a particularly dangerous raid in hopes of hastening death. The reason might be anything: maybe the person was very critical of the commander, hesitated in battle, or just made problems within the unit.

"Maybe trials were not so common, but these sorts of things happened a lot," said one PKK militant, who fought mainly in Botan between about 1995–1998. In the area where this militant was based— one of Botan's five zones—"maybe 20 people in three years died like this [by deliberately being sent to the front lines]." It can be safely assumed that similar incidents likely occurred in the other four zones and, in fact, in the other provinces where rebels were active. "But nobody had information what was happening elsewhere," said this militant.

Ultimately, the decision to try someone, to shoot them, or to hasten their death by sending them on a dangerous mission was up to the highest-ranking PKK militant in the unit and few were called to account later. "Someone could be killed for any reason, because at the end, you make the report and you say that this person was an agent, that that person was an agent," said one provincial commander.

Killings were a form of control and a way to deal with dissent and they were not limited to the mountains. In Europe, PKK members also were killed, although the relatively high risk of running afoul of police in Europe—and possibly disrupting other activities—helped deter such actions (more popular was beating up someone or imprisoning them in an apartment).

PKK militants also were killed in Turkey's urban, western cities. In 1993, for example, a 15-year-old PKK member in Istanbul—a girl still young enough to ask for ice cream when she ran into people she knew in the city—was captured by police on her way to join an armed unit in the southeast. Apparently, she was tortured by the police, or maybe she was just young and terrified, because she told them what little she knew. Around January 1994, a few months after returning to her parents' home in Istanbul, she was taken away by PKK militants who wanted to question her about what had happened. Her corpse turned up in one of the city's forests about three weeks later. She had been strangled. PKK members in the city issued warnings that no-one should ask any questions. And apparently, nobody did.[7]

"Even the funeral, no-one came to the funeral," said one person. "They were all warned by the PKK."

It was near impossible to question such murders, and this was even more difficult for those fighting in the mountains, where they were completely dependent on the PKK. Besides, raising doubts about the killing of someone who was called an agent was risky and admitting that one knew the accused traitor was dangerous. "People got afraid, they were afraid that afterwards someone might ask them why they were friends with that person," explained one man.

PKK militants viewed as close to a so-called traitor—including being related by blood—also were at risk of being executed. In the early 1990s, for example, two brothers in the Behdinan region along the Iraqi border, Cafer and Ferik, were executed after their third brother fled the PKK. Mehmet, the militant who had delivered the nearly one dozen university students "unmasked" as agents, was himself killed in the spring of 1990. "Since everyone he had brought was an agent, they assumed he was an agent as well," said Mehmet's former university friend.

But first, Mehmet was tortured. A piece of nylon was burned and dropped on his stomach to get him to talk.

"At this time, torture was fashionable," said the man who knew Mehmet and who had asked around to find out what happened to him. "There were things you heard. About a high school student buried alive. . . . Even as he was being buried he was screaming 'I'm not an agent.' He was from Van and this happened in Iran, in the Zagros Mountains. Who knows why. Maybe he asked too many questions."

Starting in 1995, as the PKK's military hold over the southeast started to decline, so did these internal executions. But they never stopped. "Somebody's child would be killed and the family would be told he was somewhere where he couldn't be reached," recalled one former high-level militant. "And they would think their son or daughter was still alive. The PKK," he added matter-of-factly, "was a party that rested on the people, but people weren't important to the party."

Those inside the PKK had no choice but to adapt to these killings, unless they wanted to put themselves in danger of being executed as well. It was not always hard to adapt. The rough mountain life not only demanded quick response, but also the ongoing war and fear of infiltration hardened most militants to such killings. Those who did feel uncomfortable—or at least wondered whether the accusations were true—shrugged this off and focused on their personal reasons for joining. They were fighting for a Kurdish state and even if there were some mistakes here and there, the goal remained true.

"You don't accept everything, but you want to take part in the struggle," said one man who joined in 1988. "I came to carry out a struggle and I didn't think about leaving."

Serhildan

The Kurds later called it their *Serhildan*, or people's uprising, and it broke out in the spring of 1990, starting in Nusaybin, a small town right up against the Syrian border, quickly spreading throughout the southeast.[8] The spark was the killing of thirteen guerrillas in mid-March in their cave hide-out near Savur, north of Nusaybin, a few days after they had secretly crossed Syria into Turkey. It was unclear exactly how the guerrillas were ambushed. One story had it that their local contact was in fact working for the state, and one evening, he slipped a sleeping potion into the *ayran* (a yogurt drink) that he brought the rebels, leaving them unconscious by the time the soldiers showed up. More likely, however, was that they simply were taken unaware by the Turkish military, as was reported in local newspapers.

At the time, relatives of PKK militants killed in fighting rarely claimed the bodies. First, it was hard to positively identify those who had died. PKK militants abandoned their Turkish identity cards when they joined the group, and the code names they adopted were not necessarily known to their families. At the same time, rebels might be killed far from where their families lived, further complicating the identification of bodies. But even families who knew their sons or daughters had died in a clash were hesitant to ask state authorities for the bodies, fearing that admitting to having a relative in the PKK would put them at risk of state retaliation.

The PKK, however, wanted people to claim their bodies. These martyrs—Turkey used the same word for its soldiers killed in the fighting—were an important symbol of Kurdish resistance and getting families to publicly bury them would be a sign of sympathy and respect for the PKK fight. The problem was, the PKK itself did not have a good system in place for tracking who was killed and where: Apart from everything else, commanders did not always know the real names of their fighters. But the PKK got lucky in Savur. One of the rebels killed, 20-year-old Kamuran Dundar, was from nearby Nusaybin and his family was very nationalistic. Dundar was an important enough fighter, and the killing of so many rebels at one time a big enough event, that the PKK was able to pass word on to the family. Dundar's father immediately went to the local state authorities and demanded the body.

"That night, we waited for Kamuran's father at a relative's house," said Helin, a 14-year-old relative of Kamuran. "There were hundreds of people there, pulling their hair and crying. We children were told to go and hide all the Kurdish music cassettes, they weren't PKK cassettes, just Kurdish music, because the police were certain to come now that they knew who had been killed."

Initially, state authorities resisted Dundar's request to take possession of his son's body, but ultimately they relented. "At 4 A.M., Kamuran's father returned with the body and said he was told we had to bury him by 7 A.M., but only with family members," said Helin. "But we had to wait for Kamuran's mother to come from Izmir. We children went out and told everyone to come and join. One of Kamuran's relatives said to us, 'don't cry, this is war. Be strong.'"

Dundar's funeral procession set out in the early afternoon. The body was carried to the mosque at the far end of town—there was a mosque closer to the house, but the family wanted to give more people the chance to join the procession—and from there to the cemetery. On the way back from the cemetery, the atmosphere turned violent. The mourners, who numbered in the thousands, threw stones at the police, who in turn pulled together to block the mourners-cum-demonstrators from continuing down the street. Then someone, possibly a demonstrator, opened fire.

"A fight broke out, people were shooting, and on both sides people were wounded," recalled Dundar's young relative. A curfew was slapped on the town, but nobody obeyed it. Tanks were called in and helicopters ferried in special forces. One Turkish newspaper warned that "in Nusaybin, there is an air of revolution."[9]

The demonstrations spread to other cities and towns in the region —the timing, right around the Kurdish Newruz new year, helped boost tensions. In Nusaybin, it was reported that 5,000 joined in the protests, in Cizre, another strongly pro-PKK city-town, 10,000 people took part. Fuzzy pictures in Turkish newspapers showed angry men running down streets or standing near burning tires, while women, their faces half-covered by traditional headscarves, raised their fists defiantly.

The state, taken off-guard by the riots, was unsure how to react. Criticism came especially from the opposition Social Democrats. One parliamentarian blamed the security forces for inciting the riots by challenging the protests, while another suggested the riots showed the state's policy in the region was bankrupt and they needed to consider something beyond a military approach to the problem.[10] The statements of these opposition parliamentarians notwithstanding, the military sought to tighten its control over the region in the face of the protests. More curfews were imposed and armored vehicles flooded in. "Masked people who mixed with the local people in Nusaybin and Cizre were the reason why things got bigger,"[11] said Turkish Interior Minister Abdulkadir Aksu, blaming the protests on the PKK. It seemed like the PKK's war had finally come down from the mountains and entered the cities.

But the PKK was as surprised as the state by the strength of the protests. Both 1989 and the start of 1990 had been tough on the rebels. The number of clashes with the security forces had gone up, but so had the number of rebels killed, even as the PKK was able to partly staunch this loss by the boost in new recruits. Problems within different armed units led to some shoot-outs among militants around 1988, especially in the Tunceli area, and in mid-1989, at least one regional unit was forced to regroup outside Turkey's borders to debate its plans. Apart from these internal problems, there was a sense that the militants, despite the aid they did receive, especially from villages, had yet to win the active backing of the people. The PKK, which did not realize how much pent-up support it had in urban centers, had no plan for how to react to such an outburst.

"The demonstrations broke out without any involvement of the PKK," insisted former PKK commander Sari Baran, whose claim was repeated by other PKK members. "We thought of doing something [after the demonstration started] but in the end we did nothing."

In fact, the PKK had little capability to guide or move these demonstrations forward. The rebels' presence in the cities still was limited, and the handful of PKK civilian activists or militants based there was focused on getting new recruits to fight. "We had influence, but we were not organized," said Baran.

One reason was the difficulty of operating in an urban environment; the other was that rebels were somewhat disdainful of the cities. They had not placed any special emphasis on establishing themselves in urban centers, except in order to gather recruits to send to the mountains. It seems logical to assume that PKK commanders, who saw themselves as leading the Kurdish fight, also were concerned that these protests might somehow draw attention and people away from the guerrillas' struggle. Because of this, they probably did not see any reason to encourage the demonstrators further.

The demonstrations slowed to an end over the next two weeks as protestors, exhausted and unsure what to do next, began to stay home. Local Turkish authorities, too, helped reduce tensions by ordering the security forces not to interfere in protests unless absolutely necessary. But the brief excitement of the *Serhildan* coupled with the initial heavy-handed state response—hundreds of people were detained and about half a dozen civilians shot dead—pushed many Kurds ever closer to the PKK.

"Every week after [the funeral] the police would come to our house," said Dundar's relative Helin. "I remember that Kamuran's father stopped sleeping in his home. When they found him, they would take him away and he would return all bleeding and bruised. Even the cemetery was defaced, the graves. I used to take journalists there and show them say that if things continued like this, we will all go to the mountains."

This show of mass defiance proved to be very important to the PKK. People's willingness to publicly claim their dead indicated they were less afraid of the state, which made them more likely to agree to help the rebels. The protests showed that people were no longer will-ing to remain passive. This shift within the civilian population al-lowed the PKK to overcome some of its previous difficulties. The PKK was able to expand its contacts, get better intelligence information, set up stronger networks of civilian *milis* activists, and get even more new recruits.

"These protests saved the PKK," insisted former rebel commander Celik.

A Most Dangerous Game

By 1990, Ocalan's control of the PKK appeared unassailable. The party organs functioned only at his behest. By one militant's count, the 25 members of the central committee had been changed three times in three years on Ocalan's orders. When the central committee did meet, Ocalan prepared the analyses he wanted them to make and the con-clusions he expected them to approve. Likewise, the provincial-level conferences of military commanders were orchestrated by Ocalan, who submitted his views and demands via couriers bearing tape cas-settes and letters.

This was not to say that PKK members, particularly those in the upper-echelons, were unable to make suggestions or show initiative. Ultimately, though, all actions were subject to Ocalan's approval—or disapproval—and PKK commanders operated with the knowledge that Ocalan could punish them at any time. Sometimes, they even were punished for acting on Ocalan's orders. PKK commander Halil (Cemal) Kaya, for example, was executed in 1988 after Ocalan decided he needed to blame someone for the failures of forced conscription. Simultaneously, Ocalan had strengthened the trappings of his own office. Officially, Ocalan was the PKK chairman or general secretary, but he now referred to himself as the "Party Leadership," which im-plied a collective authority but in fact referred to him alone. The PKK still had its party statutes, drawn up in 1978, and a variety of other rules and regulations that had evolved over the years. But none of these functioned independently of Ocalan, who applied, manipulated, ignored, and changed everything at will.

Nonetheless, Ocalan remained sensitive to possible threats to his authority. So much so that in preparation for the December 1990 4th

Congress he issued a number of directives aimed at protecting his leadership.[12] Foremost were instructions to the congress to investigate six experienced military commanders who were accused of misinterpreting or misapplying Ocalan's orders in the field. The accusations against them related to the PKK's failure to expand its battle and the highly criticized attacks on civilians, forced conscription and the killing of alleged agents inside the PKK. Certainly, Ocalan wanted to send a public message that such actions needed to be curtailed. Yet ultimately, Ocalan sought to insulate himself from criticism. Huseyin Topgider summed up Ocalan's thinking like this:

> If something was done correctly, then it was because of the party, and if something was done wrong, then it was an individual mistake, never the party's. Of course, sometimes the mistakes were because of the strategy [which Ocalan devised], but the strategy was not debated. Because if you debated this, it meant you were questioning the party, which meant Ocalan, and it was forbidden to question Ocalan.

Ocalan, however, was not going to be at the congress. On August 2, 1990—five months before the PKK's planned congress—Iraqi troops occupied Kuwait, an oil-rich, sliver of a country on its southern border. Over the next few months, the international community argued, wrangled, and finally threatened use of force if Iraq did not unconditionally withdraw. In anticipation of an attack, Baghdad shifted the bulk of its forces south toward Kuwait, leaving much of its border with Turkey unguarded. The sudden absence of Iraqi troops and the still-disorganized situation of the Iraqi Kurdish parties made it easier for the PKK to use northern Iraq. Ocalan, eager to stake a claim on part of the land the Kurds called Kurdistan, decided to hold the PKK's 4th Congress in northern Iraq. It was the group's first congress on Kurdish territory since its founding in 1978 and there was a real air of excitement.

But Ocalan did not dare chance leaving Syria's zone of protection or chance the still-dangerous trip across northern Iraq to the group's camp in the mountains northeast of Zakho. Instead, Ocalan named a special nine-person preparatory committee, which included his brother Osman (Ferhat) Ocalan and his close confident Cemil (Cuma) Bayik, to run the congress in Haftanin, nestled in the mountains that flowed from Iraq to Turkey. Haftanin had grown into an important gathering and training camp for the PKK. Some 300 people usually slept rough on the ground, but in anticipation of the congress, large tents were set up to sleep the 100 or so delegates.

The 4th Congress opened the last week of December with the meeting's chairmen denouncing various fighters accused of undermining the PKK's battle. Delegates raised their hands to approve proposals to detain and investigate now-disgraced fighters. One by one, the accused were taken away for questioning. PKK commander Topgider, stripped of his authority even before the meeting, was allowed to listen to the proceedings but could not take part. "Everybody had been crushed and now it was my turn," he simply said. Another high-ranking militant, Cemil (Hogir) Isik, who had fled the PKK and taken refuge in Iran before the congress, was sentenced to death in absentia.

Nobody escaped censure. Armed PKK units were criticized for failed raids against Turkish military targets and for focusing on wrong or unimportant targets. And even the reports prepared by the different military units were deemed weak on ideology and commitment to the PKK's cause.

"The person . . . would stand up and read the report, and then a debate would open up," recalled Aysel Curukkaya. "Then someone else would stand up and say they didn't accept a certain report because it did not follow the party's line. In the end, the same conclusion was drawn about all the reports. Those who had led the battle in the mountains were not sufficiently qualified or able to do their jobs." There was, Curukkaya added, an "atmosphere of terror."

The man leading these attacks was Mehmet Cahit Sener, who recently had rejoined the PKK after eight years in Diyarbakir Prison. Sener was a well-known and highly respected PKK member, who had taken part in the Diyarbakir Prison uprisings and hunger strikes. After his release from prison, the PKK helped get him out of Turkey and he arrived in the Bekaa probably in 1989. Ocalan named him a director of the training academy and picked him to the committee that prepared the congress.

Later, Sener argued that Ocalan named him to these positions in the hope of using Sener's prison popularity to boost his own image; however, it is also possible that Ocalan actually was concerned about Sener's popularity and wanted to tie Sener closer by giving him roles in the PKK administration. In either case, Ocalan made a mistake. After orchestrating the very public humiliation of PKK militants in general and certain commanders in particular, Sener turned his criticism on Ocalan. In the year or so that Sener had spent in the Bekaa, watching Ocalan in action and observing the almost hysterical attempt to root out agents inside the PKK, he had come to believe the PKK's weakness was its leadership. Now, far from Ocalan, and with the backing of at least one other man on the podium—Sari Baran, a highly respected Hakkari commander who had met up with Sener in the Bekaa—Sener made his move. Curukkaya said she would never forget Sener's speech:

> He said, "Friends, the situation has been evaluated and every action has been judged to have been wrong. I think that those fighting can make mistakes, but to take a gun and go to the mountains is a courageous act, those who have done so have made an enormous self-sacrifice. I don't think they are guilty. Apo said you helped the Turkish war effort [by your mistakes], you made it possible for the number of village guards to increase. But if what the fighters did is a crime, if the activities they carried out are crimes, then the party line itself must be looked at and judged." He said, "I simply want to make my views clear."

Sener was warned by Cemil Bayik, another congress chairman, to be careful about what he said, but the former political prisoner refused to back down from his veiled criticism of Ocalan. Instead, he later asked delegates to consider proposals that reasserted the power of the central committee and put checks and balances on Ocalan's dictatorial ways. Utilizing Ocalan's own condemnation of certain activities—like the killing of civilians—Sener demanded an investigation into the policies that encouraged militants to carry out these actions.

"Like Apo explained, all of us, the whole cadre base, we are all guilty," wrote Sener and his supporters in an open letter a few months after the congress. "But let us take note, all of our criticisms of each other [concern] activities that rest on Apo. . . . Is it not known that the groups that did the raids on villages in Mardin, the blackest stain on our party's history, were personally given the orders by Apo? . . . When Metin [Sahin Balic] . . . operated as a police chief in the Academy, and in the Academy alone 12 new recruits were killed, who made him the Academy coordinator?"[13] The answer, obviously, was Ocalan.

Specifically, Sener called for investigations of the internal executions that occurred in the Bekaa camp, which was under Ocalan's control, and in the PKK's camps near the Iranian border, which was under the control of Ocalan's brother Osman. He also insisted that the central committee be responsible for the PKK's finances, which until then were controlled solely by Ocalan. The proposals were approved by delegates.

"We didn't pick Ocalan as a target," said Baran. "We were at a point where the organization could split. We understood that we had to make changes step by step in order not to make the group split."

Given Ocalan's control over the PKK, it seems almost unbelievable that delegates would have approved measures that so obviously challenged Ocalan's authority. But Sener, who studied to be a teacher before joining the PKK in the late 1970s, was an intelligent man who carefully manipulated Ocalan's own arguments. He did this in a way that may have caused some delegates, who almost certainly did not expect anyone to try to undercut Ocalan's power, to think they were approving proposals put forward by the PKK chairman himself.

"How could it happen?" responded Azman, a former lawyer who initially had his own problems adjusting to Ocalan's ways. "It was a little bit because of the difficulties of communication [with Ocalan in Syria], and people weren't yet so used to Ocalan's ways. And Sener's decisions were things that people actually wanted," explained Azman. "Besides, people inside the PKK were used to just affirming everything, everyone just approved things automatically. Some people didn't even hear what was being said, they would see everyone raise their hands so they did it as well."

Meanwhile, tension in the region had risen. Saddam Hussein had refused to withdraw from Kuwait and the U.S.-led Coalition Forces troops were in place and ready to attack. The war was expected to start in January. The congress, which was supposed to last about three weeks, had to conclude quickly to give militants time to withdraw to safer areas. Sener stayed in Haftanin, Baran left for the Hakkari area, and Osman Ocalan traveled to Damascus to meet with the PKK chairman. Ten days after the congress ended, an order was issued for an investigation into Sener's activities. He was detained in Haftanin camp and interrogated. Ocalan made clear that Sener might be an agent out to destabilize and destroy the PKK.

Sener's arrest occurred just as U.S.-led forces launched their successful assault on Iraq. Iraq retained its sovereignty, but only just and its troops were forced to withdraw from Kuwait. In the aftermath of the allied attack, Iraqi Kurds and Shiites in the south staged their own rebellions that March, convinced they had the backing of the United States. When help did not come, Iraqi forces moved in to crush the rebellions. Rumors of Sener's arrest got drowned out in this turmoil. Around April, Baran heard from another militant, Halil (Ebubekir) Atac, that Ocalan wanted Baran to write his own self-criticism about his mistakes at the congress.

"I replied that I had said everything at the Congress and there was nothing else for me to say," Baran explained to me one afternoon in Stockholm. "But I was curious what had happened to Sener so I left Hakkari and went to Haftanin. I saw that he was under arrest, but I couldn't talk to him, he was isolated."

Abdurrahman Kayikci, head of the new, private security unit Ocalan formed after the congress, told Baran that Ocalan planned to publicly denounce Sener and then have him killed. It was likely Baran would be next. Baran and Sener decided to flee. Kayikci, who apparently had second-thoughts about supporting Ocalan's plan, joined them. From the mountains of northern Iraq, the three men announced a new group—PKK-Vejin (Revival)—and called on people to cut their allegiance to Ocalan and join the real PKK.

For the first time, Ocalan faced a real threat. In the past, those who fled the PKK only did so after being marginalized and disgraced. But Sener and Baran were members of the Central Committee's Executive Committee and chairmen of the 4th Congress. And unlike other dissidents, they were still in Kurdistan, not in Europe, and no-one could accuse them of running away from the rebel war. As they made clear, they did not want to criticize the PKK or its fight—just the PKK leader.

"Our idea wasn't to break off from the PKK, but to persuade people of our ideas and turn the organization in the right direction," said Baran. With their wide network of contacts—Baran knew many fighters inside Turkey, and Sener had contact with newly released PKK prisoners—they searched for support. Their first communiqué stressed the need for the PKK to reorganize itself. Later, they grew more critical of specific decisions made by Ocalan.

But these dissidents faced a tough battle against Ocalan. At that point, the PKK leader commanded an estimated 2,000 militants, had a wide network of supporters and activists in Europe, and had the backing or assistance of various states in the region. Attempts by the breakaway group to gather support among prisoners inside Turkey and those newly released, two groups of people still new to Ocalan's way of acting and thinking, failed. They apparently got some fighters in north Iraq to defect and picked up support in some cities inside Turkey, but the number was small.

"Sener was right in his thinking," said Topgider, who was at the congress. "But [people] didn't see it that way. Whether right or wrong, people looked at who had the power or who could fight. That's how they analyzed things. Ocalan had created such a system that by then it was impossible to establish a separate group. Sener was honest, but he didn't understand." Topgider did not think of joining the dissidents. "My feeling was that maybe things would change, that there were things more important than Ocalan, that the Kurdish struggle was more important than what Ocalan was doing [internally], and so I stayed.

Sener, Baran, Kayikci, and their supporters remained in northern Iraq for a few months. In the fall of 1991, Sener and Kayikci secretly crossed into Syria, where they hid out in Qamishli, the main Kurdish city. The PKK was well organized in Qamishli, which made it risky. Their reasons for going there were never clear. A friend of Sener's family said they were planning to pick up passports so they could go to Europe; another former PKK member suggested they may have hoped to meet with Syrian officials to arrange some sort of support; someone else insisted they went there to win support from Syrian Kurds. Regardless, things did not go as planned. Kayikci telephoned Ocalan's apartment in Damascus and begged for forgiveness, offering to give up Sener's exact whereabouts in return for being allowed to live. On November 1, Sener and a female supporter code-named Dilan were murdered in an apartment where they were staying.

"I was in Dohuk when Sener was killed," explained Baran, referring to a city in north Iraq. "I got the news the same day, somebody was sent to tell me. Sener wasn't dead yet, he was wounded and had been taken to a hospital. When I heard he died . . . I didn't think everything had been finished."

Baran and about 50 supporters from Turkey and Syria met to discuss their options. They agreed to continue their work. "We tried . . . but we had a lot of problems." It wasn't just the Turkish state that was against yet another Kurdish militant group being formed, Baran said, but PKK militants themselves. "A lot of people were killed trying to organize those who made up the PKK's base. After awhile, we couldn't go any further." Baran himself stayed under the protection of KDP leader Barzani for a few years, before giving up his opposition efforts and fleeing to Europe.

The attempt by Sener and Baran to force change within the PKK was the most serious threat Ocalan ever faced to his leadership. It also was the last. After Sener's death, Ocalan's power was complete. The "Sener *Olayi*," or incident, would go down in PKK history as a great conspiracy that sought to topple Ocalan and destroy the PKK. It allowed Ocalan to consolidate whatever power he had not yet grabbed, and sent yet another forceful message that dissent or challenges would not be tolerated. Although few believed Sener was an agent, no-one dared argue in his defense.

"When Sener was arrested, I spoke with Cuma [Cemil Bayik, who was holding him], and like others, he didn't believe Sener was an agent," said Baran. "But he said, 'the chairman says so,' and the debate ended there. Nobody thought that Sener was an agent, but they were prisoners of Ocalan."

Ocalan, his control complete and his challengers silenced, now was ready for his next step—which was somehow to force Turkey into political negotiations over his demands for the Kurds. He planned to do this by extending the PKK's control inside legal associations, taking control of any new, civilian protests, and, as he had long-promised, widening the rebel war to the point that Turkey could no longer claim to control the Kurdish region.

PART III

PKK Militants Fight for Control

Left and below: PKK rebels active in the Cudi Mountains in southeast Turkey. These young men and women were based in a valley a few hour's walk from a clutch of small villages outside Cizre. Photo by author, 1993.

Above: These armed young men were part of the PKK's extensive network of active civilian supporters in the southeast, commonly known as *milis*. They often showed their strength during protests and funerals. This photo was taken in the southeastern city of Cizre in 1992, then a stronghold of the PKK. Photo provided by an anonymous source.

Above right: Murat Dagdelen (right), a PKK activist, met with Abdullah Ocalan in Damascus in early 1993 to discuss plans for the Kurdistan National Assembly. Photo provided by Murat Dagdelen.

Right: Delegates to the PKK-organized Kurdistan Assembly learn to clean Kalashnikovs in Zeli camp, Northern Iraq, in 1993. Photo provided by Murat Dagdelen.

8

War in the Streets, 1991–1992

TWO MONTHS AFTER the Kurds in Nusaybin, Cizre, and other cities in the southeast took to the streets, chanting pro-PKK slogans and hurling rocks at state buildings and security forces, 22-year-old Ayhan Ciftci decided to join the rebels. "The *Serhildan* [uprising] created a feeling of excitement," said Ciftci, then a university student in Istanbul. "We Kurdish students believed that this time, we would be able to make a Kurdish state."

By his own admission, Ciftci did not know much about the PKK when he made his decision. The group's publications were hard to find, and local newspaper reporting, which focused on the PKK's "terrorism" and ignored its Kurdish nationalism, was neither trusted by Ciftci nor very informative. But what Ciftci did know about the group was enough. "I knew that the PKK defended independence, that its fight against the Turkish state is honorable, and that there was no alternative to armed struggle if Kurds are going to get a state."

One morning in May 1990, Ciftci and a friend who also was joining, boarded a bus headed northwest to Edirne, a city close to the Greek border. They were accompanied by the PKK's Istanbul representative, who said he would accompany them across the border and direct them to the PKK's safe-house in Athens. The three men got out of the bus in Edirne and took a taxi to the edge of one of the big rice fields outside the city. Another four people who needed to leave Turkey illegally—would-be PKK members were not the only ones who used this route—were waiting there. E. motioned everyone to follow him across the wet, marshy rice field. The men exited near the river Maritsa, which marked the border with Greece. Then they plunged into the river and half-walked, half-swam, to the other side.

"The water was up to our necks," Ciftci said, laughing. "I was watching how this was organized and I was surprised, I always thought that everything the PKK would do would be well-organized and wonderful. For example, I assumed there would be a boat to take us across, or when we got across [into Greece] there would be some-one to meet us."

Instead, when they climbed out of the river, E. directed them to-ward the shadow of houses down the road. "He told us to wait at the edge of the town, until the Greek police noticed us, and then we should tell them that we are PKK sympathizers and had to leave Tur-key." Ciftci shook his head at the memory. "He said the police would arrest us and hold us for awhile, but that they would then send us to Athens and when we got there, we had a phone number to call and someone from the PKK would come and get us." Ciftci was worried that the police might simply hand them back to the Turkish authori-ties, but E. insisted that would never happen. "He told me not to worry, saying they had done this many times."

The men huddled by the side of the road, waiting to be noticed. Around dawn, Ciftci heard a dog howl and from behind a window curtain, a woman's face briefly appeared. A few minutes later, the po-lice came. "We looked like what we were, wet [illegals], but it seems they were used to this. The police chief even spoke a little Turkish." Ciftci and the others were detained for close to 20 days, then sent to Salonika and then Athens. In the Greek capital, they were held an-other 10 days before being released. "We were asked if we had a place to stay and the guide from Istanbul said we had a place to go in Athens. We left with him."

Turkey always listed Greece as one of the many countries that supported the PKK, a claim Athens denied. But there was no question that the Greek authorities found it convenient to ignore people's PKK links—actually, an approach rather common throughout Europe—es-pecially as long as the people focused on nonviolent activities such as recruitment, political training, and propaganda. In Greece's case, the country had a number of conflicts with Turkey, ranging from control of the sea between the two countries to Turkey's occupation of part of Cyprus. Ignoring the PKK was a way to irritate Turkey. The PKK, for its part, benefited from the tension. The border was porous and per-fect for PKK sympathizers who needed to flee Turkey fast, or for new members recruited in the nearby western cities like Istanbul and Izmir. By the time Ciftci arrived in 1990, the PKK was well-set up in Athens, with at least four apartments it used for propaganda and political training.

"There were about 20 people in the apartment where I was

brought," recalled Ciftci, "and I recognized quite a few of them from university." Most of them were about Ciftci's age, although there were some older people who had recently been released from prison. None of them knew how long they would be there. Some people were supposed to be sent back to Turkey to work for the PKK in different cities, while others would be sent to fight. Everyone insisted they wanted to be a guerrilla fighter. "Even those who might have wanted to do something else didn't say anything," explained Ciftci, "because everyone wanted to appear courageous."

The men and women in the apartment slept in separate rooms, but every morning they got together to read and discuss PKK history and Ocalan's analyses of the PKK's actions and its mistakes. As his control over the PKK had grown more secure, Ocalan had taken to issuing sweeping statements on everything from traditional Kurdish society, which he criticized, to his own leadership, which he praised. These speeches either were typed up and published as books, or else they were taped and the cassette tapes were sent to PKK offices for training purposes.

"I thought the PKK training would be very serious, but what would happen was that someone would read Ocalan's speeches and Ocalan would swear at different people in his speeches," Ciftci said. Ocalan's sometimes coarse, patronizing and even threatening way of talking could be tempered by a vigorous defense of the Kurdish struggle and the sacrifice of armed rebels, but it still took some getting used to. Ciftci said that Ocalan's way of speaking made him a little uncomfortable.

> You start to wonder if you have come to the right place. But of course, you didn't say this, and it did not mean you wanted to leave and return to Turkey, that's not something you would think. But whenever there was a break, people always grabbed the books on Marxism, no-one wanted to read Ocalan's analyses.

Ciftci was in Athens over the hot and muggy summer. Occasionally, some of the men went out to the beach, but mainly, they stayed in the overcrowded apartment. In the afternoons, when Greeks napped to escape the heat, the new recruits had to suspend training to avoid disturbing anyone. One afternoon, Ciftci went to a public telephone on the street and called his brother in Turkey. Ciftci had not told anyone he was leaving Turkey to join the PKK—in case the police asked about him, it was better his family didn't know his plans—and now he told his brother he was in England studying English.

"I could have said I was on holiday in Greece, but I couldn't come up with a reason why I would be taking a holiday and not in school." Meanwhile, Ciftci adjusted to the political training. "At first it sounds strange, but if you hear something 40 times, slowly, slowly, you start to accept it. In any case, the whole time from Istanbul I kept thinking that things could only get better. No matter what, we would be returning to our land to be fighters. To be a guerrilla in the mountains."

New people were constantly coming and the old ones started to leave on their new assignments. Two people decided they didn't want to join the PKK after all, and they were sent to the Lavrion refugee camp to apply for asylum. The others waited. After almost five months in Athens, Ciftci was told that he was going to be sent on a flight to Syria, and from there he would go to the Bekaa camp for military training.

In Syria, Ciftci was met by a PKK member and taken to an apartment already crowded with militants. The next day, Ocalan telephoned his greetings and said that as soon as he finished his work, he would come to the Helwe camp to meet the new recruits. That afternoon, Ciftci and some others took a bus to the edge of the Syrian-occupied Bekaa Valley. They followed a courier over the hills to the PKK's Mahsum Korkmaz Academy, also known as Helwe camp.

The PKK's operations in the Bekaa were constantly expanding. Turkish Kurds, emboldened by the PKK's ability to keep up its attacks on the Turkish military, angered by the military's harsh treatment of civilians, and frustrated by the lack of democratic alternatives, were streaming toward the rebels. When Ciftci arrived in the fall of 1990, Helwe camp held about 300 new recruits. Hundreds of others were gathered in PKK bases along the Iraqi border. Syrian Kurds and even Iraqi Kurds, whose own political parties were not yet very active again in north Iraq, also were joining. Meanwhile, some of the well-known PKK commanders had come to the camp to prepare for the December 4th Congress.

"There was a real atmosphere of excitement," said Ciftci, who still keeps a small, framed picture of PKK militant Mahsum Korkmaz, killed in 1986 in a Turkish ambush, in the living room of his Cologne apartment. "Everyone was in military clothes, everyone had weapons, there was a flag in the Kurdish colors. It was a very exciting time for me."

The program at Helwe was similar to that in Athens, except that here the new recruits also did military training. "Everyone thought the education sessions were boring, we just wanted to go to the mountains," said Ciftci. Ocalan, as he promised, came to the camp to talk to the new recruits. "He asked people where they were from and he explained about the academy. Generally he was very polite." Ocalan also gave lectures on PKK history and the rebel fight. Sometimes he called Semdin Sakik, already a military commander of some fame, to the podium and berated him for alleged mistakes.

"I once asked [camp director] Cemil Bayik why, if everyone is so bad and so guilty of mistakes, then how come the PKK has gone so far and done so much?" Ciftci said. "But Bayik would just say I didn't understand, and that I need to try and understand what Ocalan was saying. That's what they always said, that you didn't understand."

Ciftci and the other newcomers did not always pay that much attention to Ocalan's speeches. "As soon as Ocalan left the room, we would forget what he had said," Ciftci said. "What made us excited was when someone would come and lecture about the fighting, about what it was like. The younger PKK militants, like me, we were interested in Sakik and what he had done in the mountains. Everyone would rush up and ask him questions."

Around April 1991, Ciftci was ordered to join an armed unit operating near Diyarbakir. Syrian soldiers, who claimed they were operating without the knowledge of their commander, gave him and some other PKK rebels a ride to Damascus. In Damascus, Ciftci and the others—nearly 60 in total—split into groups of four or five people and took buses to the main Kurdish city Qamishli near Turkey's border. From there they went to a small village near the border with Iraq and picked up their guns—Kalashnikovs—and changed into the heavy, baggy green pants and shirts uniform of the rebels.

The plan was to cross the Tigris River into Iraq, floating on makeshift boats of planks lashed to tires. But Syrian border guards, probably unsure who exactly were these armed people, opened fire and Ciftci's team was forced to turn back. One week later, they set out again for Iraq and this time made it. After a short stay in the PKK's Haftanin camp near Zakho, they crossed into Turkey and began the long trek west toward Diyarbakir.

"Inside Turkey, the people were very friendly. Wherever we went, we would inform the *milis* [PKK civilian force] and they would get us food. We would go to a village and the villagers would argue among themselves, everyone wanted to take you into their homes. We were getting enormous support." Ciftci paused.

"In the one year since I had joined the PKK, my morale had dropped by what I saw inside the PKK . . . the way things were organized, Ocalan's way of speaking, things like that." He shook his head at the memory. "But during the three months it took us to get to Diyarbakir, I pulled myself back together and I felt it was the right decision to have joined the PKK."

Ciftci was not the only one to think like this. The same year that he slipped back into Turkey, thousands of other young Kurdish men and women began to throw their support behind the group, helping turn the PKK into a mass organization. One reason for the shift was the PKK's relentless guerrilla war, which finally did win it mass trust and respect. The other reason was the group's decision to move into legal, nonviolent activities, giving the rebel group a reach far beyond the war. Over the next three years, the PKK solidified its hold over legal Kurdish politics, Kurdish publishing, and cultural events. This created a new and more varied support base for the PKK and helped it establish full dominance over Turkey's Kurdish national movement. In this same period, Ocalan struggled to use the PKK's dominance to wrest something concrete from the Turkish state. This period, 1991–1993, was a critical time for the Kurdish rebels and the Turkish state—and the PKK's wins and losses during these three years continued to influence Kurdish politics and PKK activities in 2006 and beyond.

Joining the Party

One of the accusations against Mehmet Sener, the PKK militant assassinated by his own group after he challenged Ocalan's authority, was that he tried to undermine the guerrilla struggle by demanding the PKK shift some attention from the war to the political field. But in fact, Ocalan's own views on legal politics had started to change. He began to suggest that there might be ways apart from armed struggle to address the Kurdish problem. Specifically, he noted that the new, legal Kurdish political party, commonly known by its Turkish initials HEP, might be able to play a role in bringing about a negotiated solution. "[W]e want to give them the chance to reach a solution,"[1] he said before Turkey's October 1991 national elections.

Ocalan had not always spoken so positively about HEP. He had never really tolerated Kurdish organizations outside his sphere of influence—the other, now much-smaller groups still complained of PKK harrasment—and initially he had warned his supporters to stay away from the new political party. But sometime in late 1990 or early 1991, Ocalan changed his mind.

Mahmut Kilinc, one of HEP's founding members, explained that Ocalan started to say " 'This party is not our party. . . . But if it is able to address Turkey's fundamental problems, as it says it will, if it wants to institutionalize democracy and if it supports a view towards dealing with the Kurdish issue within this framework, then we look warmly on it.' And with this, our party's organizational work in the region took off."[2]

HEP, which until then had problems getting support in the southeast, where the PKK dominated public opinion, suddenly was inundated with new members. Many of them were PKK sympathizers and supporters. The independent members of the political party—that is to say, those who did not see themselves as operating within Ocalan's sphere of control—hoped to maintain a separation between their legal work and the PKK's illegal struggle, even if they recognized that many of their long-term interests overlapped.

"[Our] view was that we are all Kurds," Kilinc, who now lives in Germany, told me. "We have our beliefs, [the PKK] has its views and on some things we don't agree, or we have differences. . . . But in the end, the Kurdish people have the same goals, so there did not have to be a contradiction in [having PKK sympathizers in the party]."

This was a hard balance to maintain. These new members viewed the PKK as the leader of the Kurdish national movement, and they believed the PKK's interests should take precedence, even in a legal, political party. This view, which was aggressively promoted by PKK loyalists inside the political party, gave Ocalan an important sway over the party through its membership.[3] "The masses had been affected by the PKK," noted Kilinc with a shrug, "and they took their views there."

Ocalan also refused to let go. Faced with the choice of leaving the party alone—in essence, allowing it to become an independent political force, one sympathetic and responsive to the PKK's fight, yet not part of it—or trying to dominate the party, he chose the latter.

"Ocalan was unable to say, 'Here is a political party' and let it be free," said Mehmet Emin Sever, one of the party's leading independent figures. "He would say that nobody but him could do anything."

Ocalan soon named certain PKK members as his special envoys, telling them to make clear his views to the legal political party and to keep him updated on what was happening inside the party. Some of these envoys already were party members, while others operated from the outside as so-called political commissars. The few PKK members within the party exploited their positions, contacts, and offices to collect money and recruit for the rebels. While independent members of HEP opposed this, they could not easily stop it.

"The PKK's view was to take over HEP, to have people inside the group with direct ties," said Murat Dagdelen, a former senior HEP official who doubled as one of Ocalan's envoys to the party. "Not everybody had to be PKK. But someone who accepted the PKK's approach." Dagdelen shook his head. "HEP's biggest weakness was that it could not institutionalize itself, it could not grow into its own organization."

Despite all this, it would be wrong to call HEP a front organization for the PKK. The desire to control something, after all, is not the same as actually controlling it. Certainly, the PKK exerted a strong influence over the party. But this did not mean that all senior party officials (or even most) were directly tied to the PKK or shared all its views.

"The presence of PKK supporters inside the party was very large, but in terms of offering a political approach, they were not very active [in the early years]," added Kilinc, who counted himself as one of the independent members of the party. "Let's say there was a meeting and Ocalan's people would come and make slogans. All right, he was using us for his own politics. But overall, HEP was a Kurdish movement and these sorts of things could be expected to happen."

The political party gave Kurds a new, more acceptable way to articulate their demands. For once, the Kurdish problem was being debated and promoted by a legal, nonviolent entity. Turks, who until now associated the Kurdish problem with terrorism, suddenly were forced to face demands made in the legal arena.

"Someone in [the Black Sea town] Yozgat, what does he know

about the PKK, he sees them as bandits," said Dagdelen, who now writes essays for Kurdish websites. "But with the HEP, then it is clear there are Kurds, that they want certain things. It forced people to hear things."

Ocalan's decision to moderate his approach to legal activities—without abandoning the armed struggle—also was good for the PKK. It helped the PKK grow into a mass movement. It gave the rebel group a legal way to promote its views, allowing it to reach more people. Simultaneously, it helped the PKK attract a new group of supporters—people who either could not or did not want to go to the mountains and fight but who were willing to work for a legal political party. Equally important, the influx of PKK sympathizers into HEP gave the PKK an influence over political developments, thereby ensuring that the rebel group could not be marginalized by events in the legal field.

But it was not so clear that all this was good for Kurdish politics. In the 1990s, the legal field for Kurdish activism in Turkey widened, but activists themselves were limited by Ocalan's desire to control and direct activities. Over time, the development of a politically experienced and savvy Kurdish class was hobbled. The next generation of politicians often were people who grew up side by side with the PKK, meaning their experiences, outlooks, and willingness to take chances were more limited.

The New Stage

Turkey's political system had never shown a real willingness to grapple with the Kurdish problem, but late in 1991 it was forced to pay attention.[4] The Motherland Party's new leader, Mesut Yilmaz, hoped to cement his position by calling early elections for October 1991, but the plan backfired. The Turkish public was unhappy with the Motherland Party, partly because of unease with the government's decision to side with the United States in support of the 1991 Gulf War that pushed Saddam Hussein's troops out of Kuwait. Turkey had gained little concrete from this: Economic sanctions against Iraq ended up costing Turkey, a major trading partner, billions of dollars; and in northern Iraq, now off-limits to Iraqi forces, the PKK was expanding its military camps. Uncertainty over the long-term implications of Ankara's support for U.S.-led military actions, coupled with Turkey's more immediate economic problems, helped push the Motherland Party to second place in the voting. The center-right True Path Party came in first.

The True Path Party's chief, Suleyman Demirel, was a veteran political leader and former prime minister ousted two times by military coups. Lacking enough seats to rule on his own, Demirel tapped the third place Social Democrats, headed by the mild-mannered physics professor Erdal Inonu, for a coalition government. This center-left party brought with them a most unusual partner: 22 deputies from the Kurdish party HEP. The two parties had joined forces for the elections—HEP was blocked from running because of a technicality; the Social Democrats hoped an alliance would enhance their standing in the southeast—and officially, the new HEP deputies were still members of the Social Democrats. As a result, the governing coalition now included almost two dozen outspoken, some very radical, Kurdish members.

The Kurdish problem rarely was discussed in Turkish news reports, but it clearly dominated the country's political and military agendas. The previous parliament's decision to lift the military-era's broad restriction on the use of Kurdish (although other legal limitations on use of the language remained) was a sign that things could not continue as they always had; now Kurds wanted even more and the PKK's war was a constant reminder of the dangers of ignoring peaceful demands. The True Path Party and the Social Democrats promised to institute democratic reforms, which was interpreted to mean addressing the Kurdish problem. The government's protocol shied away from mentioning Kurds by name, but it did state that people had the right to develop their different cultural identities.

One Turkish newspaper announced "The first focus is the southeast."[5] This appeared to be the case. After the government was announced, Prime Minister Demirel and Deputy Prime Minister Erdal Inonu set off for the southeast, where they assured the cheering crowds that the people in the region were their "brothers."[6] Inonu, whose party had touched directly on Kurdish demands in a report issued a year earlier calling for changes, stressed this new government was serious about reforms. "Don't be timid," he told crowds. "You can tell us all your problems."[7]

The problems were not a secret. Torture was rampant, especially of Kurdish detainees suspected of helping the PKK; Turkish security forces had started to threaten to burn down people's houses if they did not join the state's village guard system, now seen as proof of loyalty; village guards used their weapons and ties to the state to violently settle scores with neighboring villages; Kurds who tried to protest were accused of working for the PKK. The state's ban on Kurdish-language education, television, and radio broadcasts was still in effect, and a vaguely worded anti-terror law was used to jail journalists, writers, and public speakers who delved into Kurdish history or complaints.

Just to make the complaints clear, the 22 Kurdish deputies (there were other Kurds in parliament, but this phrasing refers to those originally linked to HEP) had drawn up a list of what needed to be done before they agreed to the coalition. Among other things, they wanted Kurds to be recognized as Kurds. This meant full freedom to speak and learn their language, express their culture, and celebrate their history.[8]

"Our goal was to get Turkey to recognize Kurdish democratic rights, change the laws, to start solving [the Kurdish problem] this way," said Mahmut Kilinc.

The day parliament was sworn in, each member carried a red, green, and yellow handkerchief in their pockets. These colors represented Kurdish identity throughout the region, but they also were the same as those in the PKK flag.

New deputy Hatip Dicle, mumbling through the oath the new deputies had to read, added, "My friends and I read this under constitutional pressure."[9] Dicle's protest reflected the oath's promise to uphold Ataturk's principles, the very principles that activist Kurds blamed for the denial of their identity.

The only woman in the group, Leyla Zana, whose thick, shoulder-length black hair was held in place by a red, green, and yellow-colored handband, followed her oath with a similar protest, adding her hope that Turks and Kurds could work together: "I underwent that formality under duress. I will fight for the fraternal coexistence of the Kurdish and Turkish people within the context of democracy."[10]

Some of the Turkish deputies yelled at Zana to pull the flag off her head. Others banged on the table tops in protest. There were immediate calls for Zana and Dicle to be kicked out of the Social Democratic Party. A few days later, the state security court announced it was looking into whether these two deputies could be charged with treason, which carried the death penalty, for their actions in the parliament.

The Kurdish deputies remained unapologetic. "If we are going to be executed because we wanted brotherhood,"[11] began Dicle, an engineer who chaired the Diyarbakir Human Rights Association before entering politics. He came from the party's more radical wing—during the campaign, he called on Ankara to open talks with the PKK—but he did not express ideas that different from those of his voters.

"We want to be the voice of Kurdish people in parliament," Orhan Dogan, a soft-spoken lawyer from Cizre, told me a few weeks before the election. We spoke in his living room, joined by about a dozen men who nodded in agreement to his pronouncements. "Up until now, the parliament has not done anything," he continued. "There was an empty space [when it came to Kurds] and we hope to fill this space."[12]

But it seemed that when Prime Minister Demirel and Deputy Prime Minister Inonu invited Kurds to talk about their problems, they did not expect them to be so blunt or honest. Inonu joined calls to force Dicle and Zana out of the Social Democrats. Demirel accused them of making rebel propaganda. The new deputies refused to apologize for their behavior. "I am fighting for my existence, but I remain face to face with not being recognized," insisted Leyla Zana. "[R]emember, those who elected me are Kurds."[13]

Trouble in the Wings

The tension in the parliament mirrored the rising tension between Turks and Kurds throughout the country. On December 24, in the southeast town of Lice, security forces opened fire after thousands of people gathered on the streets demanding to be allowed to bury three PKK rebels killed in the nearby mountains. Seven civilians were killed. The next day, PKK supporters firebombed a store in Istanbul owned by the brother of the Turkish regional governor for the emergency rule provinces in the southeast, killing 12 people. During the same period, seven soldiers and three officers were killed in a PKK attack on a gendarmerie station in a rural town in Sirnak province. Turkey's Chief of General Staff, speaking at the funerals for two soldiers killed by the PKK, promised bloody revenge.[14]

When Kurdish deputy Mahmut Alinak, speaking as head of the Social Democratic parliamentary group, tried to address the joint pain felt by Turks and Kurds—he invoked the deaths of two brothers, one a

Kurdish rebel, the other a Turkish soldier—he was physically forced off the podium by deputies from the coalition's True Path Party. Even President Turgut Ozal, who had hinted he was interested in a nonmilitary solution to the Kurdish problem, could not accept the deputies' show of Kurdish nationalism. The day Alinak took to the podium Ozal complained, "The PKK . . . has entered parliament."[15]

The Turkish political establishment's refusal to tolerate the Kurdish deputies did not appear to bother Ocalan. The PKK leader had suggested that HEP might be useful in addressing the Kurdish problem, but he always made clear he remained committed to armed rebellion. Equally important, he appeared to have mixed feelings about how much he wanted the party to accomplish. During the election campaign, Ocalan had ordered PKK rebels to do what they could to support the Kurdish candidates in the Social Democratic Party, and rebels passed on the message to their civilian supporters in the cities and their backers in the villages.

But now that these people had won seats in the parliament, Ocalan seemed uncomfortable. The reasons were many. He certainly did not fully trust the party which, despite its large number of PKK sympathizers, still operated outside his direct control. And while he struggled to be heard in the Turkish media, the new Kurdish deputies appeared on the front-page (even if sometimes in unflattering articles). These new deputies were a mix of loyalties and links: A few clearly admired the PKK, a few were slightly hostile, and the majority strove to operate independently of PKK pressure.

Perhaps to underline the fact that he was the leader of the Kurdish national movement, Ocalan started to speak of forming a war-time government that would rule over a section of Kurdistan that covered both southeast Turkey and a sliver of northern Iraq.[16] More pointedly, he began preparations to form the Kurdistan National Assembly (KUM for short) that was modeled after the Palestine National Congress, which operated as the parliament-in-exile of all Palestinians. The message was clear. Regardless of what the Kurdish deputies in parliament managed to accomplish, it was Ocalan who was going to lead the Kurds to political independence. So far, the Turkish establishment's refusal to tolerate the Kurdish deputies ensured that they could do little to rival Ocalan's authority.

"The democratic path was closed by the state," said Kemal Parlak, an independent activist who started working with the Kurdish party in 1993, when legal and illegal pressure on the party was peaking, "and this ended up strengthening the PKK."

The Arrival

Ciftci, the gangly young man who dropped out of university to fight for a Kurdish state, arrived in Amed (Diyarbakir) region in July 1991. Before he left the PKK's camp in the Bekaa, he had been named commander of a seven-person *manga*, the smallest fighting unit inside the PKK. By the time he arrived at the rebels' hide-out north of Diyarbakir City—a journey that took him three months on foot after he crossed the Turkish-Iraqi border—he was promoted to head a *takim* unit of about 30 people. His quick rise probably reflected the PKK's lack of experienced fighters at the time, but the decision clearly was a good one. Ciftci had the calm demeanor of a man who likely stayed cool under the worst firefight and a certain self-assuredness that no doubt commanded the respect of other militants.

"It was a very mobile situation, one day I would be in Lice, then Genc and then Diyarbakir," explained Ciftci, referring to the areas around different cities. "The details were left to us. When something happened, the villagers would later exaggerate the story. If one Turkish soldier was killed, villagers would say 10. They would get very excited."

Turkish soldiers, usually new to the region, were hampered by their inexperience, the foreign terrain, and a certain uncoordinated approach to fighting the rebels. The technological advantages of the Turkish military—fighter jets, helicopters, and tanks—were not that useful against highly mobile, small guerrilla teams who knew their way around the mountains and dense forests.

"The soldiers would come to the edge of the mountains, but they wouldn't enter," said Ciftci. Nor were the Turkish security forces really prepared to fight at night. "At night, we were in control," Ciftci insisted.

Years later, a senior military official blamed this on the lack of proper training and necessary equipment, like high-powered binoculars, and the reluctance of commanders to order their soldiers to conduct night operations. "The terrorists used the night like a weapon," said retired lieutenant general Hasan Kundakci in his memoirs. "And the soldiers didn't go out much [at night]."[17] Instead, soldiers stayed inside their fortified barracks, leaving the PKK rebels free to move around the region after dark. Kundakci bitterly quoted the rebels as saying, "'The nights are ours, the days are the soldiers.'"[18]

After dark, the PKK set up checkpoints on main roads and checked identity cards. Kurds were subjected to nationalist lectures; state workers and security personnel were pulled from their vehicles and often shot. While suspected state agents hunted down Kurdish activists and PKK sympathizers—killings also were carried out by the seemingly state-tolerated Islamist, right-wing Hizbollah group (no relation to Hizbollah in Lebanon)—PKK militants hunted down the state's supporters. Those targeted included village guards, police, and others who actively opposed the rebels. In 1992, PKK rebels were blamed for killing about 210 so-called state supporters; in 1993, the PKK gunned down more than 300 of them.[19]

At the same time, the rebels challenged the military's defenses by raiding urban centers and shooting up state buildings and police stations. They studied the fortifications and travel patterns of remote military bases and attacked luckless soldiers as they traveled back and forth or stood guard. The situation grew so severe that between 1990 and 1992, the military retreated from its more isolated compounds in the southeast.

"One by one, they were being abandoned," complained Kundakci in his memoirs. "As this happened, the terrorists did not stay put, but every day they took another step forward."[20]

But the PKK's successes came at a high price. Of the 300 PKK rebels based in Amed province the year Ciftci arrived, nearly half died that same year in clashes. That figure excludes those who were wounded or ran away.

"The Turkish soldiers were very inexperienced, but so were we," said Ciftci. "I was 21, 22 years old, and others in the group were even younger. Late in 1991, we started to get a lot of new people. None of them had ever shot a gun before." The PKK liked to boast of its military training camp in the Bekaa, but those who completed the program frequently complained that it was not very useful. "I remember, they showed us how to jump out of jeeps," laughed Ciftci, "and I said, 'vallah, as far as I know, in Kurdistan we don't have jeeps.'"

Besides, not everyone was sent for training. The burst in recruits in the 1990s made it hard to find the space and time. And those who joined in the southeast needed to survive long enough to at least make the long trek to PKK bases in north Iraq.

"Sometimes, as you are returning from a village with a new member, there would be an attack and they would die even before getting a chance to change their clothes," added PKK rebel commander Huseyin Topgider.

The PKK always lost a lot of rebels in fighting—it is a staggering experience to look through the group's "martyr albums," where the dead are memorialized—but in the 1990s the losses seem heavier. The main reason was that the flood of new recruits included more urban-based supporters, especially university students, and teenagers as young as 14 or 15 from villages in the southeast. Their youth and relative inexperience not only made them more likely to die in battle, but also more likely to run away. Regardless of where one had grown up, the rebel life was a difficult one. It could be hard to find water, the food was monotonous and starchy, people slept rough on the ground, and there were lice.

Neval, the code-name of a woman who joined the rebels out of university in 1992, remembered how she first rejected the food, even though it was luxurious by PKK standards—bread smeared with tomato paste and oil. "It's possible you won't find this type of food again,"[21] warned Ocalan's brother Osman, when he offered it to her at the PKK's Hakurk base in north Iraq.

Late in 1991, a PKK rebel known as Dr. Suleyman—so-named because he dropped out of medical studies to join the rebels—arrived in Amed province to take command of a rebel unit based in the forested area around the town Genc. Dr. Suleyman had done his political training in Athens and his military training in the Bekaa, including a special, Palestinian-organized course in urban guerrilla warfare. A small, muscular man, he first was sent to organize PKK sympathizers in Adana, the city where he had attended university. But less than a week after he arrived, the other newly arrived PKK operative was arrested and informed on the group's budding operations. Dr. Suleyman, whose real name is Sait Curukkaya and who then was nearly 23 years old, soon had no choice but to leave the city. When the PKK ordered him to the mountains to fight, he was thrilled.

"All I was thinking about was the fight and going to Kurdistan," he recalled.

Curukkaya was given command of a 30-person unit in Genc,

north of Diyarbakir city. The unit was once much larger, but fighting had been fierce in Genc over the previous six months and more than half the unit's members either died or ran away. By the time Curukkaya got to Genc it was winter, when both the PKK and the Turkish army were forced by weather conditions to suspend fighting. In Genc, so much snow fell that it was impossible to move around.

"We lived under a tent that covered a sort of rocky outcropping," said Dr. Suleyman. "We had a small toilet outside and there was one village not too far away with 120 houses. Every day, a different house would prepare food supplies for us." It was boring and uncomfortable and when the PKK guerrillas emerged at the end of winter, more than half of them ran away, including three commanders. A few days later, the Turkish military launched an assualt against the remaining 13 militants.

"It was my first clash," said Dr. Suleyman, laughing, "and I thought it would be like in the films. I remember, I threw myself out from behind a rock and sort of rolled into position, like you see in a film, and I ended up with cuts all over my back from the rocks in the ground." He shook his head. "The fighting lasted a whole day, from morning until night. The soldiers were about 100 or 200 yards away, but it was a forested area and they didn't enter. They called in F-16s and helicopters, but they didn't do anything to us either. And when it was dark, they left."

The loss of so many rebels in Genc did not hurt the PKK's ability to recruit. Either new recruits did not know about the risks or, more likely, they did not particularly care.

"You get these ideas in your head, like Rambo, and you want action and the state pressure pushes you towards the PKK," said Dr. Suleyman, who has since split from the PKK and is enrolled in a German university. "You understand that anyway, you have no right to life [in the Turkish state] and you want revenge, and all this feeds support for the PKK."

That spring, for example, more than 100 new people joined up in the Genc area and by the end of 1992, the number of rebels in Genc was about 500. The increase was mirrored throughout Amed province, where the number of rebels went from about 300 to around 1200 by the end of 1992. "There were so many people coming that we started to send them elsewhere, to Mardin, Cizre, other parts of the southeast," said Dr. Suleyman. All over the region, in fact, PKK commanders noted a boost in recruitment—quite apart from the active support they received from civilians—bringing the total number in the southeast to around 10,000.

"We had lit a fire with the armed struggle and you couldn't put this out, it just got bigger," said Azman, who returned to southeast Turkey late in 1992 after six months in the Bekaa. "Our morale was very high."

Women

Kurdish villagers often were surprised to discover women among the gun-toting rebels who descended on the villages at night to make propaganda and collect supplies. Aysel Curukkaya, who rejoined the rebels in 1986 after her release from prison, recalled that village women could not believe another woman had gone to the mountains to fight. One young girl insisted on running her hands under Curukkaya's shirt and screamed in surprise when she realized Curukkaya really had breasts. Men, on the other hand, were shamed into action when they realized that women also were fighting.

"There were these older people, and they would say, 'look, we haven't done anything since [the Dersim uprising of] 1938, and look at how there are women now doing this,'" Curukkaya told me when we met in Hamburg, where she lives with her husband, former PKK member Selim Curukkaya, and their daughter.

Because young Kurdish women in villages usually did not go out by themselves—making it hard for them to meet PKK activists—and because the PKK was not very active in urban areas in the 1980s, the group did not have a lot of female members in this period. This changed after 1989, when the PKK made inroads into universities and urban centers. Similarly, the PKK's move into publishing and politics in the early 1990s helped it attract support from more women, who sometimes found it easier (and more acceptable to their families) to work in an office instead of leaving home and plunging into an unknown life in the mountains.

Women also had changed in the years following the military coup. The detention of tens of thousands of Kurdish men forced women to take a more active role in family and society. They not only had to worry about feeding their family, but also they were thrust into the unruly, difficult bureaucracy of Turkey's judicial and prisons systems, where rough treatment by guards and police radicalized them.

Leyla Zana, for example, the only woman elected to parliament from the Kurdish political party, had been married off in 1975 at the age of 15 to a much-older cousin.[22] At the time, she did not speak Turkish—her father, a municipal worker, did not believe in educating girls—and after she married her husband ruled her life. "For the next five years it was the same," she explained, "it was still not my own life, it was controlled by [my husband] Mehdi."[23]

Her husband's arrest after the military coup, he had been mayor of Diyarbakir, forced Zana to live on her own with two small children. She took part in prison protests and learned Turkish.

"I had changed, become different, I had an identity," she continued. "It was terrific. . . . I was able to tell myself, 'Here I am. I do exist.'"[24] When she was arrested in 1988 after a melee broke out between waiting families and prison guards, she was tortured and sexually humiliated. The experience only strengthened her conviction. "It was about that time that I began to be a political activist, and when I learned there were Kurdish women fighting with guns I was moved to action," said Zana. "This changes everything, I told myself, a woman is also a human being."[25]

While Zana channeled her energy into legal activities, some women left for the rebels. By 1993, women comprised about a third of the PKK's armed forces. The jump in female recruitment coincided with Ocalan taking a more vocal stance in favor of women's rights, and it seems one fed off the other. Whether he truly believed in equality for women is unclear, but he certainly understood that he could gain a powerful ally in women if he defended their rights.

Ocalan began to insist that the Kurdish movement's "basic responsibility is to . . . liberate women,"[26] and he repeatedly complained that women in Kurdish society were treated like slaves, their lives governed and restricted by their fathers, brothers, and other male relatives. It might have been an exaggeration, but it played well with women, many of whom did not feel like they had real control over their lives nor that their lives had any real value. His insistence that the PKK's revolutionary fight would be impossible without the presence of Kurdish women, specifically those who had broken with the prejudices of traditional life, gave women an immediate sense of worth.

"Where we were, it was hard for women," said Batufa, who came from the conservative city-town Yuksekova. "Joining was a reaction to that [pressure on women], it was a step for freedom, the PKK books I read spoke about women's freedom."

But many young women simply saw the PKK as an acceptable form of escape from their day-to-day lives. In a society in which most girls were not educated beyond primary school and many were married before age 15—and then to a man picked by their family—joining the PKK might be the only way to take control of the direction of their lives.

"Because we have a closed social structure," explained a city official in the southeastern city Batman, "when young girls are being pressured by their families, they see going to the mountains as a way to express themselves."[27]

A Kurdish father could block his daughter from working, from walking to the store alone, from going to high school, or even from wearing pants, but it was not easy to criticize her decision to fight for Kurdish freedom. Doing so could raise questions about a family's real loyalties, which in turn could put the family at odds with the PKK. There also was the chance that such comments could raise questions inside the PKK about the loyalties of the girl who had joined, possibly endangering her life. Besides, the PKK was said to protect a girl's virginity with the same zeal as her family, something that helped shore up support for the PKK even among the most conservative Kurdish families.

One young woman, let us call her Zilan, joined the PKK out of a Turkish university in 1992. The next time she saw her family was four years later in Europe, where she had been sent by the PKK. What Zilan's relatives really wanted to know, before everything else, was whether she was still a virgin. And Zilan very proudly could assure them that she was.

9

Fueling the War, 1992–1993

THE PKK'S ABILITY to operate successfully in southeast Turkey was due to careful planning and courage—and no small amount of stubbornness and luck. Huseyin Topgider, a commander in the region Kurds called Garzan, once managed to cross a particularly dangerous strip of territory—land mines and Turkish military maneuvers had closed the planned route near the city-town Siirt—because sympathetic villagers insisted on loading the rebels on five trucks and driving them down the road past the police station. It was late in the summer of 1992, and villagers assured the doubtful rebels that the security forces never bothered to check cars.

"The soldiers know the rebels usually use a different route through this area," Topgider recalled one of the villagers saying, trying to convince him it could work. "It was a crazy idea," said Topgider, laughing at the memory, "and we later said that if the interior minister knew that 80 guerrillas in cars crossed the mountains near a police station, he would have had to resign."

The villagers had made the offer to help unasked and their willingness to take such a risk underscored the explosion of civilian support for the PKK in the early 1990s. Militants constantly tested the extent of their backing by calling on civilians to organize funerals for rebels who died in clashes, demanding that shops and schools go on strike to protest the military's offensives and encouraging people to take to the streets to mark the August 1984 anniversary of the war's start. In towns across the region, funerals for PKK rebels drew thousands of angry mourners. In Diyarbakir, the regional capital with an estimated population of 500,000 at the time, the rebels could shut down the whole city with just a few days notice, using civilian supporters to inform people of the plan. The Kurdish new year became an excuse for a week of near-violent demonstrations, in which tens of thousands of Kurds took to the streets throughout the region to taunt the military and shout PKK slogans.

The PKK's ability to mobilize so many people was a direct challenge to the state's authority and Turkish security forces reacted harshly, making little distinction between civilian sympathizers and the armed rebels themselves. In 1992, for example, Turkish security forces in the southeast shot and killed two dozen people in 13 separate demonstrations, some of which were held to protest state violence against civilians.[1] The mysterious murder of activist Kurds—usually gunned down in the street or abducted and their bodies dumped elsewhere—jumped to more than 250 that year and just over 450 the next year. The choice of victims, mainly people connected to the human rights movement, HEP political party members, or apparent PKK sympathizers, caused Kurds to speak of a shadowy, state-backed force they called the contra-guerrillas.[2]

Turkish security forces reacted to PKK attacks with shows of force that seemed aimed at frightening people into turning against the rebels. After PKK militants in August 1992 fired mortars at state buildings in the city-town Sirnak, where about 25,000 people lived, the security forces went on a three-day shooting spree. The electricity and phones were cut and the army barred people from entering or leaving. More than 70 percent of the houses and shops were ruined and 22 townspeople killed. Within a few days, thousands of residents had loaded up their belongings and fled. Among those left behind were the corpses of five children.[3]

"One of the corpses [in the hospital corridor] was that of a four-year-old child," recounted journalists Faruk Balikci and Namik Durukan, who managed to enter Sirnak before the military's blockade on journalists was lifted. "From the eight-year-old boy's body, half of the jaw was gone and there was a hole in his throat the size of a fist. His eyes had been left open. Right next to him was his 12-year-old sister, her beautiful black hair scattered. I [Balikci] went to press the shutter of the camera but my eyes were filled with tears and everything was cloudy."[4]

Elsewhere in the hospital, a father clutched his wounded three-year-old daughter to live, begging God to let her live, while he grasped the hand of his wife, also wounded. About an hour's drive away, in the city-town Cizre, where refugees from Sirnak crowded into already overcrowded cinder-block houses, young Kurdish men debated leaving for the mountains. "Maybe we will go to the rebels," said one young man, crouched on the bare concrete floor in a small house off one of Cizre's muddy backroads. His brothers nodded their heads in approval. "There, everything is good. In the mountains, the fighting is one-on-one. You see what happens to us when we have no weapons."[5]

Smaller-scale, but otherwise very similar, military counterattacks occurred elsewhere: in the border city-town Cukurca, a brief PKK attack was followed by four hours of gunfire from the security forces, leaving a 14-year-old boy dead and many houses and shops damaged. During an overnight clash near an Agri district village—five soldiers and 20 PKK militants died in the clash—security forces opened fire on houses, apparently at random, killing two young children and wounding three.[6] In Kulp, a town known for its PKK sympathies, soldiers responded to an attack on a military vehicle by shooting at the town center. One local complained that, "[The soldiers] burn our houses, although it was the PKK that opened fire [on] them."[7]

The independent Turkish Human Rights Foundation, which had no links to the PKK, warned that the violence was destroying people's trust in the state: "People living in Nusaybin, Cizre, and Sirnak believe that the state does not take them into account and persecutes them. Those people now have no expectations from the state."[8]

This actually was what the PKK wanted. In the areas where it was most powerful, it already had set up a parallel, if rudimentary, system of administration. PKK rebels not only collected taxes, but they were also an influential presence in many aspects of daily life. In Nusaybin, the PKK burned a construction supply shed to protest plans to pave streets. When the mayor arranged a meeting with the PKK provincial commander, he was unable to convince the commander to lift his ban.

"We say to you. . . let the streets stay muddy," the PKK militant said, "that way, the tanks can't enter; you don't listen to us, that's why we burned the shed."[9]

In Cizre, a dusty city-town on the edge of the Cudi Mountains, militants held trials for people accused of transporting food to the army and harming local morals by selling whiskey and gin.[10] They also handled complaints like bad debts and land disputes, warning people against using the local courts because this recognized Turkey's authority in the region.

In Idil, a town northwest of Cizre, the situation was the same. "We have not had a single application to the courts in the past six months," the local governor told Turkish journalist Ismet Imset in 1992. "The people prefer to go to the [PKK's] popular tribunal instead."[11] In Diyarbakir, a prosecutor complained to his old lawyer friend, Azman, now a rebel commander, that the state's cases had dropped off dramatically.

"People no longer accepted the authority of the courts," said Azman. "They saw us as providing more justice and as being the power in the region."

The PKK had supplanted more than the state's authority. Kurds in the region were used to appealing to local, influential figures—tribal leaders, sheikhs, and wealthy landowners—for help in addressing everyday family problems and adjudicating other disputes. Now, in areas where the PKK was strong, Kurds instead appealed to the rebels. This shift underscored the extent to which the rebel war had changed social dynamics in the region, siphoning off authority even from people not necessarily linked to or supported by the state.

One reason simply was that the PKK had proven itself to be a group that could back up its decisions by force. The other reason was that in many areas, the rebels were viewed as representing the real interests of the Kurds. As such, they were more trusted and respected than the traditional authority figures—even those with no ties to the state—who symbolized the nonnationalist, nonrevolutionary forces that so far had failed the Kurds.

"Once, a Laz girl who was married to a Kurdish boy complained because he was beating her," said Azman. "She sent us a letter telling us of the problem. And so someone went and threatened him, or something." Azman shrugged. "After that we got a letter from her thanking us for solving the problem."

The PKK's level of control was sufficiently strong that some fighters started to wonder when it would be time to call for a general uprising.

"This situation, where we split the power with the state, it couldn't go on for very long," said rebel commander Sait Curukkaya, better known by his code name Dr. Suleyman, mixing a bit of Mao's theory with his own reflections. "Either the situation starts to regress, or else the next step is a strategic attack."

Talk of an Uprising

The PKK commanders' interest in a mass uprising was sparked in part by the Iraqi Kurdish experience across the border. In early 1991, after U.S.-led Coalition Forces pushed Saddam Hussein's troops out of Kuwait, the Iraqi Kurds staged their own popular uprising. The Kurds believed they would get support from the United States—then-President George H. W. Bush had indicated as much when he called on the Iraqi people to get rid of their dictator—but the United States was wary of getting involved. Its close ally, Turkey, opposed an independent Kurdish state because of fears that this would further enflame Turkish Kurdish separatists; other states in the region also had serious concerns about what would happen if Iraq collapsed into two or three ministates. In the end, the United States and the Coalition Forces ignored Baghdad's brutal counterattack on the Kurds and close to two million Iraqi Kurds fled to Turkey and Iran. The pictures of bedraggled, hungry refugees—among them small children and babies—crowding the muddy mountains led, for the first time it seemed, to a real international interest in the Kurds. Unfortunately for the Turkish Kurds, this did not extend to their plight.

Ankara, unhappy with the influx of Kurdish refugees and equally displeased by the international attention, supported creation of a protected "safe haven" in northern Iraq to get the Iraqi Kurds to return home.[12] Turkey envisioned something close to the Iraqi border and not very permanent, but the Iraqi Kurds got much more. The allied-protected zone ended up encompassing most of the Kurdish region of Iraq and, because Iraqi troops were not permitted into the safe haven, gave the Kurds a type of de facto autonomy. Now, the Iraqi Kurds were readying to hold elections in May 1992 for their own Kurdish parliament. Some PKK commanders figured that even a failed mass uprising of Turkey's Kurds might be a success if it won them similar international protections.

"Basically, either control would pass into our hands or this would become a big international issue," said Dr. Suleyman.

PKK rebels numbered about 10,000 total during this period and they claimed to have about 60,000 armed civilian *milis*, about two-thirds the strength of the Turkish soldiers normally stationed in the region (excluding police, special forces, and village guards).[13] Even if the *milis* figure was slightly inflated, the rebels also estimated that they had the sympathy of more than half the region's people, many of whom were armed as a matter of course. Any sustained uprising would draw in these people as well, posing a challenge even for the better-equipped Turkish security forces.

In February 1992, rebels in Amed province gathered for a meeting in the PKK's military headquarters outside Kulp town. Semdin (Zeki) Sakik, who commanded that province, chaired the meeting. Like the others, Sakik seemed to think it was time to encourage and support a sustained popular uprising throughout the region. Ocalan certainly had spoken about this enough to make rebels believe it was the goal. But the discussion in the Kulp headquarters did not get very far.

Participants quickly realized that Ocalan already had made his own decision on the next phase of the military battle (he apparently made his views clear in messages to senior commanders). Instead of encouraging a popular uprising, which by its very nature would not be totally under the control of the PKK, Ocalan wanted the guerrillas to focus on getting people to join or otherwise directly support the PKK's guerrilla army.

"According to Ocalan, the most important thing was to build a guerrilla army and fight the Turkish army in the mountains," Ciftci, who attended the Kulp meeting, told me.

Similar discussions took place among rebel commanders in at least four other provinces. Given the PKK's secure position in the region, waiting a little bit longer did not seem a problem. "We thought all right, later on, the situation will just be better," said Dr. Suleyman.

But in a sign that the people themselves might be ready, that March marked the most violent Kurdish new year (Newruz) celebrations the country had experienced. In Kurdish towns and cities, the PKK's local backers organized street celebrations that turned into nationalist demonstrations. Men, women, and children taunted the security forces with pro-PKK slogans and upraised fists. In some places, armed civilian backers of the PKK opened fire on soldiers and police, sparking violent clashes that lasted for days. About 90 people, mainly civilians, were killed.[14] But Ocalan's refusal to let PKK guerrillas direct the demonstrations and turn them into a mass uprising—something like the Palestinian *intifada* that broke out at the end of the 1980s—left the protests to dwindle until they stopped.

"Our approach at Newruz wasn't clear," said Dr. Suleyman. "We wanted people to take part, but not to start a people's uprising. If we had wanted that, we would have told them all to bring their guns."

Later, some of the PKK commanders started to wonder why Ocalan shied away from approving a popular uprising in the first half of the 1990s. Some wondered whether Ocalan might have been afraid of Syria, which certainly would have been opposed to any action that could end with the flight of millions of Kurdish refugees to stream across its own border, disrupting its internal control and possibly sparking new, international interference in the region. They also began to have suspicions that Ocalan may have spoken against a mass uprising because he feared that it would remove the Kurdish fight out of his direct control. A sustained uprising, whether violent or not, could cause new actors and interest groups to emerge, challenging Ocalan's authority and the PKK's hegemony. Directing resources to the guerrilla army, and insisting that an uprising could only take place under tight PKK control, kept the struggle firmly in Ocalan's hands.

"The PKK was against anything outside of its control," stated Azman. "But the real problem was what was the program? . . . What was the goal? Without a clear strategy the tactics could not be clear."

Ocalan always had great trust in his plans and abilities and he seemed to believe his own propaganda. He was so convinced of the PKK's ability to lead the Kurds to a victory that he apparently no longer saw the need for a people's uprising. On the one hand, he insisted he could build a guerrilla army big enough to wrest control of the southeast from Turkish forces. On the other hand, he believed that with a big enough guerrilla force, the Turkish government would agree to sit down and negotiate with him.

But Ocalan's analyses took a lot for granted. Mainly, it assumed a static situation, one in which the Turkish army did not learn from its mistakes and Ocalan did not make any.

Financing the Fight

PKK rebels fighting in the rural southeast, and those doing organizational work in Turkey's urban areas, were expected to finance their own operations.[15] PKK operatives in the cities might have jobs that helped cover their basic costs, but the guerrillas relied on money and goods they collected from individuals and businesses. The goal was not only to pay for supplies like replacement weapons, extra ammunition, food, and clothing, but also to show their authority.

"The idea was that whatever the state does, we do, that we should sort of share authority, they operate during the day, and we operate at night," said Ayhan Ciftci, then known as Kucuk Zeki, a good enough fighter and leader that early in 1994 he was named commander of Erzurum province, the highest rank one could reach in the field. "So if the state taxes, then we have to tax too."

The idea of taxing people was not new. The plan was announced at the 1986 3rd Congress, but at that time the rebels were not yet strong enough to do more than demand money on an ad hoc basis as they swept through the region. The situation since had changed. Now, the PKK's support network was so wide, and the rebels so well entrenched, that their demands were more regular and few dared turn down a request. Some people wanted to give, others certainly felt forced, but overall, quite a few probably figured that at least it made sense to help the rebels, who were fighting for Kurdish rights, rather than the state, which was intent on repressing Kurdish identity. Besides, as the matriarch of a wealthy Diyarbakir land-holding family once explained to me, the rebels wanted flour, while the state wanted Kurds to join the state militia and fight the rebels. In this balance, the rebels were much more sympathetic.

In small towns where the PKK held sway and had semipermanent bases nearby the rebels tried to collect money regularly from companies, municipal authorities, and the wealthy. One commander said he imposed a tax rate of 10 percent in Kulp, north of Diyarbakir. Once a month, or once every few months, PKK backers came to the mountains carrying bags of cash. "Apart from the commander of the military base, everybody paid the tax, from officials in the administration down," boasted Dr. Suleyman, perhaps only in slight exaggeration.

But while wealthy Kurds were expected to give—and give well—the average Kurdish worker in the region was not regularly tapped for money. "There was no policy to go and take from individuals," said one PKK rebel, "although if someone had a shop that was different."

To be sure, the PKK was strong enough to demand money from everyone, but that was not necessary. They already had enough money for what they needed. "It didn't even come to our minds," said Kucuk Zeki.

The PKK's ability to demand revenue from individuals and small businesses in the southeast was limited by the fact that people were poor and business slow—a small business in an average-sized town might take in just a few hundred dollars profit a month. Amed province, for example, one of the largest and wealthiest, produced about one million dollars annually in so-called tax revenue for the PKK, a good sum, but not enormous. "It's hard enough for the Turkish government to collect taxes, so how could we manage to get money from everybody?" joked Kucuk Zeki.

Most of the money collected in the southeast came from private companies hired by the state to fix roads, lay down pipes, expand the electricity grid, and build buildings. Public state companies that did upkeep in the region also paid. Paying ensured that rebels would not attack them at the work-site or blow up their machinery. One successful professional in Ankara recalled that when he wanted to build a school in his former village in the southeast, the foreman handling the project made clear extra money was needed to pay off the PKK. "Otherwise, they would destroy the tools, or just destroy the building," the professional recounted.

In areas where the rebel group was strong, local companies checked with the PKK commander before bidding on a state contract for work in the area. The PKK sometimes warned contractors off projects to build police stations or pave roads that Turkish troops used. They also fixed bids for a fee that might run 30 percent of the contract. Assuring that a certain contractor received the contract was done by warning rival bidders to drop out of the bidding or, more commonly, telling them to submit a bid that was too high to win.

"This work sometimes was hard," one rebel commander noted. But, as another added, "We did have the guns."

One very profitable source of local financing was the PKK's tax on smugglers operating between Turkey, Iran, and Iraq. Like other Kurdish groups in the region—Iraqi Kurds, for example, enforced a so-called customs duty on trucks coming in from Turkey—the PKK exacted payment from those seeking to cross territory it controlled by virtue of its armed presence.

"We got money for allowing smugglers to pass through the mountains with their goods," recalled Sari Baran, who operated in the Hakkari area through 1990. "With animal smugglers, we would take three percent of the flock as tax. Sometimes we ate the animals, or more commonly, we sold them."

It was an open secret that a number of Turkish Kurds were in-volved in the drugs trade, particularly heroin smuggling from Iran to Turkey (and from there to Europe). And in the 1980s the trade really started to boom, said a former city official from the border region. Kurds involved in the drugs trade, either because they truly believed in the PKK—or because they thought it a good business practice—fre-quently donated money to the rebels. There are also reports of PKK supporters in Europe who used their positions and contacts to trade in drugs—and then handed some of the profits to the PKK. And when PKK activists needed more money, they had no qualms about ap-proaching Kurds who trafficked in narcotics.

However, it does not seem that the PKK, as an organization, di-rectly produced or traded in narcotics.[16] "The PKK was not directly involved," stressed Kucuk Zeki, underlining what others in the PKK said. "But for example, [name withheld] would give an ad to the PKK's newspaper and pay a lot of money. Or [name withheld] would pay money for something the PKK needed. The party knew where their money came from."

As necessary as money was, most PKK rebels viewed it as just an-other tool in their struggle. Money was something to be used to get what was needed to continue the fight, but apart from that it had no real value to their lives. "Money was not important to us," recalled Neval. "It was just something to trade for our supplies, it was not real money."

Getting Supplies

The sudden jump in people joining the rebels in the early 1990s cre-ated unexpected logistical problems. PKK rebels usually relied on villagers to provide food—mainly bread, rice, chickpeas, macaroni, sugar, tea, and cooking oil—but these larger units of 30, 40, or even 100 people could not simply turn up at the nearest settlement and de-mand assistance. First, not all villages were friendly or approachable. Second, the goal was to build support, not bankrupt supporters. Vil-lagers often were poor, and what stocks they did have they needed for their own families.

Besides, there were no shops in these small settlements, meaning it was impossible just to show up and order from—or raid—the local market. Apart from their daily food requirements, rebels needed to build up food depots to free themselves from the daily search for food and help them make it through the winter months. They also needed a steady supply of items not easy to find in rural settlements. These included a variety of medicines to treat illnesses, batteries for the walkie-talkies they first acquired around 1991, heavy shawls and extra shirts for chilly nights, and, above all, shoes to replace the ones that were quickly ruined climbing over sharp rocks and wading through streams. And, of course, they needed replacement weapons and extra ammunition.

PKK commanders employed creative solutions to address their logistical needs. Dr. Suleyman once tasked a chronically ill rebel with the job of arranging supplies for the rebels. The young man suffered from fainting spells and it proved impossible to keep him in the mountains. Instead, he was ordered to set himself up in Istanbul, where he apparently hired or borrowed trucks to ship clothing to the southeast, where supporters arranged for the goods to get to the mountains. It helped that the young man was related to a wealthy, pro-PKK reputed heroin smuggler, ensuring both his trustworthiness and his ability to finance the supply operation.

"This was in 1992, when we had a lot of problems getting enough supplies," explained Dr. Suleyman, referring to the year when the number of recruits really jumped. "We told him we wanted him to get two trucks full of supplies and one thing we asked for was 500 shirts. Sure enough, we soon got a couple of truckloads of goods from Istanbul. It worked out very well. If he had stayed in the mountains it would have been a big problem for us."

In most cases, however, PKK rebels relied on their regular network of supporters in different cities and city-towns in the southeast and elsewhere in Turkey. In areas where the PKK was strong, supporters set up so-called neighborhood committees that collected money, handled recruitment, and helped buy what the rebels needed. Thanks to the money PKK rebels collected in the southeast, it was easy to pay for what they needed. Once a year, villages were expected to donate a certain amount of mainly food supplies to the rebels—poorer villagers might be reimbursed for what was taken—but other items had to be picked up in cities.

In regions far from the Iraqi border, getting and securing supplies was a difficult job. If the Turkish military was very active, rebels might be cut off from their depots, or their depots might fall into the state's hands, or villagers might be too frightened to help arrange for the delivery of supplies. Things were easier for rebels based along the Iraqi border. They ordered supplies from Iraqi Kurds, who could drive the goods almost right up to the PKK's border camps. The depots in north Iraq sometimes were destroyed in Turkish raids, but the depots still were that much harder for the military to reach. Ultimately, the ability of PKK commanders to ensure necessary supplies of food, clothing, and ammunition did not depend on money, which was easy to get, but on the local contacts they developed to ensure the collection and transport of the supplies.

Once the military realized that the villages that dominated the southeastern landscape were critical to the rebels' well-being, they turned their attention toward the PKK's civilian backers and fatally disrupted the PKK's logistical supply network. "When they [Turkish soldiers] burned villages and lots of villagers were killed, things started to turn bad for us," recalled Kucuk Zeki.

Finding Arms

PKK rebels always stressed to me that it was inexpensive to make war. The weapons they used—mainly Kalashnikovs, BKC machine guns, Dushka anti-aircraft guns, and rocket-propelled grenades—were easy to find and fairly cheap, and this was assuming they had to pay.[17] After U.S.-led Coalition Forces established a safe haven in north Iraq, huge stocks of old Iraqi army weaponry and equipment were there for the taking.

"The cities, towns and villages that Iraqi soldiers abandoned are filled with gear, guns and foxholes,"[18] wrote Turkish Kurdish journalist Namik Durukan, a veteran regional reporter, as he toured north Iraq late in March 1991.

PKK rebels gathered up what they could, substantially boosting their stocks on the cheap. "They left behind so much," marveled rebel commander Huseyin Topgider, who at the time was based in the mountains outside the northern Iraqi city Zakho.

In any case, the region always was awash in weapons and dealers in weapons. Most of the weapons were Russian-made items passed on or sold to Middle East allied countries and sympathetic rebel groups during the Cold War era. Iraqi Kurdish fighters had never been picky about who gave them armed assistance, and the PKK was similarly willing to take weapons from just about anyone willing to provide them. At different times, the PKK almost certainly received weapons from Tehran and Baghdad, in addition to whatever assistance Syria regularly provided. But the weapons trade in the region was so brisk that it would be wrong to assume the PKK was dependent on any one country, or even a group of countries, for its weapons.

"Our strongest ties with Iraq were in 1991," said Topgider, a slight hint of complaint creeping into his voice, "and even then all the help they were going to give stayed on paper."

Iraq was then under a U.N. embargo, which limited its own access to new weapons. Whatever the PKK could get—or did get—from Baghdad was not much different from what it could pick up on its own in the cheap, open market.

"After the Gulf War, there were a lot of guns on the market, so many that the price of a Kalashnikov fell to the price of a pack of Marlboros," noted Azman, the lawyer-turned-rebel.

For all the reported help that PKK rebels received, they never had much more than basic light weaponry, grenades, and land mines. Some items, like the anti-aircraft Russian-made Dushka gun, were too heavy for a mobile force traveling on foot and mainly were used in the PKK's semipermanent bases in north Iraq and the Turkish Kurdish province they called Botan, where the thick mountain ranges hid rebel forces well.

When it came to keeping themselves armed in the field, PKK rebels needed to be self-sufficient. Everyone who was trained in the Bekaa was sent off with a gun, bullets, and grenades, but once these were finished they had to resupply themselves. The PKK kept enormous weapons stocks in its semipermanent bases on the Iraqi border, but it could take weeks if not months to make it there from deep inside southeast Turkey. To assure steady supplies, they carefully built up depots of weapons in the mountains—in the Bitlis-Mus-Siirt-Batman area (called Garzan) where Topgider operated, he created some 80 storehouses of food and weapons—and when they needed more, they made their own arrangements with local dealers.

Weapons were not so difficult to buy in southeast Turkey, thanks to the smugglers who plied the Middle East weapons trade routes, picking up items in north Iraq or former east bloc countries, for example, and reselling them in Turkey. PKK rebels paid for what they needed with the money they collected or extorted from individuals and local businesses in the Kurdish region.

"There was a big arms trade," recalled Kucuk Zeki. "We would meet with smugglers and tell them what we needed."

The weapons the PKK relied on in southeast Turkey were limited by what was available on the local market and what they could carry on their backs. As a mobile guerrilla force that staged hit-and-run attacks, they did not need to keep enormous stocks of weapons with them at all times. Instead, after an attack, they withdrew to the mountains, where they already had scattered weapons depots that easily kept the small fighting units resupplied. This system worked well in the first half of the 1990s, but eventually the Turkish military learned how to better use air strikes against the rebels, relying especially on U.S.-supplied Cobra helicopters. When Turkish tactics shifted, the PKK's lack of advanced weaponry started to hurt.

"The one thing we needed were missiles against helicopters and airplanes," said Topgider, bemoaning that none of the PKK's backers made such items available.

The PKK's lack of shoulder-fired, surface-to-air missiles (SAMs) frustrated the rebels. The issue was not money—the PKK collected tens of millions of dollars annually from Kurdish businesses and individuals in Europe—and they certainly could have afforded the cheaper, Russian-made versions that circulated in the region. But the PKK always had trouble acquiring such weapons.

"Syria didn't want us to have them," insisted Selim Curukkaya, a former PKK member.

Curukkaya probably was right. The PKK's foreign supporters—foremost Syria and then Iran—wanted the PKK to hurt Turkey, but had little interest in the PKK actually succeeding in its battle. There also was the risk that successful PKK attacks against Turkey's air power might so enrage the Turkish military that it would retaliate against those countries it knew were supplying the PKK. And, as the United States learned after it supplied Stingers to the anti-Soviet Mujahadeen fighters in Afghanistan in the early 1980s, one could not ask for the weapons back. Surface-to-air missiles were too effective a weapon for a guerrilla group.

Nonetheless, in the mid-1990s, PKK rebels began to get their hands on Russian-designed SA-7 Strela shoulder-fired missiles. Russian or former Soviet-state military advisors apparently trained the PKK to use these missiles, but one rebel said this consisted of little more than showing them what to push to fire the missile.

"The problem was not whether we had enough of these," said one PKK rebel, who did not want to be identified, "but that we didn't get real training."

The PKK also did not always bring these missiles into Turkey, where they could be the most effective. The reason why was never clear, but some rebel commanders believed that Syria had warned Ocalan not to let the missiles across the border.

The problem with weapons availability—and the freedom to move Strelas, for example, across the border—pointed to an inherent contradiction in the PKK's dependence on foreign alliances, something that Ocalan preferred to ignore. In the early 1980s, when he decided to concentrate on building up good ties to Syria, he told a Turkish leftist acquaintance that he realized it could be a difficult balance. But there were not a lot of options for a Kurdish rebel leader in the Middle East, and Damascus had proved a safe haven and a loyal backer. Besides, the PKK had grown so strong in Turkey and Europe that things like SAMs seemed almost unnecessary.

Political Big Brothers

Ocalan always had been dismissive of Kurdish activists who focused their attention on publishing revolutionary theories instead of making revolution, but now that the PKK's war was well underway, he and his supporters looked at things differently. PKK members, particularly those already working in the group's internal party newspapers in Europe, realized they needed their own, broader-reaching publications to help legitimize the PKK's image and expand the group's influence. And Ocalan was interested in a forum for addressing potential negotiating partners in the Turkish establishment. The PKK did have its own party magazines, but they were illegal inside Turkey and risky to distribute. Besides, their narrow focus on Ocalan's propagandistic speeches limited their readership to those already convinced of the PKK's cause. "It was time to have a real newspaper," said Selahattin Celik, then working on the PKK's party newspapers in Europe.

Yeni Ulke (New Country), a weekly newspaper headquartered in

Istanbul, was founded in October 1990.[19] Former PKK members and independent Kurdish journalists said the PKK arranged for the start-up funding. Kurdish activists who had spent much of the previous decade in prison, not all of them for links to the PKK, were among the most enthusiastic backers of the new venture. In prison, they had experimented with their own publications—tiny, handwritten pieces of rolled-up paper secretly passed among cells—and they understood the importance of maintaining channels of communication.

"The idea was that a newspaper would give the Kurds a voice to the world and inside Turkey, but in a legal way," said Ramazan Ulek, who got involved in the newspaper after his release from prison on charges of PKK membership.

The new newspaper, with its polemical columns by PKK prisoners and glorified accounts of young men and women joining the rebels, remained too closely linked to the PKK to gain a varied readership. Nonetheless, the newspaper's relative popularity—circulation was said to be about 50,000—soon led people involved to consider a daily newspaper. The PKK, which wanted more coverage of the war and the Kurdish problem, again agreed to organize start-up financing, according to people once closely associated with the venture.

The planned daily attracted the interest of both unaffiliated Kurds eager to write about the Kurdish problem and leftist Turkish journalists looking for a more radical outlet for their reporting. The former had little chance of finding space for their articles in the mainstream media, while the latter had long since jettisoned their opposition to the PKK's nationalist ideology, partly out of grudging admiration for Ocalan's ability to launch the revolution they had failed to make. PKK supporters assured interested journalists that while the new publication would be pro-Kurdish—that is to say, sympathetic to the PKK's fight—the staff would be left free within this framework to report and write as they saw best. Many leftist Turkish and Kurdish journalists jumped at the chance to work at *Ozgur Gundem*, founded in May 1992.

"[The PKK] was a strong organization . . . they had a lot of resources," said C., a Turkish journalist who requested that his name not be used. "This organization had the need for a newspaper and we had the desire to work for an opposition newspaper. These two needs fit each other perfectly."

But the PKK's interest in supporting a mass appeal newspaper soon collided with its inability to tolerate independent actors or critical views. "At first we were very happy with the situation . . . but then their [the PKK's] patience declined and they started to look negatively at articles that did not mention 'Kurd' or 'Ocalan,'" said the same Turkish journalist. "And over time, tension started to rise between the 'political big brothers' at the newspaper and the journalists."

The first editor quit before the new newspaper even appeared and the second lasted 10 weeks before resigning. The third editor held on for a few months before being replaced in December 1992 by veteran PKK member Sukru Gulmus. Gulmus, a one-time teacher, had spent more than 10 years in prison for his tie to the PKK, and after his release in 1990, he worked briefly at *Yeni Ulke*. Ocalan subsequently invited him to the Bekaa for talks. During their talks, Gulmus said, Ocalan named him responsible for the Turkey-based publications and cultural activities affiliated—by want or design—with the rebel group.

Gulmus, already older and more experienced than most when he took over editorship of *Ozgur Gundem* newspaper, figured he knew how to balance the needs of a newspaper with the needs of Ocalan. Years later, Gulmus laughingly explained that, "When there were problems [at the newspaper], I used to joke . . . that God is above, [Hafez] Assad is in Syria, after Assad comes Apo and after Apo, I'm here."[20]

It was not difficult for the PKK-affiliated editors to ensure the newspaper's direction. The coverage, heavy on news of rebel clashes and on reports of human rights abuses by soldiers sweeping through the region, certainly followed the PKK's political interests. The features, focused on cultural, health, and history issues specific to the Kurdish region, matched the PKK's identity interests. Even Ocalan, writing under the pen name Ali Firat, made an appearance as a columnist offering philosophical analyses of international political trends and developments.

But did this make the newspaper a mouthpiece of the PKK? Not exactly. *Ozgur Gundem* offered Kurds—for the first time—a regular outlet to read news that directly affected them. In the Turkish mainstream press, the Kurdish problem did not exist, the war in the southeast was a problem of terrorism, not identity, and people who claimed otherwise were out to destroy the state. The Turkish mainstream press —excluding some columnists and some rare exceptions—did not investigate Kurdish complaints and ignored news critical of Turkish military operations in the southeast.[21] *Ozgur Gundem,* in contrast, focused on the southeast: on the war, on the human rights abuses, and on cultural issues of specific interest to Kurds. It was hard to say that this was not legitimate news.

"There was a big war, and the Turkish press didn't cover this," Yasar Kaya, *Gundem*'s former official owner, told me in his Cologne apartment, overflowing with the books and framed interviews attesting to his long-life in Kurdish publishing and politics. "We had a perspective, and in this we published the reality of the war. In the whole history of the Kurds, there was never a newspaper this successful. And that's why we had so many problems from the Turkish state."

The Turkish state never really distinguished between armed militants and unarmed critics and the newspaper's journalists and editors faced constant legal problems. Numerous laws existed solely to circumscribe free speech and the press. In particular, article 8 of the 1991 Anti-Terror Law specifically barred what it called oral or written propaganda aimed at damaging the unity of the state. Because the law did not take into account intent, it potentially made almost any discussion of Kurdish ethnic identity, the PKK, or state human rights abuses a crime.

"In Turkey, the philosophical concept 'I think, therefore I am' is understood as 'I think, therefore I am a terrorist,'" Haluk Gerger, a middle-aged Turkish intellectual with an English made fluent at Johns Hopkins University, told me in 1995 from his prison cell, where he was serving a 15-month sentence under the anti-terror law. Gerger, who contributed to *Gundem*, was jailed for a public statement in which he argued that Turkey's denial of Kurdish existence fueled the PKK's war. "I was trying to understand the reasons for the war [with the PKK], but even trying to understand this has become a crime of terrorism."[22]

Certainly, the state agreed. Official and unofficial pressure on *Ozgur Gundem* mounted.[23] Offices in both western and eastern Turkey frequently were raided by police. Reporters and others detained during these raids complained they were threatened or tortured. The paper's distributors and news-dealers were under similar pressure.

"'You are servants of the PKK,'" police officers reportedly warned two people detained in Mersin in September 1994. "The duty of the police is to kill terrorists, that is to say, to kill you.'"[24]

This was not an idle threat. Nine Kurdish journalists for *Yeni Ulke*, *Ozgur Gundem*, and like-publications were gunned down in the southeast in 1992 and one was seriously paralyzed; in 1993, two journalists from these newspapers were killed in the southeast; in 1994, one *Ozgur Gundem* journalist went missing and is presumed dead; and in 1995, a journalist from the successor newspaper, *Yeni Politika,* died under mysterious circumstances in police detention.[25]

Police investigations into the murders dragged on. Local human rights officials and the dead men's colleagues suspected the perpetrators either were linked to or encouraged by the security forces. Senior Turkish officials dismissed the murders as unimportant.

"Those killed were not real journalists," Prime Minister Suleyman Demirel stated a few days after the fifth journalist mysteriously was gunned down in August 1992. "They were militants in the guise of journalists."[26]

No proof ever was made to back up this claim. In fact, the real PKK members at the paper knew enough to go underground or start switching apartments when things got rough. It was the others at the newspaper, the journalists, the distributors, and news-dealers working out of sympathy or need, who were the ones most at risk of assassination.[27]

"I went to 26 funerals," Kaya, the paper's official owner, soberly recounted. "These killings were to make the rest of us afraid. But it didn't stop us."

Legal problems—including heavy fines, temporary closure orders, and jail sentences—forced the paper to shut in April 1994. It reopened two weeks later as *Ozgur Ulke* (Free Land).

"Activities of certain publications, in particular *Ozgur Ulke,*" warned Prime Minister Tansu Ciller in a secret memo dated November 30, 1994, "have become clear attacks on the permanent and spiritual values of the state. . . . With the aim of eliminating such an important threat . . . I ask the Ministry of Justice to determine and pursue the organs that have such publications."[28]

Three days later, a bomb blew up the Istanbul offices of *Ozgur Ulke.* One person was killed and around 20 wounded. The prime minister's office issued a statement denying state involvement, but quickly turned attention back to the dangers of *Ozgur Ulke*'s articles, reiterating the need for a judicial inquiry into the paper. Yet, the newspaper kept on publishing.

"Our journalists were people who stuck their hands into the fangs of the snake to pull out the news," Gulmus told me. "It was difficult, and they were brave. When the killings started, the leftists, the Turks, they all left the paper. But we had hundreds of people who wanted to do this work, they ran to take jobs with us."

There is no question that Kurds gained from the opportunities created when the PKK, starting in the early 1990s, carved out or otherwise gave its backing to new, legal Kurdish institutes and publications. A whole generation of journalists developed in *Ozgur Gundem* and its related newspapers, and for the first time, Kurds could read news of direct relevance to their lives; Kurdish playwrights, actors, and directors found support in new cultural centers. The PKK's willingness to back the Kurdish party HEP made it a mass political party, in the process creating opportunities for politically minded Kurds, while the move in 1995 of PKK supporters into legal satellite television in Europe brought, for the first time, news and information to Kurds, in Kurdish, worldwide.

But the gains always were offset, at least in part, by the PKK's usually successful attempts to block independent initiatives or decision-making. Kurdish politicians felt pressure to accede to the PKK's political interests, knowing otherwise the PKK would call on voters to withhold their support; the singers and actors at the cultural centers were expected to focus on overtly nationalistic themes and subtly praise the guerrilla war; the satellite television station would not allow reporting that veered from the PKK's line. "The PKK acted as if they didn't send someone to the paper, it wouldn't come out like they wanted," complained the paper's former owner Kaya.

And when Gulmus, editor of *Gundem*, hesitated to publish a fawning interview with Ocalan—variously described as being 15, 100, and 500 pages long—the PKK leader summarily ordered the newspaper temporarily shut down (it reopened three months later in April 1993). The story may be apocryphal: others, including the paper's legal owner Kaya, said *Gundem* temporarily closed for a variety of reasons, including heavy legal fines. But it certainly would not have been out of character for Ocalan to act like this. And the PKK's man then at the paper—the editor, Gulmus—insisted this was the reason he and the others suddenly found themselves out of work.

"One of the Turkish writers on the paper came to me and said, 'I thought I understood the PKK, but after this, I don't know,'" Gulmus told me as we sat in an Essen café, drinking coffee and waiting for the rain to stop. "I told him that I've been in the PKK for 15 years, and I still don't understand."

Love and War

Huseyin Topgider was almost 40 years old when he fell in love. The woman was a much-younger rebel named Hevidar, a new recruit who had been sent to the mountains of Garzan, where Topgider commanded a unit of about 100 fighters in 1992. "I remember the day she arrived," Topgider wrote in his unpublished memoir, which he gave to me a few months after our first meeting. "She had this air about her of being easily startled, of being timid."[29]

Hevidar, then about 18 years old, was the second in her family to join the PKK. A sister had joined before her, but nobody had heard news of her since and it seemed likely she had died in a clash. Perhaps because of this, Hevidar had not told her parents about her plans—in fact, as she later told Topgider, one reason she joined was to escape her parents, who argued constantly—but now that she was inside the rebel group she was having second thoughts. She had grown up in a city in central Turkey and she found it difficult to adjust to living in the open in the mountains. There was no opportunity to take a bath and she missed her normal, everyday clothing.

One day, Hevidar came to Topgider's tent and told him, "I can't do it, I can't stand it." She sat near the small, wood-burning stove that kept Topgider's tent warm and cried. "This life is too hard for me."

It was not the first time Topgider, a veteran commander, had faced such a problem. New recruits, especially those like Hevidar who arrived at the start of winter when fighting dwindled and the living conditions worsened, often were bored and unhappy and some wanted to quit. "[People] romanticized the guerrilla life from books they had read and films they had seen," he wrote, "but the situation was not at all like that. The life was difficult."

All commanders struggled with the question of what to do with rebels who wanted to leave. There were no easy answers. Militants who returned home might be detained by police and forced to give up information about where their units were based and which villages helped them. Or they might offer up the information on their own to avoid a prison sentence. "Every time someone ran away, our supply depots were uncovered [by the soldiers] . . . the villagers who helped us were captured," complained Topgider.

Because of this—and because the PKK's ideology did not allow for anybody to reject the struggle—rebels rarely were allowed to quit the group. Topgider tried to convince the young woman that she would adjust to the life. When she still seemed unhappy, he promised that once spring came and the rebels could move around again, he would send her to a city to work for the PKK there. She was so pleased with this news that she relaxed and the two soon were just talking—"we talked a lot," Topgider recalled fondly in his memoir.

The rebels split up into four, small groups for the duration of the winter and settled in and around a thickly forested valley about an hour's hike from a Turkish military base. It was not as dangerous as it seemed. The closely packed trees offered natural protection and the heavy snow made it unlikely soldiers would stray too far from their base. Topgider's fighters strung up large tents—three for the men, one for the women—made of thick, nylon sheeting anchored by thin, wooden poles and warmed by wood-burning stoves. Days, they cleaned the snow off the tents, gathered wood, baked bread, collected water, and held political seminars. Nights, they crowded into one tent and entertained each other with songs, theater pieces, and stories. With roads closed by the snow and the mountains of Garzan impassable, it sometimes seemed as if they were the only ones in the world.

"In this narrow valley, a world was created out of 30 people and four tents," Topgider wrote. "In some ways, we forgot the enemy and they forgot us."

Rebels fighting inside Turkey rarely had the luxury of relaxing or the time to develop close ties. The constant struggle to ensure supplies, secure temporary bases, plan attacks, and defend against Turkish attack left little energy for anything else. Besides, rebels constantly were coming and going—they were shifted around in small groups for reconnaissance and operations, sent to other parts of the region to deliver messages, or left behind somewhere to arrange shipments of food and clothing—and they died frequently and unexpectedly in battles and in accidents. But in the winter months, when fighting basically was suspended, life fell into an almost monotonous routine that suddenly gave room for friendships, and more, to develop. Topgider, for one, started to notice Hevidar, who herself seemed to be noticing him. "During the [political] lessons, we frequently looked at each other," wrote Topgider. "When we ran into each other we would stop and talk."

Hevidar had adjusted to the guerrilla life and she now was energetic and enthusiastic. She eagerly joined in the hikes to nearby villages for supplies and easily scrambled over the snow-covered paths. Her enthusiasm encompassed Topgider as well. On the nights she had guard duty—the guards' main duty was to make sure the stoves in each tent stayed lit, otherwise the air immediately froze—she usually arranged to be assigned to the tent where Topgider stayed. If he was awake when she arrived, she would drop her gun and sit down next to him. If he was asleep, she noisily shoved firewood into the stove until he woke up. Their conversations did not veer much off the normal topics of politics and war, but Topgider was certain they were trying to say something else.

"How we talked and how we looked at each other was completely different," Topgider explained. "Maybe between us an emotional relationship started, I do not know this for sure, but inside me, there was a sort of mixed up feeling, something between compassion and love."

Love was not unknown in the PKK, but it was a forbidden and dangerous luxury.[30] Fighters needed to be on guard constantly and love got in the way. "Feelings softened us, they drew us away from the painful realties of our lives," wrote Topgider. "The enemy had no compassion. We had to be on guard all the time."

Love, of course, could not really be forbidden. But close relationships between members of the opposite sex were looked at suspiciously—even repeatedly greeting someone of the opposite sex could invite questions—and sexual relations were not allowed. There were, of course, rumors of exceptions. It was fairly well-known that certain high-powered commanders, all men, had sexual relationships with some women fighters in their groups; there were similar rumors concerning Ocalan.

But such relations were done on the sly. For a commander, rumors of a sexual relationship could endanger one's reputation as a committed, dedicated PKK member.

"What you would hear sometimes was that someone had relations with a certain girl and then his career was finished, his respect was lost," said Neval, a female commander.

Respect was not the only thing lost. Sexual contact was reason to be arrested and put on trial. Sometimes, the punishment was death.

"There were some stories," added one militant, "some people were arrested, there were some people killed [because of love]."

Execution was an extreme way to punish people for love and sex, but it was imperative to maintain some sort of boundary between the young men and women in the PKK. Before they joined the rebel group, many fighters lived sexually sheltered lives. Girls and boys did not normally mix unless they were close relatives; girls were expected to remain virgins until marriage. Now, young men and women were operating side by side, even sleeping not far from one another in their makeshift mountain camps. Some sort of moral control had to be exerted. Otherwise, not only would there be chaos, but also Kurdish families would not allow their children to join.

"I think that in one way, it had to be forbidden," admitted Batufa, herself a sheltered 15-year-old high school student when she joined the PKK. "If not, the Kurdish people never would have joined. But it was extreme. Even for saying hello to someone [from the opposite sex] you could be arrested."

Some commanders took a soft line, either ignoring or gently warning couples to restrain from physical contact, but all tried to keep this under control. Now Topgider, who had often rebuked fighters who he believed were getting too close, found himself falling into the same situation. One day, Hevidar showed him photographs of herself from before she joined the PKK.

"She was rather pretty," Topgider wrote, an almost-embarrassed tone seeping into the sentence. "She looked very pretty in those other clothes."

Another day, Topgider noticed that her clothes—the rebels all wore similar loose, green pants and shirts, with heavy shawls and extra sweaters in the winter—had rips in them. He suggested she take something new from their storage supplies. "We had a lot of clothing, our depots were full," he recalled. But Hevidar shrugged off the suggestion. "It doesn't matter," she told him, "I've gotten used to things."

Topgider was unsure how to respond. "I didn't want her in such old clothing," he admitted. Once, after she ate an onion for the vitamin C, he offered to show her how to identify other, less smelly plants, that also contained vitamin C. In that world, it was one of the few ways he could show he cared.

On the morning of the 55th day in their valley camp, Topgider went out of his tent to smoke a cigarette. He noticed a helicopter passing overhead. In a region full of military bases and snow-blocked roads, helicopters were not unusual. But this one hovered at the valley's edge—as if signaling—and then two Cobra attack helicopters swept up from behind the first and headed toward the PKK camp.

From the sky, the Cobras opened fire on the valley, ripping into the tents. Topgider, who had not put on his white snow camouflage coveralls before leaving the tent, stood rooted to the spot, afraid that any movement would attract attention. The helicopter gunships continued to pound the valley and the hillsides around it, cutting off escape routes. Two rebels ran to Topgider and motioned him to follow them up a half-hidden, narrow mountain pass. It led to the top of the hill, where Turkish soldiers would least expect them to flee. As the men began the difficult ascent, rebels in other parts of the valley began similar climbs. Once on the hilltop, they quickly dug trenches in the snow and crouched low, hoping to blend in.

When the attack helicopters finally withdrew, Topgider counted and recounted his fighters. Some were missing. One was Hevidar. More time passed. Two more rebels turned up, a man and a woman, and then another man. "What's the situation?" Topgider asked the last arrival. "What's happened?" A look of distress passed over the new arrival's face. "Two dead . . . Hevidar and Canda. The helicopters first opened fire on the women's tent. They probably left the tent too late." There was no time to mourn. Fighter jets had turned up in the sky and were passing overhead, dropping bombs on the valley. It was daytime and hard to hide. The rebels scattered, with a plan to meet in a certain village after dark. A helicopter caught sight of Topgider and opened fire; he retreated into the mountain pass, throwing himself into a narrow pit. When the Turkish air force finally quit, Topgider slowly got up. Some rebels, meanwhile, went back to the valley and scavenged what they could, including Hevidar's rifle. Topgider took the rifle.

Topgider never told Hevidar that he was in love with her; he barely admitted this to himself. "I didn't want to tell her about my feelings," Topgider wrote in neat, blue-inked words that move evenly across the unlined pages of his unfinished memoir. "To love is something beautiful, but we had no choice but to adjust our feelings and our behavior according to [two things], death and killing. Or else we would not be able to survive."

10

Mixing War and Politics, 1991–1993

BEFORE SNOW STARTED to fall in the mountains that cut across the Kurdish regions of northern Iraq and Turkey, Turkish jets began their counterattacks on PKK bases in northern Iraq. The bombing raids, which stretched from August 1991 to May 1992, were aimed at driving PKK rebels away from the Turkish border. But it was hard to pinpoint targets. The deep gorges and mountainside caves offered impenetrable shelter. Turkish ground troops, who sometimes took part, had little luck dislodging the rebels.

The Turkish attacks raised some uncomfortable questions for the United States and allies Britain and France. These three countries had agreed on a safe haven for Iraqi Kurds to protect them from Saddam Hussein's wrath and, specifically, the Iraqi air force was barred from flying over the safe haven. Yet meanwhile, Turkish jets were streaming across the northern Iraqi skies to attack PKK bases. And Kurds in Turkey were complaining of state repression of their identity and of military attacks on their villages. It was hard for Turkish Kurds to understand why Kurds in Iraq deserved protection while those in Turkey did not. Some international commentators, equally perturbed by the distinction, floated the idea of the good Kurd/bad Kurd syndrome. Kevin McKiernan, who made a film by the same name, explained: "'Good Kurds' are those in Iraq: they are Saddam Hussein's victims, whom we want to help. 'Bad Kurds' are those waging an armed insurrection against Turkey, an American ally: they are the receiving end of US weaponry."[1] It was that simple.

But the Turkish military attacks sometimes were sloppy. Iraqi Kurdish villages got hit and civilian Iraqi Kurds were killed or wounded. Iraqi Kurdish officials, struggling to build up their own administration, assumed the accidents were on purpose. They believed that the Turkish military wanted to send them a warning: Either they help push the PKK out of the region, or they would be treated as part of the problem.

"The Turkish government's goal is to make us fight with the PKK,"[2] complained Celalet Taha Mazhar, an official of Talabani's party in Zakho. Barzani reportedly called on Ankara to guard its own border, rather than make the Iraqi Kurds responsible for ensuring a level of security that apparently even the Turkish army could not provide.

The Iraqi Kurdish leadership was reluctant to be dragged into the conflict between Turkey and the PKK, but Massoud Barzani and Jalal Talabani knew that the stability of their safe haven depended at least partly on Ankara's goodwill. Turkish support for the safe haven was necessary. The allied flights that patrolled over northern Iraq took off from a NATO base inside Turkey. Every six months the mandate for the operation, called Operation Provide Comfort, had to be renewed by the Turkish parliament. Besides, Iraqi Kurds relied on Turkey as their main outlet to the world, using the Habur border crossing to get goods and people in and out. "We consider relations with Turkey to be extremely vital,"[3] noted Barzani.

Ankara, too, saw the benefit of direct relations with the Iraqi Kurdish leadership, even as it sought to crush the Turkish Kurdish rebel movement. This shift in attitude was led by Turkish President Turgut Ozal, who had come to believe that Ankara needed to jettison its fear of all things Kurdish if it was to play an active role in the Middle East. Ozal had dragged a reluctant Turkey into siding with the U.S.-led coalition in the 1991 Gulf War and in March of the same year he secretly met with Talabani and a representative of Barzani. Ozal admitted to the meeting a few days later, shocking a country used to viewing all Kurdish leaders as implacable foes.

"Everyone meets with these leaders, if we don't meet, we won't be able to control what is happening, we will be left off the stage,"[4] argued Ozal.

The Turkish political and military establishments had not abandoned their suspicion of Kurdish national demands, even outside Turkey's borders, but Ozal believed that close ties to the Iraqi Kurds would give Turkey influence over north Iraq and over any political accommodation later forged with Baghdad. The Iraqi Kurds seemed likely to end up with at least low-level autonomy, if not some sort of federation, in which they managed most of their own affairs.

This sort of solution was anathema to the Turkish establishment, but Ozal was appeared willing to risk that even a federated Iraq, with a Kurdish federal state, might not be a danger to Turkey's interests.

He also thought that forging relations with the Iraqi Kurds might show Turkish Kurds that their government was not implacably opposed to Kurds, in general, only to the PKK's violence.[5] For Ozal, the key was to reduce the armed strength of the PKK by pushing the Iraqi Kurds to deny the PKK use of northern Iraq.

Ankara made clear to the Iraqi Kurdish leadership that they needed to help halt PKK attacks from northern Iraq and Talabani, after his first meeting in Ankara, alluded to the usefulness of a nonviolent struggle. "If you are asking what sort of politics I would make if I were in the PKK's place," Talabani told *Yeni Ulke,* a Turkish-Kurdish newspaper close to the PKK, in the summer of 1991, "I would say, leave aside the armed struggle for one year and I would propose solving the Kurdish problem with dialogue."[6]

But the PKK showed no interest in halting its attacks and Ankara sought to use the power vacuum in northern Iraq to its advantage. Turkey's military cross-border raids between late 1991 and early 1992 accomplished little concrete. The PKK's strength inside Turkey was growing and its ability to use northern Iraq as a base camp and a staging ground for attacks was unimpeded. Barzani and Talabani, worried about the effects of continued Turkish cross-border raids, hinted to the PKK that they should at least relocate away from the border. But this only worsened tensions between the Turkish and Iraqi groups. In the summer of 1992, a series of apparently tit-for-tat killings of Iraqi Kurds linked to the PKK and those opposed to the PKK took place in the border town Zakho. Subsequently, Barzani's fighters, seeking revenge for the death of one of their men, threatened to attack a nearby PKK camp.[7]

PKK militants, convinced that Turkey was using Barzani's fighters as a proxy force, clamped a blockade on the one road leading into north Iraq from Turkey. The Turkish and Turkish-Kurdish truck drivers who plied the Habur crossing took the PKK's threats seriously and traffic dropped from about 500 trucks daily to less than a dozen. Not only did this underscore the PKK's power, but it also hurt the Iraqi Kurds' newly formed Kurdistan Regional Government, which received a great deal of revenue from the fees levied on trucks crossing at Habur.

When the PKK lifted its blockade a month later, neither Barzani nor Talabani were in the mood to negotiate.

"The PKK has to make a choice," Talabani said. "Either they will stop using north Iraq as a military base . . . or they should go to their own areas [inside Turkey] and operate according to their own strategy."[8]

Ocalan simply ignored him. Northern Iraq was too important for the PKK to quit, and even more so now that Syria finally had acceded to Turkey's demands and ordered the Bekaa Valley Mahsum Korkmaz Academy closed in September 1992. The PKK received some walled-in parcels of land in Damascus, but these were not suited to military training and could not hold nearly as many people as the Bekaa camp. Besides, the PKK needed its camps in northern Iraq to ensure easy access to Turkey.

Birakuji: The Bloody Fight Between Kurds

The PKK staged an enormous raid inside Turkey at the end of September. Hundreds of rebels streamed across the border from northern Iraq and attacked the Turkish Derecik Jandarma border outpost. Twenty-three soldiers and five village guards were killed. Turkish soldiers pursued the rebels back across the border into Iraq, killing more than 100.[9] A few days later, on October 2, some 5,000 Iraqi Kurdish fighters attacked PKK positions along the border. Soon, Turkish planes were carrying out bombing raids over the same areas.

PKK military commanders in the border region were unprepared for the onslaught. Their supplies had long since been arranged in nearby depots designed to carry them through the harsh winter, leaving them little choice but to defend their encampments. Their fighters, too, were less than perfect for such a war. The more experienced rebels were inside Turkey, and half of the estimated 2,000 militants in the border camps were not really fighters. Either they were too young, too ill, or simply too inexperienced to fight.

Neval, a university student who joined the PKK about a month before the war broke out, remembered how she ran around the Hakurk camp south of the Turkish-Iraq-Iranian border triangle, fearlessly delivering supplies back and forth to fighters. "I didn't know how people die yet," she recalled, sitting in her apartment in Germany, holding her new baby on her lap. "I would see the [Turkish] jets overhead, and I just kept going. After I saw a woman die, I felt differently."

Kurds fighting Kurds was not very popular, especially not when they appeared to be doing so on behalf of a country that repressed its own Kurdish minority. Within two weeks, Talabani, always more interested in negotiating than fighting, started to moderate his tone. But Barzani, whose traditional area of control inside north Iraq overlapped with the PKK's expanding military encampments, reasserted his intent to push the PKK out of the border region.

The PKK, meanwhile, was suffering. The group did not have the strength or supplies to defend its camps, yet militants could not abandon their depots. Turkish ground troops, backed by fighter jets, entered northern Iraq around the middle of the month. In the camps close to the Turkish border, the number of PKK dead rose.

"People were exhausted, they hadn't slept, these weren't the same people you had met the month before when first arriving in the camp," said Orhan, a rebel in the Haftanin encampment, which saw the brunt of fighting with Turkish and Iraqi Kurdish ground forces.

The situation was not much better in other encampments, even those closer to the Iranian border. By the end of the month, Ocalan's brother Osman, commander of the Hakurk camp closer to Iran, announced that supplies were almost finished. They had two choices: Either to admit defeat and strike a deal with the Iraqi Kurds or die fighting. "He told everyone that either we fight until we commit suicide, or we do a political deal," recalled Neval.

Under normal circumstances, Abdullah Ocalan would make the final decision, but contact with him was difficult to establish. The chief of the Cukurca camp, Faruk (Nasir) Bozkurt, accepted Osman's proposal; Murat (Cemal) Karayilan, commander of Haftanin, refused, calling the decision opportunistic. But Osman—described by many who know him as a political realist—refused to back down. Neval said Osman was not happy about his decision but that he saw no other way: "He said doing this was as bitter as drinking poison, but I am going to do it."

Osman sent a team to meet with the representatives of Barzani and Talabani. On October 30, Osman Ocalan and the prime minister of the regional Kurdish government signed an agreement for the PKK to withdraw from the border and halt its use of northern Iraq for military operations against Turkey.[10] In return, the PKK would receive a new camp near the Iranian border and it would be free to engage in nonviolent political activities in the area under Iraqi Kurdish control. In the beginning of November, bedraggled PKK fighters began the walk to their new camp.

"We didn't want to go, we were all depressed," said Neval. "It was like we had lost." The Turkish army kept up its own fight through the first week in November, focusing their operations around Haftanin, where some PKK holdouts initially refused to put down their weapons.

The PKK's forces relocated to Zeli, an old military encampment of Talabani's close to the Iranian border, near an abandoned village filled with half broken-down concrete houses. The PKK fighters set up tents for themselves on the barren hilltops and in the valleys.

"There were some people who ran away, people were demoralized," said Orhan. "There were a lot of problems, with food, with clothing."

The camp quickly filled up with the 300 or more wounded, some of whom were transported with the help of the Iraqi Kurdish fighters. The PKK announced that 161 of its fighters were killed in the war. The Iraqi Kurdish fighters were said to have lost about the same number. Turkish military casualties probably were not very high given the limited use of ground troops.

The Turkish military proudly hoisted the nation's flag in Haftanin, but then withdrew its forces and warned the Iraqi Kurds that it was their responsibility to keep the border secure. Attempts to create a buffer zone a few kilometers wide failed because of what one Turkish military officer later complained was the unwillingness of Barzani and Talabani to assist. But neither man was willing to be Ankara's full-time militia in the south, certainly not against other Kurds. And, as the Turkish military knew, it was impossible to fully secure the high mountains and deep ravines that ran along the border. If it had been possible, the Turkish army would have done it long ago.

The internal agreement between the PKK and the Iraqi Kurdish leadership did not last very long either. PKK fighters forced to turn over their weapons when they evacuated border camps got them back later on or picked up replacement weapons on the local market. Within a few months, the rebels started moving back into their old camps and they soon were well entrenched again along the border. Neither Talabani nor Barzani were interested in risking another war to actively block the PKK. They had their own problems, notably personal and political differences that disrupted their power-sharing agreement and less than two years later would spark a war between their own forces.

For all parties involved, the outcome underlined the near-impossibility of a military solution to the PKK's presence in northern Iraq. In this war and in subsequent large-scale Turkish cross-border raids in 1995 and 1997, the Turkish military always faced the same insurmountable problems. First, the mountains and ravines that made up the border formed natural defenses that were hard to breach. By the time they were breached, the rebels were long gone—after the 1992 war, the PKK never again tried to defend territory and instead relocated fighters as necessary. Air campaigns were only of limited success, thanks again to the rough terrain and the difficulty of pinpointing the caves where rebels took shelter. And even if the military raid did manage to disrupt PKK camps and operations, this ended the minute the troops withdraw. Then the rebels were free to relocate themselves back near the border.

Turkey's hopes that the Iraqi Kurds would help them beat back the PKK never succeeded. Talabani, while quick to criticize the PKK, was loathe to fight them. Barzani often had his own reasons for wanting to pressure the PKK, which was his rival for control of the border region, but even his fighters were reluctant to be dragged into a long battle. Apart from everything else, there was a certain plus to keeping the PKK on the border. In case Turkey ever turned its attention to the Iraqi Kurds—maybe to foment instability in hopes of undercutting a nascent Iraqi Kurdish state—PKK rebels could always be incited to attack.

"In the end, we were all Kurds," said Neval.

Failed Politics

The nationalist Kurdish deputies elected to the Turkish parliament on the Social Democratic ticket in October 1991 found it impossible to operate effectively.[11] Colleagues in the other political parties did not want them to take up the Kurdish problem. Relations between the Kurdish deputies and the others, strained ever since the Kurdish nationalist show at the oath-taking ceremony, continued to deteriorate amid the Kurdish deputies' criticisms of state policies and their demands for Kurdish rights.

"Some people in the parliament wouldn't even look at us, we couldn't talk," complained Mehmet Emin Sever, a patrician-looking man and a surgeon before entering politics. "They would point their fingers at us and say we were protecting the PKK. We were irrelevant."

Kurdish deputies who tried to address parliament were shouted down and sometimes physically threatened. When they demanded official investigations of human rights abuses—an issue of particular concern, because the majority of abuses occurred in the Kurdish region—they were accused of working for the PKK.

Any hope they had of using their position in the government to promote real change ended in March 1992: The parliament voted overwhelmingly to extend the state of emergency in the southeast, indicating no interest in a peaceful solution. And during the Kurdish Newruz new year protests that same month, Turkish security forces shot and killed some 90 demonstrators.

In a show of protest, 14 of the deputies resigned from the Social Democrats and rejoined their old party, the People's Labor Party. "We had no choice, not after the Newruz massacre," explained Mahmut Kilinc. "The Social Democrats were part of the government and we were part of them, so we had to split off." They joined Leyla Zana and Hatip Dicle, the two deputies who caused such a furor when they spoke in Kurdish during the oath-taking ceremony. Zana and Dicle had resigned a few months earlier under pressure from the Social Democratic leadership. Later, another two Kurdish deputies also pulled out of the Social Democrats and became independents, creating an 18-strong Kurdish nationalist camp in the parliament.

Quitting the Social Democrats played well in the southeast, where Kurds increasingly felt isolated and abused by the central authorities, but it did not make the Kurdish deputies any more effective. If anything, cutting ties with the mainstream Social Democrats further marginalized them. Their attempts to challenge Turkey's treatment of the Kurdish minority were seen as proof that they were traitors to the Turkish nation.

In July 1992, the state prosecutor appealed to the constitutional court to shut down the People's Labor Party (HEP), claiming it was trying to undermine the unity of the Turkish state. Meanwhile, the Ankara prosecutor unsuccessfully sought to get the deputies stripped of their immunity so they could be tried on the death penalty on similar charges stemming from speeches they had made in the election campaign and in parliament.

The deputies' relations with their constituents in the southeast grew strained and the public enthusiasm that greeted election of the country's first openly Kurdish politicians waned. When they traveled through the southeast to meet with their voters, they were harassed and threatened by the security forces. Deputies trying to investigate abuses by the security forces were refused entry into towns and villages; the houses they stayed in were raided by the security forces and the people they met with were detained. During one visit, a gendarmerie regiment commander told parliamentarians Orhan Dogan and Leyla Zana he would drink their blood and crush them like rats.[12]

Diyarbakir HEP chairman Vedat Aydin—a popular Kurdish activist who was not a member of the PKK—was found murdered a few days after men claiming to be police took him from his apartment in July 1991. His killing marked the start of what many suspected was a new state-backed approach to use murder to do away with Kurdish activists.[13] Officials linked to HEP were at particular risk. The next year, 27 HEP officials were mysteriously murdered in the southeast. In 1993, the number of HEP officials murdered was 17, including one of the party's parliamentarians; in 1994, another 18 HEP officials were killed.[14] The inability of the Kurdish deputies to protect themselves —let alone members of their party and other Kurdish activists— weakened the legitimacy of both the political party and the political struggle.

"We go to the state, the state closes the doors," complained Kurdish deputies Mahmut Alinak and Orhan Dogan. "We go to the people, but because we can't solve our own problems, by now their trust in us is broken. . . . Sometimes, the state does not even allow us to go to our own electoral regions. Under these conditions, we no longer think it will be useful to stay as parliamentarians. That's why we are thinking of resigning from parliament."[15]

The Assembly

Ocalan had a somewhat related idea. Ever since the 1991 national elections, Ocalan warned that if the Turkish state refused to work with Kurds to find a solution to the Kurdish problem, then Kurds could set up their own national assembly in Kurdistan. The assembly, envisioned as an umbrella group for all Kurds, would issue laws, make political decisions, and represent the Kurds internationally. It would be PKK-dominated, but not an arm of the rebels: the goal was to make it a legitimate governing body for Kurds everywhere, but especially Turkey's Kurds. PKK activists argued there was no reason for further delay.

"The Kurdish parliamentarians could not make their voices heard in the Turkish parliament," said Murat Dagdelen, a PKK activist who favored withdrawing from the Turkish political system. "This was one reason why the idea of building up institutions belonging to Kurds gained strength among Kurdish intellectuals and politicians."

There was another, important reason to consider moving ahead with a national assembly. The Iraqi Kurds created one in 1992 and this helped gained them political respect and legitimacy. "Such an assembly could help Ocalan win international legitimacy," Dagdelen pointed out. "And Ocalan had the need for legitimacy."

In November 1992, red, green, and yellow-colored posters were slapped up across Europe, calling on Kurds to vote in PKK-organized elections to pick 15 delegates for their own national body. Ballot boxes were placed in PKK-affiliated cultural centers and associations across Europe. Rival groups were invited to take part, but none accepted. Their experiences with the PKK to date had not been very positive, and they had doubts about Ocalan's willingness to respect the authority of an assembly. Kemal Burkay's Kurdistan Socialist Party was particularly brusque in its refusal. "Their criticisms of the PKK were very harsh," recalled Dagdelen, who handled some of the negotiations. "They explained they would not make any ties with the PKK under any circumstances."[16]

Ocalan envisioned the assembly as replacing any Kurdish representation in Turkey's parliament, but he did not think it necessary for the deputies in the People's Labor Party to immediately join in. Instead, PKK activists sought out other candidates to represent Turkey's Kurds, tapping them individually to take part. They focused on leading members of the Kurdish nationalist community—lawyers, intellectuals, human rights workers, and former members of rival groups—hoping to come up with a list that would give the assembly legitimacy.

"They asked me but I refused," said one man, then an official with the nongovernmental Human Rights Association. "I just did not think it would work. Not that I said that openly," he added hastily.

Zeynel Abidin Han, a high school teacher approached about joining the assembly, also wondered whether the PKK really could follow through on such a seemingly democratic endeavor. Han had spent three years in the Diyarbakir prison for membership in the more intellectual Kurdish group Rizgari and, like other unaffiliated activists considering the proposal, he was uncomfortable with the PKK's violence against dissenters and Ocalan's cult of personality. Still, it was obvious that the PKK's war had raised the profile of Kurds in Turkey in a way that Rizgari's clandestine publications never did.

"My thinking had not changed and the PKK had not changed, but the fact was, there was no other Kurdish group," Han earnestly explained to me one afternoon in the print shop he runs in Berlin. "It was either the PKK or the state. We couldn't support the state, so that left the PKK."

In early March, Han packed a small bag and said good-bye to his wife and small child. "This sort of departure was normal in Kurdish families," laughed Han, when I asked whether he minded leaving his family for an unknown period of time. "I saw this as a historical duty. This was the mentality driving people at the time."

PKK militants guided Han and some of the other delegates across the border into northern Iraq—Turkey's planned new border controls notwithstanding, the trip was easy—and from there they hiked to Zeli camp. The camp, which straddled the Iraqi-Iranian border, now contained about 1,600 rebels. During the day, delegates debated the planned parliament in an enormous tent filled with rough-hewn benches. At night, they slept outside like the rebels or in scavenged U.S. military tents.

Ocalan had indicated the assembly would be free and democratic and the delegates, about 80 percent of whom had no direct link to the PKK, took this seriously. So did some of the PKK militants who wandered into the tent to listen to the sessions. Han remembered one session in particular:

> We picked a minister for women's affairs, for religion, for trade and even human rights. I remember some people said we didn't need a human rights ministry because we were fighting for human rights and one person, a PKK militant, stood up and said, "there is torture, I

have tortured people and we need a ministry and we need sanctions for this."

The delegates, 130 in all, drew up hundreds of pages of laws and formed committees for everything else. Meetings lasted hours at a time and discussions continued after hours. On their days off, they walked in the mountains of Kurdistan. The scenery was beautiful.

"Except for the food, it could have been a holiday," joked Han.

Making Peace—Briefly

Ocalan could be paranoid about protecting his leadership and obsessive about his own importance, but he also could be politically savvy and reasonable. Ocalan's plan for the Kurdistan National Assembly (KUM) made sense as long as the Turkish political system refused to engage the Kurds' newly elected representatives, but it was a second-best solution. Although Ocalan promised his guerrillas they would fight until they pushed Turkish troops out of the Kurdish region, he was smart enough to realize the most likely solution was a negotiated one. For years he made clear his interest in political talks with Ankara, issuing statements in which he hedged his demand for a separate state and focused on the need for Turks and Kurds to work out their differences together.

"We believe that there is no problem we have with the Turkish people that we cannot solve,"[17] Ocalan stated as early as 1988.

Turkey's political establishment, already hostile to engaging the elected Kurdish parliamentarians, was unwilling to consider something as radical as direct talks with people they called terrorists. But Ocalan believed that Turkish President Turgut Ozal, who turned into a maverick liberal reformer after moving out of the prime ministry, was leaning toward a political settlement.

Ozal also hinted at this in a meeting with three of the Kurdish parliamentarians late in 1992, reportedly telling them that he could do nothing unless the PKK ended its armed battle: "If the guns can fall silent, I can start working on convincing certain circles and on developing some projects."[18]

There was good reason to believe Ozal was serious about reform. He successfully pushed to end the military rule-era ban on written and spoken Kurdish in 1991. Around the same time, he broke with tradition and established direct relations with the Iraqi Kurdish leadership. He seemed unafraid of the powerful military and made public comments that challenged Turkey's official silence on Kurdish identity, once even announcing that he himself probably had Kurdish blood.[19]

Ozal repeated his interest in a ceasefire to Iraqi Kurdish leader Jalal Talabani, who maintained cordial relations with both the Turkish president and the PKK leader.[20] Talabani again suggested to Ocalan that he take steps to ease the atmosphere. "I said to him, 'Are you ready to stop the war and make peace?' He said to me, 'yes.'"[21]

Ocalan did not mean he was going to end the war and disarm. It would take more than whispered hints for him to do that, but he had little to lose from a ceasefire. In mid-March, Ocalan declared a 25-day unilateral ceasefire, starting on March 20, a day before the Kurdish New Year. In addition, he promised that the celebrations, usually a time for violent, pro-PKK demonstrations, would be peaceful. Ocalan, who made this announcement at a news conference with Talabani in Bar Elias town in the Bekaa, appealed to the Turkish government to use the lull in fighting to start reforms.

Turkish officials reacted to the ceasefire announcement with suspicion mixed with disinterest. "The state does not negotiate with bandits,"[22] Interior Minister Ismet Sezgin noted, not bothering to offer up any new ideas on how to handle the situation.

Turkey's Chief of General Staff, General Dogan Gures, repeated the well-worn observation that there was no Kurdish problem, just a southeast problem, and the military kept up its operations in the southeast. Some state officials insisted that the PKK was on the verge of collapse, causing columnist Mehmet Ali Birand to remind people that the "basic problem . . . is not Apo and the PKK, but the Kurdish problem."[23]

When Ocalan had made his ceasefire announcement—dressed seriously in a suit and tie, instead of the khaki pants and loose sport shirts he usually favored—he made clear he believed his real interlocutor was Ozal. "Is Ozal sincere or not? I hope he is," Ocalan said. "Has Ozal got the power behind him to take a courageous approach to developments? Does he really want to take some steps forward in this matter?"[24]

Ozal was not saying. The Turkish president had hinted to Kurdish deputies that he had a plan—at a second meeting in early March, he apparently spoke even more directly about his desire to solve the Kurdish problem[25]—but he needed to take care not to appear to be engaging in any dialogue with the PKK chief, no matter how indirect. And he could not be sure that Ocalan—or the "lunatic," as Ozal sometimes referred to him—was serious about halting the fighting. "Keep pushing that lunatic," Ozal told Talabani after the ceasefire was announced. "Go push that lunatic not to start fighting [again]."[26]

Using Talabani as an indirect, unofficial go-between, Ocalan passed on the message that the ceasefire would be extended. Ozal received word of this as he returned from a state visit to Central Asia in mid-April. His pleasure apparently was muted by his concern that the coalition government was neither inventive nor courageous enough to take advantage of the situation.

"Because of these pompous fools, a very important opportunity will be lost,"[27] Turkish journalist Cengiz Candar recalled Ozal as telling him. When Candar asked whom he meant, Ozal said he meant the government. "Don't they see what the problem is?" Ozal complained to Candar. "I have a path to a solution in my mind."[28]

Ocalan formally announced an extension of the ceasefire on April 16 in a second news conference in the Bekaa. He called on Ankara to grant the Kurds cultural rights, end abuses, issue a general amnesty, and lift all restrictions on Kurdish broadcasting and education. This did not mean that Ocalan had abandoned hopes of a Turkish-Kurdish federation, or even the dream of independence, but it showed that he well understood the political limitations within which Ozal would have to act. He also understood, even if his speeches sometimes spoke otherwise, that Kurds might have to settle for a lot less than independence.

The next day Ocalan, eager to hear the government's reaction, switched on a television. The news was unexpectedly bleak: Ozal had suffered a heart attack. By midday, he was declared dead.

Hoping not to lose the political momentum, Ocalan immediately reaffirmed his commitment to the ceasefire. But Turkey's politicians were busy with the domestic political shifts that came with the death of their charismatic and forceful president. Meanwhile, the loss of Ozal's restraining vision left the security forces freer to assert themselves.

During the first ceasefire period, PKK rebels complained that the

Turkish soldiers did not halt their attacks and now the attacks seemed to be better coordinated and fiercer. On May 19, about a dozen rebels were killed in an attack near Kulp, which was under provincial commander Semdin Sakik's control.

Sakik warned Ocalan that the guerrillas were losing respect. Ocalan, speaking by wireless, told the rebels they were free to retaliate if attacked.

"Apo sent a message that you could defend yourself," said Dr. Suleyman, at the time Sakik's deputy.

Not long afterward, Sakik decided on a coordinated show of strength and ordered rebel units in Amed (Diyarbakir) to cut all the province's main roads. This sort of operation was favored by the rebels because it asserted their authority—they checked identity cards, lectured drivers about Kurdish nationalism, and shot the luckless state employees they found—with a low degree of risk. The Turkish military was not eager to confront PKK rebels on these remote stretches of highway and sometimes sent off-duty soldiers on unmarked buses to reduce the chances they would be identified at any roadblock.

The same night that Sakik ordered the main roads cut, one of these unmarked buses was on its way from Bingol to Elazig. Aboard were 35 off-duty unarmed soldiers, along with a few civilians. The bus was stopped at a PKK roadblock set up by rebels operating under the command of two battalion commanders. The Turkish soldiers were ordered off the bus, lined up on the side of the highway, and shot. So were the four teachers on the bus. Only two soldiers survived. When news broke a few hours later, even Ocalan was stunned.

The killing of the 33 soldiers in late May marked the end of the ceasefire.[29] Ocalan insisted the PKK would still honor the ceasefire, but there was nobody left to believe him. Some Kurds argued that forces within the state deliberately sent unarmed soldiers on the bus that night, hoping for such an attack to break the ceasefire. But even such an unlikely scenario did not absolve the rebels of their responsibility. The PKK officially ended its ceasefire on June 8, but by then the Turkish military was already carrying out its own offensive.

"The killing of the soldiers was a turning point," said Kucuk Zeki, who had just been named to head a 200-strong person *tabur* in the Mus area, not far from where the attack took place. "The state launched a very big operation against us. . . . The war got much worse."

Innocents in the Mountains

The delegates to the PKK's planned Assembly came to Zeli camp thinking they were engaged in important work to build up the basic, governing institutions of a new state. The ceasefire Ocalan declared in March made them believe the Assembly could play a role as an interlocutor between the PKK and Ankara; when the ceasefire essentially collapsed in May, they returned to their initial program of creating an authority to peacefully promote Kurdish political demands.

But the delegates had difficulty getting support for their work. PKK rebels in Zeli camp viewed the newcomers as opportunists and accused them of trying to profit off those willing to die for a Kurdish state. The delegates, some of them elderly activists with their own long histories of political fighting, were pressed to trade in their civilian clothes for military garb and join in armed training.

"We [militants] saw them as unimportant," said Neval, who had made the long trek to Zeli from Hakurk with Osman Ocalan's forces at the end of the October 1992 war with the Iraqi Kurds. "We were revolutionaries and we were fighting for revolution for our people. They were engaged in a type of politics we saw as paralyzed, ineffective."

Ocalan's interest in the Assembly also waned. Syria had made clear that it was uncomfortable with the Assembly—probably because it smacked too much of a real, independent Kurdish movement—and Ozal's death had left Ocalan without any clear political interlocutor. Besides, a functioning Assembly would cut into Ocalan's dictatorial powers. Around August, Ocalan ordered the Assembly disbanded.

The PKK chief faced unexpected opposition. Murat Dagdelen, the Assembly's chairman and a former HEP official, believed the Assembly offered Kurds the chance to internationalize their demands and broaden their appeal. Despite Dagdelen's loyalty to the PKK—and by association, Ocalan—he had started to think Kurds would be better off with a more varied leadership and he saw the Assembly as a way to balance Ocalan's authority. Dagdelen's concern had been sparked by a visit to the Bekaa the year before, when he met Ocalan for the first time and sat through one of his speeches.

"The speech had nothing to do with my questions or the political issues," recalled Dagdelen. "There was something like 500 people there, the whole speech was about him, how wonderful he was. It went on for four hours. I thought to myself, what will I do? I have fallen into the hands of a madman."

Dagdelen, who has a New York-styled self-deprecating sense of humor (although he has never been there), laughed. "But on the one side there is the struggle, on the other side are your plans and then there is this man. I tried to convince myself things were not so bad. Besides, how long could he live? It's enough if we just go ahead with the struggle and succeed."

But now, Ocalan's decision to disband the Assembly directly challenged not just Dagdelen's plans, but his authority as chairman of the Assembly. Dagdelen refused Ocalan's order that all delegates write a report saying they agreed with the PKK leader's decision.

"I wrote that I didn't accept this and that no-one can disband the Assembly on their own, that this body reflected the will of the people," Dagdelen explained. A new vote was held and Dagdelen said more than 100 of the some 130 delegates voted to keep the Assembly going. Still, it was hard to stand up to armed guerrillas. "A commander named Osman came to me and said, 'you have to say you don't know why you wrote this.'" When Dagdelen did not back down, the Assembly simply was dispersed. Nobody argued back.

The Assembly's start was well planned but its end was chaotic and brutal. The delegates had taken big risks in coming to northern Iraq, now they faced new risks returning to Turkey. Some instead fled to Europe; at least four who went back—and probably closer to 12, said Dagdelen—were murdered by suspected state-backed forces.[30] Others stayed in Zeli, either joining the guerrilla force or working in the PKK's political and press operations.

As for Dagdelen, he told Osman Ocalan that he was quitting the group. "I told him there was no way of thinking except Ocalan's thinking and I don't want to stay in the party anymore."

Dagdelen is convinced the PKK wanted to kill him, but he believes the group hesitated because of concern that this would reverberate badly among the other Assembly members: Ocalan could be sensitive to things like this. Instead, PKK rebels escorted Dagdelen to a safe house in Urumiye, Iran and then unceremoniously kicked him out. By chance, at a cheap Iranian border hotel, Dagdelen ran into two Turkish Kurdish border guards looking for information about a relative in the PKK. Dagdelen offered them a phone number in exchange for help crossing into Turkey and the switch was made. In Ankara,

Dagdelen arranged for a false passport and fled to Europe. "They warned me not to talk," said Dagdelen, referring to the PKK, "but I always said everything I could."

The Assembly's collapse was to be expected. Since the mid-1980s, Ocalan had two goals: promoting the PKK's battle and protecting his own authority. When there was a conflict between the two, he always chose to protect himself. Sometimes, Ocalan took steps even before there was a conflict, just to make sure.

The problem was that not everyone knew this. Ocalan's approach was not a secret, but it was well shrouded behind claims of conspiracies against the PKK and threats to the leadership. Besides, Ocalan could be persuasive and convincing and his ideas, like the one to form a political body to promote the Kurds internationally, often were good ones, at least in theory. It helped that the PKK was the only Kurdish nationalist organization fighting the Turkish state, making it hard for Kurdish nationalists to ignore it and still be active.

Unaffiliated, or loosely affiliated, Kurdish nationalists inside Turkey were not the only ones to believe Ocalan's promises. Even Kemal Burkay, Ocalan's long-time rival, briefly changed his mind following the PKK's first ceasefire declaration. Burkay agreed to make an alliance with the PKK, hoping their two groups could work together now that Ocalan was pushing for peaceful negotiations.

"We couldn't ignore him," shrugged Burkay, "It doesn't mean we accepted everything the PKK did." Burkay's hope lasted just slightly longer than both the ceasefire and the Assembly. In the summer of 1993, the protocol collapsed. "In our protocol it said that if there were problems between the two groups, nobody would resort to violence. But the PKK didn't hold to this."

Ocalan's unwillingness to give up absolute authority was not an obstacle when the PKK was just beginning its war. But as the PKK grew bigger and its activities stretched into politics and culture, this changed. In the early 1990s, the PKK grew from a guerrilla force into a real political force, complete with associated publications, cultural institutions, and a political party. Its backers were not only villagers but also teachers, trade unionists, and lawyers. It had a strong presence in urban centers in western Turkey. All this gave the PKK enormous influence and power. But instead of taking advantage of this presence to develop even semiautonomous Kurdish institutions that could have strengthened Kurdish identity and power, Ocalan sought to harness directly these forces to promote himself and protect the PKK's dominance. As a result, Kurds were unable to develop lasting institutions that could fill the gap when the war turned against them.

The forced demise of the Kurdistan National Assembly was not only a blow for Kurdish political development, but also a blow to the autonomous or semiautonomous Kurdish activist community in Turkey. The forced flight of so many Kurdish activists not only hurt the activist community, but also was a warning to others of the limits of their power and influence.

The Final Step

PKK rebels were intent on driving Turkish state forces out of the Kurdish region and showing their authority to the few Westerners who still dared to come to the region. Tourists who wanted to visit the region's breathtaking mountains, ancient churches, and ornate mosques were warned that they needed a PKK-issued visa, available from the group's front offices in Europe. Most tourists wisely ignored the demand and the PKK retaliated in 1993 by kidnapping 20 tourists. Some were picked up when their cars were stopped at PKK roadblocks, others when they wandered too close to the mountains. All were released unharmed, but the kidnappings underscored the state's loss of control.

The main Western business in the region was small-scale oil drilling and production and foreign concerns became targets. The year before, three Turkish engineers from the international oil giant Mobil Oil were executed by the PKK. By 1993, the company had reduced staff in the field and moved out the families of Turkish workers who lived in the Batman city compound. Foreign archeological teams, plentiful in the region, were next. The PKK warned them that it was dangerous to be there; the Turkish military warned them that it could not guarantee their safety.

"The military told us in no uncertain terms not to be at the site before 7:00 A.M. and not to remain at the site past mid-afternoon," recalled American archeologist Michael Rosenberg, who was digging at a site near Batman in the summer of 1993. "The virtual admission that Turkish forces had lost control of the area at times other than full daylight came as a rude surprise." The team packed up at the end of July after being warned that the PKK was tracking their movements. "We heard recurrent rumors all along that the PKK, which obviously knew of our presence in the area, would soon demand protection money from us or even do worse."[31]

The PKK also worked to destroy what remained of Turkey's civil authority in the region.[32] Many teachers assigned to the region never showed up for work, preferring to resign rather than chance PKK threats. Hundreds of schools never opened for the school year: Some were burned down by the rebels, most shuttered because they had no teachers. In November, the PKK issued a blanket ban on all schools, warning both students and teachers to leave. In some schools, the numbers of students dropped severely, but it was mainly teachers that were targeted. That year, 34 teachers were murdered, compared with 10 the year before. Dr Suleyman's team delivered the message in a manner designed to underscore that PKK rebels could move around at will.

"We would give a letter to the village *mukhtar* [headman], and he would go to the police station the next day and tell them the PKK had come and left a letter for them," recounted Dr. Suleyman, with a grin. The letter contained the warning to the teacher. "Sometimes, the soldiers would come and set up in the village to protect the teacher. We would open fire that night and the next day, the teacher would leave and then the soldiers would leave as well."

The Turkish military clearly was on the defensive.[33] Many of its mountain bases had been abandoned and its armored convoys were attacked during daylight patrols. At night, the situation turned worse: soldiers, fearful of venturing into the unfamiliar terrain and unsure about the real loyalties of the villages they would pass, abandoned the region to the rebels. "In many places," admitted Turkish military commander Kundakci in his memoirs, "the initiative had passed into the hands of the terrorists."[34] Even the state's proxy soldiers, the village guards, were trying to turn in their weapons.

The PKK, confident of its military hold over the region, sought to tighten its already-strong political grasp. Editors and reporters who staffed local, Turkish newspaper offices in Diyarbakir, the headquarters for the Turkish press, were invited to talk to the PKK in October.[35] Such an invitation could not be ignored. Local media representatives were taken in the middle of the day by car from the city center to a mountain camp east of the city near Silvan. The PKK warned them to shut their offices or face armed retribution. Almost every newspaper closed down its local operations.

The final target was the local Turkish government. The PKK already controlled much of the state's local authorities: They had excellent informants in the municipalities and issued demands with impunity. Many municipal authorities were sympathetic to the PKK, but even those who were not acceded to the demands of the rebels. "It did not matter which party was in office," explained Dr. Suleyman, "they all helped us." But the rebels wanted to destroy Turkey's authority completely and in early 1994 they ordered people to resign their positions.

"That road we had gone on, to close newspaper offices, to get all colonialist parties to resign . . . it was because we planned to make a new state," explained Dr. Suleyman, who in 1994 was promoted to command the whole of Amed (Diyarbakir) province. "But if you do this, if you push out all colonialist powers, the uprising had to start soon."

11

Change in Fortunes, 1993–1997

THE TURKISH MILITARY turned more aggressive after the PKK broke its own ceasefire in May 1993 and killed 33 unarmed soldiers on a bus stopped at a rebel blockade. PKK attacks now were met with all-out shows of force that made little distinction between civilian and rebel. In October of that year, rebels attacked a transformer, kidnapped two workers, and burned a school in the area around the town of Lice. In the ensuing clashes, a Turkish gendarmerie commander was shot dead. The military retaliated with a blunt show of force.[1] Lice, a town of 10,000 people, was closed off to outsiders while soldiers raked the houses with gunfire. More than 30 civilians were killed and 100 wounded; houses and shops were destroyed. Turkish politicians who tried to enter the town to investigate were turned back by the military. Over the next few weeks, most of the residents fled the town. "What did happen in Lice?" An old man from Lice repeated, responding to a journalist's question. "Well, the military solution was applied in Lice."[2]

These sorts of attacks grew more frequent in 1994, driving out more and more people from the villages and towns that dotted the region.[3] In Cizre, centrally located between PKK camps in northern Iraq and its main area of operations in the Cudi Mountains, a Turkish tank brigade shelled the city-town after the gunshots were heard. One elderly man and two children, one a baby, were killed. Four others were wounded. A few days after the January incident, another Turkish shell hit a house, killing six people and wounding five, apparent retaliation for what security forces claimed was PKK gunfire. When the PKK did stage an assault on state buildings in March, the security forces opened fire, seemingly at random, on houses; village guards burned down 11 shops and gunfire destroyed the office of the pro-PKK Kurdish newspaper.

Similar Turkish attacks took place in other towns across the region, driving more and more Kurds out of their homes and into cramped quarters in Diyarbakir and cities in Turkey's west. Villages, which supplied the PKK with most of its food and intelligence information, were particularly hit hard. A clutch of five villages in the Cudi Mountains were bombed by fighter planes in March, killing a total of 24 people, almost all of them elderly or children. There was no question that many villagers sympathized with the rebels, but nor was there any attempt to differentiate, anymore, between unarmed sympathizers and the armed rebels. The only distinction was whether Kurds in the rural areas would join the military's proxy village army, and so prove their loyalty, or whether they would leave their villages.

In stories repeated with increasing frequency and despair, Kurdish villagers complained that security forces (sometimes accompanied by their proxy army) turned up in the early hours of the morning, forced everyone into the center of the village, and told them to join the armed guards or to evacuate the settlement. Villagers were beaten and their houses burned: often men were taken away for questioning, some later turned up dead. The pressure and the threats were too much for most and whole villages now packed up and left.[4]

At the peak of this policy, in 1994, some 1,000 settlements were forcibly evacuated, compared with another 1,000 settlements emptied under mainly state pressure between 1990 and 1993.[5] Forced evacuations continued through the end of the decade, the numbers decreasing as less villages remained to be targeted. In total, somewhere between 300,000 and more than one million Kurds were driven out of their homes, only to crowd in shantytowns and slums in Diyarbakir, Adana, and cities further west, like Istanbul and Izmir. It was a tried—and often true—method for breaking guerrilla resistance and, gradually, it began to work.

"The evacuation of the villages really helped the state," Topgider admitted. "The villagers provided everything to us, supplies, material and information. When the villages were emptied, all this was taken away from us."

The army also boosted its checkpoints, especially on the smaller roads that wound their way past towns where PKK sympathizers organized supplies and the hand-off of new recruits to PKK contacts in the hills. People, especially young people whose identity cards showed them to be from another area, were pulled off and questioned. Cars filled with an unusual amount of sweaters or shoes were stopped on suspicion the goods were for the PKK. Those carrying more food than seemed necessary for a large family were closely questioned. PKK rebels began to run out of food and the number of new recruits dropped, largely because of the difficulty of reaching the rebels.

Dr. Suleyman, who in 1994 had been promoted to command rebel forces in all of Amed province, sketched a simple map for me, roughly laying out the new checkpoints and abandoned villages. "The psychological situation that created support for the PKK didn't change," he said, "but the state managed to change the physical situation. They emptied all the areas between the cities and mountains."

The Turkish army's more aggressive approach to PKK supporters occurred as part of an overall change in counterinsurgency tactics.[6] Turkish soldiers, who used to stage quick forays into the mountains and retreat by dark, now stayed for weeks at a time, sending out small, mobile units to track the guerrillas like guerrillas. The rebels, unable to move far without being sighted by the soldiers, began to lose contact with their supporters and had trouble reaching their supply depots.

"The soldiers being sent now were very professional soldiers, they knew tactics," said Azman, the former lawyer who rose in the PKK to be commander of Serhat (Agri) province. "They held huge parts of the terrain, they tried to engage us in fighting continuously. . . . You couldn't move around as easily. After a while, people's morale broke, they started to give themselves up [to the soldiers]."

The changed tactics were not limited to Agri province, a particularly difficult stretch of mountains bordered on one side by Iran. Throughout the southeast, PKK commanders were surprised by the Turkish army's new tactics. "The soldiers got experienced in mountain fighting, they used good air power and land forces," explained then-Erzurum commander Kucuk Zeki, a hint of admiration in his voice. "They started to enter areas they hadn't entered until then."

PKK rebels were still very active—in July 1994, for example, the military commander in Hakkari reported more than 20 separate guerrilla actions, including one PKK attack that killed 14 soldiers—but the Turkish retaliation took its toll.

"Unit after unit was destroyed," said Neval, a female commander who operated in Zagros, a province that straddled the Turkish-Iraqi border close to Semdinli. "You would attack a military outpost and another one was built in its place. You killed a soldier and another was sent. In 1993, we had been very successful, but in 1994, we lost a lot."

PKK fighters tried to convince Ocalan and senior commanders close to him of the need for new tactics, but their suggestions were rebuffed. "We said the people are gone [from the villages] and we need to strengthen ties with people in the cities," recalled Kucuk Zeki. "They said no, stay in the mountains. . . . We ran out of bullets, our losses grew."

PKK fighters were left with little room to maneuver.

"The military fight was not being carried out well," conceded Topgider. "If you are a commander, you have to be responsible for your area, but only Ocalan was really in charge."

Problems in Politics

The Kurdish political party HEP was important for promoting and focusing debate on the Kurdish problem and it could easily have acted as an unofficial stand-in for the rebel group, if Ankara decided on a negotiated solution. But Turkey's political establishment, especially in the wake of President Turgut Ozal's unexpected death in April 1993, never was comfortable with the outspoken HEP politicians, who refused to accept the state's claim that the problem was one of poverty and terrorism. In July 1993, the Turkish Constitutional Court closed down the HEP political party, ruling 10–1 that the party's calls for ethnic-based rights contradicted the constitution. "HEP's aims," explained the court, "resembled those of the terrorists."[7]

The court's decision had been expected—the case started nearly a year earlier—and Kurdish politicians took steps ahead of time to protect their seats in parliament. A new party, the Democracy Party (DEP), had been registered in the spring of 1993 and by the time HEP was closed, most people had transferred their membership. However, while HEP began as a party of Turks and Kurds and then was overwhelmed by PKK sympathizers, DEP was envisioned from the start as a heterogeneous Kurdish party, in which PKK sympathizers would have a role, but not necessarily the defining one.

"When HEP was closed, they [PKK activists] said to me, OK, let's build a big party," remarked one senior member of HEP. "I met with [independent] Kurds and they said to me, no, we know what will happen." They were convinced the PKK would end up trying to take over the new party, similar to what happened in HEP. "I said no, they [the PKK] understand things now, they realize it can't go on like this, that the situation has changed. I managed to convince some people."

The new Democracy Party started off with a decisive public call for democratic changes in how Kurds were treated in Turkey: Kurds needed the right to learn and broadcast in their own language; they needed the freedom to develop their own identity; the heavy-handed military measure in the southeast needed to be lifted; a ceasefire had to be arranged; and a general amnesty had to be declared. But before the problem could be addressed, the party noted, the problem had to be named: "The problem is a political one and its name is the Kurdish problem."[8]

But with the death of President Ozal earlier in the year, the political direction of the government had shifted in favor of hardliners. Prime Minister Tansu Ciller, a political novice who took office when Suleyman Demirel moved into the presidency, had little interest in grappling with the difficult and unpopular Kurdish issue. Instead, she handed it over to the military, which was eager for the freedom to crush the PKK without civilian interference or concerns.

"From now on, we will act differently,"[9] she noted in a speech she made promising reinforcements for the military's Special Forces.

In the second-half of 1993, the targeting of Kurdish activists—harassment, arrest, and death squad-styled assassinations—grew worse. DEP officials complained they were threatened by police, soldiers, and their proxy village guards, blocked from moving freely through the region, and sometimes, detained for allegedly aiding the PKK. The unsolved murders of Kurdish activists jumped. In September, DEP parliamentarian Mehmet Sincar was assassinated during a visit to Batman to investigate exactly these sorts of murders. DEP officials who accompanied Sincar accused the security forces of being behind the attack, noting that the police, who otherwise had followed them throughout their visit, did not turn up that day.[10]

These attacks radicalized the party membership. Some DEP supporters dropped out of the party, fearful of the repercussions of staying active. Others fled their hometowns, emptying local offices of the most experienced members. Younger and angrier members might choose to join the PKK's armed units, rather than wait to be arrested or gunned down in the street by hit men.

"These people don't leave you alone to make politics," complained then-DEP parliamentarian Mahmut Kilinc, referring to the Turkish state. "They force people to go to the mountains."

In December 1993, Hatip Dicle, a member of parliament viewed as representing the DEP's more radical wing, was voted chairman. For some observers, Dicle's win was a sign that the PKK had changed its mind about remaining in the background,[11] a change probably spurred by the group's belief that its dominance in the southeast was unassailable, meaning it did not need partners.

Following Dicle's election, the political party's offices were bombed and shot up; the party's secretary general, Murat Bozlak, was shot and wounded in the capital Ankara; and in the southeast especially, party officials and supporters complained of threats and attacks.[12] Meanwhile, in December, the Constitutional Court began to hear a case to close down DEP—again for alleged separatist activity and PKK support—and a parliamentary commission began to approve requests to lift the immunity of some DEP deputies, the first step to charging them with treason. The proof almost solely was based on statements they made for Kurdish rights, their willingness to address their supporters in Kurdish, and their refusal to condemn the guerrilla fight.

"Maybe [name of former DEP parliamentarian withheld] was close to the PKK, but no-one was ever caught with a knife or weapon, the party never called for war," said former DEP parliamentarian Kilinc, insisting that the issue was not the sympathies of political party members, but whether Ankara was willing to tolerate any nonviolent activism on behalf of the Kurds. "If the state was serious, if they had wanted a reconciliation [with the Kurds], they would have said okay, we will give a space for the party to operate, but it didn't happen."

Nor was the PKK willing to wait. Its military offensive, which peaked around the end of 1993, spilled more and more into Turkey's western regions. In February 1994, rebels bombed Istanbul's Tuzla train station, killing five military students and wounding 31 others. Dicle, interviewed by telephone for Turkish television, refused to condemn the attack, arguing that "during wartime, soldiers in uniform are targets."[13]

Dicle later claimed he was making a legal point, but his statement was taken as proof the party supported the PKK's war. Two days later, DEP's provincial office in Ankara was bombed; four days later, a bomb ripped through the party's Ankara headquarters. Dicle blamed the state's security forces—and Prime Minister Ciller—for the attack, pointing out that DEP's headquarters was located 100 meters from a police station and 500 meters from the heavily guarded parliament building.

Turkey's interior minister insisted that DEP bombed its own building, adding that Dicle, anyway, was a traitor. The general chief of staff, General Dogan Gures, suggested that instead of looking for the bandits in Bekaa, they should search them out in the parliament.[14] Prime Minister Ciller agreed.

"The time has now come to remove the PKK's existence from under the roof of parliament,"[15] she announced at the end of February.

In this atmosphere, it was difficult for DEP members to focus on the upcoming March 1994 local elections. A debate broke out over whether or not to take part. The real problem was pressure in the southeast against DEP's voters and candidates. There were fears this would make it impossible for DEP to do well in the polls.

"Because we don't think like them, some organizations . . . are trying to strangle DEP,"[16] cautioned Dicle.

But many inside DEP wanted to go ahead and take part in the elections. Pulling out accomplished nothing; in fact, if the state wanted to push out DEP from the political process, which seemed to be the case, then withdrawing from the polls only helped the state. Ocalan apparently thought differently. According to reliable sources, PKK supporters made the decision to boycott the elections, a rare example of outright PKK pressure on DEP to take a certain policy line.[17]

"The PKK was opposed to the elections," said one former DEP parliamentarian. "The PKK was afraid that people wouldn't use their votes and this would make it [the PKK] look weak."

Pressure on the party mounted. In the beginning of March, parliament voted to lift the immunity of six DEP deputies and an independent Kurdish deputy. One by one, they were detained by police and ordered held for questioning. The expected charge was treason. The remaining deputies knew their time was limited. In June, the Constitutional Court ordered DEP shut down, announcing that similar to HEP, the party's statements calling for Kurdish rights were contrary to the constitution and constituted separatism.

Just before the decision was announced, the other deputies debated whether to stay and face likely arrest or flee the country. They were uninterested in trying to switch to yet another new party to get around yet another attempt to silence them.

"The state played with us like a mouse," complained Kilinc. "You make a party and then they close it and then it happens again." On the morning of June 16, the day the court decision was expected, five of the deputies got on a plane and left for Brussels (another deputy was already in Europe). "We thought, if [the state] doesn't want us to represent the Kurdish people, then let them [the international community] see this," added Kilinc.

The flight of the DEP deputies, the closure of the party, and the subsequent treason trial opened against eight of the former parliamentarians focused international attention on Turkey's Kurdish problem. But Ankara withstood pressure to make concrete changes, and in retrospect, it was Kurdish politics that suffered the most. With its leading figures in prison or in exile, it was hard for Kurdish politics to recover. The new party that formed in DEP's place, the People's Democracy Party (HADEP)—eventually was closed down by the Constitutional Court in 2003 and replaced by yet another—never had the stature or the influence of its predecessors. This made it even harder for the party to carve out a political line independent from that demanded by its mainly PKK-influenced supporters.

Nor did the state allow independent Kurdish politicians to fill the gap. When Serafettin Elci, a former cabinet minister in the Turkish government, formed a party in 1997, the Constitutional Court closed it down two years later. A different Kurdish party, the Democracy and Change Party (DDP), lasted less than a year before being ordered shut in 1996. The real problem, it seemed, was not real or alleged PKK influence in Kurdish politics, but Kurdish political demands. The state's approach, which was to treat all Kurdish politicians with equal suspicion, effectively strangled any chance of independent, effective Kurdish politics, leaving the field for the PKK. Kurdish politics, stuck between the PKK and the state, did not have much of a chance.

"From the outside, it looked like we couldn't do anything," said one former DEP parliamentarian. "All right, maybe we didn't have the [right] experience, but also, we weren't free. We would have an idea and then an idea would come from there [the PKK]."

The former parliamentarian paused. "But look at the other side, the other [Turkish] parliamentarians also had to think about what the National Security Council wanted," he said, referring to the military-dominated body that advised the government. "I remember one [Turkish] parliamentarian came to me and said, 'if only you didn't listen so much to this Apo and the PKK.' And I said to him, 'look, 75 years have passed [since Turkey was founded], are you prepared to stand up to the MGK [National Security Council]?'"

Politics Abroad

A few times a year, PKK officials in Europe rented an empty farmhouse in a remote stretch of land, often in the Netherlands, and brought about 50 new members there for political training. These young men and women, recruited from the Kurdish community in Europe, stayed at the so-called camp for nearly three months. They started their mornings by running and doing sports and followed this with lectures on Kurdish and PKK history and Marxist theory. In the afternoons, they read books on the same subjects. Toward the end of the training period, they held their own self-criticism session, in which people stood up and discussed their weaknesses and strengths and the others commented.

"The atmosphere was very serious, very heavy," explained Orhan, the pseudonym of a former PKK official in Europe who was about 29 years old when he attended the program in the early 1990s. "No joking, very disciplined, like a military high school but without weapons. The objective was to teach you how to talk about certain things, how to listen. They teach you . . . to respect whatever the organization wants of you."

Although most of the people tapped to go on the program were familiar with the PKK—some already worked in the group's European offices—the restrictive atmosphere still could be a surprise. Before going to the farm, participants agreed not to have contact with their family and friends for the duration of the training, something designed to help them make an easier transition to being a part of the PKK. "This was to make a rupture with your past life," explained Orhan. "Because you are starting a new life and these months will teach you how to make a new life." It was not unusual for one or two people to be kicked out before the end of the program.

"These were either people who were not following the rules, or were difficult to get along with," said Orhan. "But before they left, it would be explained that these people were bad Kurds, that they didn't have the right consciousness. From this, you understood that you can't leave the group and if you do, you leave under this cloud of being dishonored."

Toward the end of the program, the PKK decided who would go to Kurdistan to fight and who would stay in Europe to work on the PKK's diplomatic and organizational initiatives. Most people were eager to see the battle up-close. Orhan, fluent in French and English, was sent to one of the PKK's information centers in France. He was a little disappointed. "I wanted to go to fight. But like everyone, I said I would respect whatever decision the PKK made for me."

The PKK's network in Europe had grown tremendously since the early 1980s, when a handful of supporters considered themselves fortunate if they could raise a few thousands dollars or get a few hundred people to a rally. Just a decade later, the PKK operated an extensive network of cultural clubs, political offices and publishing ventures, spread out over half-a-dozen countries. Its annual fund drive raised about $30 million a year, and the group collected another $20 million or so from its festivals, which drew tens of thousands of people, from magazine subscriptions, which sympathizers bought as a show of support, and all the concerts, coffees, and plays that PKK activists staged.[18]

"Our goal was to organize people here and tie them to the PKK's struggle," explained Akif Hasan, a fast-talking former spokesman. "This meant everything from getting new people for the war to getting them out to marches."

Working for the PKK was not always easy, but it commanded respect. The rebel group's fight against the Turkish military had won it support, especially among the disaffected Kurdish youth in Europe, where integrating was not easy and finding jobs even harder. Those who were willing to go and sacrifice their life for the nationalist cause were viewed with a certain jealous respect; those who worked to promote the PKK in Europe were their representatives. Other Kurdish groups did little more than run one-person offices that published dense newspapers. The PKK, in contrast, backed a popular newspaper, a satellite television (that started broadcasts in 1995 under the name Med-TV), and an academic-styled institute that held conferences on Kurdish issues. Associations helped gather journalists and businessmen together, and students and women had their own venues.

Kurds could get involved without joining the PKK, but these activities all helped tie more people to the organization. By one estimate, the PKK controlled up to 90 percent of Kurdish opinion in Germany alone, where half of the continent's Kurds lived.[19]

"When you are inside the PKK, people respect you, they see you as someone who is ready to go to Kurdistan and fight," explained Orhan. "At the same time, it is a career. A lot of people were nothing before joining the PKK. Or others are afraid of you because they know that you are now protected by the PKK. When those who were really high up went to a [Kurdish] restaurant, they were treated very well."

But the work itself was hard. PKK activists were expected to be on duty 24 hours a day and, like the rebels in the mountains, they were barred from sexual relations. PKK officials in Europe usually did not have their own apartments—their monthly stipend, between $150 and $300, was barely enough for coffee and cigarettes—and they were expected to spend their nights at the homes of sympathetic Kurdish families.

"You have to give confidence to the families that the PKK people won't bother the girls in the family," said Orhan. "And basically, if you didn't have this rule, then families wouldn't let their girls take part."

The PKK measured its support in Europe in different ways. The number of new recruits for the armed struggle always was important, but perhaps even more important was the number of people they could get out for public demonstrations and the number of people who donated money when asked. By all of these measures, the group was successful, but it took constant work to maintain the support, noted Hasan:

> You have to convince people, it can be difficult. Once, we made a play about a guerrilla who was wounded, he goes to a tent hoping to get help from a doctor, but it's too late, he dies. Before he dies, he says, "tell my children I am sorry I can't see them before I die." The message was that he died because the guerrillas did not have enough bullets [for lack of money]. People would cry watching it.

Activists usually approached families for a small donation every month—sometimes, in the form of a magazine subscription—and once a year, everyone was expected to make a big contribution. When necessary, threats were employed, but often, the PKK's reputation (both for violence and for being serious about fighting the Turkish military) was enough to ensure people gave. In Germany, where many workers received what was known as a 13th month salary, PKK activists pushed people to think of the needs of the fighters.

"We would say, you work 12 months for yourself and one month, you should think of the struggle," explained a PKK official from Europe. "You try to create that sort of atmosphere." When that did not work, there was another route. "Sometimes, the money was coerced."

The PKK had a complex bookkeeping system to track where money came from and how it was spent, but it did not really think long term. "The PKK didn't have a good business perspective, it didn't have an economic plan," said Hasan. "Money came and went." The group used the money to pay its own expenses in Europe and sent some to Ocalan in Damascus. When they ran short of funds, they simply asked people for more. PKK members did try to invest in small businesses, like grocery stores or tailor's shops, but these rarely succeeded.

"The idea was they [the owners] would give the profits back, but usually, they went bankrupt," said a PKK activist familiar with the process.

The PKK's other main source of funding was a tax on Kurdish businesses, and some Turkish businesses as well. More nationalistic Kurdish businessmen were asked to plug up specific deficits in the PKK's own operations, like its invariably loss-making publishing ventures. This made it very difficult for law enforcement agencies to track these ventures directly to the PKK, because the financial backers were not PKK members. Some of these businessmen were involved in the narcotics trade, which did not really bother the PKK.

Turkish officials frequently complained about European governments' willingness to tolerate the PKK, whose intertwined mix of political, cultural, and financial activities was not a secret. Certainly, when activities tipped over into the criminal realm, like extortion, drug running, and murder of dissidents, the police stepped in when they could and made arrests. But it was not easy—nor was there any real interest—in shutting down the group as a whole. One reason was that that in Europe, the PKK operated as a political front, making it hard to ban. Many Europeans generally were sympathetic to the plight of the Kurds in Turkey, partly because of the PKK's work to publicize Turkey's human rights abuses.

But PKK activists wanted more than sympathy, they wanted Europe to take concrete action. In Turkey, Kurdish villagers were being forced out of their homes by soldiers. The Kurdish politicians were being harassed and threatened. Ocalan's 1993 ceasefire was ignored by the security forces. Kurdish human rights workers and journalists were being abducted and killed. It seemed that Europe, a staunch supporter of Turkey despite the occasional criticisms and warning, could do more.

"Europe was just observing this, sometimes even giving support to Turkey," explained Hasan. "When the PKK [in Europe] did a peaceful action, like a hunger strike, nobody paid attention. There were meetings with European parliamentarians, but nothing came out of this. We made brochures to explain things, but we couldn't get serious responses. This creates a certain hopelessness and so you have to do something."

On June 24, 1993, activists in France, Switzerland, and Germany staged well-coordinated attacks on Turkish businesses in more than a dozen cities and stormed Turkish consulates in three of them.[20] In November, PKK supporters carried out a new wave of attacks against Turkish businesses in Germany, killing one man. That same month, the German interior minister responded by banning the PKK and 35 affiliated organizations. France followed suit. The bans had little effect.

"In democratic countries, it's not so easy to stop these things," noted one former PKK activist. "You just change your name. The people's rights club becomes the human rights club, the 'Ozgur Politika' newspaper becomes the 'Yeni Ozgur Politika' newspaper."

But the PKK had not counted on how the ban would affect its contacts with European parliamentarians and national politicians. Some of the PKK's contacts lost interest in further meetings, concerned about being linked to a banned group, even if it now operated under a new front organization. European journalists, who before might have treated the PKK like a legitimate voice of the Kurds, now gave space to the group's violent, terrorist attacks.

"People stopped meeting with us, saying they don't meet with terrorists," recalled Hasan. "On a practical level, we still had our masses and support, but we couldn't do lobbying anymore, some people didn't want to come to our festivals. We still made activities, but we were limited."

Life Abroad

The flight of DEP deputies to Europe after their party was shut down by the Turkish court was a propaganda boon for the PKK.

"The arrival of the DEP people provided a certain gas to the diplomatic activities," noted Hasan, the spokesman in Europe. "That was the state's mistake, to ban DEP."

Many DEP officials had struggled hard inside Turkey to act independent of PKK pressures, but now that they were in Europe, it no longer seemed so important. Nor was it that simple. They had arrived with little money, few contacts, and limited foreign languages, making it hard for them to operate on their own. The PKK controlled the Kurdish community in Europe and directed the debate. It had offices everywhere and money to match. Unless a person wanted to join up with a rival group—none of which had any real support in Europe or Turkey—there was little choice but to work alongside the PKK.

The former DEP mayor of Yuksekova, Nejdet Buldan, for example, fled Turkey after his brother Savas Buldan, a reputed PKK financier, was abducted in Istanbul and killed. The 44-year-old former mayor became fixated on how he could exact revenge for the murder of his younger brother, Savas, last seen being led away by men believed to be police. Nejdet Buldan had no interest in joining the PKK, but he saw them as a group that could help him realize his goal.

"They [the state] took the best from my family and killed him," explained Buldan, who escaped Turkey in September 1994 by hiding his lanky frame in the luggage compartment of a bus going to Bulgaria. "I couldn't go fight [but the question was] how can I put the Turkish state in a harsh position? How can I do something for the Kurdish problem? What can my role be?"

DEP officials considered various initiatives, finally settling on a parliament-in-exile, a potent symbol of Turkey's refusal to let Kurdish politicians operate inside the Turkish national parliament.[21] The Kurdish Parliament in Exile, with 65 members drawn mainly from PKK-affiliated associations and the PKK's own ERNK political front, was inaugurated in a ceremony in the Hague in April 1995. Among the members were eight DEP officials, including five former parliamentarians, and their presence gave the PKK-dominated body a certain legitimacy the rebel group could never get on its own.

The timing for such an endeavor could not have been better. Turkey's insistence that the Kurdish problem was solely one of terrorism was beginning to sound more and more forced, even to its closest allies. Ankara's decision to ban the legal Kurdish party DEP and try the eight who did not flee the country (in December 1994, they received prison sentences that ranged up to 15 years) had shocked many European countries and raised unease inside the U.S. government. Germany briefly suspended military assistance after DEP was closed, and the European Union postponed signing a customs union with Turkey. Meanwhile, some members of the U.S. Congress had started to take a closer look at weapons sales to Turkey and the link to human rights violations.

Ankara wanted the parliament disbanded, arguing it was nothing more than a PKK front. But even if so, the parliament was a nonviolent PKK front, one that included well-known, unaffiliated figures, and it was not engaged in any violent activities. In fact, it called for dialogue to settle the conflict peacefully.

The refusal of European officials to clamp down on the parliament enraged Turkey. When the Kurdish parliament convened for the first time in the Hague, Ankara expressed its displeasure by briefly recalling its ambassador and suspending military purchases. Turkey's reaction to the meeting, where the main call was one for peace, certainly underlined its inability to tolerate free debate on the issue. It also gave the meeting a publicity boost that no speech or press release could have accomplished.

"Every time we met in another country, there was a crisis with Turkey and this put the Kurdish issue again on the map," Buldan, a member of the parliament, said with a smile. "In the diplomatic field, despite all the deficiencies, the parliament in exile was the most successful [Kurdish endeavor]."

DEP officials, eager to make politics, envisioned a real political body, one that drafted laws and plans and had the authority to direct political talks. In the long run, they hoped to build a truly national body, one that incorporated Kurds from all parts of Kurdistan.

Ocalan, as always, seemed interested in everything, even initiatives that on the surface appeared to threaten his dictatorial leadership.

"He said, 'even if I am just one representative in such a [national] body, I will agree,'" recalled Buldan, who traveled to see Ocalan in Damascus in 1995. "Of course, in practice, he wouldn't even put up with the brochure of another party. . . . I think he knew that we would never make a national congress."

Thanks to the PKK's majority presence in the parliament, its financial backing of the body, and above all, its dominance of Kurdish public opinion and sympathy, the parliament had no chance to carve out a more assertive program for itself. In essence, it became a publicity stunt, albeit it a very effective one.

"The PKK saw [the parliament] as a tactic, something to make Turkey uncomfortable," explained former Europe-based spokesman Hasan. "The PKK did not say to the Kurdish people that these were the representatives of the Kurds, that they would be the ones to debate the Kurdish issue. That wasn't the plan."

Ultimately, the parliament had some successes, but it would be hard to call the parliament itself a success. Like so many of the PKK's democratic-styled endeavors, there was a big gap between what the parliament could have done and what it was allowed to do. Similar to the Kurdish newspaper in Turkey, the satellite station broadcast out of Europe, and the many Kurdish political parties in Turkey, the Kurdish Parliament in Exile began with certain plans and promises. But Ocalan's refusal to hand over any authority—or his attempts to grab authority—coupled with his difficulty tolerating independent thinkers, limited the effectiveness of all these groups.

"Outside the PKK there was nothing," Hasan said bluntly. "If there was no money, where would they go? The building came from the PKK, the tickets, the travel. Even the pens came from the PKK. The PKK was that sort of organization [that did everything]."

PART IV

Ocalan's Capture and After

Right: As part of their attempt to break the PKK's control over parts of the southeast, Turkish soldiers conducted frequent house raids, looking for signs of PKK support and weapons. This photo shows them preparing to enter the gates to a house—or a group of houses—in the southeastern city of Cizre in 1992. Photo provided by an anonymous source.

Above left: Kurdish demonstrators in Diyarbakir in 1996 celebrate the Newruz new year. Photo provided by an anonymous source.

Above right: Abdullah Ocalan, a few months before he was forced to flee Syria. Photo by Michael Gunter, March 1998.

Left: PKK commanders, left to right, Zeki Ozturk, Huseyin Topgider, and Ayhan Ciftci meet up in February 1999 in the Kandil Mountains near the Iraqi-Iranian border. They were there to attend the PKK's 6th Congress. Photo provided by Ayhan Ciftci.

12

The Decline, 1995–1998

SAIT CURUKKAYA, THE medical student turned PKK rebel, set off for northern Iraq in July 1995 to attend a meeting of senior military commanders. It was not an easy trip. Stepped-up Turkish military operations forced his team of 17 fighters to make long detours. Depleted supply depots—and very few friendly villages left—meant they never had enough food. By the time Curukkaya reached the city-town Siirt, about halfway to the border, he had no choice but to chance entering the urban center to get provisions. "We found a shop in one of the outlying neighborhoods," said Curukkaya. "The owner was shocked when he saw us. We told him we would pay, and we just filled our bags with everything we could. Flour, sugar, chocolate, whatever 17 men could carry." But a few miles away, they got stuck behind a clash between Turkish soldiers and rebels.

> I was listening to the enemy on the wireless and I could hear that there was an operation but I wasn't sure exactly where. We spent two nights on the river bank. . . . When we crossed and I saw vultures, I knew that meant there were bodies somewhere. . . . We came across three guerrillas dead and one man, still alive, but his leg was broken and filled with maggots. He had been lying there for three days without water or anything. If I hadn't seen the vultures we never would have known.

Curukkaya's team carried the injured rebel to the closest village, looking for a donkey. They found one, but the owner did not want to give it up—he was afraid Turkish soldiers would find out and accuse him of helping the PKK—but Curukkaya could be persuasive. "I told him that if we did not get the donkey we would leave the wounded man there and then the state would come and kill the rebel and him. Or, we could give him money for the donkey and he could say the donkey got lost. So he gave it to us for 500 [German] marks."

They strapped the wounded man to the donkey and continued across the Besler and Gabar Mountains, where they left him with another unit. Turkish tank fire halted them just at the Cudi Mountains, their last stop before crossing into northern Iraq to the PKK's Zap camp. The situation in Cudi was even more difficult—so many villages had been emptied that rebels were lucky when they could scavenge from abandoned fruit and vegetable gardens—but Curukkaya already was thoroughly dispirited from what he had seen during his two-month trek across the region.

"Everyone spoke of the same problems, not enough supplies, no contact with the local people, constant attack by village guards," said Curukkaya, who sounded still frustrated years later. "I couldn't think of a solution because the answer did not lie with me." He believed it lay with Ocalan.

Ocalan liked to boast that although he had never fired a gun he understood war better than his most experienced military commanders and he ignored suggestions that the PKK review its armed tactics. He refused to listen to the concerns of his senior commanders in the field, nor was he willing to consider that the PKK's military strategy might be to blame for some of the difficulties. He refused even to acknowledge the difficulties.

This was made clear during the PKK's 5th Congress in January 8–27, 1995, when Ocalan instructed delegates to approve a plan of action that did not take into account the PKK's reversal of military fortunes. Instead, he demanded that rebels prepare people for a general uprising and redouble their efforts to take control of northern Kurdistan. As in previous congresses, a handful of senior commanders were accused of misapplying Ocalan's orders and harming the PKK's fight—one of them was Huseyin Topgider, whose rebels had been pushed out of much of the Garzan (roughly bordered by the cities of Batman, Mus, Bitlis, and Siirt) region by Turkish soldiers. To the extent that mistakes had been made, Ocalan stressed, they were made by rebels who were too weak or too cowardly to properly implement his orders.

"There is no place in the military for the concept of inadequacy," Ocalan stated in the report prepared for the congress, which was held in Haftanin camp in northern Iraq. "To say, 'Because of this internal or external reason we could not reach the target or were prevented from being successful' is a crime. In the military, the only proper approach and statement is, 'For success I did everything and I succeeded.'"[1]

But many senior field commanders had begun to believe that Ocalan's military directives were at the root of their failures. The PKK chief had not been inside Turkey in 16 years and he seemed to understand little of what was going on. When commanders raised the problem of the forcible evacuation of Kurdish villagers, Ocalan exhorted them to press the villagers to return. But PKK rebels could barely protect themselves anymore, let alone unarmed civilians. When commanders complained that the large battalions Ocalan wanted them to set up hurt their fight—it was easier for Turkish soldiers to track and kill large groups of rebels—he accused them of being cowards. When they said that long firefights depleted the ammunition they could carry—Ocalan wanted them to hold their ground like a regular army instead of using hit-and-run guerrilla tactics—he told them they did not know how to fight.

Years later, Neval expressed her frustration:

> Ocalan would say the tactic is not the problem, that the problem has to do with the individual. But we didn't have enough military supplies, what does that have to do with it? You get blown up by a landmine—that has nothing to do with the individual—that has to do with the lack of mine detectors. We would discuss instead that the individual was not attached enough to the party. . . . Ocalan would say, everything is fine, the problem is you.

Eight months after the 5th Congress, the PKK's Amed (Diyarbakir) commander, Sait Curukkaya, arrived in Zap camp in northern Iraq after his two-month trip across the region. He was there to attend a central committee meeting to decide how to implement the decisions issued at the 5th Congress. But Curukkaya, who still answers to his old PKK code-name Dr. Suleyman, was not interested in what the 5th Congress decided. Nor were many of the other experienced field commanders who made the same long, difficult trek for the meeting. They had read the congress's concluding report and they were shocked by the decisions, which reflected more Ocalan's control over the PKK than the realities that the guerrillas were living.

"It was as if nothing had changed, as if no villages had been emptied, as if there had been no rebel losses, as if we still had the same number of people joining," complained Ayhan Ciftci, then commander of Erzurum province. "I read the decisions and was devastated." Semdin Sakik, chief of the Dersim (Tunceli) province and one of the most experienced and prominent commanders, was said to have thrown the report on the ground in disgust, saying, "This can't be."

The meeting in Zap offered PKK commanders, who usually communicated via wireless or in hurried meetings in mountain hideouts, a rare chance to sit together and speak at length. Ciftci, Sakik, and Curukkaya—whose combined area of authority covered about half the area where PKK fighters remained very active inside Turkey—believed the time had come for a serious reevaluation of the armed struggle.

"Sakik, Dr. Suleyman and me, we had our views, which was that the situation was very different [than what Ocalan was describing] and that this was not because of the way we were applying the tactics, but because of the tactics themselves," said Ciftci emphatically.

The three men tried to promote a real discussion of the problems PKK rebels faced. They were careful to avoid blaming Ocalan—Sakik, in fact, did not think Ocalan was at fault, he instead accused Ocalan's senior advisors of mishandling the war—but they insisted the rebel group needed to rethink its tactics if it was going to regain the military initiative.

"We had to operate with smaller and more experienced groups," insisted Curukkaya. "We needed to choose targets more carefully."

Some of the commanders at the meeting suggested taking the fight to western Turkey, specifically, Turkish villages in the rural Black Sea region.

"We fought in our land and we lost our land, the villages were burned, so why not take the fight to the Black Sea and see if the Turkish army treats Turkish villagers the same way," Ciftci recounted.

Another idea was to focus on economic targets—factories, public utilities—in order to hit Turkish interests more directly. Commanders also debated trying to move the fight to Turkey's urban centers, both in the Kurdish region and in the west.

"Our conclusion was that the way we were doing the war, we couldn't continue like this," explained Curukkaya. "We called up Ocalan and told him what we were considering, and the answer was clear: This isn't an issue of tactics. The problem is that you have not yet unified yourself with the party."

This phrase, which Ocalan often used when faced with a complaint, meant that the person speaking did not properly understand the PKK, which really meant he did not properly respect Ocalan. "He said we needed to be closer to the party . . . and he said that me and Kucuk Zeki [Ciftci] should come to Syria."

As they readied to leave for Syria, they understood that the ideas proposed at the meeting would, for now, have to be put on hold.

"Once Apo issued his decision, everyone made the same conclusion," said Curukkaya. "When he spoke, everyone knew the discussion was finished, there was no chance to change Apo's mind."

No Exit

The 5th Congress and the Zap Conference set the focus for the PKK's military fight over the next few years. Bereft of a serious strategy—that is to say, one that honestly addressed both the rebels' armed strengths and weaknesses—the fight continued, but never recovered its old strength. Armed units remained in the mountains and still moved, with surprising ease, back and forth between the Turkish and Iraqi parts of Kurdistan, but they also remained on the defensive.

The military changes that Ocalan did implement spoke more about his need for self-glorification than anything else. Apart from the women's army, which was directly tied to him, he also encouraged limited suicide bombings. Extolling the bravery of women who blew themselves up rather than fall into enemy hands was nothing new—in 1992, a rebel called Berivan was glorified for blowing herself up with a grenade rather than be taken prisoner, sparking a rush on that name by new recruits. But in 1996, the emphasis shifted to staging such attacks, rather than falling back on them in desperation to avoid capture. At the end of June, a PKK militant named Zeynep (Zilan) Kinaci strapped a bomb to her body and blew herself up next to a military ceremony, killing herself and six soldiers.

"Comrade Zeynep, my commander, I will carry your name with honor," former *Ozgur Gundem* editor and PKK militant Gurbetelli Ersoz, who also had the code name Zeynep, wrote in her diary upon hearing the news. "I will be someone who lives up to the name."[2]

A few months later PKK militant Leyla Kaplan blew herself up at the entrance to a police station, killing three police. Over the next three years, another 14 attacks were staged, mainly by women (perhaps because in Turkey, and especially the southeast, suicide is a frighteningly common way for women to settle their unhappiness[3]) and almost always targeting security personnel.[4] The attacks were praised by Ocalan but they never really took hold. One reason might have been that women in the PKK often felt empowered—and suicide bombing was more a sign of weakness. Certainly, the turn to suicide bombing underscored something Ocalan refused to publicly admit: that the rebels had lost the initiative and without some radical, tactical, and strategic change, had no way to regain it.

But Ocalan's inability to analyze honestly the PKK's military strengths and weaknesses was in marked contrast to his relatively strong grasp of the need for political changes, underscoring the very practical, ideological elasticity that had helped the PKK survive and grow so successfully over the years. In 1995, for example, congress delegates approved stripping the PKK's flag of its hammer and sickle. Marxist-Leninist thought, anyway, had always been secondary to the PKK's nationalist drive, and the collapse of the Soviet Union made such a symbol almost beside the point. But the fact remained that many leftist groups kept it as a sign of their revolutionary zeal: Ocalan, in contrast, was as focused on revolution as he was on political gain. The changing of the flag did not change the fact that the PKK was a revolutionary group committed to armed struggle, but it did show that Ocalan was, above all, practical.

Similarly, Ocalan began to think more about religion and its uses. The PKK, despite its Marxist-Leninist ideology, never took an open stand against Islam.[5] However, in line with Ocalan's moderating approach to religion, the 5th Congress issued a statement affirming that Islam was not contrary to Kurdish nationalist goals. The congress referred specifically to a new group, the Kurdistan Islamic Movement (KIH), which was created with PKK backing. The PKK had never shown an interest in linking up with religious Islamic movements— which downplayed Kurdish identity in favor of Islamic identity—and it seemed the PKK hoped to undercut other Islamic groups by forming its own. The difference was this new group was openly nationalist, asserting that different Islamic nations have the right to live independently and develop their own culture, a reference to the Kurds.[6] The conciliatory statements issued by the 5th Congress, which emphasized that fighting against oppression was not anti-Islamic, reflected more

Ocalan's attempts to gain new support where he could, rather than any serious interest in religion.

But ultimately, Ocalan's tactical political leadership was limited by two factors. First, his constant efforts to protect his leadership and the PKK's dominance over Kurdish activity, which usually worked counter to his public political maneuvers. Second, the Turkish government's refusal to accept him as a negotiating partner. His claims that he had abandoned hope of independence in favor of a federation, or autonomy, also were ignored by his potential interlocutors. Turkish leaders, especially military leaders, were not interested in accommodating Kurdish nationalist desires in any form.

Back in Iraq

The Turkish military sent 35,000 troops across the border into northern Iraq to wipe out PKK bases in March 1995, hoping to finally end the rebels' ability to use the border strip to launch attacks.[7]

Turkey had not sent a major armed force into northern Iraq since 1992, when its soldiers fought alongside Iraqi Kurdish militias in what ultimately was a failed, four-week drive to oust the rebels. This time, Turkish officials promised they would not leave until they had rid northern Iraq of the PKK and its some dozen main bases. Immediately, Turkey came under pressure to limit the operation, which appeared like a possible land grab to its Middle Eastern neighbors and worried Turkey's Western allies. There were fears Ankara might try and carve a security zone for itself by settling Turkish troops just inside the border, or that it might try and spread out over much of northern Iraq, using problems faced by its ethnic kin, the Turcoman minority of northern Iraq, as a rationale.

Ankara, in the midst of lobbying for the customs union accord with Europe, quickly understood the need to act carefully to balance its political and military goals. Six days into the operation, Demirel was forced to soften his initial comment and stress that this was a limited action: "We're not thinking of solutions like a security zone."[8]

The operation made sense in theory—certainly from the perspective of the Turkish military—but it blundered in practice, underscoring the problems of fighting the PKK in Iraq. Turkey's military buildup was noted in advance by rebels, who relocated the bulk of their fighters and supplies further south before the operation's launch. At the same time, Turkish troops had trouble operating in what really was a foreign environment, especially under the scrutiny of an already suspicious West. What Ankara could somehow justify, coverup, or just ignore when it happened on its own land—like death-squad-styled murders and the bombing of villages—was front-page news when it happened in northern Iraq, which was supposed to be under the protection of U.S.-led forces and the United Nations.

Aerial bombing raids sometimes hit Iraqi Kurdish villages, forcing people to flee and set up tent camps along the main roads. Iraqi Kurds also complained of mistreatment—early on, seven shepherds were found dead after they had been detained by the Turkish military for questioning. Turkish soldiers manning a checkpoint outside Zakho had trouble telling who was friend and foe, given that most could not read the Arabic-script identity cards people pulled out when stopped. Meanwhile, just an hour's drive away from the Turkish military's operation to clear out Haftanin and Kani Masi of rebel camps, PKK fighters strolled openly in the mountains, seemingly unconcerned about the Turkish troops a few miles away.

The Turkish operation inside northern Iraq ended less than two months after it started. Turkish troops claimed a great victory, throwing out what the PKK claimed was an inflated number of militants killed—555 rebels dead compared with 11 Turkish soldiers killed—and showing more credible pictures of the stockpiles of weapons, medical supplies, and food captured. But there was no way to stop the PKK from returning to its bases once the soldiers retreated, and within a few weeks, PKK militants again were staging hit-and-run attacks on border outposts, killing handfuls of soldiers.

The PKK's relative freedom to operate inside northern Iraq always was helped by a power vacuum within a power vacuum: Baghdad's authority over the Kurdish region was cut in 1991 and then, in May 1994, fighting broke out between the militias' of Talabani and Barzani, paralyzing the power-sharing Kurdistan Regional Government. The fighting started because of a land dispute, but quickly spread to encompass questions of revenue sharing—Barzani's KDP was accused of pocketing all the fees collected at the Habur crossing into Turkey— and at the end of the year, Talabani's forces captured Erbil, seat of the now-frozen Kurdistan Regional Government.[9]

The fighting between Barzani and Talabani was of particular concern to the United States, which worried that one or another of the parties might call on Baghdad or Tehran for help. In August 1995, Washington arranged a meeting of the two Iraqi Kurdish parties in Dublin: The goal was not to deal with Turkey's security concerns, but the preliminary agreement did include a reference to Turkey's legitimate security interests.

Ocalan, always fearful of a possible international plot against him, took this to mean that the United States was going to push the Iraqi Kurds to attack PKK rebels. Four days after the conclusion of the Dublin meetings, and even before the agreement was implemented, Ocalan declared war against Barzani's KDP, which nominally controlled the border areas where the PKK rebels were based.

It was clear from the start that neither side could best the other: While the KDP had more fighters, the PKK was based in well-fortified mountain camps. But the PKK's unprovoked attack on Barzani's militia shocked Iraqi Kurds, who had viewed the PKK as a rare example of a unified, stable Kurdish movement—so unlike their own groups, which were busy fighting each other instead of building a state. The PKK's offensive turned Iraqi Kurds against the Turkish Kurdish group and cost the PKK real support.

"No one won that war," remarked former PKK militant Huseyin Topgider, who was in northern Iraq at the time. "But in a way, we lost, because we lost lots of prestige."

The clashes between the PKK and the KDP ended in December 1995—winter always was a good time to suspend fighting—when the two groups signed a ceasefire agreement. The PKK was allowed to maintain its military bases, but encouraged to do political work instead inside northern Iraq. Ankara took this as a sign of betrayal by the Iraqi Kurds, but the KDP, which needed to focus attention on the ongoing war with Talabani, was being practical.

"We could overcome the PKK easily if we had arms and ammunition," boasted KDP foreign relations chief Sami Abdul-Rahman in the middle of the clashes with the PKK. "[But] the ammunition especially is important because we do not wish to use up our ammunition in fighting the PKK and then end up in a weak position if we are attacked by the PUK."[10]

Meanwhile, U.S. fears that Iraqi Kurdish in-fighting would further destabilize the region and shift the balance of powers were realized.

Iran, now closer to Talabani than to Barzani, used its ties to stage a quick foray inside northern Iraq in July 1996. The target was Iranian opposition forces based across the border, but Barzani's men complained that the Iranians were there to prop up Talabani's forces. This set off a new round of Kurdish in-fighting and outside support. At the end of August, Baghdad sent in troops to help Barzani retake the Kurdish regional capital Erbil from Talabani's fighters. Turkey grew ever-more concerned about the PKK's ability to gain strength from the chaos.

Repeated efforts by the United States to quiet the situation were unable to settle the differences between Barzani and Talabani and end the fighting. It was not until May 1997, when Turkey launched another enormous operation against PKK bases (and again in September), that the Iraqi Kurdish leaders realized that their own conflict might end with the partitioning of the Kurdish region among its neighbors Turkey, Iran, and Syria. It took another bout of Iraqi Kurdish in-fighting in October—this time, Turkish forces helped back up Barzani's fighters against Talabani's—to get the Iraqi Kurdish leaders to negotiate. In September 1998, after a flurry of U.S. peace proposals, the two Iraqi Kurdish leaders met in Washington and announced a new accord to end their four-year-old civil war.

Turkey immediately complained about reference in the accord to a federative structure for Iraq, something that smacked of a Kurdish semistate. Turkey also was concerned about anything in the agreement that might constrict its ability to attack PKK targets in northern Iraq. The PKK, for its part, probably saw the agreement as a threat, or at least a betrayal, because it again was being ignored as a regional player, but Ocalan's attention was elsewhere. Turkey had upped its threats against Syria, warning that if Ocalan was not forced out, the Turkish army might invade. In this environment, it was hard for Ocalan to focus on imagined threats; there was a real one in front of him.

The Kurdish Problem Remains

By 1995, Ankara was spending as much as $11 billion[11] a year to fight the war, part of which went to building new military outposts and paying premiums to state workers in the region. In addition to special forces, police, and village guards, Turkey also deployed some 220,000 troops in the region—tying up a quarter of NATO's second largest army in a domestic battle.[12]

What was surprising was that despite this massive show of strength—and Ocalan's tactical errors—Ankara could not finish off the PKK. The number of rebels declined precipitously between 1994 and 1996, but then stabilized to around 5,000–6,000 fighters, of which half were based inside Turkey. Perhaps more critically, the PKK retained its dominant political presence within the Kurdish community in Turkey, primarily through its sympathizers in the Kurdish political party HADEP and the Kurdish daily newspaper.

The state's inability to eradicate the PKK undermined its argument that the problem was one of terrorism, not Kurdish identity. Kurdish activists, many of them well-known opponents of the PKK, had long claimed that it was the state's repression of the Kurds that helped make the PKK so powerful. Now, more than a decade into a war that had proven so costly, one Turkish newspaper columnist daringly suggested that maybe the problem was more one of logic than terrorism.

"What if Mustafa Kemal had been an Ottoman pasha born not in Salonika, but in [the Kurdish region of] Mosul . . . and the republic formed was called the Republic of Kurdey?" Ahmet Altan, a columnist for the *Milliyet* daily, mused in a published piece in 1995. "What if it were said that in Kurdey there were no Turks and everyone in fact was a Kurd and those who thought themselves Turks were, in fact, sea Kurds," referring to the myth that Kurds were mountain Turks who had forgotten their true language and culture. "Would we Turks have agreed to this . . . Or would we have insisted that our Turkish identity, our language, our culture be accepted, that we be accepted as equal citizens in this country? . . . Democracy is accepting that what we Turks would have wanted if we had lived in the Kurdey Republic, are the same desires that Kurds today are raising."[13]

Altan, who hoped to get his readers thinking, was charged with the state security offense of inciting ethnic hatred (the legal logic was that by claiming Kurds were oppressed by Turks, hatred between Kurds and Turks was provoked), given a suspended prison sentence, and fired from his job. Still, the column signaled that Turks, too, were tiring of the state's approach that demanded wholesale repression of Kurdish identity.

"The PKK is still recruiting people," noted state minister for human rights Algan Hacaloglu, a member of the government's social democratic junior partner, in June 1995. "Why? Because there is widespread alienation, because despite talk [the government] have not been able to apply real progress for rights, democracy."[14]

Part of the reason for the more outspoken attitude, especially among mainstream Turks, was the cost of the war. The cost had turned almost unmanageable, and not just in terms of government spending. There was the lost investment, the lost tourism (the PKK routinely warned foreigners to stay away from Turkey and occasionally set off bombs in resort cities), and, increasingly, the cost to Turkey's image abroad.

The United States, usually Ankara's strongest ally, had started to face internal debates and hesitations over aid packages and military sales to Turkey. Reports of Turkey's human rights abuses and the repression of the Kurds, publicized with the help of a Washington, D.C.-based Turkish Kurdish activist named Kani Xulam, was eating into Ankara's appeal. In 1994 Congress held back 10 percent of the aid to Turkey pending a special inquiry into alleged human rights abuses, and already, a sale of cluster bombs had been cancelled and much-needed Cobra helicopters were being held up. Turkey's bid for closer European ties, too, suddenly seemed in jeopardy. The European parliament, upset at the jailing of the Kurdish parliamentarians, delayed signing a much-anticipated trade union with Turkey at the end of December 1994. Around the same time, the Council of Europe threatened to suspend Turkey's membership unless democratic changes were made, something that seemed to threaten Turkey's bid to start accession talks for full European Union membership.

The Turkish business elite issued a flurry of reports in 1995 calling on Turkey to take a new approach to the Kurdish problem. One report suggested Ankara learn from the experiences of Spain, Italy, and Britain in dealing with minorities; another stressed that allowing Kurdish-language education and cultural freedoms could be a good thing. While these reports—including a first-ever survey of Kurdish opinions[15]—looked good on paper, they either were largely ignored or fell afoul of accusations of secret goals and mysterious supporters.

Ankara was not ready to accept bold ideas, but it was clear some change was needed. Not necessarily to satisfy Kurds, but to ensure that Turkey's international standing was not further harmed. The customs union with Europe, especially, had become a symbol of Turkey's aspirations to join the European Union. In fact, it had become a symbol of Turkey's desire to be accepted as a Western nation—something of which much of Europe remained unsure—and Turkey's prime minister ominously warned in the summer of 1995 that the country's Islamists would be strengthened if the European Parliament voted against this trade deal. The U.S. Administration, too, echoed this warning—Richard Holbrooke, the assistant secretary of state for Europe, was "cracking heads all over Europe to get Turkey the vote"[16]— even as it hoped that Turkey's desire for the customs union might force the country to make positive change.

Prime Minister Tansu Ciller, who had gone from political novice to political calculator in two years in office, had staked her political future on this trade agreement and now, with pressure mounting, she went into action. The change she chose to make was high-profile: the ban on separatist propaganda, commonly known as article 8 of the Anti-Terror Law. More than 100 writers, publishers, Kurdish activists, and others were in jail because of this law, which was used to punish nonviolent discussion of Kurds and their demands; some 2,000 cases were pending. Ciller, looking to make a splash, successfully called on parliament to strip the law of the phrase "regardless of intent," forcing prosecutors to at least prove that the defendant had wanted to dismember the state. The change, approved by Turkey's parliament about six weeks before the European Parliament was set to vote on the customs union, allowed Ciller to declare that she was tackling the Kurdish issue. Some 80 people were freed from prison immediately, while others were having their sentences reviewed.

The change to the Anti-Terror Law was part of the slow erosion of limits on political activity and criticism, limits that were bending and relaxing as more people challenged the system. Yet Turkey still maintained a host of laws that were used to punish those who criticized the state's treatment of Kurds and its human rights abuses. Their use depended on the political climate and, despite Ciller's willingness to change article 8, the political climate still insisted that those who challenged the system in speeches or writings be punished.

The European Parliament approved the customs union in mid-December. But it did not win Ciller much. Kurds did not feel like their problems had been tackled, and the rest of the country remained unhappy with allegations of corruption in the government, among other things. National elections at the end of December pushed the Islamist Welfare Party to first place with 21 percent of the vote, while Ciller's party fell to second place with 19 percent. The Kurdish party HADEP, still the favorite in the southeast, could not break the 10 percent minimum national vote threshold needed to enter parliament—although it commanded over 50 percent of the vote in parts of the southeast—and its seats went to other parties.

Over the next year-and-a-half, Turkey's mainstream politicians and opinion-makers focused on the Welfare Party and questions of whether the party wanted to weaken the secular state. After a minority government failed, Welfare Party chief Necmettin Erbakan formed a government in mid-1996 with his old rival, Tansu Ciller, as the junior partner. The Welfare Party, in theory, was more amenable to relaxing rules on Kurdish identity, which it saw as less critical than the religious tie of Islam. Like Kurds, they also were critical of aspects of the secular-based Kemalist state.[17] But precisely because Erbakan was an Islamist, he was even more constrained than other politicians. He could not chance doing something that might anger the powerful security establishment, which already was suspicious that he might try to weaken the secular state.

In February 1997, he was warned by the military-dominated National Security Council (MGK) to initiate certain measures to limit Islamist activity and freedom in the country. In June 1997, amid veiled threats of armed action by the Turkish military, he was forced to resign.

The new government, a minority coalition of three parties led by Mesut Yilmaz, of the Motherland Party, made clear at the start its indifference to Kurdish concerns. The coalition protocol stated that the problem in the southeast was not one of ethnic identity, insisting that it was economic, geographic, and social in nature. Yilmaz may have been driven by desire not to anger the military so soon after Erbakan was deposed, or he and his partners may have believed that because the PKK's armed fight was in decline, so was ethnic identity.

As Turkish politics moved into the end of the 1990s, its static approach to the Kurdish issue could not stop change. The legal restrictions on Kurdish identity remained, but applying them grew more difficult. The PKK's fight had emboldened Kurds, not all of them PKK sympathizers, and the huge increase in activists—or people interested in their Kurdish identity—simply forced creation of more space to act. The Kurdish legal party, HADEP, could not break into national politics, but in 1999 municipal elections it swept many of the major mayoral seats in the region. This gave the Kurdish party enormous influence, even as the main power in the region, the PKK, had lost military momentum.

Nonetheless, as the second half of the 1990s drew to a close, two things were clear. Ocalan was not going to change his unrealistic analyses of the PKK's strengths and the Turkish state's weaknesses, even as it became clear that he was losing military ground; and the Turkish state was unwilling to change its unrealistic approach to the Kurdish problem, even as it grew clear that while the PKK could be contained militarily, it could not be destroyed. What remained was the Kurdish problem.

13

Searching for a New Way,
1995–1998

DR. SULEYMAN, KUCUK Zeki, and about a dozen other PKK militants left Zap camp for Syria at the end of 1995. Crossing the border was more difficult than expected—Syrian soldiers, who usually ignored the traffic, opened fire—but the militants got past safely. It had been almost five years since either man had seen Ocalan, and they were hopeful they could discuss the PKK's deteriorating military situation with Ocalan face-to-face. But Ocalan made clear he would not accept challenges to his views.

"He wasn't the same Apo I had seen before," explained Dr. Suleyman. "I saw more his real face. When he greeted us, he started going on, saying, 'do you see how strong I am, if you are alive today, it's because of me.' A man, Ali K—— came up to Ocalan, and Ocalan started to swear at him, telling him he was a good-for-nothing bum. The man sort of wilted in front of us. But Ocalan was giving us a message, he was saying, you could be next."

The PKK's main activities in Syria took place in two, high-walled compounds on the edge of the capital Damascus. Each compound held about 200 people who spent upward of a year for political training. One compound was for Kurdish speakers, mainly Iraqi and Syrian PKK members, and the other was for Turkish speakers. The compounds contained more or less the same things. There were buildings where militants slept in single-sex dormitory-styled rooms, playing areas for volleyball and Ocalan's favorite sport, soccer, a swimming pool that never was filled with water, and a large garden where Ocalan lectured. Dr. Suleyman and Kucuk Zeki, who were expected to stay in Damascus for six months or more, were appointed to serve on the administrative committee for the educational program at the Turkish camp.

"[By now], the training was just reading Ocalan's analyses and listening to cassettes [of his speeches]," explained Dr. Suleyman. "Sometimes, Ocalan would come to speak and then we had to make sure everybody was ready."

When the PKK leader lectured, a certain protocol was demanded. Militants were warned not to sneeze, laugh, or otherwise act improperly. Those called on by Ocalan to answer a question were supposed to rise to their feet before doing so. More unusually, they were not supposed to sit down afterward—no matter how much Ocalan pressed them—and had to remain standing through the whole lecture, which could run six or seven hours.

"This was all explained before hand," said Neval, a three-year veteran of the PKK who was called to Damascus for the first time in 1995 to give Ocalan a report about the Woman's Congress that same year. After she spoke at the start of one of his lectures, Ocalan insisted she sit down again. But she knew to refuse. "I kept saying no, no, I will stand and he responded, 'You are still young.' And for five hours I stood."

Ocalan's lectures were supposed to be opportunities for militants to understand him, which he insisted was the same as understanding the PKK. He was a tireless speaker who often mixed historical reflections, childhood reminiscences, and PKK history. He was good at recalling people's names and he publicly delved into the details of people's lives before they joined the rebels, weaving their experiences into his lectures to underscore his points. Militants often reported feeling enervated and excited after spending time at the PKK's educational camps in Damascus, saying that his lectures helped focus their minds and built up their courage.

But Neval was taken aback when she first heard Ocalan speak.

Ocalan could talk without stop for three or four hours. He would talk about his childhood, how when he was a boy he would guard the fruit in the garden. After his lecture, everyone would sit around and analyze it, like, when he talks about a garden, he is really talking about socialism. To me, I understood that he was talking about a garden. . . . I thought everyone else understood but me and I couldn't figure out what was wrong, after all, I am not a stupid person, I am not an agent [out to undermine the PKK]. In the end, I decided the mistake was his . . . and that everyone was tricking themselves [into thinking they understood him]. I decided that in the shortest period of time, I needed to go back to [the fight].

It took Neval a few months to come to this conclusion and she knew that she could not say this to anyone else. Besides, what she cared about was the PKK's battle for a Kurdish homeland, not the PKK's leader. "Ocalan was the official leader, let him be the official leader," Neval explained. "What was important to me was fighting and that's what I was doing."

This view, that the PKK's fight was more important than Ocalan's leadership, grew increasingly popular in the second half of the 1990s among senior militants. Yet they also knew that Ocalan's analyses and his decisions were the only ones that mattered. Kucuk Zeki and Dr. Suleyman had arrived in Damascus intent on changing Ocalan's mind about PKK tactics and short-term goals in the aftermath of their discussions in Zap. But within a few months, they realized this was impossible.

"We told him the guerrillas couldn't find food and he would just deny it, he wasn't interested in listening," recounted Dr. Suleyman. "No-one could explain the true situation to him."

Instead, Ocalan called yet another conference in early 1996 to announce the next phase of the battle. Senior field commanders, many of whom had criticized the rebels' fight at the Zap Conference, again tried to put forward their views. "The limit was just not to criticize him personally," explained Kucuk Zeki. Ocalan refused to accept that the war had turned against the rebels. Instead, he repeated his demand that the rebels create enormous armed units, dig in to the mountains, and wait for the Turkish soldiers to attack.

"And then we would destroy them," said Kucuk Zeki, pausing. "We didn't believe that. Nothing came out of this meeting. He couldn't change our minds."

Someone Tries to Kill Ocalan

Kucuk Zeki was sitting in the garden of the Turkish-speakers' school one evening in April 1996, typing up the minutes from the conference. Suddenly, he heard a loud blast and shrapnel rained down on the garden. A bomb had gone off on the road that ran past the compound's entrance. No one was hurt, but a huge crater opened up in the road.

Ocalan immediately denounced this as a Turkish-plot to kill him, but if so, it was very poorly planned. The chance of the bomb killing him or any PKK rebels was so slight—Ocalan rarely used the road at night and the compound's walls protected the interior from damage —that it seemed more like a warning from Syrian intelligence to ensure Ocalan stayed in line. Nevertheless, the bombing proved useful to Ocalan.

"He came to the school afterwards and said to us, 'see, you didn't carry out my orders, if you had, then the [Turkish] state wouldn't have been able to get this far,'" said Kucuk Zeki, marveling at Ocalan's audacity. "He turned it around to use it against us."

Kucuk Zeki and Dr. Suleyman had joined the PKK as young university students, eager to take part in the national struggle. Four years later, they were prominent, experienced field commanders, who had survived not only Turkish bullets, but also the suspicions, intrigues, and rivalries that had led other PKK militants to be arrested or executed by their own organization. Now, after six months at Ocalan's side, they understood that the PKK was in a bottleneck.

"Ocalan would go on MED-TV and say things, he would speak to *Ozgur Gundem* [the Kurdish newspaper in Turkey] about everything he was doing, he thought it was all going well," said Kucuk Zeki, "but it was not."

That summer, Kucuk Zeki left to go back to Turkey.

> I didn't want to leave the PKK. So the best was to go far away from Ocalan. First I went to Zap and in June I went to the Cukurca border and crossed with about 70 people and another 70 crossed elsewhere. Meanwhile, clashes were breaking out. We were hungry, we had nothing. As I crossed the region, I saw the situation. In Botan, for three months they couldn't get bread. The same in Garzan. In another area, they only had some sheep they had taken from the village guards.

Things only worsened. The absence of villages meant they had almost no ties with the people and no way to get the supplies they desperately needed to run an effective war. Kucuk Zeki's team, based in Erzurum province, ran out of batteries for many of their wireless radios and could not get enough shoes to replace ripped and torn ones.

Their stocks of medicines finished. Sometimes, when Kucuk Zeki contacted the PKK's military headquarters in Zap, northern Iraq, he tried to explain what was going wrong. The commanders in Iraq, where the situation was much calmer and it was easy to resupply, responded by calling on armed units inside Turkey to redouble their efforts to ambush Turkish military brigades.

"We didn't have rockets, I said we didn't have enough strength," said Kucuk Zeki.

Worse, local people began to complain. They wrote letters to guerrilla commanders in the mountains, asking how much longer the situation could go on. The rebels were pressing the people and the Turkish military was pressing the people.

"There were constant attacks and we always had to defend ourselves," said Dr. Suleyman, who had returned to Amed province. "Yes, there were still some clashes at our initiative, but usually, we had to run and hide."

PKK rebels argued among themselves what to do.

"The question was, who would put the bell on their neck," explained Kucuk Zeki, drawing on a Turkish proverb. "This meant, who would be brave enough to tell Ocalan. I tried to tell people, look, the problem is not my fault, I work with what I have, but by 1998, even I wasn't working so hard. And the people were in a miserable state."

Semdin Sakik's Turn

Neval once noted that a militant needed three things to survive: cold-bloodedness, because it was imperative to stay calm under fire; luck, because sometimes, that's what it took to avoid getting killed; and physical stamina, because it was demanding to hike through the rugged Kurdish mountains day after day. But there was one thing she did not include—perhaps because it was so obvious—one had to make sure not to fall afoul of Ocalan.

This was something everyone in the PKK knew, from the newest recruit to the most senior, battle-tested commander. Dr. Suleyman, for example, who wanted to raise his concerns with Ocalan in 1996 about the direction of the war, was careful how he did it.

"If you spoke freely," he said with a shrug, "you could be pushed out and killed."

Dr. Suleyman's friend and neighbor (the provinces they commanded bordered on one another), Kucuk Zeki, also knew just how far he could go in trying to convince Ocalan that the PKK needed to change its armed tactics.

"He sort of gave me the chance to talk, but I knew the limit, the limit was just not to criticize him personally," said Kucuk Zeki.

Similarly, Batufa, a 15-year-old high-school student when she joined the PKK in 1993, picked up very quickly exactly what and was not allowed. The list included trying to run away, appearing to want to run away, having sexual relations, or simply falling afoul of one of the more senior commanders. "Someone would be gone, and they [commanders] would say they went to Paris," recalled Batufa, "this meant the person was killed."

But at some point, Semdin Sakik, the PKK's most experienced military commander, forgot this.[1] Perhaps it was because Sakik, a slightly built, almost shy-looking man who joined the PKK in 1979 (he later claimed he joined after his father refused to pay the money he needed to get married) had survived so much: he survived countless Turkish military operations; he survived Ocalan's internal political machinations to consolidate power; he survived the doubts that caused other PKK militants to flee or left them isolated or killed; and he managed to do this while creating formidable fighting forces and logistical networks in the provinces he commanded, proving himself not only brave and capable, but also lucky.

Sakik had become a popular symbol of the PKK's fight—in the southeast, his nickname was Semo, a name that connoted a beloved outlaw or slightly wayward, but still-respected family member. Like other senior commanders, Sakik was desperate for a solution to the PKK's military dead-end in the mid-1990s, or at least a debate, and he turned his frustration on four high-level PKK members who oversaw military operations. His outburst, which occurred during the 1995 Zap Conference, shocked even those who agreed with him.

"Sakik got up at the meeting and blamed [Ocalan's senior lieutenants] Duran Kalkan, Mustafa Karasu, Murat Karayilan, and Ebubekir [Halil Atac], saying that they didn't know war," recalled Dr. Suleyman. "I said to Sakik later, 'what are you saying? The problem is not linked to these people.' I said, 'if the war is going badly, it's not their fault, it's Apo's.' But this meeting basically was Semdin's end, because he spoke openly, he targeted certain people and so what happened? They wrote reports to Apo that Semdin wanted to take over the organization."

Ocalan was an expert at anticipating threats, but he perhaps was even better at creating them, a tactic he employed when he needed a public justification to get rid of or isolate someone he viewed as troublesome. This tactic he especially employed against senior-level militants, because simply announcing that they were traitors and executing them would have hurt morale and raised questions about his leadership. Instead, he created situations in which the person's own actions doomed him.

Perhaps most notably, he did this in 1993 to his brother, Osman Ocalan, who had gained loyalty and respect for his handling of the 1992 war that Turkish army-backed Iraqi Kurds launched against the PKK. In response, Abdullah Ocalan accused his brother of mishandling the war and the ceasefire negotiations—when to the contrary, he had done a respectable job—and then ordered a whole conference to explore his brother's "collaborationist" mistakes.[2]

The goal was to cut into Osman's credibility and when a very dispirited Osman fled to Iran around the summer of 1993, the PKK chief probably was thrilled. He could use this to claim his brother, who was forcibly returned from Iran by PKK members, was not loyal to the group. Osman subsequently faced the death sentence for vaguely defined disloyalties to the party, a charge he escaped only after he submitted a number of humiliating self-criticisms, including one that ran for 106 pages. By the time he was pardoned at the 1995 5th Congress he had been so thoroughly isolated and discredited that little remained of his position in the PKK, except as defined by his relationship to his brother. In other words, he could never be a threat, which is probably why in 1996, he was allowed to return to his old area of responsibility in Hakurk camp.

The Fall of Sakik

Now it was Sakik's turn. At first, Ocalan seemed to praise the experienced military commander. Following the 1995 Zap Conference, Ocalan transferred Sakik to the three-person executive committee that was supposed to oversee the activities of the PKK's Zap military headquarters. Members of the executive committee clashed constantly: Neval, in charge of women's activities, could not get along with Sakik, who believed his wider field experience gave him final say. The third member of the committee, Ali Haydar (Fuat) Kaytan, had almost no military experience but was a long-time Ocalan loyalist, and he also clashed with Sakik. Part of the problem was that the committee's authority was not clearly defined—Ocalan did this deliberately—making it impossible for it to function effectively. The executive committee members had no choice but to appeal to Ocalan to intercede.

"We spoke with Ocalan everyday on the phone," recalled Neval, "and told him of the problems."

To make things worse, the winter of 1995–1996 was a harsh one and the some 500 militants in the camp could do nothing but wait it out.

"It was very cold, we stayed in caves, sometimes it was so cold you couldn't speak," said Neval. "We ate lentil soup, but there was no fruit or vegetables. But Semdin wanted us to live like the rebels lived inside Turkey and he even forbade us from lighting the stove to keep warm." She shook her head in disgust. "We did anyway."

It was not long before relations among the three totally broke down. In the logic of the PKK, an inability to carry out one's responsibilities was a sign of insufficient loyalty to the PKK—or a sign that one was a traitor. In November 1996, Neval, Fuat, and Sakik were put under arrest. Stripped of their weapons—for Sakik, this must have been the worst insult—they were ordered to Damascus.

Presumably, like Neval, Sakik had to write a detailed report criticizing his own actions and thoughts and then a trial was held, during which other PKK members shouted out their criticisms and forced the defendant to admit to all sorts of real and imagined faults. But Sakik, unlike others forced to undergo this process, had a strong reputation.

His military experience could not be assailed, nor could his bravery be questioned, no matter how hard Ocalan may have tried to discredit him personally.

Late in 1997, Ocalan came up with a solution. He ordered Sakik to go fight in the region the PKK called the South-West, which bordered on Syria's far-western border and included the Hatay. The Hatay was the region that Syria claimed for itself, although it had long been incorporated into Turkey, and on occasion the PKK had staged a few small attacks there, most likely on Syria's orders. But in general, it was an area in which the PKK had never established a serious force. One reason was that it was not a wholly Kurdish area— there were a lot of Turks and Arabs, and a sprinkling of Armenians —but the main reason was the terrain. More flat than mountainous, it was hard to hide. In the South-West area, the PKK did not have any support infrastructure to speak of. By the late 1990s, one militant estimated the PKK's total force in the South-West at about 50 or 60 people.

"That's the same number of fighters that Sakik used just for his own personal protection," said Neval, scoffing at Ocalan's plan. "And Ocalan sent Sakik there accompanied by [just a few men] and they were the newest recruits."

Sakik had survived many a difficult battle, but this was one he realized he could not beat. He may have crossed the border and then retreated in the face of a large Turkish military operation or, according to another version, he never even went that far.

"Instead of crossing into the South-West, Sakik camped out on the border," explained Neval, who ran into Sakik a few weeks later. "He was immediately called back to Damascus and arrested."

Now Ocalan had him. There was no longer any need to throw out vague claims of lack of commitment to the PKK. Sakik had refused a direct order. He had refused to fight. He was sent, in handcuffs, to Gare camp in northern Iraq.

By coincidence, Neval also was at Gare, a PKK camp somewhat north of the Iraqi Kurdish city Dohuk. She was disillusioned and depressed by the criticisms leveled at her in Damascus and she felt trapped in an organization that she believed was stuck by Ocalan's leadership. But unlike Sakik, she was not under arrest and she carried a gun.

"Semdin came to Gare, he was thin, not the same Semdin," said Neval, who could not help but feel sorry for the PKK's once-great military commander. Sakik was finished in the PKK, Neval said. It did not even make sense to have him killed. "If he was killed, people would have reacted. But he had been made ineffective. There was no reason to kill him."

A day after running into Neval, Sakik fled the PKK. It was the middle of March 1998.

"I found out from Cemil Bayik," explained Neval, referring to a long-time PKK loyalist. Bayik, who had been in charge of guarding Sakik, was worried how to explain this to Ocalan. "Everyone runs from my side," he complained to Neval. "[Mehmet] Sener fled, Semdin fled, what will I say [to Ocalan]?"

Sakik hid out in the mountains for a few days before taking refuge with Barzani's KDP. The Iraqi Kurdish group had long been a sanctuary for former PKK militants, starting in the early 1980s, and KDP leader Massoud Barzani personally guaranteed Sakik's safety.[3] But four weeks later, on April 13, four Turkish military helicopters swooped down on a car carrying Sakik, his brother Arif who also fled, and a few Iraqi Kurdish guards. Within a few minutes, Sakik and his brother were bundled into a helicopter and flown to Diyarbakir. The man viewed as the second most important in the PKK was in Turkish custody.

The tale of Sakik's fall from grace said a lot about Ocalan. The PKK leader put protecting his leadership first, to the point that he would destroy his chief military commander. Ocalan did not consider that this might hurt the PKK's ability to wage war, because he believed that only his leadership mattered.

But Sakik's capture and the aftermath also said a lot about the Turkish state's inability to face up to the reality of the Kurdish problem. Sakik's capture could have been an opportunity to investigate the PKK—what it wanted, why it increasingly was unlikely to succeed, and what political steps could help wrest Kurdish support away from the group. Instead, the arrest of Sakik was seen as an opportunity to discredit those people, mainly Kurds but many Turks as well, who had proven themselves troublesome by questioning the state's Kurdish policy.

Within two weeks of Sakik's arrest, statements purporting to be from Sakik were leaked to the Turkish media, which did not question their authenticity. Each day brought publication of new, devastating claims by Sakik: Akin Birdal, the Turkish chairman of the nongovernmental Turkish Human Rights Association, which Turkish officials long accused of being allied with the PKK, took orders directly from Ocalan; two Islamist-oriented newspapers, not uncoincidentally linked to Islamist-based parties the military mistrusted, had promised not to criticize the PKK; the weekly meetings in Istanbul of mainly Kurdish women whose husbands had "disappeared" was a PKK operation; various Kurdish politicians, some from mainstream political parties, supported the PKK. And then there was the real shock: Ocalan had paid some Turkish journalists to write articles in favor of the PKK. It almost seemed too good to be true.[4]

"The PKK has no secrets left," boasted Turkish *Hurriyet* newspaper columnist Oktay Eksi. "Even if the Turkish public does not yet know, the state knows with whom the PKK had connections and what sort of support they secretly gave, from the evil names given in Semdin Sakik's statements." Eksi, who also was chairman of the Turkish Press Council, warned especially about those journalists who had turned on their motherland. "It is necessary that we learn which lowlives are stabbing us in the back, [while] posing as 'responsible intellectuals' or 'honest journalists.'"[5]

The answer was surprising: Mehmet Ali Birand, the internationally respected *Sabah* newspaper columnist who distinguished himself with thoughtful pieces about the Cyprus problem, relations with the European Union, Turkey's role internationally, and, now and then, the domestic Kurdish problem. Cengiz Candar, another well-known *Sabah* newspaper columnist with a liberal bent, also was said to have been named by Sakik.

"I don't believe it," Hasan Cemal, a colleague of the two men, later wrote in a book that combined his extensive reporting on the Kurds with astute political observances. At the time, Cemal wanted to write a column in response. But, "it is understood that we will not write about this in Sabah. . . . I can't do my job," he painfully noted. "I can't write what I think."[6]

Sabah newspaper immediately fired Birand. Candar was put on a sort of leave. A few days later, the deputy chief of the Turkish General

Staff, General Cevik Bir, apparently incensed that Birand still was doing his television news show, phoned the owner of the station and demanded Birand's program be stopped. It was. Akin Birdal, meanwhile, was seriously wounded by two gunmen who burst into the Human Rights Association's Ankara office. After all this, when Sakik appeared in court and denied making these statements, it almost seemed irrelevant. The damage was done.[7]

Sakik received a death sentence, which later was commuted to life imprisonment. He apparently has few visitors—most Kurds are not willing to risk visiting a PKK traitor, even if they do not like the PKK.

Ecco Homo

Ocalan's life in Syria grew very comfortable over the years. He split his time between two large villas—one on the edge of Aleppo and one on the edge of Damascus—each with a big garden, a swimming pool, and a place to play volleyball. The villas were taken care of by female militants, who did the cooking, cleaning, and also worked on transcribing Ocalan's speeches. The PKK leader also had various apartments, where he held interviews and meetings, but the villas were places to relax. In the one in Aleppo, for example, he liked to walk in the garden, which he dubbed the *ulke*, the Turkish word meaning country, the same word Kurds used to refer to their Kurdish homeland. He also kept a falcon, which he named Mahabad, after the short-lived Iranian Kurdish republic, and he used to stroke and talk to it while feeding it raw lamb meat.

Ocalan did not live a luxurious life, at least not by Western standards, but some PKK militants still were surprised to see how he lived, especially after the hardships they faced in the mountains.

"Between 1992 and 1995 I saw terrible things in Iraq," recalled Helin, who stayed in one of Ocalan's villas in 1995. "There were people without proper clothing, not a lot of food, sometimes not enough shoes. In Damascus, I saw this beautiful house and some contradictions came into my mind. Apo always was talking like he did everything, but what about the people in the mountains?"

But inside the PKK, Ocalan had created a world that revolved around himself and it was hard for him to imagine it could be otherwise. When he spoke, everyone clapped. When he entered a room, everyone stood up. When he made a decision, nobody contradicted or questioned him. All his speeches were taped, transcribed, and distributed for study. Even his phone calls to PKK commanders, calls that could last over an hour, were taped and then transcribed for later use.

His narcissism spilled over into every activity. When he played soccer with men in the PKK, as he often did at the group's Damascus-based compounds, players took care to pass the ball to him and equal care not to block his goals. But he insisted that someone keep track of each goal he scored. Once, the PKK militant tasked with keeping track of Ocalan's goals forgot to count four of them. Ocalan blew up at the man—an experienced fighter from the very-tough Botan province. Neval, who was watching the game, explained that Ocalan just couldn't stop screaming:

> He asked Mehmet how many goals he had made and Mehmet said 12. Ocalan started shouting, "You bum, how could you forget four of my goals." Mehmet apologized, saying he only counted 12, but Ocalan kept shouting. Later that day, when Ocalan came to give a lecture, the first thing he said was, "Where is that low-life? How could he forget four of my goals? To forget four goals is like forgetting four fighters. And to forget four fighters is to forget to kill four [Turkish] soldiers and that means to forget the revolution and to forget Kurdistan." After that, I thought all right, now it's over. Then that night he was interviewed on [the Kurdish satellite television] MED-TV, and he started complaining again, saying, "That bum, that bum commander, he forgot four of my goals, how could he do this?"

Ocalan was so convinced of his strength, which to him equaled the PKK's strength, that he began to believe that the PKK's actions were behind many world events. Neval, who stayed a month in Ocalan's villa in Aleppo (Ocalan asked her to write a novel, never completed, about the PKK's Zap camp), used to hear him all the time:

> Ocalan saw himself as the center of world events. If there was a minister talking on the television, from any country, the United States,

Germany, Ocalan would say that the person speaking had been influenced by Ocalan's own speeches. He wasn't exaggerating. He really believed this. Of course, some things were affected by what the PKK was doing, but not the way he saw things. He assumed that everything was done by him or because of him. He was a man in love with himself. Really. He used to say what the United States and Germany should do in general, as if he was making revolution for the world, not just for the Kurds.

Ocalan's belief in himself was reinforced by the esteem with which many PKK members did hold him. While some were disillusioned when they met him, especially those who came to Syria after years fighting inside Turkey, where they could see for themselves the PKK's problems, there were many more who did feel empowered by getting to meet him. After all, he was the leader of the biggest, most powerful Turkish Kurdish national movement, a movement that had helped lift the Kurds from national oblivion and forced Turkey to at least admit that it had a problem.

"Last night I saw the party leadership in my dream," PKK militant Zinarin, a well-educated young women in her early twenties, wrote in her diary a few months before dying in a clash inside Turkey in September 1997. She had just spent a year in Damascus, where photographs show her tearfully grasping Ocalan before leaving to fight. "It was a beautiful dream. . . . You must know how much I miss him! Everything that he said echoes hundreds of times in my brain, it resonates with the sound of his voice, it pierces my heart."[8]

Gurbetelli Ersoz, the one-time editor of the Kurdish newspaper *Ozgur Gundem*, who apparently desperately wanted to leave the legal field and take part in armed activities (despite physical problems that made it hard for her to walk), was very harshly criticized by Ocalan after she arrived in Damascus around early 1995. Yet she accepted the criticism as something that could help make her a better PKK member.

"The Party Leadership [Ocalan] stressed that I must not be afraid of facing up to the ways in which I have been stained by my liberal views. . . . This criticism was very difficult for me, but I have been strengthened by this," she wrote in her diary, describing a phone conversation she had with Ocalan after she was sent to a PKK military camp in northern Iraq. "I feel like I have been reborn. All the troubles I lived before have been left behind . . . I have found the answer to my question: The PKK."[9]

14

Ocalan, Caught by Surprise, 1998–1999

IN THE SUMMER of 1998, Ocalan turned tense and short-tempered. He had a lot of mysterious meetings. Suddenly, he ordered the PKK's two training compounds disbanded and militants were sent to other parts of the country and northern Iraq. "Syria told Ocalan there was a lot of pressure from Turkey and we have to change places," recalled Batufa, a PKK fighter ordered to Ocalan's villa in Aleppo. "And the camps were closed."

This was not the first time Syria ordered Ocalan to close down a PKK training facility or tried to limit his movements inside Syria. In 1991, he reportedly was detained briefly after meetings he held with Iraqi Kurdish representatives; in 1992, Syria shuttered the PKK's military training facility in the Bekaa; and in 1997, Ocalan apparently was told to close down the houses he used in the Bekaa's Bar Elias town for meetings. But this was the first time that Turkey seriously pressured Syria. Toward the end of the summer, Turkish officials even started to hint that, if necessary, military force might be used to dislodge the PKK leader.

The capture of PKK commander Semdin Sakik not only had emboldened Ankara, but also Sakik likely provided new, damning details of Syrian support to the rebel group. At the same time, Turkey clearly had gained the military advantage in the southeast and knew it had the military advantage over Syria. With the arrival of a new Turkish military command in August, Turkey's rhetoric only grew more heated. For the first time, Ankara seemed serious about using military force.

Syria must have made its worries known to Ocalan, because late that summer, the PKK chief began raging against the international and internal conspiracies trying to bring him down. Unable to believe that he might be abandoned by his long-time backer, he insisted the real problem lay with PKK supporters and sympathizers who were plotting to destroy him. He claimed that a well-known Kurdish journalist in Germany was an agent of the German state, which in turn was working with the PKK's enemies. In fact, he told Batufa and the others at the Aleppo villa, the whole of the PKK's European committee needed to be put on trial because they were no longer doing their jobs.

"Exactly at the point . . . the situation got even worse," Batufa explained.

In the middle of September, Turkish Land Forces Commander General Atilla Ates turned up at a Turkish military base near the Syrian border and accused Damascus of exploiting Turkey's good will: "At this point, our patience is finished."[1] A few days later, Turkey's Chief of General Staff, General Huseyin Kivrikoglu, spoke about an undeclared war, implying that Ankara had to defend itself. Meanwhile, there were rumors that Turkey had moved some 10,000 troops to the Syrian border.[2]

Members of the PKK's European Committee (officially known as the ERNK Front), flew to Syria to discuss the situation with Ocalan. The PKK's main spokesman in Europe, Akif Hasan, was himself from Syria and he warned Ocalan that Damascus might not be able withstand the pressure. One problem was that even Arab countries, which might normally be expected to stand up for another Arab country, appeared disinterested in backing Syria in a fight over a Kurdish revolutionary leader.

"But Ocalan insisted he was following the situation, he argued that they will try to take this [military] base, but that he had taken precautions and no-one could push him out," said Hasan.

When Hasan noted at the meeting that if Ocalan were kicked out, the PKK would find itself in a very bad situation, someone else dismissed his concerns.

" 'Oh, they always come to the border and threaten us, it's nothing,' " he recalled one woman as saying. Hasan, whose fluent English allowed him to follow what was happening on the international scene, believed that Ocalan needed to consider worse-case scenarios. "The problem was, Ocalan did not take any precautions."

Ocalan's problem was that he could not accept that maybe he was not so important after all. He could not imagine that his longtime backer might kick him out. He had been based in Syria for nearly two decades and over the years, he had been useful to pressure Turkey and as a way to redirect Syrian Kurds away from their own surroundings. More recently, PKK attacks on Iraqi Kurds helped keep the region unstable, making it even harder for an Iraqi Kurdish state to emerge and limiting U.S. influence there, two things of interest to Syria. But Damascus also was very logical about its support for such militant groups and its primary rule was that these groups could do nothing that threatened Syria's national integrity. It was not Ocalan's fault, but it was enough that Turkey was making serious threats to force Syria to reconsider. Taken all together, Syrian President Hafez Assad began to think that sacrificing Ocalan made the most sense.

In early October, as Egypt warned Syria that Turkey was serious about its military threats, Syrian officials told Ocalan that they faced an unpleasant choice and it would be best if he left. "Either war is going to break out between us and Turkey," Ocalan later recalled the Syrians telling him, "or we will arrest you and turn you over to the Turks, the choice is yours."[3]

On October 9, 1998, Ocalan quietly slipped out of the country—as quietly as he had arrived 19 years before. It took Ankara a few days to believe Ocalan really was gone. PKK supporters heard the news piecemeal, as Ocalan's driver traveled through northern Syria, passing on the news.

"Ocalan's driver came and said Ocalan was gone," recalled Batufa. "That was it."

But Ocalan's driver did not have any more information.

"I was in Qamishli when I got the news," said Azman. "We didn't know where he had gone. After about 15 days, groups of militants were organized to leave Syria and go to Kurdistan [northern Iraq]."

Because of the PKK's most recent round of clashes with Iraqi Kurdish leader Barzani's fighters, Azman and the others were unable to use the normal crossing route. Instead, they cut into Iraq closer to Mosul, where Saddam Hussein's troops were in control.

"The Iraqi guards acted like they didn't see us," he recalled. "We would walk around the outpost, and then get back into the car."

Slowly, PKK militants gathered in Hakurk camp in northern Iraq, the PKK's main base near the triangle where the borders of Turkey, Iran, and Iraq meet. There, they met up with newly arriving militants from Turkey, who were coming to prepare for the January 1999 6th Congress. Most of them heard about Ocalan's disappearance on their way, but like everyone else, they were confused about what this meant and where he was. One of those who came to Hakurk was Ayhan Ciftci, who was certain that it was his turn to be arrested and blamed for the PKK's latest round of military failures.

"But I decided I had to go, because otherwise, the choice was to take a group of fighters and leave, and I wouldn't be able to do much then," said Ciftci, usually called Kucuk Zeki. He paused for a moment. "I thought that maybe I wouldn't be killed, just blamed. They had to blame someone for the way the war had declined."

Kucuk Zeki's journey out of Turkey initially took him to Zap camp, where his arrival was supposed to be reported to Ocalan in Damascus. Duran (Abas) Kalkan, one of Ocalan's trusted lieutenants, gave Kucuk Zeki a phone number to call.

"I called the number and spoke with Ocalan, he was in Russia," said Kucuk Zeki.

Ocalan, Surprised Again

Akif Hasan, who had returned to Europe by the time Ocalan fled Syria, received a phone call around November 10, 1998, informing him that a "guest" was on the way. The guest was Ocalan, and the destination was Italy.

"[PKK European spokesman] Kani Yilmaz said to me that a guest was coming and that I should do whatever I had to, but a guest was coming and we needed a solution," recalled Hasan.

Ocalan's situation was critical.[4] He had fled Syria six weeks earlier and was still on the run, unable to find a country to grant him refuge. Initially, he assumed he could get asylum in Greece, where the PKK had broad sympathy, and on October 9 he had flown directly to Athens on a commercial airliner out of Damascus. But when he arrived, Greece "showed its ugly face,"[5] as he later called it, and gave him three hours to get out of the country.

That same night, Ocalan secured permission to fly to Moscow, thanks to the patronage of ultranationalist leader Vladimir Zhirinovsky. But despite strong support in the Russian parliament to grant Ocalan asylum, Russian government officials did not want him to stay. Turkey had since discovered, reportedly with the help of U.S. intelligence services, that Ocalan was being sheltered in Moscow. Russian officials, eager to avoid a showdown with Turkey, denied Ocalan's presence, but at the same time made clear to the PKK that their leader had to go.

Hasan and other PKK representatives frantically worked with sympathetic leftist Italian politicians to come up with a solution. Their contacts in the Communist Refoundation Party, an offshoot of the old Communist Party, suggested they speak with the party's president.

"They said, 'What if we introduce you to the leader of the [re-formed] Communist Party, he is a close friend of the prime minister of Italy,'" explained Hasan, describing the hurried two days before Ocalan flew into Rome's airport. "We went to his house. This man was very happy, and asked what he could do for us. He said, 'Should I call the prime minister?' And we said, 'If you do this, we will be very happy.'"

The Communist Party leader picked up a telephone and called Prime Minister Massimo D'Alema, himself formerly from the Communist Party. Hasan heard one side of the conversation, and afterward the man repeated what the prime minister had said. Hasan explained:

> The Communist Party president said [on the phone], "Listen, Abdullah Ocalan, president of the PKK, is coming today or tomorrow." And D'Alema replied, "Who is this Abdullah?" And the other man said, "He is the PKK president." And then D'Alema asked, "So, and what sort of passport?" He spoke like he had no information about who Ocalan was. So the other man said, "I don't know, but in any case, it will be a false one." By this point, they were laughing. And the prime minister responded, "Ok, let him come, but please have one of your people coordinate this."[6]

On November 12, Ocalan flew to Rome, announced his real identity and demanded asylum. Certain of being arrested and held in prison—Italian foreknowledge of his arrival only assured him entry into the country, not freedom—he claimed chest pains and was whisked off instead to a hospital under heavy guard.

News of Ocalan's arrival broke slowly over the next few hours and then exploded. While Kurds rallied on his behalf, Turks assumed that Europe would not protect a man they saw as a terrorist leader.

"Apo's capture is the biggest blow struck against the PKK," stated Turkish Prime Minister Mesut Yilmaz, clearly gleeful at the news. "We do not consider it likely that Italy will shelter Apo."[7]

Ocalan's arrival plunged not just Italy, but all of Europe and also the United States into a dilemma. With Turkey clamoring for Ocalan's immediate extradition, Washington pressuring Rome not to give the PKK leader political asylum, and many European countries clearly relieved that Ocalan was not in their hands, the PKK leader's fate became a question of relations: between Europe and the United States, which not only viewed Ocalan as an unrepentant terrorist leader, but always was mindful of the interests of its close ally Turkey; and between Europe and Turkey, which viewed European hesitation as a sign that it was not serious about fighting terrorism. Ocalan's leadership of a violent group made it near-impossible for the West to embrace him, yet few were under any illusions about Turkey's treatment of its Kurdish minority.

Le Soir newspaper in Brussels, the political capital of Europe, noted, "Much imagination will be required to reconcile legality, ethics and political appropriateness [to end this crisis]."[8]

Turks refused to accept any delay and as days passed and Ocalan remained under heavy guard in Italy, the mood in Turkey turned angry. Demonstrations were held outside the Italian embassy in Ankara. A boycott of Italian goods was launched and lucrative defense contracts were threatened. One Turkish newspaper columnist suggested that Ocalan was being protected by the Italian mafia. Another noted that if Europe learned more about this baby-murderer (as Ocalan often was called), it would certainly make the right decision.

It was no surprise that Turks were frustrated by Italy's inaction on deporting Ocalan. But apart from everything else, the first obstacle was that Italian law blocked extradition of suspects to countries with the death penalty, which Turkey had. Ocalan's request for political asylum, which Italian authorities delayed, also complicated the situation. One thing was clear: The Italian decision to allow Ocalan in the country, a decision probably borne out of sympathy and late night exhaustion, did not take into account the day after.

Rome soon appealed to Germany to take Ocalan off its hands. The PKK leader, formally arrested in Italy because of an outstanding German warrant that dated back eight years, should have been extradited to Germany to stand trial instead. But Germany announced it was not interested in prosecuting him. German officials, mindful of the PKK's organizational network on its own territory, openly admitted they were afraid that putting Ocalan on trial would spark violence among their 2.5 million-strong Turkish and Kurdish communities.

Italian officials imposed a type of house arrest while they struggled to come up with another plan. Ocalan was moved to a three-story building—rented by PKK supporters—on the edge of Rome. Two floors were filled with Italian police and their surveillance equipment and one floor housed the PKK leader and his assorted guests.

In many ways, Rome was pleasant and life in the villa was good. Ocalan was not free, but he was free to contact whom he wanted. And he did. He ran the PKK via the telephone, calling militants in Syria and northern Iraq. He issued orders: who should go where, what decisions should come out of meetings. In the villa, he entertained a nonstop roster of guests: There were PKK officials from Europe with whom he discussed his future, journalists eager to get his views, and a bevy of foreign and Kurdish figures who came to show sympathy for the embattled leader. Ocalan's access to the media was so great, and the Kurdish issue so widely debated, that some Turkish commentators morosely suggested it would have been better had Ocalan been left alone in Syria, where at least he was isolated from the world.

"There was a lot of support for him," recalled Hasan. "On the Italian houses there were banners saying 'Ocalan, you are welcome in our country.' You could see PKK flags and his pictures. People asked for his autograph."

But Italy's delay in reviewing Ocalan's request for asylum was worrisome. Ocalan thought it would be much easier in Italy and was surprised, even depressed, to be treated more like a criminal than a political leader. The fact that he was in Europe, where all attention was focused on the Kurdish issue, did not console him. Nor did the fact that his plight, such as it was, had rallied almost all Kurds to defend him. The PKK leader was unused to any restrictions on his movements—save for the general guidelines Syria gave him—and he was even more used to doing exactly what he wanted, observed only by very loyal PKK militants.

"Some days, his mood was good, sometimes he was down," said Hasan, who met with Ocalan frequently. "He was afraid of going to prison and he worried he would be killed. He worried that he would lose his presidency, that he would lose control of the PKK, that he would lose his authority." Hasan also thought Ocalan was uncomfortable in a democratic country. "I think he was afraid of European democracy and power, because in Europe, everything rests on law [and not his will]."

Ocalan's mood turned increasingly grim and his pronouncements erratic. He referred darkly to international plots, which the PKK's *Serxwebun* party newspaper claimed were led by the United States and Israel. One minute, he decided to flee Italy. The next, he announced he was going to stay and transform the PKK into a true political movement. He warned he might resign as chief of the PKK and then backed down. He called an end to the armed struggle but did not offer a new, coherent political plan for the PKK. In telephone calls to PKK militants in northern Iraq, he swore at them for mistakes that he blamed for leading to his expulsion from Syria.

Gradually, as the weeks went by, Ocalan spoke more and more of finding a country more receptive to his presence. Other Kurdish figures, including Kemal Burkay, the only rival whom Ocalan took at all seriously, pressed Ocalan in phone calls to use Europe to his advantage.

"I told him it was good to be there, that Rome was a big chance for him," recounted Burkay. "But the problem with this man is that he expected he would get political asylum right away. When he saw it might be different, he changed his mind."

Ironically, the support Ocalan received from Kurds across the political and national spectrum probably frightened him. The idea of a broad, national movement was in the air, even among PKK supporters, yet in truth, Ocalan never wanted this. In the past, when he suggested creating such a body, he was careful to strangle or destroy it before it could challenge his rule. Now, it began to seem like unity might be imposed on him, with no chance to resist. He knew this would mean a dilution of the PKK's power, which in turn would mean a loss of his own power.

Ocalan insisted that his representatives find a more hospitable country. Some of the PKK's European representatives, either because they were afraid to tell him the truth or because they, too, misjudged international support, agreed this was possible.

The final decision came down to Ocalan.

"One day I called E——," said Hasan, referring to a former PKK European representative who did not want to be interviewed. "It was around 2 A.M. and I said, it's settled, our president has decided to stay. And E—— said, 'that is good, but is there any guarantee he won't change his mind at 6 A.M.?'"

On January 16, 1999, Ocalan changed his mind for the last time. The PKK rented a plane and Ocalan flew to an airport just outside Moscow. His arrival was approved after negotiations between PKK representatives and the Russian authorities. But Russia immediately reneged on this deal, which Ocalan had believed would allow him to stay six months (it is quite possible PKK operatives in Moscow either misunderstood, were talking to the wrong people, or just assumed things would work out), and threatened to return him to Syria forcibly. On January 29, after a week of being held under Russian Security control in Tajikistan, he was flown to St. Petersburg, where he was picked up by a private plane apparently arranged by a retired Greek navy admiral, long sympathetic to the PKK. The plane flew Ocalan back to Greece.

Greece was supportive of the PKK when there was no risk—a progovernment newspaper, for example, had demanded Ocalan receive asylum in Italy, conveniently ignoring that Athens kicked him out rather than do the same. But when there was risk, Greece balked. News of Ocalan's return panicked the government and Prime Minister Costas Simitis reportedly fainted when he heard the news.[9] He had reason to be afraid. The Turkish National Security Council had indicated that any neighboring country that sheltered Ocalan could face military attack.[10] And thanks to the outstanding tension between Turkey and Greece over Cyprus and the Aegean Islands, Athens could be a very attractive target.

Greek officials told Ocalan to leave the country. To encourage him, they promised him and his Greek backers that they would arrange asylum for him in Holland. This was enough to convince Ocalan to get back on the plane, but after he was dropped off in Minsk, Belarus, the expected follow-up plane never arrived. He later complained that he waited "four hours in the freezing cold."[11]

Just after midnight on February 1, Ocalan returned to Athens on the same plane that brought him. Greek security officials refused him entry and immediately whisked him to Corfu island. It was suggested to Ocalan that he go to Kenya and use this as a base for getting political asylum in an African country. Until he got that permission, he would stay under Greek protection in the ambassador's own villa. It was a crazy idea and later Ocalan argued this all was a plot; but if anything, the plan just showed how desperate Greece was to get rid of Ocalan, yet how it did not want to be the country that handed him over to the Turks. At least not unless they absolutely had to.

A Greek plane flew Ocalan to Kenya on February 2 and he was swept through passport control. At the ambassador's villa, Ocalan prepared his request for political asylum. Meanwhile, Turkish and U.S. intelligence services—and maybe others—were trying to pinpoint his location. It turned out not to be very hard. Word was out about Ocalan's brief stay in Greece. And in Nairobi, he used his cell phones all the time and took walks in the residence's garden. Within two days of his arrival, a Kenyan newspaper ran his photograph with the headline: "Do you know this man?"[12]

On February 5, a Greek government official called the embassy and, using code-words, told them Ocalan had to leave. New promises were made, again about finding refuge in Holland. Pressure mounted from Athens on Greek embassy officials and Ocalan, who refused to leave the building. On February 12, Kenya informed the Greek Embassy that they knew Ocalan was there and they wanted him gone. It seems U.S. intelligence services, which after the August bombing of the U.S. embassy set up a huge presence in Nairobi, had given them proof of Ocalan's presence. Certainly, Ankara received the same information and probably much earlier. Greek officials, feeling pressure from all sides, suggested to Ocalan that he take refuge in a church in the city center.

Ocalan could sense the situation was grim. He phoned frantically, trying to find another country to take him, issuing last minute orders to militants. Around this time he telephoned his old villa in Aleppo, where PKK fighter Batufa was still based, and ranted against militants he blamed for his predicament. He accused Neval, one of the senior female commanders, of being a Mata Hari and insisted she and others previously assigned to the Zap headquarters—including Semdin Sakik—had tried to form a power bloc against him.

"He spoke really fast," recalled Batufa. "He said he wanted us to write the truth, he said, 'Write me. There is a conspiracy against me. Nobody even lets my plane land.'"

Then Ocalan was informed by Greek officials that Holland was willing to accept him. He had no choice but to believe them. On February 15, a Toyota Land Cruiser drove up to the residence. Kenyan police emerged from the car to escort him. When the Greek ambassador said he would drive Ocalan to the airport, he was told this was impossible. He was told he could meet Ocalan at the airport instead. The Greek ambassador waited for hours at the airport. The car carrying Ocalan never arrived.

From the start, the car was under the control of Turkish agents or people working for them. They drove directly to a separate part of the airport, where a private plane—rented from an unsuspecting Turkish businessman—stood by. Ocalan later said he realized early on something was amiss, but also knew there was nothing he could do. Yet he didn't know exactly what was going on and according to one version, until the last minute, he really believed he was flying to Holland.[13] Then he boarded the plane. He was handcuffed, restrained, blindfolded, gagged, and belted in, and probably sedated.[14] A military doctor on board ensured his health.

The Turkish intelligence agents on board recorded at least part of the journey and later released segments to television stations. In one segment, played over and over again, masked Turkish agents remove Ocalan's blindfold and gag. Ocalan squints heavily and moves slowly. Then one agent speaks:

"Abdullah Ocalan, welcome home."[15]

Ocalan was on his way to Turkey.

Kurds believe that Ocalan fell victim to a plot, which they variously have blamed on the United States, Israel, and the whole of Europe. Certainly, the United States played a role, as did Europe (the case for Israeli involvement appears weak). The United States provided intelligence information and, perhaps more importantly, pressure to ensure no European country gave Ocalan asylum. Europe, too, played its role, turning its back on the leader of a group that many countries had sheltered or tolerated out of sympathy for Kurdish demands.

But Ocalan ultimately fell victim to himself. The same single-minded focus and absolute belief in himself that made it possible for Ocalan to build the PKK into a powerful and popular movement also helped destroy him. Unable to see that he was not all-powerful, that he was not always right, and that, in the end, not everyone saw him as he saw himself, led Ocalan to one fatal mistake. He fled Italy. At that point, there was nothing left to do but wait.

Jail

Turkey expected that Ocalan's capture would cause the PKK to collapse and, just in case militants in the mountains had not heard the news, officials reportedly wanted to blanket the region with photographs of a handcuffed Ocalan standing in between two Turkish flags.[16] The assumption was that senior PKK commanders, afraid that news of Ocalan's capture would demoralize militants and cause them to flee, had collected people's radios to ensure they could not follow Ocalan's flight.

But in fact, news of Ocalan's capture, which was widely known inside the PKK, initially boosted support for him.

"We heard the announcement of his arrest on the radio," said Kucuk Zeki, who was at the 6th Congress in northern Iraq. "Everyone was in shock. Despite all the problems, this was Turkey's gain and it was not something to be happy about. It was like the world had been destroyed. Everyone got upset."

Kurds everywhere were shocked and angry. In major cities throughout Europe, stretching from London to Vienna, Kurds went on violent rampages, aiming much of their wrath against the embassies and businesses of the two countries they blamed for giving up Ocalan —Kenya and Greece. Quickly, anger turned on Israel as well—amid rumors the Mossad played a role—and in Berlin, three Kurds were shot dead as they stormed the Israeli consulate. Some people tried to burn themselves alive in protest. In Iraq and Iran, Kurds held rowdy demonstrations; and in Turkey, where protests had to be expressed carefully, shops in the main city Diyarbakir were shuttered.

In the United States, Kurds and their supporters gathered outside the White House to condemn Ocalan's arrest. The soft-spoken president of the independent Washington Kurdish Institute, Najmaldin Karim, an American Iraqi Kurd, tried to explain this show of support. "There has really not been any other venue for the Kurds to express their opinion, explain themselves, and try to gain their rights like equal citizens in Turkey with preservation of their Kurdish identity," he told Voice of America two days after Ocalan's capture. "The PKK has become a rallying point."[17]

Ocalan in captivity became a symbol of the Kurdish nation—oppressed, imprisoned, used, and then discarded by nations with other interests at heart. The publicly released pictures of him—slumped clumsily in the airplane that returned him to Turkey, grimacing in front of Turkish flags in an unnamed interrogation room—seemed designed to humiliate not just him, but Kurds themselves. Turkey had reason to rejoice in the capture of Ocalan, and it was not unusual to photograph Kurdish and leftist suspects in front of the Turkish flag, but the government appeared eager to use this to discredit the whole of the Kurdish "problem."

"The issue Turkey faces is not ethnic or Kurdish, as the Europeans like to call it,"[18] Prime Minister Bulent Ecevit said soon after Ocalan's arrest. Instead, insisted Ecevit, who presided over Turkey's military invasion of Cyprus in 1973 after a Greek-backed coup, the issue was one of regional underdevelopment and poverty.

But there were some Turks who said that now was the time to act. For many years, it was generally understood that Ankara would not substantially change its approach to its Kurdish minority while the PKK's war raged. Even the late President Turgut Ozal, who was interested in instituting reforms, had made clear he first needed a PKK ceasefire. The conundrum Ankara faced, like any country dealing with such an uprising, was that while reforms might lessen support for the rebels, it might also strengthen the rebels because they could claim this as a win. But Turkey faced a very different situation now. With Ocalan in prison and the PKK clearly scrambling to figure out its next move—and how to govern itself—the time was right to undercut the group and its demands.

"This is the time to act in a cool-headed manner, however difficult that may be," noted political columnist Cengiz Candar, one of the journalists smeared the year before, mainly for being too even-handed on the Kurdish issue. "I think that the 'Kurdish problem' created the PKK and Apo, rather than vice versa. The solution lies . . . in making democratic arrangements which would enable [Kurds] to fully express themselves politically and culturally."[19]

Kurds did not appear to have any great hope that Ocalan's capture would spark real change. If anything, they appeared convinced that Turkey would use this exactly to wipe out, again, the small gains Kurds had made over the years. But politically active Kurds, even those independent of the PKK, thought Ocalan's trial might at least be a way to make their case heard. An impassioned defense by the PKK leader of the armed struggle, mixed in with his explanations of what drove people to such extreme measures, would underscore the repression Kurds faced and the need for change. At the same time, international attention on the trial—while no European country wanted to try Ocalan, they all were eager to demand he got a fair trial in Turkey—had already forced the government to begin to discuss various legal changes related to its state security courts. Ocalan as a rallying cry appeared almost a stronger draw than Ocalan as the PKK leader.

"They are trying to put the Kurdish people on trial in the person of Abdullah Ocalan," said Kurdish lawyer Ahmet Zeki Okcuoglu, who in the 1990s distinguished himself by his unrelenting criticism of Ocalan. Now, he had volunteered to lead the PKK leader's defense team, a symbol that Ocalan had become a symbol. "I could not simply remain an observer in this situation. I decided to put on my lawyer's cap and defend my people in Ocalan's person."[20]

The problem, however, was Ocalan. His first statements aboard the airplane were confused and slurred and it was not clear how the video had been edited, but he did seem to be taking a rather conciliatory stance: "I love my country. My mother is a Turk. If I can be of service, I will."[21] Perhaps the only hint that he was speaking under duress—apart from the fact that he was tied up—was that he sharply told the special agents not to ask him anything else. This caused one of the Turkish agents to sorely remark that if Ocalan answered their questions, then he would be of service.

Within days of Ocalan being in custody, the Turkish media was full of reported confessions, in which Ocalan gave details of the rebel group's operations and supporters, criticized the militants, and spoke glowingly of Turkish history. PKK sympathizers first assumed Ocalan had been drugged, and then thought that many of these so-called statements were faked. After all, the year before, newspapers printed so-called confessions from PKK commander Semdin Sakik, who then repudiated everything in court.

But soon Ocalan began to release similar statements directly to his supporters via his lawyers.[22] He praised his prison conditions, spoke respectfully about the soldiers guarding him, and stressed how well he was being treated. He mixed political musings on the Turkish state —which he proudly noted was founded with the help of Kurds—with direct orders to PKK supporters. He called on the PKK to hold to the ceasefire he last announced in September; he indicated the negotiating tack senior PKK officials should take on his behalf; and he instructed the supposedly independent Kurdish satellite television MED-TV on how to report his capture and Turkey's politics. When he did refer to the Kurds, it was mainly to assure them that Turkey already provided them with the rights they needed and it was only their ignorance and fear that held them back from taking advantage of this. The important thing, he stressed, was to protect the Turkish state's unity and territorial integrity.

Both PKK sympathizers and the rebels were unsure of how to react. They could only assume that Ocalan had some larger plan. Possibly he was negotiating with the Turkish state and these statements were part of his tactics. Or perhaps he had been forced, even tortured, into making the statements. It was hard to imagine otherwise.

Ocalan, the Captive

Ocalan's trial for treason began on May 31, 1999. It took place in a specially constructed courtroom on Imrali Island in Turkey's Marmara Sea, where Ocalan was now the sole inmate in the uninhabited island's small prison. Speaking from a bullet-proof glass box, Ocalan opened his defense with an apology. But first, he wanted to assure everyone that he was not speaking under duress.

"I want to make clear," he announced, "that the day I was captured I promised I would live for peace, and since the day I was brought to Turkey, I have not been subjected to torture or rough treatment."[23]

The PKK leader immediately launched into a call for peace in Turkey. He promised to respect and honor the democratic Turkish Republic, his officious words seemed chosen to underscore his new allegiance to the state. He stressed that to bring "peace and brotherhood" to Turkey, he had to stay alive. And then he paid his respects to the families of those soldiers his rebels killed: "I share the sadness that they have lived, I share their pain."[24] When the court asked Ocalan if it would be correct to transcribe this as an apology to the families of soldiers, he did not disagree.

What he did not mention was that Kurds, too, had suffered. That Kurds had been killed by Turkish soldiers. He did not mention that Kurdish families were grieving and still waiting for someone from the Turkish side to apologize. He also did not bother to go into Kurdish demands or complaints; he did not explain why Kurds so willingly followed his call for revolution for so long. Later on, when he did mention this, it was to assure the court that he realized the war's direction was wrong, even if he somehow failed to mention this to others in the PKK at the time.

Ocalan did remember to praise Ataturk, who was the founder of the Turkish Republic (normally, PKK militants referred to the Turkish state either as the "enemy" or by its Turkish initials, T.C.); he referred often to the joint fight of Kurds and Turks to build the Turkish state in 1923; and he dismissed human rights concerns, insisting that the PKK should have given up armed struggle long ago.

"In Turkey in the 1990s, together [for Kurds and Turks] there were positive developments in human rights," he told the court. "After this, the uprising was wrong. There was a way of solving the problem."[25]

Ocalan's turnaround seemed shocking, except to those who knew him.

"He is a coward," Kemal Burkay, leader of the Kurdistan Socialist Party and Ocalan's long-time rival, told me. Burkay was more used to criticizing Ocalan for his violence than for trying to make peace, but he saw Ocalan's defense statements as a sign of capitulation.

"It is possible to accept that since being arrested, Abdullah Ocalan thinks that he has been mistaken and that he has accepted [the idea of] a peaceful solution," said Burkay, in a statement released to the German media during the trial. "But Ocalan's statement to the court and to the state that 'whatever you want, I will do,' and his extending his respects to the Turkish Republic, and stressing many times his wish to be of service, this shocked Kurds and [the PKK's] members."[26]

Ocalan most likely did not believe that he really was giving up. He had long hoped to enter into direct negotiations with the state, now it seemed like they were talking. He believed he was so important that he probably could not imagine otherwise. Some of his supporters, too, hoped this was the case, but they had to struggle through his long praise of the Turkish state. The pro-PKK Kurdish newspaper in Europe, *Ozgur Politika*, insisted there was something of worth in what he was saying. "Ocalan's message of peace and brotherhood must be approached with respect and prudence," the paper wrote. "T.C. officials have to take on a more serious and responsible approach."[27]

Regardless of whatever tortured argument PKK supporters used to explain Ocalan's statements, the PKK chief's decision not to defend the Kurdish struggle was an attempt to win over his captors and save his own life. Such a betrayal should not have been a surprise. After all, Ocalan could have taken refuge in northern Iraq after being kicked out of Syria—many other Kurdish leaders had based themselves there— but that would somehow have implied that the PKK was more important than Ocalan's personal survival. And he did not believe this. Nor did Ocalan ever fixate on one plan or one goal—this versatility had always been part of the PKK's strength. Now that he was in Turkish captivity, it perhaps appeared to him most logical to join forces with the state. Whether he saw this as a real betrayal of the PKK's fight and the Kurdish problem is unclear, but others did.

"For dictators, their own lives are more important than everything," complained lawyer Ahmet Zeki Okcuoglu, who resigned from Ocalan's defense team when it became clear the PKK leader was not going to defend the Kurdish fight or Kurdish rights. "There is nothing that can't be sacrificed for this."[28]

Unfortunately for Ocalan, the state did not really care. Ocalan's sentence was read out on June 29—not uncoincidentally, the day Kurdish nationalist leader Sheikh Said was hanged in 1925 in Diyarbakir. Ocalan was sentenced to death. And just in case, the judges also barred him from public service work for life. At the end, spectators and the prosecuting lawyers burst into the Turkish national anthem. The PKK, left without its dynamic leader, now struggled to plan its next steps.

15

The PKK Saves Itself, 1999–2007

IN AUGUST 1999, two months after Ocalan was sentenced to death, he publicly called for PKK forces to withdraw from Turkey and give up the armed struggle. His demand was made via statements released by his lawyers, who regularly made public the transcripts of their meetings.

"People thought Ocalan was making this call to end the fighting for a purpose," said Neval, who was in northern Iraq at the time. "People didn't want to think he had given up." Neval hoped the PKK's Presidential Council would reject Ocalan's leadership. "The issue was not the war for me, it was the actions [of Ocalan]."

But regardless of the personal views of some members of the Council—formed after Ocalan fled Syria to coordinate implementation of Ocalan's decisions—the Council was ill-prepared to challenge Ocalan.[1]

"There were people on the Council who had been with Ocalan since the beginning and they were the ones who helped bring Ocalan's system to the point where it was," noted Neval. "Ocalan would have finished them off as well if they tried to stand up to him."

Instead, the Presidential Council heralded Ocalan's announcement as a sign of the new phase in the PKK's fight, a political step in line with Ocalan's new approach to winning Kurdish rights by working peacefully with the Turkish government. Those in the PKK who saw this as a capitulation to Turkey, which had not given any indication that it was considering changes in policies toward the Kurds, had no choice but to accept the decision. Unless they wanted to chance quitting the group.

"[Council member] Cemil Bayik read out the orders from Ocalan saying we should withdraw our forces from Turkey," recalled Kucuk Zeki, who went to the PKK's Kandil camp in northern Iraq for the meeting. "I felt this was an order from the Turkish military and I said that if we withdraw our forces we will never be able to start [fighting] again. I tried to figure out how many people were on my side . . . but while everyone thought like me, no-one wanted to say anything."

The PKK had about 2,000 rebels inside Turkey at this point—and about the same number in northern Iraq—and pulling them back was a dangerous and messy affair. Turkish soldiers laid ambushes for the retreating rebels and then kept up the chase with cross-border attacks that continued over the next few months.

"There was almost nobody, from the highest level to the lowest, who thought this was the right thing to do," said Rozerin. But it was impossible to counter the order without being accused of disloyalty. She and the 15 others in her team reluctantly began their trek backward, cutting back and forth in a desperate attempt to avoid the traps laid by Turkish soldiers. "Most of the routes that would be used to pass to the south [northern Iraq] were known," she said. "You could be a really good guerrilla commander, but it didn't matter . . . a really bad clash broke out on a completely flat piece of land. The fight went until dark and we lost eight fighters and three were wounded."[2]

Next, Ocalan demanded that a number of senior PKK members, among them European spokesman Ali Sapan, turn themselves in to Turkey. Ocalan claimed this would underscore the PKK's desire for peace. It was a strange and unpleasant demand, yet again, nobody refused.[3] In October, Sapan and seven others turned themselves in to Turkish border guards near Semdinli; a few weeks later another group of eight senior militants flew into Istanbul airport. They all were arrested, imprisoned, and put on trial for membership in the PKK. Ocalan's hope for peace did not materialize, but he did succeed in proving that prison was no barrier to his running the PKK.

Ocalan had not ordered the PKK to disband or even to disarm—without the PKK, Ocalan had no leverage over Turkey, nor would he be important at all—and rebels now regrouped in half-a-dozen or so camps in northern Iraq. Brief Turkish incursions and unrest with Iraqi Kurdish militias sometimes had them on the defensive, but in between, they held official meetings to discuss the various international plots that they believed led to Ocalan's capture and approve Ocalan's changing theories. Ocalan had come up with something he called the "Democratic Republic," which was his new goal for Kurds and Turks. Instead of struggling for autonomy, a federation, or independence, Kurds now would fight for a truly democratic Turkey, in which Kurds and Turks would be unified in the way that Turkey's founder, Ataturk, had imagined—so Ocalan claimed.[4]

Some of the militants, especially those who were experienced in war and had watched their friends die for an independent Kurdistan, grew more and more appalled by Ocalan's ideas. Rozerin, for example, had worked for the PKK as courier when she was 12 years old; after the police detained and questioned some PKK supporters who knew her, she was forced to flee to the mountains to escape arrest around 1992. She had been a fighter since. What bothered her the most was Ocalan's decision to renounce an independent Kurdistan and replace it with vague hopes of equality in a strong Turkish state.

"I joined for an independent, free Kurdistan and to protect this I also would leave the PKK," explained Rozerin. "According to me, the king was naked but we couldn't say this."[5]

In January 2000, the PKK held an extraordinary 7th Congress in northern Iraq to approve Ocalan's new approach and analyses. The Congress was important to ensure that as a whole, the PKK had shifted direction. Ocalan was well aware of unhappiness inside the PKK; the group's chief ideologue, Mehmet Can Yuce, imprisoned since 1980 for his unwavering support for the PKK, had angrily renounced Ocalan in September, among other leading, imprisoned PKK members. Ocalan warned militants not to be tricked by the conspiracies of Yuce and other so-called agents.

"The approach I took in my interrogation and trial should be evaluated as offering a political road. . . . The whole world, and you as well, was in shock. But this is the right way,"[6] he insisted.

Dropping Out

Even before the Congress approved Ocalan's new ideas, some militants were planning their escape from the PKK. Those with long experience fighting inside Turkey, where they struggled to survive as their friends died for the idea of a Kurdish state, were the first to go. Neval, for one, decided to wait until after the Congress. She knew she was going to receive some new duties at the Congress—she was given an armed unit to command—and she wanted to prove she was not splitting because she had been sidelined.

"They always said people ran away because they did not have any [high] responsibility," explained Neval, "so I figured I would wait until I got a new responsibility, and then leave."

But it was not easy to flee the PKK. Those who quit the group always were in danger of being killed and especially now, with internal tension high over Ocalan's leadership, PKK loyalists were on guard for any public shows of dissent. Besides, there was no easy place to hide. Iraqi Kurdish villages in the area were loathe to get involved in internal PKK fights; Iranian forces, as of late, had taken to handing over PKK militants to Turkey. Giving up to Turkey was not an option for most rebels and finding a way to get to Europe, while preferable, was difficult without money for a false passport and even then, one still needed a visa.

"I did not have any plan in my mind," said Neval, who finally found a chance to flee late in 2000. "I spoke to some people, those who knew me well, because I knew after I fled the party would question them. Five people agreed to come with me."

Just before Neval fled, the PKK had launched an attack against the Iraqi Kurdish forces controlled by Jalal Talabani. The reason never was clear—the PKK claimed Talabani's PUK party attacked first, the PUK claimed the PKK broke an agreement to stay in its mountain redoubts —but it probably had a lot to do with maintaining group unity and giving PKK fighters some sort of armed focus. Whatever the reason for the fighting, this made it hard for Neval to find a way out.

"We couldn't go straight to the PUK," said Neval, explaining that Talabani's fighters might assume she and the others had come to attack, not to give up. Instead, Neval and her five comrades slipped out of the PKK camp at night, while the others slept, and walked about an hour to the closest Iraqi Kurdish village, where they knocked on a door, planning to ask whomever opened to escort them to the Iraqi Kurdish front lines. But the old man who answered refused their request, insisting he did not want any trouble from the PKK. The six PKK militants had few options. At any moment, others in the PKK might realize they were missing and come after them. Without an Iraqi Kurdish guide, they probably would be shot as they approached the PUK fighters. They needed the man's help.

"I put my gun to the back of his neck and said, 'Think about this, we don't want much,'" recalled Neval. "And he took us."

It was about a 40-minute walk to where the Iraqi Kurdish fighters had their front line. The elderly villager went first and explained the situation. Then two peshmerga, as Iraqi Kurdish fighters were called, came down to speak with the PKK rebels. It was a strange and uncomfortable feeling to be giving up, even if they were not really giving up, just trying to get away.

"They were very friendly," admitted Neval, "they offered us tea, cigarettes. We didn't take it," she said, "it was like a soldiers' psychology." Giving up did not feel good, even if it was necessary.

Neval wanted to be taken to a city, figuring there she could lose herself, maybe make new contacts, and figure out what to do next. She really had no plan, no idea of what to do beyond escaping, and nothing with her except the clothes she was wearing, a gun, and a wireless radio to keep track of PKK militants who might pursue her. But the commander of the Iraqi Kurdish unit suggested she instead meet the others from the PKK who had fled. "Your friends, Kucuk Zeki and Dr. Suleyman are here too," Neval recalled the commander saying. "We can bring you to them if you want."

It was a brief, happy moment, being reunited with others from the fight. Then reality set in. They lived in a hardscrabble camp outside Suleymania—nominally under PUK protection—under constant threat of PKK reprisals. Plans to start up a new nationalist battle never got any further: Their split with the PKK had been because of Ocalan, not because they abandoned their dream of a Kurdish state, but they quickly realized they could not fight both at the same time. Their presence, too, was complicating things for PUK chief Talabani. Turkey wanted PKK militants turned over and Talabani was struggling to maintain good relations. In May 2001, after some wrangling, the now-former PKK rebels managed to arrange to fly to Europe, where they all applied for political asylum. It was an empty, almost brutal end to their dreams.

"Right now, I want to live again the 10 years I was in the mountains," said Rozerin, who quit in 2000. "If there was a chance to turn back history, I would have wanted to live again those 10 years, getting rid of February 16 [when Ocalan was captured]. I want to live this again, until the end of my life." But to stay inside the PKK now, she continued, would be a betrayal of "my friends who died, of my country."[7]

■

Senior militants in the field were not the only ones leaving the PKK. Fighters, too, began to flee the group, many of them setting up new lives for themselves in the Kurdish cities of northern Iraq; between 1999–2004, their numbers rose to the thousands. Most of the PKK's European organizers left after Ocalan's trial; some of them briefly tried (and failed) to set up new Kurdish groups to claim the mantle of the PKK struggle. In all cases, these splits were risky and in some cases, bloody, as PKK militants sought to punish their former comrades.[8]

But the PKK did not collapse. Thousands of armed militants, around 3,000 men and women, remained loyal to Ocalan and stayed in the northern Iraqi mountain camps. PKK-backed associations in Europe and in Turkey retained a core group of supporters that enabled them to retain their dominance. Most critically, many PKK sympathizers inside Turkey refused to turn their back on the organization. They maintained their belief in the PKK; they supported its positions; and their children continued to trickle into PKK camps. The rate was much lower than years before, and the support sometimes was tinged with a hint of uncertainty, but the support remained. And this support allowed the PKK to keep setting the agenda for the Kurds, even as its own political positions grew less coherent.

PKK sympathizers did not—or could not—believe that Ocalan had abandoned the Kurdish people and the nationalist struggle. It was not easy to think otherwise. Tens of thousands of Kurds had died fighting for the PKK and they all had parents, uncles, aunts, sisters, and brothers. To give up on the PKK was to give up on the blood of one's relatives; to turn their backs on Ocalan was to say their sacrifices had been in vain. After all the suffering, after all the deaths, after all the hopes, it was easier to keep believing in the PKK. And besides, when Ocalan talked about democratic rights, about Kurdish-language education, and about being treated as equal citizens, well, after so many years of bloodshed, it did not sound all that bad.

The Party, Still Powerful

Two months before Ocalan's trial, the Kurdish HADEP Party swept local elections in southeast Turkey, capturing dozens of mayoral seats and getting more than 60 percent of the vote in the regional capital Diyarbakir.[9] This victory gave HADEP a critical role over people's lives.

And because PKK sympathizers made up the majority of the party—and because voters viewed HADEP as the PKK's legal representative—HADEP's victory was a vote of confidence in the PKK.

HADEP's control of so many municipalities in the Kurdish region was one reason why the PKK was able to retain its dominance and much of its popularity, despite Ocalan's political capitulation and the subsequent disarray within PKK ranks. The mayors were not directly linked to the PKK-although Turkish officials claimed otherwise—but they had to be responsive to their constituents. This meant not only dealing with the day-to-day problems of running their municipalities, but also taking on issues of broader relevance to the majority of their voters: The mayors criticized Ocalan's imprisonment; they did not contradict Ocalan's new political positions; and they echoed calls for a full amnesty for the armed rebels in the mountains of northern Iraq.

Their stance reinforced the image of the PKK as a still-viable and relevant organization and, in turn, this helped keep it as such. In March 2004 elections, the Kurdish party (running under the name DEHAP [Democratic People's Party], after Turkey's Constitutional Court closed down HADEP in 2003 for links to the PKK) lost a few big mayoral seats and dropped about two percentage points in Diyarbakir. Privately, some party officials blamed the losses on DEHAP's convoluted positions on Kurdish rights, mirroring Ocalan's own positions. But the party's ability to retain a hold over many municipalities in the southeast—and over the unofficial regional capital Diyarbakir—was what counted. Currently, the party goes by the name DTP or Democratic Society Party.

The PKK's grip over Kurdish public opinion was reinforced by the Kurdish daily newspaper and other media. The newspaper—currently publishing under the name *Ulke'de Ozgur Gundem* (and *Ozgur Politika* in Europe)—remained sympathetic toward the PKK and supportive of the group's official positions. The newspaper's reporting helped turn Ocalan into a symbol of the Kurds: His imprisonment was portrayed as the imprisonment of Kurdistan itself and his freedom was a condition for Kurdish freedom. Turkey continued to exert legal pressure and the newspaper was shut down about five times between 1999 and 2006. But each time, its journalists regrouped and reopened the newspaper under a new name.

Likewise, the PKK retained many—but not all—of the cultural

institutes, publishing houses, and other associations in Turkey that it backed in the 1990s. The few associations that tried to operate independent of the PKK did not have the funding nor the backing to make much of a name for themselves. Often, former PKK activists-turned-independent were too dispirited or simply unwilling to put in the necessary effort. Those that did do something did so by carving out a narrow, mainly apolitical position for themselves, where they do not clash with PKK demands or positions. This has helped reinforce the PKK's position as the dominant political voice of Turkey's Kurds—despite the fact that a growing number wish they could have more of their own voice.

The PKK had other ties that proved equally important. The most popular television station for Kurds in Turkey is a satellite station that, most recently, was called Roj-TV. Currently broadcast out of Denmark —despite Turkish pressure to get the license revoked—Roj-TV mixes Kurdish- and Turkish-language programming with a sympathetic stance on the PKK. It is where Turkish Kurdish politicians debate Turkey's policies and where PKK commanders get their say via telephone hook-up. There are also special children's shows and movies. At once political and entertaining, Roj-TV ensures that Kurds keep updated on the latest news, at least as it relates to the PKK.

But the main reason for the PKK's ability to maintain its political hold was perhaps Turkey. Instead of using Ocalan's capture and the subsequent disarray inside the PKK to undercut the nationalist group by making reforms and seizing the political initiative, Ankara chose to claim victory and leave it at that. The reforms that did follow Ocalan's capture were made grudgingly and largely to please the European Union, which demanded that Turkey meet the so-called Copenhagen criteria for democratic and human rights before formal membership talks started (they officially opened October 3, 2005 and may take 10 years or more to conclude). But the state's fundamental approach did not change: In front of every, even limited, reform, the state put obstacles to slow down implementation.

Kurdish-language broadcasting was allowed in 2002, for example, but it took Turkey another two years to make the necessary regulatory changes to allow broadcasting by the state-run station. The U.S.-based Human Rights Watch, while praising Ankara for taking this step, noted that the state's weekly half-hour show was "uninspiring."[10] (In a somewhat unscientific poll—basically, the author querying everyone she met during a June 2006 trip to Diyarbakir—it turned out that most Kurds were not aware of the state-run television program and those who did know about it said it was too dull to watch.) Private television stations had to wait another two years to get their paperwork approved. When it was, in March 2006, they were limited to 45 minutes a day of Kurdish-language programming (totaling no more than four hours a week) and even this was made difficult. Among other things, each segment must be subtitled in Turkish, which makes it impossible to do live or even near-real time shows (the mainstay of these stations). For the region's small and poorly financed television stations, these are time-consuming and costly burdens, leaving the broadcast field open for the pro-PKK satellite station and the new Iraqi Kurdish ones.

Turkey made similar, grudging changes in education. Kurdish-language classes were allowed in the same set of August 2002 reforms approved by parliament, but only as special, after-school private classes and then only for people over the age of 18. It also took two years for language schools—six in the southeast, one in Istanbul—to get permission to open their doors. (State officials spent a long time making sure door-frames were wide enough and that enough pictures of Ataturk were hanging.) The classes opened April 1, 2004 and closed just over a year later. Few Kurds could afford the classes and adults neither had the time nor inclination to study. Besides, the real demand was that Kurdish, and by extension Kurdish identity, be nationally recognized and accepted, without restrictions that aimed to marginalize the language while fulfilling the letter of European law.

The peace that followed the suspension of the PKK's war did create space for some real change. Kurdish cultural festivals were organized, books on Kurdish history appeared in stores in Diyarbakir, and Kurdish music blared, unimpeded from small storefronts. The discussion level, among Kurds at least, was raised. But these were changes that Kurds grabbed for themselves, without fundamental legal reforms to ensure these freedoms by recognizing that Turkey is a country of both Turks and Kurds. Coupled with ongoing human rights abuses (albeit at a much lower level); continued pressure against politically outspoken Kurds; and, crucially, the gains made by Kurds in Iraq, the Kurds in Turkey still want more. So does the PKK, the only spokesman the Kurds have.

■

In June 2004, frustrated by the lack of dialogue or serious political movement on the Kurdish issue and eager to reassert the PKK's relevance, Ocalan called an end to his ceasefire. The PKK, which during the previous three years had gone through various name changes, took back its old name and restarted its war.[11] An ostensibly independent, but in fact PKK-linked, Kurdish group called TAK (Kurdistan Freedom Falcons) announced a new campaign of violence, which for the first time, successfully and relentlessly targeted civilians in western Turkey.[12] At the same time, the PKK's guerrilla war picked up dramatically in 2006, with clashes reported weekly and the number of dead on both sides, once again, climbing. Bigger and more violent public demonstrations in support of the PKK were staged, underscoring the group's ability to mobilize Kurds. In March 2006, after 14 rebels were killed by Turkish soldiers, masked youth rioted in Diyarbakir, shutting down much of the city for three days with stones, Molotov cocktails, and burning tires. While some older, former PKK sympathizers were appalled at the violence, which targeted state offices as well as local shops and banks, they stressed that this was to be expected. For the most part, even PKK sympathizers do not want another war: But in the absence of any political dialogue, it is hard for Kurds to oppose one.

Ocalan, Still in Control

Abdullah Ocalan, nearing 60 years old, lives in semi-isolation on Imrali Island, where he is the sole prisoner. The only way to get to the island is via special ferry and very few people are granted permission to see the PKK chief. He is allowed regular contact only with close family members—his parents are dead and his surviving siblings, who live far away, visit about once a month—and his lawyers. Ocalan's lawyers try to come every week, but poor weather conditions often keep the ferry from making its scheduled run. Requests that Turkish authorities replace the boat with something more seaworthy have been ignored.[13] The limited visits, coupled with some apparently minor health problems that have been checked by Turkish doctors, are things about which Ocalan routinely complains.

When Ocalan was arrested, there was a brief moment where it seemed that his hand-picked Presidential Council might take over control of the PKK, leaving him as the titular head. But Ocalan refused to accept this and the Council backed down. Being in prison did not dull Ocalan's ability to run the PKK. He used his meetings with his lawyers to issue orders and to give his analyses of international and Turkish politics, which in turn made clear to supporters what positions they should take. But he always was concerned that his messages were not getting through properly. "Ocalan would complain, saying, 'Why don't you repeat what I am saying,'" explained a lawyer who used to be part of Ocalan's defense team. "Once, when he complained that the Council was not listening to him, he demanded their phone number."

Ocalan's lawyers always denied that they transmitted information to the PKK for Ocalan, but until prison regulations were tightened they regularly released transcripts of their meetings in which Ocalan laid out his views.[14] And certainly, Kurdish activists who wanted to know what Ocalan was thinking could always approach his lawyers for more information. Ocalan, after all, did not want his views kept secret. Nonetheless, Ocalan could not exert the same, tight, day-to-day control that he once did. But he had created such a system that it worked even in his absence. If anything, Ocalan's imprisonment and the PKK's relatively weaker position has made the group even less tolerant of any independent initiative or dissent. At the same time, PKK supporters have developed their own litmus test of loyalty to the PKK: To be a true Kurdish patriot, which means supporting the PKK, one has to demand Ocalan's release from prison.

Ocalan's chances of being released from prison are, absent a special amnesty, zero. However, he no longer needs to worry about being executed. In 2002, as part of Turkey's legal reforms to prepare for European Union membership, the Turkish parliament revoked the death penalty. Ocalan's sentence was commuted to life imprisonment. Ocalan has long insisted his trial was unfair—his lawyers had little time to prepare a defense and there was a military judge on the tribunal—and he appealed to Europe. In 2005, the European Court of Human Rights ruled in favor of Ocalan's claim but its ruling was nonbinding on Turkey. A Turkish court turned down Ocalan's request for a new trial in 2006. Ocalan's supporters insist that without his freedom, there can be no solution to the Kurdish problem.

Topgider's End

Huseyin Topgider had known Ocalan a long time. True, the two men had spent little actual time together, but Topgider felt he understood him because for more than 20 years, Topgider indexed his life to the PKK's nationalist struggle and this meant following Ocalan. Topgider was there in 1978, when Ocalan inaugurated the PKK into existence at the meeting in Fis village. Two years later, he was arrested by Turkey, and after eight years in prison, his first thought upon release was to rejoin the PKK. After that, Topgider's life in the PKK followed the rise and fall and rise and fall of so many others. He fought inside Turkey, then returned to Damascus. He spent time in northern Iraq, then went back into Turkey. At one point, he was put on trial for misapplying orders, then he was given new responsibilities. He saw his friends die and friends leave (some of whom, like Mehmet Sener, were killed by the PKK) and he even once fell in love. The PKK was everything he knew and all he knew. But as Ocalan spoke up in the Turkish court, apologizing to Turks for killing their soldier-sons and berating Kurds for a feudal fight, Topgider also knew it was time to leave.

Topgider was far away from everything when he made this decision. He was in Moscow running the PKK's local operations, a job he was assigned a month or so before Ocalan went on trial. He had walked from northern Iraq all the way to Armenia, then crossed a few more borders before he could fly to Moscow. In the Russian capital, he tried to watch the trial, but he could barely manage half of the opening session. Ocalan's apology to the families of the Turkish soldiers was too much.

"When I went to light my cigarette, I put the wrong end in my mouth before lighting it," he said, by way of expressing his shock at the trial. "I didn't think he would shout out slogans but to bend his neck to the martyrs' mothers, this I did not expect. To take [Turkish nationalist] Ziya Gokalp and [Turkey's founder] Mustafa Kemal and praise them, I didn't expect this."

Topgider did not want to make a hasty decision. He thought that maybe the PKK's Presidential Council would take some action, maybe even decide that as long as Ocalan was in prison, he could not be expected to direct the PKK. But then Bayik, the Council's leading figure, called up Topgider in Moscow and proudly informed him that Ocalan had bested the Turkish state.

"The enemy came out empty-handed," Topgider recalled Bayik telling him. Topgider lit another cigarette—the right way this time—and blew out his disgust in the smoke. "As if Ocalan had grabbed something out of the hands of the state and used it for his own purposes. And as if Ocalan had done something else, the enemy would have reacted differently."

Topgider found that it was impossible to maintain this fiction in his meetings with Kurds or others in Moscow. "I tried to say what I was supposed to, which is Ocalan did what he had to do and so on, but who could I convince of this? I couldn't even convince myself."

The decision was at once impossible and easy. Topgider had given almost half his life to the PKK. His fervor for Ocalan—which meant his fervor for the PKK—had long since waned, precisely because of Ocalan's leadership, but he never could bring himself to quit. At least not while the PKK still represented, whatever its own problems, Kurdish nationalism. But when Ocalan defended Turkish politics, spoke glowingly of Ataturk, and defended Kurdish-Turkish brotherhood in a united Turkish Republic, it was too much.

"I didn't sign up for these ideas," said Topgider, referring to those secretive meetings in Fis village, 21 years before Ocalan's court appearance. "In fact, the PKK was formed with completely opposite ideas." Leaving the PKK was not easy—Topgider knew this as well as anybody, but he believed he had no choice. "It's not an issue of being afraid or not, I could not go on like this."

Sometime that summer, Topgider, along with a Russian-speaking Kurd who assisted him in the Moscow office, split from the group and went underground. Topgider needed to make arrangements to get out of Russia. He had arrived in Russia with a false passport, which the Russian authorities apparently knew was false, and it was unclear what would happen now that he had split from the group. After a few months, he managed to make arrangements to ensure he could leave safely. He and the Russian-speaking Kurd drove a car across the Russian border, heading west. When Topgider left Moscow—left the PKK, that is—he had with him the clothes he was wearing, two bottles of Russian vodka for friends, and some money his relatives had sent to help him flee. This was the material sum of 22 years in the PKK.

Some six years later, sitting in a department store cafeteria in Hamburg, where Topgider lives the life of a political refugee, the former PKK militant reflected on his life. In the end, it was not a bad one, he had to admit. He fought for what he believed in and fought as well as he could.

> We wanted something and we thought we could push out the enemy and take our country. We had courage, we had ideas, we had millions of people behind us. I don't regret what I've done. History brings people to a certain place, there is no point in wondering what if or why not. I don't regret it and if it were the 1970s again, I would do it again. But in retrospect, we were unprepared for things in the region, political changes, other changes. We didn't win what we wanted, maybe that's for the next generation.

Six years after Ocalan's capture, what remained of the PKK seemed empty, bereft of a focus. "The PKK's tactics change all the time, but in the middle there is nothing," Topgider complained. "The PKK doesn't know anymore what it wants. It says it wants freedom, everyone wants freedom. It says the Kurdish problem must be solved, but what does this mean now?"

Left: A Kurdish
girl dressed up
to celebrate the
Kurdish new
year, March 2005.
Photo by Mark
Campbell.

Right: Kurds, in-
cluding a woman
holding the PKK
flag, crowd the
center of Dogu-
bayazit, in south-
eastern Turkey,
to celebrate the
Kurdish new
year, March 2005.
Photo by Mark
Campbell.

Conclusion

"TURKEY'S KURDS USED to face Istanbul," remarked a friend of mine, Tayfun Mater, a former activist in the militant Turkish left, a current activist in the Turkish peace movement, and an often-prescient commentator. He meant that many Kurds, whether or not they backed the PKK, once believed that the answer to the Kurdish problem lay in the multicultural streets of Istanbul, that Turks and Kurds might jointly come up with a mutually agreeable solution. "But these days, they face Iraq," he said.

In 2003, the United States and allied troops invaded Iraq, overthrew Saddam Hussein, and disbanded the country's military. In the political vacuum that followed, Iraqi Kurds pulled their political forces together and demanded self-rule in the new Iraqi state forming under U.S. tutelage. After much heated negotiation—Iraqi Arabs were uneasy with Kurdish autonomy, all the more so because of the oil reserves in the Kurdish region—the Kurds received approval for their autonomous region in the historically Kurdish north. This Kurdish ministate, enshrined in 2005 in Iraq's new constitution, has only grown stronger as the rest of Iraq descended further into sectarian violence. The Kurds have their own schools, their own taxes, their own oil exploration laws, their own flag, and their own army—former Kurdish peshmerga fighters. In theory, the autonomous Kurdish government supports a federated Iraq; in practice, the Kurds of Iraq are creating an independent state.

Iraqi Kurdistan, as it is now called, has become a magnet for Kurds from all over the region, but especially from Turkey. The Kurds of Iraq and Turkey always were close—many share linguistic, family, or trade ties—and now ties are tightening. Some Turkish Kurds go to northern Iraq to visit their relatives—many of them former PKK militants who have since settled in Iraqi Kurdish cities but cannot return home for fear of arrest. Others go to attend university—the Kurdistan government gives out special scholarships for such students. Others want to find work—unlike southeast Turkey, where unemployment is high, the economy of Iraqi Kurdistan is booming. Turkish Kurdish businessmen prefer to invest in northern Iraq—they trust more in the stability of northern Iraq than they do in their own region's future.

The border between Turkey's Kurdish region and the new Iraqi Kurdish autonomous region is fast fading. In the summer of 2006, I was introduced to a Turkish Kurdish architect in Diyarbakir, who had been commissioned by the Iraqi Kurdistan Regional Government to create a monument to Mulla Mustafa Barzani. The architect described his frequent travels between Turkey and northern Iraq with the air of a seasoned and jaded commuter. For him and many other Turkish Kurds, there is no real border anymore.

The Iraqi Kurdish autonomous state has given Turkish Kurds a chance to evaluate their own situation. And they have not found much to like. The Turkish government has no clear policy for addressing the Kurdish problem and it has refused to engage in any dialogue with the main Kurdish political party, now called the Democratic Society Party (DTP), or any other Kurdish representative.

Nor do Turkey's Kurds, who make up an estimated 20 percent of Turkey's nearly 70 million people, retain much hope in the European Union. Turkey's bid for membership used to be viewed as the way to force the country to reform. But the reforms have been so piecemeal and so grudging that Kurds are losing trust in the effectiveness of EU influence. Simultaneously, Kurds wonder whether they should depend on a political process that may ultimately fail. Turkey's candidacy still faces opposition from some EU-member states, who worry that the country will never become democratic—or Western—enough to fit in. Besides, the accession process could last two decades or more, a timeframe that does not encourage waiting for a solution.

No matter how strong the ties between the two Kurdish groups, Turkish Kurds know that a solution to their problem does not lie across the border. Still, they take their cues and views from what is happening in the first nationally accepted, Kurdish self-rule region. "It's the dream of every Kurd," remarked a Kurdish politician from the DTP party, whose name I will withhold because he could be charged with separatism for saying this. "Why shouldn't we also have the same thing, if that's what we want?"

■

The PKK, based in the Kandil Mountains in southeastern Iraq, not far from the Iranian and Turkish borders, uses these mountains as their political training, media, and war planning centers. The PKK's base camps are not that hard to reach, but afterward the rebels melt away into the harsh landscape. Their presence is no secret—Iraqi Kurdish villagers help supply them, foreign journalists visit them, and every so often the PKK sponsors visiting days for families of the rebels.

Abdullah Ocalan has adjusted his rhetoric to smooth relations between the PKK and the Iraqi Kurdish leadership, to placate supporters in Turkey (who admire the Iraqi Kurdish ministate) and to help ensure the PKK can stay where it is in Kandil. The PKK chief no longer dismisses Iraqi Kurdish autonomy as an imperialist trick to weaken the region, and he has moderated his verbal attacks on Massoud Barzani, president of northern Iraq. In turn, the Iraqi Kurdish leadership steadfastly insists that the PKK is not its problem and that the solution to Turkey's PKK problem lies in dialogue and official recognition of the country's Kurdish minority.

The Iraqi Kurds have good reason to avoid making an enemy of the PKK. One, it is near-impossible to dislodge the PKK from the border mountains, something the Iraqi Kurds, who used to wage their war from the same mountains, know well. Two, despite past problems between the PKK and Iraqi Kurdish parties, Iraqi Kurds are sympathetic to the demands of Turkish Kurds for ethnic-based rights, if not more. Three, the Iraqi Kurdish leadership does not trust Turkey, which is unhappy with Iraqi Kurdish autonomy and is implacably opposed to an independent Kurdish state. If Turkey ever employed its armed forces against a nascent Iraqi Kurdish state, the PKK would be a welcome addition to the defense. While the Iraqi Kurdish regional government is unlikely to actively aid the Turkish Kurds—or the PKK— in their quest for broader freedoms, they are even more unlikely to actively oppose them.

Turkey is very unhappy about the developing political and military situation across its border—as concerns the Iraqi Kurds and the PKK. Ankara is suspicious of the long-term intentions of the Iraqi Kurds and angered by the PKK's ability to maintain a foothold in northern Iraq. But Turkey has few options. The Iraqi Kurds can be warned (and perhaps influenced through Turkish business investments in the autonomous region), but the PKK cannot be kicked out of the Kandil Mountains. Turkey does not like to admit this: Turkish military officials always insist that one more operation will shut down the PKK forever. But barring some sort of concerted, regionally united raid on the PKK, itself almost inconceivable, forcing the rebels out of Kandil is near-impossible.

Nonetheless, Turkey demands some sort of action against the PKK. The problem is it cannot find a partner. The Iraqi Kurds refuse to get involved; the United States has so far demurred support and both have made clear that a sustained, cross-border raid would not be tolerated. Washington's position is doubly frustrating for Turkey. The United States has said it is fighting a global war on terror, yet it refuses to fight the PKK.

U.S. officials have tried to finesse this issue. They often note that, among other things, their troops are tied up fighting the Iraqi insurgency. But the fact remains that the United States does not see the need to fight Turkey's war, all the more so after Turkey refused to take an active role in America's war. The PKK, while viewed by Washington as a terrorist group, is not a group that has ever deliberately targeted Americans or American interests. (If anything, PKK rebels complain of not getting support from the United States.) American officials may condemn the PKK as a dictatorial, violent, and repressive organization, but this does not mean they do not understand why Kurds are unhappy with their treatment by Turkey.

Nonetheless, should Turkish demands for a U.S. military attack on the PKK ultimately find support in Washington, then it will be the Turkish Kurdish rebels who come out the winner. Because Kurds throughout the region, including Iraqi Kurdistan, will see this as an unjust war fought on behalf of a repressive regime (Turkey), and they will turn against the messenger. And the PKK will become a symbol of Kurdish resistance everywhere, giving Ocalan just what he always wanted. And in the end, the Kurdish problem will remain because the answer lies in Turkey opening a real dialogue with Kurds, and taking it from there.

The PKK

Some people like to say that the reason the PKK remains popular is that Kurds have no other options. Independent Kurdish politicians who have tried to build up a political base have been harassed by the Turkish state, leaving the PKK with little legal or illegal competition.

But this is a little disingenuous.

The Kurdish political party that is backed by the PKK—currently called the Democratic Society Party—always was under attack by the state; its supporters were jailed, some mysteriously killed, and the party itself has been closed down four times by Turkey's Constitutional Court. Each time, Kurdish activists, many sympathetic to the PKK, managed to regroup.

Others insist the PKK's violence toward its opponents explains the inability of other groups to garner support among Kurds. Certainly, there is some truth in this and former PKK activists who have tried to form their own party have been most at risk. Hikmet Fidan, a long-time Kurdish activist and HADEP member, was murdered in Diyarbakir in July 2005. He was the Turkey-based representative for the year-old breakaway party formed by Ocalan's younger brother Osman, who split from the PKK and formed the Patriotic Democratic Party (PWD) in August 2004. At least three others from PWD also have been killed.[1] The PKK denied all the attacks, but circumstantial evidence (and the arrest in northern Iraq of one PKK member) point to the rebel group's involvement.

These accounts cannot fully explain the PKK's ability to maintain its dominance. The PKK survives because it is popular among Kurds in Turkey. It is popular because it fought for so long and the PKK's fight tied people to the party and gained it Kurdish respect. Now, Kurds in Turkey are loathe to turn against it, because this smacks too much of betraying their dreams. Ocalan has turned into a symbol of Kurdish desires. What he says or what he does is not that important, because he is a symbol. So is the PKK.

The PKK's fight, whether one thinks it is good or bad, put the Kurdish problem on the agenda in Turkey and in front of the world. It helped Kurds define themselves as Kurds. It gave them a sense of honor. For Huseyin Topgider, and many of the other former militants interviewed for this book, this is enough.

Timeline

October 1923—Turkish Republic is founded.

1925–1938—Turkey puts down a series of Kurdish uprisings.

1949—Abdullah Ocalan is born.

May 1960—Turkish military stages coup, ushers in a new, liberal period.

1965—The Kurdistan Democratic Party of Turkey (TKDP), the country's first underground Kurdish party, is formed.

1969—Ocalan finishes high school and moves to Diyarbakir to work in a state office responsible for title deeds.

1970—Ocalan arranges to be transferred to Istanbul, where he is exposed to leftist activism.

March 1971—Turkish military stages its second coup, revokes rights and freedoms previously allowed, shuts down Kurdish and leftist groups.

1971—Ocalan relocates to Ankara to attend university.

March 1972—Ocalan is arrested for joining a leftist demonstration and he is sent to Mamak prison, where many leftist militants are being held.

October 1973—Democratic elections in Turkey are held and Prime Minister Bulent Ecevit takes office in January 1974, ushering in a new, relatively liberal period.

1973—Ocalan and some friends hold the Cubuk Dam meeting in Ankara, where they make very tentative plans for a Kurdish group.

1975—Ocalan holds the Dikmen meeting in Ankara, where he and his expanded group of supporters decide to focus their activities in the Kurdish southeast to win backing. They start to call themselves the Kurdistan Revolutionaries.

March 1975—Mulla Mustafa Barzani's forces are forced to admit defeat in their fight against Baghdad. The Iraqi Kurdish movement falls into disarray.

December 1976—Ocalan and close supporters hold the Dikimevi

meeting in Ankara and begin to formalize the nascent Kurdish nationalist group's plans.

1977—Ocalan sets out for the southeast, where he holds clandestine lectures for supporters.

November 1978—The PKK is founded at the Fis meeting.

Summer, 1979—Ocalan flees across the border into Syria. He soon leaves for Beirut, where he begins to make contact with Palestinian militant organizations.

September 1980—Turkish military stages coup, ushers in period of intense repression.

April 1982—PKK announces united front with Turkish leftist group Dev-Yol, among others.

1982—PKK receives permission from Massoud Barzani to relocate some PKK fighters to northern Iraq.

November 1983—Turkey holds limited democratic national elections, in December Prime Minister Turgut Ozal takes office.

1983—Relations between the PKK and Dev-Yol unravel.

August 1984—The PKK launches its war. Ocalan is now living in Damascus.

November 1985—Former PKK member Cetin (Semir) Gungor, who had publicly turned against Ocalan, is assassinated.

October 1986—PKK holds its 3rd Congress in the Bekaa Valley. Ocalan begins to consolidate his power.

May 1987—Massoud Barzani formally cuts all relations with the PKK.

June 1987—PKK rebels kill two dozen Kurdish children and women in an attack on Pinarcik village in the southeast.

1987—PKK receives permission from Iran for limited use of Iranian territory near the Turkish border. Ocalan's brother Osman is placed in charge of these activities.

May 1988—PKK establishes a nonaggression pact with Jalal Talabani. The agreement falls apart a year later.

October 1989—Independent Kurdish Institute in Paris holds an international conference on the Kurds, attracting Kurds from throughout the region.

March 1990—Mass demonstrations against the state break out in southeast Turkey following the killing of 13 PKK rebels near Savur.

June 1990—HEP, the first legal Kurdish political party in Turkey, is founded.

August 1990—Iraqi President Saddam Hussein invades Kuwait.

December 1990—PKK holds its 4th Congress in Haftanin camp in northern Iraq. Ocalan faces a serious leadership challenge from Mehmet Sener, who is assassinated a few months later in 1991 by PKK operatives in Syria.

January 1991—U.S.-led Coalition Forces launch attack against Iraq, pushing out Iraqi troops from Kuwait.

March 1991—Iraqi Kurds stage unsuccessful uprising for control of their territory. Iraq stages brutal counterattacks and about half the Kurds in northern Iraq flee to Turkey and Iran. To encourage their return, the United States, Britain, and France establish a safe haven in northern Iraq, warning Iraqi troops to stay out.

April 1991—Turkey rescinds military rule-era law banning spoken and written Kurdish and Kurdish names, but use of the language for broadcasts and education is still forbidden, while use in general remains highly restricted, despite the legal change.

October 1991—National elections in Turkey. Twenty-two deputies from the Kurdish political party HEP are elected.

May 1992—Iraqi Kurds elect their own regional administration.

October 1992—Turkey and Iraqi Kurdish forces launch an assault on PKK bases in northern Iraq. Fighting ends in November, with the PKK still entrenched in the region.

March 1993—PKK offers a limited, unilateral ceasefire.

April 1993—Turkish President Turgut Ozal suffers a fatal heart attack just as PKK extends its ceasefire.

May 1993—PKK rebels kill 33 unarmed Turkish soldiers traveling on a bus in the southeast.

July 1993—The legal Kurdish political party HEP is banned. Most members switch to a new party, DEP.

November 1993—Germany bans the PKK.

March 1994—The immunities of six DEP parliamentarians are lifted in anticipation of trying them for links to the PKK.

January 1995—PKK's 5th Congress is held in Haftanin camp in northern Iraq.

March 1995—Turkey stages a six-week cross-border operation in northern Iraq to root out PKK rebels. The rebels remain entrenched in the region.

April 1995—The Kurdish Parliament in Exile is formed in Europe. Its members include prominent Kurdish deputies forced to flee Turkey to escape arrest and trial for alleged links to the PKK.

Around October 1995—Zap Conference. Senior PKK commanders gather in the rebels' northern Iraqi Zap camp to discuss strategy amid the Turkish military's new gains. Their ideas are rebuffed by Ocalan.

1997—PKK's strength in the southeast is sufficiently weakened that Turkey lifts the state of emergency in three provinces, Batman, Bingol, and Bitlis.

April 1998—Disgraced PKK commander Semdin Sakik, who had been offered protection by Iraqi Kurdish leader Massoud Barzani after he fled the PKK in March, is captured by Turkish forces in Iraq.

September 1998—Rival Iraqi Kurdish leaders Jalal Talabani and Massoud Barzani sign a peace agreement in Washington, D.C., ending four years of intermittent fighting between their forces.

October 1998—After weeks of Turkish threats against Syria if the PKK leader is not handed over or kicked out, Ocalan flees the country.

November 1998—Ocalan arrives in Italy and is arrested.

January 1999—Ocalan slips out of Italy and embarks on an increasingly frantic journey in search of asylum. One month later he is captured by Turkish forces, who find him hiding out in the Greek Embassy in Kenya.

January–February 1999—PKK holds it 6th Congress in the Kandil Mountains in northern Iraq, agrees to support Ocalan as its leader despite his capture.

May 1999—Ocalan's trial on the heavily guarded Imrali Island begins. He faces the death penalty for treason. The nine-day trial ends the next month, with Ocalan given the death penalty.

August 1999—Ocalan, isolated on a special island prison, calls on his rebel force to suspend fighting.

2000—PKK holds extraordinary 7th Congress. Loyalty to Ocalan is reaffirmed.

April 2002—PKK holds 8th Congress in northern Iraq.

October 2002—Ocalan's death sentence is commuted to life imprisonment when the death penalty is abolished, part of legal changes Turkey made to meet European Union criteria for membership.

March 2003—U.S.-led forces invade Iraq and overthrow Saddam Hussein.

August 2004—Ocalan's brother Osman splits from the PKK and, with some other high-ranking members, forms the Patriotic Democratic Party (PWD).

July 2005—Hikmet Fidan, a long-time Kurdish activist, former HADEP member, and the Turkey-based representative of the new, breakaway PWD, is assassinated in Diyarbakir.

October 2005—The European Union opens accession talks with Turkey.

October 2005—Iraq's new constitution is formally approved. It includes recognition of a Kurdish autonomous region in the north, with wide powers of self-governance.

July 2006—Turkey threatens military action against PKK rebels in northern Iraq after 13 Turkish soldiers are killed in two separate PKK raids in the southeast.

August 2006—The United States names retired US Air Force General Joseph W. Ralston as Special Envoy for Countering the PKK. His job is to work with Turkey and Iraq to coordinate activities against the PKK in northern Iraq.

Notes

Notes to the Prologue

1. Because of the tensions between Kurdish demands for minority rights and states' policies, the countries in question generally do not release official figures. As a result, it is no surprise that even the number of Kurds in each country often is disputed. For figures relevant to this period, see van Bruinessen's *Agha, Shaikh and State,* 14–15.

2. McDowall, *A Modern History of the Kurds,* 347; for specifics on support and countersupport for Kurdish rebel forces, see 326, 343–344.

Notes to Part I, Chapters 1–4

Primary interviews: Qais Abdul-Karim (Abu Leila), Mesut Akyol, Selman Arslan, Umit Askin, Ibrahim Aydin, Vehbi Aydin, Sari Baran (Cangir Hazir), Nejdet Buldan, Kemal Burkay, Kamuran, Selahattin Celik, Aysel Curukkaya, Selim Curukkaya, Serafettin Elci, Kamiran Hajo, Ertugrul Kurkcu, Mamdoh Nofal, Ahmet Zeki Okcuoglu, Selahattin, former PKK militant S., Huseyin Topgider, Ramazan Ulek, Hatice Yasar, Mehmet Can Yuce.

Published sources: Ahmad, *The Making of Modern Turkey*; Balli, *Kurt Dosyasi*; Birand, *Apo ve PKK*; Birand, *The Generals' Coup*; van Bruinessen, *Agha, Shaikh and State*; Celik, *Agri Dagini Tasimak*; Cubukcu, *Bizim '68*; Info-Turk, *Black Book*; Imset, *the PKK*; Kizilyaprak, ed., *1900'den 2000'e Kurtler*; Maoz, *Asad: The Sphinx of Damascus,* Metz, ed. *Turkey*; McDowall, *A Modern History of the Kurds*; Montgomery, *The Kurds of Syria*; Ocalan, *Ilk Konusmalar,* Cilt II; Olson, *The Emergence of Kurdish Nationalism*; Ozcan, *PKK*; Randal, *After Such Knowledge*; Seale, *Asad*; Yuce, *Dogu'da Yukselen Gunes,* Cilt I, II; Zurcher, *Turkey*.

Publications: *Milliyet* (European edition), *Cumhuriyet, Serxwebun*, "Haki Karer ve Halil Cavgun un Anisi Olumsuzdur," No. 1, May 1979; *Serxwebun*, "Teslimiyet Ihanete Direnis Zafere Goturur," No. 4, September 1979.

Notes to Chapter 1

1. This section relies on two main sources: A wide-ranging interview Ocalan gave Turkish writer Yalcin Kucuk, published as *Kurt Bahcesinde Soy-*

lesiler in 1993 and cited in Vamik Volkan, *Bloodlines* (New York: Farrar Straus and Giroux, 1997), 168–180; *Dogu'da*, Cilt I, 83–169, a history of the PKK's early years written by former PKK member Yuce; and Kucuk's *Dirilisin Oykusu*, apparently based on the interview in *Kurt Bahcesinde*.

2. Ocalan said this shortly after he was captured by Turkish special forces in 1999 in a video released by the government to the news media.

3. Paraphrased in McDowall, *Modern History*, 419.

4. Birand, *Apo ve PKK*, 31.

5. Volkan, *Bloodlines*, 168–180.

6. Cited in ibid., 171.

7. Ibid., 172.

8. Ibid., 173–174.

9. Birand, *Apo ve PKK*, 80.

10. Ibid., 80.

11. The book's title in Turkish is always given as *Sosyalizmin Alfabesi*. It refers to U.S. socialist Leo Huberman and Sybil H. May's 1953 pamphlet, "The ABC of Socialism," published by Monthly Review Press.

12. The main sources for this section are McDowall, *Modern History*, 397–410; Zurcher, *Turkey*, 231–274; and Ahmad, *Modern Turkey*, 121–157.

13. McDowall, *Modern History*, 402.

14. See Ahmad, *Modern Turkey*, 121–137 for description of 1960 coup and aftermath.

15. McDowall, *Modern History*, 405.

16. Information on the TKDP is taken from an interview with Kurdish politician Serafettin Elci, who was close to the group, in Balli, *Kurt Dosyasi*, 599–607.

17. Ibid., 603.

18. See description of the 4th Congress in Lipovsky, *The Socialist Movement*, 75–82.

19. Ibid., 78.

20. Ahmad, *Modern Turkey*, 145.

21. See Ahmad, *Modern Turkey*, 148–157 for details on the coup and aftermath.

22. Birand, *Apo ve PKK*, 81–83. Ocalan's role in and his views on the Turkish left are described in Yuce, *Dogu'da*, Cilt I, 169–177.

23. Birand, *Apo ve PKK*, 81.

24. Yuce, *Dogu'da*, Cilt I, 201.

25. Birand, *Apo ve PKK*, 84.

26. This section relies on interviews with Kurds, representing a variety of groups active in the 1970s, including PSK, Kawa, Rizgari, TKDP, and the PKK. It also draws on Ahmad, *Modern Turkey*, 159–164.

27. McDowall, *Modern History*, 404.

28. Details of the Cubuk Baraji, or Cubuk Dam meeting, are found in Birand, *Apo ve PKK*, 84 and Yuce, *Dogu'da*, Cilt I, 234–238.

29. Birand, *Apo ve PKK*, 84.

30. Ocalan's experiences in ADYOD and how it affected his developing ideology are described in Birand, *Apo ve PKK*, 84–85 and Yuce, *Dogu'da*, Cilt I, 243–250.

31. Ocalan describes the meeting and decisions taken in Birand, *Apo ve PKK*, 85; also Yuce, *Dogu'da*, Cilt I, 280.

32. Birand, *Apo ve PKK*, 86.

33. For a description of the origins of the groups and others, see Imset, *the PKK*, 380–398.

Notes to Chapter 2

1. Information on Barzani's defeat comes from David Korn, "The Last Years of Mustafa Barzani," *Middle East Quarterly*, June 1994, Vol. I, No. 2; and Ghareeb, *The Kurdish Question*, 160–176.

2. For details of U.S. assistance, and also aid by Israel, see Ghareeb, *The Kurdish Question*, 138–146.

3. Information on Ocalan's speeches come from the speeches themselves, in Ocalan, *Ilk Konusmalar*, Cilt II; also interviews with former PKK militants active in that period.

4. This section incorporates information from Celik, who attended the meeting, also the description in Yuce, *Dogu'da*, Cilt I, 371–377, and interviews with early PKK members and rival figures.

5. For a breakdown of the groups and their ideologies, see Imset, *the PKK*, 380–398.

6. Ocalan, *Ilk Konusmalar*, Cilt II, 84.

7. This section relies heavily on interviews with former PSK leader Kemal Burkay, former Rizgari member Kamuran, former KUK militant Selahattin, and former PKK militants active in the southeast then.

8. Description of KDP-PUK conflict taken from McDowall, *Modern History*, 343–345.

9. Factual details of Yildirim's life are drawn mainly from Yuce, *Dogu'da*, Cilt I, 327–371; and Ocalan's comments in *Dirilisin Oykusu*. Interviews with Celik, Yuce, and Arslan also were helpful, as were sections of Celik's *Agri*, especially 149–153.

10. Quoted in Yuce, *Dogu'da*, Cilt I, 356.

11. Ibid., 356.

12. Ibid., 361.

13. Ibid., 363.

14. *Dirilisin Oykusu*, 91.

15. This section utilizes the following sources for information on the Hilvan fighting: Yuce, *Dogu'da*, Cilt II, 75–113; and *Serxwebun*, "Haki Karer ve Halil Cavgun," 31–51. Ulek (who was from the same area where the fighting took place) was interviewed for this section, along with PKK militants active at the time. The PKK's general approach to landowners uses material from McDowall, *Modern History*, 418–420.

16. This section relies on Yuce, *Dogu'da*, Cilt II, 226–244; Birand, *Apo ve PKK*, 96–99; and interviews with former PKK members active during the period.

17. Parts of the PKK founding manifesto are reprinted in Yuce, *Dogu'da*, Cilt II, 293–298.

18. Yuce, *Dogu'da*, Cilt II, 174, 190.

19. Ibid., 219.

20. Ibid., 375.

21. Ibid., 244.

22. Pope and Pope, *Turkey Unveiled*, 135.

23. Yuce, *Dogu'da*, Cilt II, 245.

24. This section draws its information from Birand, *General's Coup*; Zurcher, *Turkey*; and Ahmad, *Modern Turkey*.

Notes to Chapter 3

1. This section utilizes interviews with PKK and other militants who fled Turkey after the coup.

2. McDowall, *Kurds of Syria*, 10–11.

3. Marvine Howe, "Turks Say They are Gaining on Kurdish Nationalists," *The New York Times*, Dec. 12, 1980.

4. The reconstruction of Ocalan's activities draws on Birand, *Apo ve PKK*, 108–118; Yuce, *Dogu'da*, Cilt II, 257–260; and interviews with former PKK members and others who met with Ocalan during this period.

5. For an overview of Kurds in Lebanon, see McDowall, *Kurds of Syria*, 93–104.

6. Birand, *Apo ve PKK*, 110.

7. Description of the camp provided by Kurdish militants who trained there and the DFLP's Nofal and Abu Laila.

8. Additional information on Syrian attitudes toward militant groups comes from Reuven Ehrlich, "Terrorism as a Preferred Instrument of Syrian Policy," Institute for Counter-Terrorism (Israel), www.ict.org.il and interview with Ely Carmon of the ICT.

9. Information on Syrian-Turkish discontent largely drawn from Makov-

sky, "Defusing the Turkish-Syrian Crisis," and Daniel Pipes, "Hafiz al-Asad Should be Careful," *Turkish Times,* Dec. 15, 1994.

10. This was a frequent complaint of Syrian officials, who made their views clear to many Turkish and Kurdish militants. Jalal Talabani also discusses this in Birand, *Apo ve PKK,* 199.

11. For details on Syria's general approach and policy goals see Ehrlich, "Terrorism . . . Syrian Policy" and Maoz, *Asad,* 170–177; information on Syrian-Iraqi relations is taken from Maoz, *Asad,* 112–113, 146–147.

12. Details taken from McDowall, *Modern History,* 343–347; see also Montgomery, *Kurds of Syria,* 136–139.

13. For details see Montgomery, *Kurds of Syria,* and McDowall, *Kurds of Syria.*

14. The analysis of Ocalan's activities and plans during this period is based on interviews with those who had contact with him during this period. It also draws on the unpublished English-language copy of Mesut Akyol's political autobiography, "A Slice of My Life." Information about the 1st Conference comes from Birand, *Apo ve PKK,* 116–117, Imset, *the PKK,* 32–33, and Celik, *Agri,* 53–54.

15. Quoted in "Express" dergisi, Sept. 2005, 58.

16. Birand, *Apo ve PKK,* 111.

17. Akyol, "Slice of Life," 6.

18. Ibid., 6

19. Quoted in Birand, *Apo Ve PKK,* 194.

20. For further details on the Front, see Celik, *Agri,* 63–64; for information on internal Dev-Yol debates on the alliance by a leading member, see Aslan, *Devrimci-Yol,* 63–99.

21. Details on PKK operations and other militant groups in Europe in the early 1980s benefited from interviews with Kemal, Burkay, and former Turkish leftist leader Ertugrul Kurkcu. General information on the situation of political refugees taken from Info-Turk, *Black Book.*

22. About 110,000 people applied for political asylum in Europe after the military coup, *Black Book,* 234.

23. The description of abuses inside Diyarbakir prison was taken from Zana, *Prison No. 5,* and interviews with former prisoners. There are numerous books in Turkish about Diyarbakir prison; see especially the personal memoir of lawyer Kaya, *Diyarbakir'da Iskence,* and the Internet site about the prison, www.diyarbakirzindani.com, organized by former PKK prisoner Selim Curukkaya.

24. Zana, *Prison No. 5,* 26.

25. Ibid., 19.

26. Details on Barzani and the situation of the Iraqi Kurdish groups at this time draws on McDowall, *Modern History,* 335–347; Gunter, *Kurds of Iraq,*

37–39; and Ghareeb, *Kurdish Question in Iraq*, 14–28, 187–193. The description of developing PKK-KDP relations utilizes also Ozcan, *PKK*, 228–229; Birand, *Apo ve PKK*, 123–124; and Dagli, *Birakuji*, 20–32.

27. Balli, *Kurt Dosyasi*, 447.

28. This section draws primarily on interviews with Kurdish and Turkish activists in Syria at the time. Information on Syria and the Palestinians uses Seale, *Asad*, 378–396, and Maoz, *Asad*, 119–122, 167–169.

29. Burkay, *Devrimcilik Mi Terorizm Mi*, 207.

30. For a full discussion of Ala Rizgari's activities during this period, see the interview with Yasar, one of the group's leaders, in Balli, *Kurt Dosyasi*, 83–106.

31. Akyol, "Slice of Life," 7.

32. Ibid.

33. Ibid., 6.

34. Ibid.

35. Ibid., 7.

Notes to Chapter 4

1. In 1985, the national average of people living in Turkey's urban centers stood at 53 percent. In southeastern Turkey, the percentage of people living in urban centers ranged from a high of 50.5 percent in Diyarbakir province to a low of 23.1 percent in Mus province. All figures from the *Il Gostergeleri, 1980–2003* (Ankara: T.C. Basbakanlik Devlet Istatistik Enstitusu Yayinlari, 2004).

2. In 1980, the average literacy rate in Turkey was 67.48 percent. All figures from *Il Gostergeleri, 1980–2003*.

3. A handful of unidentified militants, apparently from Dev-Yol, who took to the mountains in Turkey after the coup, described similar experiences in Uyan, *Gerilla Kartaldir*.

4. Extensive details on the practical planning, along with information on who took part in the attacks can be found in Celik, *Agri*, 73–98.

5. The Eruh attack was recreated based on descriptions in Celik, *Agri*, 90–92, and Ozcan, *PKK*, 95–96, and an interview with Celik, one of the people responsible. The Semdinli attack was recreated thanks to details provided by participant Baran and information from Celik, *Agri*, 92–95. The third team, which was supposed to raid Catak, failed to carry out the plan. A member of the team told me they received the final instructions too late to proceed.

6. *Cumhuriyet*, October 5, 1984.

7. Some details taken from Imset, *the PKK*, 41–42, 130–131, Birand, *Apo ve PKK*, 135.

8. This section relies on the following: Ahmad, *Modern Turkey*, 181–190;

Barkey and Fuller, *Turkey's Kurdish Question*, 143–145; Harris, *Turkey*, 64–68; Heper and Evin (eds.), *State, Democracy*, 63–80, 177–200, 159–176; Helsinki Watch, *Human Rights* (Nov. 3, 1983); Helsinki Watch, *Destroying Ethnic Identity* (March 1988); Pope and Pope, *Turkey*, 141–157; and Zurcher, *Turkey*, 292–298.

9. Birand, *Apo ve PKK*, 126.

10. Quoted in Pope and Pope, *Turkey*, 148.

11. Political Parties Law No. 2820, section 81. See anayasa.gen.tr/2920sk.htm.

12. *Cumhuriyet*, October 18, 1984.

Notes to Part II, Chapters 5–7

Primary interviews: (Some names withheld to avoid complications related to information on internal executions.) Mesut Akyol, Selman Arslan, Ibrahim Aydin, Sari Baran, Batufa (code name), Nejdet Buldan, Selahattin Celik, Ayhan Ciftci, Selim Curukkaya, Aysel Curukkaya, Mehmet Ali Eren, Ahmet H., Helin (pseudonym), Recep Marasli, Neval (code name), Zeki Ozturk, Kemal Parlak, former PKK militant Rafik (pseudonym), former PKK militant S., Ismet Sivirekli, Huseyin Topgider, Ramazan Ulek, Mehmet Can Yuce, Zilan (pseudonym). Also author interviews conducted in 1993 in a PKK camp in Cudi Mountains.

Published sources: Birand, *Apo ve PKK*; Barkey and Fuller, *Turkey's Kurdish*; Buldan, *PKK'de Kadin*; Celik, *Agri*; Chubin and Tripp, *Iran and Iraq*; Dagli, *Birakuji*; Ersoz, *Gurbet'in Guncesi*; Genc, *PKK'de Kadinin Anatomisi*; Gunter, *Kurds of Iraq*; Halis, *Batman'da Kadinlar*; Helsinki Watch, *Destroying Ethnic Identity* (1988, 1990); Imset, *the PKK*; McDowall, *Modern History*; Ocalan, *3. Kongre Konusmalari*; Ocalan, *PKK'ye Dayatilan Tasfiyecilik*; Ozcan, *PKK*; Pope and Pope, *Turkey*; Yuce, *Bildirgesi*; *Zinarin'in Guncesi*.

Publications: *Milliyet* newspaper (European edition), *Cumhuriyet* newspaper, *Serxwebun*.

Notes to Chapter 5

1. This section relies on extensive interviews with former PKK militants with firsthand or credible secondhand information on these internal executions. Because of the sensitivity of the subject, I withheld most names. A variety of unpublished sources were critical to this section, including the open letters of Cetin Gungor to the PKK, dated April 15, 1983, May 10, 1983, Oct. 19, 1983, March 18, 1984, and August 16, 1984, and an unsigned, undated eulogy for Enver Ata in 1984. Also used was a pamphlet from Die Gruenen/GAL, "Politische Mord in Europa," 25/6/87.

2. Semir, open letter to the European committee, April 15, 1983.

3. Ocalan, *PKK'ye Dayatilan*, 47.

4. From the German-language translation of a November 1985 brochure issued by the PKK in Europe: "PKK-Vertretung in Europa," November 1985.

5. Birand, *Apo ve PKK*, 163.

6. This figure is my own. Hatice Yasar, writing in the magazine *Sterka Rizgari*, No. 21, 2002 (Istanbul), 89fn12, names many of the same people; Birand, in his *Apo ve PKK*, 121, came up with a figure of 10, but did not specify names.

7. The men arrested for the attacks on Ata and Gok had worked in the PKK's *Serxwebun* newspaper according to the Gruene/GAL report, "Politische Mord in Europa," 14.

8. *Cumhuriyet* newspaper, Nov. 12, 1985.

9. In his letter dated August 16, 1984, Semir identifies her as Ayten Yildirim, a name I also was given.

10. This section utilizes especially the firsthand experiences in the region of Baran, Celik, and former PKK militant S. The main published sources were Birand, *Apo ve PKK*, 134–143, and Imset, *the PKK*, 41–44, 107.

11. Birand, *Apo ve PKK*, 136.

12. Birand, *Apo ve PKK*, 138.

13. Sources for this section included Syrian Kurds, Ely Carmon, an Israeli expert on Syria and the PKK, and former PKK members active in the Bekaa. Some details relied on Makovsky, "Defusing the Turkish-Syrian Crisis"; Seale, *Asad*, 427; and David Barchard, "Ozal Signs Security Agreement with Syria," *Financial Times*, July 18, 1987.

14. Birand, *Apo ve PKK*, 177.

15. Information on Iraq and Iraqi Kurds relies mainly on McDowall, *Modern History*, 347–352.

16. They also were reported to be providing information on Turkish troops movement: See McDowall, *Modern History*, 426.

17. This section utilizes interviews with former PKK militants active in Iraq and the Bekaa during this period; and also non-PKK sources familiar with events at the time, including Mesut Akyol and Paris-based Kurdish Institute chairman Kendal Nezan. Published sources: Celik, *Agri*, 119–120; Dagli, *Birakuji*, 29–47; McDowall, *Modern History*, 347, 350–351; and Chubin and Tripp, *Iran and Iraq*, 142. Barzani's comment on the PKK, probably half in jest, was made in 1982 to Nejdet Buldan, who had crossed into Iran to avoid an unrelated jail sentence in Turkey.

18. See Birand, *Apo ve PKK*, 130–133.

19. Attacks cited in Dagli, *Birakuji*, 44–45.

20. Quoted in *Yeni Gundem*, 27 Sept.–3 Oct. 1987, 14.

21. Birand, *Apo ve PKK*, 197.

Notes to Chapter 6

1. Description of the 3rd Congress draws mainly on Celik's recollections, along with information provided by PKK members who later received information about the proceedings. Published sources include Birand, *Apo ve PKK*, 141; and Yuce, *Bildirgesi*, 233–234.

2. Ocalan, *3. Kongre*, 378.

3. Yuce, *Bildirgesi*, 219.

4. Information on Diyarbakir prison relies on interviews with former prisoners. Published sources include Zana, *Bekle Diyarbakir*, 336–346 and *Prison No 5*, 3–36; Yuce, *Zindan Direnisi*; and Helsinki Watch, *Destroying Ethnic Identity* (1988).

5. Details are given in Yuce, *Zindan Direnisi*, 191–220 and Zana, *Prison No 5*, 28–35.

6. Helsinki Watch, *Destroying Ethnic Identity* (March 1988), 15.

7. Description of Pinarcik attack taken from reports in *Milliyet* and *Cumhuriyet* newspapers; other information uses Birand, *Apo ve PKK*, 141–145; Ozcan, *PKK*, 99–100; Imset, *the PKK*, 49–78; Helsinki Watch, *Destroying Ethnic Identity* (March 1988).

8. *Milliyet*, June 24, 1987.

9. From a 1987 issue of *Serxwebun*, quoted in Birand, *Apo ve PKK*, 142.

10. *Cumhuriyet*, June, 26, 1987.

11. *Milliyet*, June 24, 1987.

12. The best analysis on Kurdish tribal structure and behavior remains van Bruinessen's *Agha, Shaikh*. See pages 64–73 for an overview of the history of blood feuds.

13. Imset, *the PKK*, 100fn92.

14. The TIHV (Turkish Human Rights Foundation) included a comprehensive report on attacks on teachers in its 2001 *Turkiye Insan Haklari Raporu*.

15. McDowall, *Modern History*, 423.

16. *Milliyet*, June 16, 1988. Ocalan told this to Mehmet Ali Birand, the first mainstream Turkish journalist to interview him. The series of articles Birand later wrote was banned before it could run in full.

17. A good overview of the PKK's difficulty of holding forced recruits is given in Ozcan, *PKK*, 121–127.

18. This section draws on interviews with a number of former Kurdish militants with firsthand information about relations with Iran. Books used include Dagli, *Birakuji*, 49–57; Ozcan, *PKK*, 231–237, 262–264; Imset, *the PKK*, 138, 184, 205; McDowall, *Modern History*, 272–275, 351–360, and 372–373.

19. Robert Olson, in *The Kurdish Question*, argues that Iran feared that a Turkish presence in northern Iraq would allow Ankara to exert a destabilizing influence over Iran's Kurdish and Azeri populations.

20. Ozcan, *PKK*, 263fn217.

21. Talabani recounted the details in Birand's *Apo ve PKK*, 193–197.

22. McDowall, *Modern History*, 351.

23. Birand, *Apo ve PKK*, 197.

24. Birand, *Apo ve PKK*, 198.

25. TBMM (Turkish Parliament), Tutanak Mudurlugu, Birlesim: 10, Tarih: 19/1/1988. Copy provided by Mehmet Ali Eren. See also *Cumhuriyet*, Jan. 20, 1988, for coverage of the speech.

26. *Milliyet*, Jan. 21, 1988.

27. This section draws heavily on an interview with Mehmet Ali Eren. Published sources include Ahmad, *Modern Turkey*, 194–197; Olmez, *DEP*, 55–109; McDowall, *Modern History*, 357–360; and *Cumhuriyet* and *Milliyet* newspapers (January 1988).

28. *Hurriyet*, Jan. 22, 1988.

29. Cited in Olmez, *DEP*, 60.

30. For details of the conference, see the Institute's Bulletin: "International Conference on the Kurds" (February 1990).

31. Details on events before and after the conference are found in Olmez, *DEP*, 67–84.

32. This section draws on Olmez, *DEP*, 85–109, where the interactions between Kurdish and Turkish supporters of the planned new party are described in detail. I also relied on interviews with Kurdish politicians Mahmut Kilinc, Mehmet Ali Eren, Serafettin Elci, and Mehmet Emin Sever; the views of former PKK militants Selim Curukkaya and Zeki Ozturk; and rival Kurdish leader Kemal Burkay.

33. *Milliyet*, April 19, 1988.

34. The provinces were Bingol, Diyarbakir, Elazig, Hakkari, Mardin, Siirt, Tunceli, and Van. In 1990, the newly formed provinces of Batman and Sirnak were added. Adiyaman, Bitlis, and Mus also fell under emergency rule as "neighboring" provinces.

35. Further details on Decree 413 and the effect on the Turkish media are found in Helsinki Watch, *Destroying Ethnic Identity* (Sept. 1990), 13–18.

Notes to Chapter 7

1. The lack of census data based on ethnicity makes it impossible to know the real number of Kurds living outside the Kurdish region, but it generally is thought to be about half the country's overall Kurdish population.

2. This section relies on interviews with PKK militants active at the time. Because of the sensitivity of the subject, I withheld all names. General information on internal executions are also drawn on the interviews in Buldan,

PKK'de Kadin; from the history of the PKK in Celik, *Agri*; from the brochures issued by PKK members who broke away in 1991 and formed PKK-Vejin; and in the limited report on internal executions made at the PKK's 5th Congress, published in *PKK 5. Kongre Kararlari*, 257–264.

3. This incident, with slightly different details, also is recounted by the late PKK militant Ersoz in her diary, *Gurbet'in Guncesi*, 143.

4. Buldan, *PKK'de Kadin*, 110–111.

5. Celik, *Agri*, 161.

6. Background on the Bindal-Balic affair is given in Celik, *Agri*, 160–163.

7. This story was told to me by a number of people, including one person who knew the girl very well. The murder apparently was reported in Turkish newspapers, but without the exact dates, it proved impossible to locate the articles.

8. This section draws on interviews with PKK militants active in the region during this period. Published sources included Ozcan, *PKK*, 198–202; Birand, *Apo ve PKK*, 150–154; Imset, *the PKK*, 79–81, 219–221; Celik, *Agri*, 165–167; and *Milliyet* newspaper, March, April 1990.

9. *Milliyet*, March 17, 1990.

10. Independent deputy Adnan Ekmen and Social Democratic deputy Tevfik Kocak, respectively, quoted in *Milliyet*, March 20, 1990.

11. *Milliyet*, March 22, 1990.

12. Information on the 4th Congress draws on interviews with congress participants. Additional information in Celik, *Agri*, 169–173; Ocalan, *PKK'ye Dayatilan Tasfiyecilik*, 451–525; Yuce, *Bildirgesi*, 226–237; and the open letter issued by PKK-Vejin, "PKK-MK ve tum uye ve savasci arkadaslari" (To the PKK central committee and all comrade fighters and members).

13. PKK-Vejin, "PKK-MK ve tum uye."

Notes to Part III, Chapters 8–11

Primary interviews: Selman Arslan, Sedat Yurtdas, Ali Agbaba, Batufa (code name), Nejdet Buldan, Selahattin Celik, Ayhan Ciftci, Sait Curukkaya, Selim Curukkaya, Murat Dagdelen, Faysal Dagli, Sukru Gulmus, Nazmi Gur, Ahmet H., Zeynel Abidin Han, Akif Hasan, Helin (pseudonym), Yasar Kaya, Mahmut Kilinc, Zeynel Abidin Kizilyaprak, Neval (code name), Kendal Nezan, Yavuz Onen, Orhan (pseudonym), Zeki Ozturk, Kemal Parlak, Ruken (pseudonym), Mehmet Emin Sever, Huseyin Topgider, Ramazan Ulek, Mehmet Can Yuce.

Published sources: Birand, *Apo ve PKK*; Barkey and Fuller, *Turkey's Kurdish*; Buldan, *PKK'de Kadin*; Cemal, *Kurtler*; Imset, *the PKK*; Kirisci and Winrow, *Kurdish Question*; Kundakci, *Guneydogu'da*; Olmez, *DEP*; Ozcan, *PKK*; Ozdag,

Turkiye Kuzey; McDowall, *Modern History*; *Turkey Human Rights Report*, 1991, 1992, 1993, 1994; U.S. State Department, Turkey Human Rights Practices, 1993. Publications: *Ozgur Gundem, Ozgur Ulke* (European edition), 1994; *Serxwebun*, 1994, 1995; *Kurdistan Report*, May/June 1994, Sept./Oct. 1995; *Milliyet* (European edition), 1993, 1994.

Notes to Chapter 8

1. *Serxwebun*, October 1991, 19.
2. Quoted in Olmez, *DEP*, 119.
3. See the analysis provided in Barkey and Fuller, *Turkey's Kurdish*, 88–89.
4. This section benefited from Ahmad, *Modern Turkey*, 201–203; Olmez, *DEP*, 154–212; Kirisci and Winrow, *Kurdish Question*, 136–151.
5. *Milliyet*, Nov. 18, 1991.
6. *Milliyet*, Dec. 9, 1991.
7. *Milliyet*, Dec. 9, 1991.
8. For complete list, see Olmez, *DEP*, 161.
9. *Milliyet*, Nov. 8, 1991.
10. The controversy over Zana's statement is matched only by the myriad of versions available of what she said. I relied on her own recollection—perhaps the most radical version—that appeared in Zana, *Writings From Prison*, 2.
11. *Milliyet*, Nov. 22, 1991.
12. Aliza Marcus, "Kurd Separatists Grip Southeastern Turkey," *Christian Science Monitor*, Oct. 13, 1991.
13. *Milliyet*, Nov. 9, 1991.
14. Incidents taken from *Turkey Human Rights Report* (1991), 52, and *Milliyet* and *Cumhuriyet*, December 1991.
15. *Milliyet*, Dec. 28, 1991.
16. Imset, *the PKK*, 245–246.
17. Kundakci, *Guneydogu'da*, 223; the memoirs offer an excellent overview of the problems facing Turkish soldiers, see 195–242 especially.
18. Kundakci, *Guneydogu'da*, 224.
19. See *Turkey Human Rights Report* (1992), 63–73; and (1993), 82–89.
20. Kundakci, *Guneydogu'da*, 202.
21. Buldan, *PKK'de Kadin*, 16.
22. Information about Zana's life comes from author interview conducted in 1993 in New York City and Kutschera, "Leyla Zana."
23. Kutschera, "Leyla Zana."
24. Ibid.
25. Ibid.
26. Quoted in Ozcan, *PKK*, 161.
27. Halis, *Batman'da*, 94.

Notes to Chapter 9

1. *Turkey Human Rights Report* (1992), 37–47; hereafter *THRR*.

2. Figures come from *THRR* (1992), 63–71; and *THRR* (1993), 143–158. For a credible account by a former PKK militant of how he later worked for the Turkish security forces assassinating Kurdish activists, see Sahan and Balik, *Itirafci*; Turkish state involvement in such killings long has been assumed because of who was targeted, because victims often were taken away by people who identified themselves as police or otherwise were last seen in police custody, and because very few people were arrested and with rare exception, nobody prosecuted. The U.S. Embassy in Turkey, in its 1993 annual human rights report, referred to allegations by independent observers that the security forces were complicit; in 1997, by which time discussion turned more open, the State Department's human rights report referred to "credible reports of political and extrajudicial killings by government authorities."

3. Three soldiers and one policeman were killed in the first night; subsequently, another 60 civilians also were wounded. For figures and eyewitness accounts, see *THRR* (1992), 27–35. See also Imset, *the PKK*, 286–298, who noted that Turkish tanks moved into the city's downtown and fired on buildings.

4. Balikci and Durukan, *Olumun Iki Yakasinda*, 98.

5. Adapted from Aliza Marcus, "The Other Kurdish Revolt," *Commonweal*, Nov. 20, 1992.

6. *THRR* (1992), 35–37.

7. A Kulp resident quoted in *THRR* (1992), 36.

8. *THRR* (1992), 26.

9. Quoted in "Abdullah Ocalan'in," *Serbesti*, Mart-Nisan 2005, 34.

10. In 1993, after my car broke down on a remote road outside Cizre, I flagged down a passing taxi. It turned out to be a PKK-affiliated taxi that was taking a Kurdish shopkeeper to a rebel-convened trial for having ignored warnings not to sell food to a local army base. The man said he expected to be fined.

11. Imset, *the PKK*, 270.

12. For details see Kirisci and Winrow, *Kurdish Question*, 157–161.

13. The usual number of Turkish troops was about 90,000. By June 1994 the number rose to 160,000. Figures come from Kirisci and Winrow, *Kurdish Question*, 130.

14. *THRR* (1992), 20–27.

15. In addition to interviews with former PKK militants and Kurdish civilians who gave money or goods, published sources include Barkey and Fuller, *Turkey's Kurdish*, 29–34; Ozcan, *PKK*, 188–189; *THRR* (1993), 68–71; and Imset, *the PKK*, 201–210.

16. A European intelligence official concurred with this view.

17. A good description of the variety of weapons used by PKK rebels is found in Gursel, *Dagdakiler,* 75–76. Gursel, a Turkish journalist, was kidnapped by the PKK and held for nearly a month.

18. Quoted in Ozcan, *PKK,* 266fn238.

19. This section on media sympathetic to the PKK drew especially on interviews with PKK militants with close information about the newspaper, and former journalists and editors at the newspaper. Published sources included Ersoz, *Gurbet'in Guncesi,* and reminiscences by former *Gundem* editor Gulmus that appeared on his website, www.nasname.com.

20. The quote comes from an interview, carried out by Gursel Capanoglu, that appeared on www.lekolin.com.

21. See Barkey and Fuller, *Turkey's Kurdish,* 121–126, for a fuller overview of the Turkish media and the Kurdish issue.

22. Aliza Marcus, "Turkish writers form 'closed university' behind bars," Reuters, March 6, 1995.

23. Information on the pressures, including the killing of journalists, was drawn mainly from published sources, including Kocoglu, *Kursunla Sansur; THRR* (1993, 1994); and the Turkiye Gazeteciler Cemiyeti website.

24. *THRR* (1994), 263.

25. The PKK also exerted its own pressure. In 1992, the PKK admitted to killing Mecit Akgun, a *Yeni Ulke* journalist accused of informing on the group. The same year, Yasar Aktay, a freelance Kurdish journalist for the Turkish media, apparently was killed by the PKK for reasons still unclear.

26. Amnesty International, *Turkey: No Security,* 30.

27. It would have been unusual for someone to be a reporter and an active PKK member. First, PKK members usually were assigned to positions in the editorial staff, where they had control over the newspaper's direction. Second, a reporter who decided to join the PKK would have done so to take part in armed combat, not to stay in the same job.

28. Amnesty International, *Turkey: No Security,* 30.

29. Unless otherwise indicated, all of Topgider's quotes are drawn from the unpublished memoir he gave to me.

30. Apart from firsthand interviews with former militants, this section incorporates information from Buldan, *PKK'de Kadin.*

Notes to Chapter 10

1. See www.kevinmckiernan.com/doc.html.

2. Dagli, *Birakuji,* 67.

3. Cited in Kirisci and Winrow, *Kurdish Question,* 163.

4. Birand, *Apo ve PKK,* 264.

5. Barkey and Fuller, *Turkey's Kurdish*, 53.

6. *Yeni Ulke*, Haziran 16–22, 1991.

7. Events taken from Dagli, *Birakuji*, 68–75.

8. *Milliyet*, Sept. 7, 1992.

9. *Milliyet*, Oct. 1, 1992; Oct. 2, 1992; in *Birakuji*, 89, Kurdish writer Dagli said 50 PKK rebels were killed.

10. The agreement is reprinted in Dagli, *Birakuji*, 183.

11. Details of the problems and the deputies' reactions can be found in Olmez, *DEP*, 176–217.

12. Olmez, *DEP*, 215.

13. See chapter 9, n. 2 for explanatory note.

14. Figures of murdered HEP officials taken from Serdar Celik (Selahattin Celik), *Turk Kontr-Gerillasi* (Berlin: Ulkem Presse, 1995), 467–469.

15. *Milliyet*, September 3, 1992.

16. Murat Dagdelen, "93 Bahari Kemal Burkay ve Otekiler" (unpublished essay), Feb. 28, 2005.

17. Birand, *Apo ve PKK*, 217.

18. Olmez, *DEP*, 236.

19. This section benefited from descriptions of Ozal's approach to the Kurds in Birand and Yalcin, *Ozal*, 451–480; and in Can Dundar, "Ozal-Apo Pazarligi," *Sabah* newspaper, June 5–7, 1999 (Internet edition); and the view from the Kurdish side in Olmez, *DEP*, 219–250.

20. Talabani describes his contacts with Ozal in Birand and Yalcin, *Ozal*, 472–476.

21. Birand and Yalcin, *Ozal*, 474.

22. *Milliyet*, March 19, 1993.

23. *Milliyet*, March 20, 1993.

24. English-language transcript of news conference in *Kurdistan Report*, April/May 1993, 1–4.

25. Orhan Dogan, who met Ozal both times, described the meetings in Olmez, *DEP*, 235–243.

26. Birand and Yalcin, *Ozal*, 475.

27. Ibid., 468.

28. Ibid.

29. Some sources give May 24 as the date, others May 25. May 24 is the date used in *THRR* (1993).

30. See Celik, *Agri*, 192, for details on those killed.

31. Quotes from Rosenberg, "On the Road"; see also U.S. State Department, Turkey Human Rights Practices (1993).

32. Details taken from *THRR* (1993), 89–91.

33. Kundakci, a retired lieutenant general who was based in the region, gives a good description in his memoirs, *Guneydogu'da*, 210–219.

34. Kundakci, *Guneydogu'da,* 217.

35. Information taken from *THRR* (1993), 258–259, and an author interview with a journalist who attended the meeting.

Notes to Chapter 11

1. *THRR* (1993), 60–67, includes excerpts from a Turkish newspaper article describing the devastation.

2. Cited in *THRR* (1993), 64.

3. Examples taken from *THRR* (1994), 61–64; and *THRR* (1993), 64–68.

4. The forcible evacuation of villages is described in U.S. State Department reports on Turkey (1993, 1994), various reports of international and Turkish human rights groups, and in my own articles for Reuters 1993–1995. That it happened is widely accepted, but it remains a sensitive subject for the military, despite the fact that it contributed to the army's successes against the rebels. For a comprehensive study of forced displacements and government policies, see Jongerden, *Settlement Wars.*

5. Turkish government commissions, the Turkish Human Rights Association, and international monitors generally cite a figure of more than 3,000 villages emptied through the end of the 1990s, with most emptied between 1993 and 1995. The number of people affected is harder to ascertain. Human rights groups in Turkey usually say two million to three million people were displaced. A Turkish commission in 1997 reported that 360,000 people had been forced out of their settlements since 1990, but this is low relative to the number of emptied settlements. The U.S. State Department often cites a figure of 560,000. Based on a sampling of the populations of evacuated villages in different parts of the region, I estimate the number of those who fled their villages to be closer to one million.

6. Kundakci details the changes in the second-half of his memoir *Guneydogu'da;* see particularly 219–242.

7. For details see the European Court of Human Right's judgment related to the case in: www.worldlii.org/eu/cases/ECHR/2002/408.html; see also Olmez, *DEP,* 255–257.

8. Full statement in Olmez, *DEP,* 281

9. Quoted in Pope and Pope, *Turkey,* 273.

10. Pressure on DEP and other abuses taken from *THRR* (1993), 303–311; see also U.S. State Department, Turkey Human Rights Practices (1993).

11. For more on this see also Olmez, *DEP,* 325–337.

12. For a complete list of pressure and attacks on DEP from mid-1993 through February 1994, see Olmez, *DEP,* 358–364.

13. Olmez, *DEP,* 342.

14. Both quoted in Olmez, *DEP,* 347, 349.

15. Pope and Pope, *Turkey*, 275; for Ciller's full statement see Olmez, *DEP*, 349–350.

16. *Ozgur Gundem* (European edition), February 27, 1994.

17. For a denial of this by other DEP officials, see Olmez, *DEP*, 364–368. However, the PKK itself noted in its own party newspaper *Serxwebun* (February 1994) that a weak showing by DEP in the elections would be seen by the Turkish state as a defeat for the PKK.

18. This section incorporates interviews with a variety of former PKK Europe-based activists, some of whom did not want to be named, and information from European intelligence officers, who also did not want to be further identified. Also useful was Barkey and Fuller, *Turkey's Kurdish*, 29–34, and Ozcan, *PKK*, 288–301.

19. The estimate, made by anti-PKK groups, is cited in Barkey and Fuller, *Turkey's Kurdish*, 32.

20. See Lyon and Ucarer, "Transnational Mobilization."

21. Information on the parliament mainly drawn from interviews with former parliament members and PKK officials involved in its activities; see also Kutschera, The Middle East magazine, June 1995, on http://chris-kutschera.com/; Barkey and Fuller, *Turkey's Kurdish*, 34–39. Information on Turkey's relations with Europe utilizes also Kirisci and Winrow, *Kurdish Question*, 171–179, and Barkey and Fuller, *Turkey's Kurdish*, 157–166.

Notes to Part IV, Chapters 12–15

Primary interviews: Ali Agbaba, Ahmet H., Batufa (code name) Nejdet Buldan, Kemal Burkay, Selahattin Celik, Ayhan Ciftci, Sait Curukkaya, Murat Dagdelen, Dersim (code name), Akif Hasan, Helin (pseudonym), Serafettin Kaya, Yasar Kaya, Mahmut Kilinc, Necdet (pseudonym), Neval (code name), Yavuz Onen, Orhan (pseudonym), Zeki Ozturk, Kemal Parlak, Mukrime Tepe, Huseyin Topgider, Sedat Yurtdas.

Published sources: Barkey and Fuller, *Turkey's Kurdish Question*; Bila, *Hangi PKK?*; van Bruinessen, "Transnational aspects of the Kurdish question"; Celik, *Agri*; Cemal, *Kurtler*; Gursel, *Dagdakiler*; Inanc and Polat, *Apo, PKK*; Kirisci and Winrow, *Kurdish Question*; Kundakci, *Guneydogu'da*; Mater, *Voices from the Front*; Ocalan, *PKK 5. Kongresi'ne sunulan Politik Rapor*; Olmez, *DEP*; Ozdag, *Turkiye Kuzey*; Pamukoglu, *Unutulanlar Disinda*; *PKK 5. Kongre Kararlari*; *Zinarin'in Guncesi*; *Turkey Human Rights Report* (1993, 1994); Human Rights Watch, *World Report* (Turkey section), years 1996 and 2000 through 2006.

Notes to Chapter 12

1. *PKK 5. Kongresi*, 224.

2. Ersoz, *Gurbet'in Guncesi,* 153.

3. See the excellent study by Halis, *Batman'da Kadinlar,* on female suicides in the southeastern city of Batman in 2000.

4. For an overview of PKK suicide bombing, see Mia Bloom, *Dying to Kill: The Allure of Suicide Bombing* (New York: Columbia University Press, 2005), 101–119; list of attacks taken from Schweitzer, Yoram, "Suicide bombing: the Ultimate Weapon?" Aug. 7, 2002, at www.ict.org.il.

5. A detailed look at Kurdish views toward Islam in general and the Islamic beliefs, practices, and divisions in the Kurdish community in specific is outside the scope of this study. Probably the best and most enlightening studies of Kurds and Islam have been produced by Martin van Bruinessen. Much of his writings are available on his website: http://www.let.uu.nl/~martin .vanbruinessen/personal/publications/.

6. *PKK 5. Kongre Kararlari,* 98.

7. This section utilizes Balikci and Durukan, *Olumun Iki Yakasinda,* 132–147; Gunter, *Kurdish Predicament in Iraq,* 79–126; Kirisci and Winrow, *Kurdish Question,* 161–171; Laizer, *Martyrs,* 133–138, 149–158; and Ozdag, *Turkiye,* 126–206; also, personal observations of the author who reported on the operation for Reuters.

8. Quoted in Ozdag, *Turkiye,* 132.

9. See Barkey, "Hemmed in by Circumstances," for a broader overview.

10. The statement, which he later repudiated, quoted in Laizer, *Martyrs,* 158.

11. Estimates on the cost of the war for the years 1993–1995 vary between a low of $6 billion to a high of around $11 billion.

12. This section utilizes information primarily from Barkey and Fuller, *Turkey's Kurdish;* Human Rights Watch, *World Report 1998,* at http://www.hrw .org/worldreport/; Sabri Sayari, "Turkey's Islamist challenge," *Middle East Quarterly* (Sept. 1996); Tirman, *Spoils of War,* 215–229; and Kurdish-focused institute TOSAM's information page, www.tosam.org.

13. *Milliyet,* April 17, 1995.

14. Reuters, June 9, 1995, quoted in Amnesty International, *Turkey: No Security Without Human Rights,* 7.

15. This survey, released in August 1995 by the influential Turkish Union of Chambers and Commodity Exchanges (TOBB), was authored by Dogu Ergil.

16. Tirman, *Spoils of War,* 229.

17. See especially the excellent analysis in Barkey and Fuller, *Turkey's Kurdish,* 99–108.

Notes to Chapter 13

1. This retelling of Sakik's history in the PKK relies on interviews with

PKK militants who knew him and draws on Celik, *Agri*, 116–117, 399–409; also useful were the diaries of two militants: Ersoz, *Gurbet'in Guncesi* and *Zinarin'in Guncesi*.

2. Osman Ocalan's problems were discussed at the 5th Congress, see *PKK 5. Kongre Kararlari*, 271–274. Former PKK militants described Osman's flight.

3. For Barzani's statement and his response when Sakik was captured, see the bulletin issued by the independent Paris-based Kurdish Institute, March-April 1998, at http://www.institutkurde.org/en/publications/bulletins/bulletins.php?bul=156#2.

4. See *Hurriyet* newspaper (Internet edition), April 26, 1998, and *Sabah* newspaper (Internet edition), April 25, 26, 1998, for list of Sakik's purported claims.

5. *Hurriyet*, April 25, 1998; Eksi has complained that those who quote this column by him do not note that he later admitted he unwittingly had been used by "official offices" to spread lies. See his columns in *Hurriyet*, December 12, 1998, and February 28, 1999 (Internet editions).

6. Cemal, *Kurtler*, 425–426.

7. For Birand's personal, painful recollection of this event, plus an excellent analysis of what was dubbed the "Memorandum Affair," named for the alleged military memo planning the operation against these journalists and others, see Cemal, *Kurtler*, 424–438.

8. *Zinarin'in Guncesi*, 34.

9. Ersoz, *Gurbet'in Guncesi*, 212.

Notes to Chapter 14

1. Quoted in Cemal, *Kurtler*, 445.

2. See Makovsky, "Defusing the Turkish-Syrian Crisis."

3. Ozkan, *Operasyon*, 69.

4. This section, including the reconstruction of Ocalan's flight from Italy and afterward, incorporates information from Celik, *Agri*, 409–436; Ozkan, *Operasyon*; Ocalan's court statement in Inanc and Polat, *Apo, PKK*, 29–33; BBC and CNN news reports covering the relevant period; and a variety of other news reports collected by the online news-gathering security source, www .globalsecurity.org, specifically at http://www.globalsecurity.org/military/library/news/1998/11/index.html.

5. Ozkan, *Operasyon*, 71.

6. Italy's foreknowledge of Ocalan's arrival is described in detail in *Top Secret: il caso Ocalan*, by *La Reppublica* journalist Marco Ansaldo. See Turkish news coverage of this at http://www.ntv.com.tr/news/133072.asp.

7. *Hurriyet*, November 14, 1998, see http://arsiv.hurriyetim.com.tr/hur/turk/98/11/14/.

8. *Le Soir,* November 25, 1998, cited in www.globalsecurity.org.

9. Celik, *Agri,* 420.

10. In their January 28, 1999 meeting. Celik, *Agri,* 419.

11. Inanc and Polat, *Apo, PKK,* 31.

12. Cited in Celik, *Agri,* 423.

13. Ozkan, *Operasyon,* 157.

14. This is denied in Ozkan, *Operasyon,* 157, but videos taken of him on the plane show him overly confused and slow-moving and even his speech sounds heavy, as if he had been sedated.

15. Ozkan, *Operasyon,* 158.

16. See *Hurriyet,* Feb. 23, 1999 (Internet edition).

17. VOA at http://www.globalsecurity.org/military/library/news/1999/02/990219-kurd2.htm.

18. Sami Kohen, "Turks take hardened stance after Ocalan," *Christian Science Monitor,* Feb. 26, 1999.

19. *Sabah* newspaper, February 25, 1999 (Internet edition).

20. Gul Demir and Niki Gamm, "Okcuoglu says the Turkish legal system is on trial along with Ocalan," *Turkish Daily News,* April 8, 1999.

21. Ozkan, *Operasyon,* 158.

22. Many of the notes released by Ocalan's lawyers are available at the Kurdish opposition site http://www.welatparez.com/tr/arsiv/gorusmenotlari/.

23. *Hurriyet,* June 1, 1999, "Gundem: Yasamak Istiyorum." This and other articles are available at the newspaper's on-line archives www.hurriyet.com.tr.

24. *Hurriyet,* June 1, 1999, "Gundem: Yasamak Istiyorum."

25. *Hurriyet,* June 3, 1999, "Gundem: Aglatan Ifade."

26. *Hurriyet,* June 25, 1999, "Gundem: Apo Diktator."

27. *Hurriyet,* June 2, 1999, "Gundem: PKK'da Kafalar Karisti."

28. *Hurriyet,* June 25, 1999, "Gundem: Apo Diktator."

Notes to Chapter 15

1. At the time, members were said to be Riza Altun, Cemil Bayik, Duran Kalkan, Mustafa Karasu, Murat Karayilan, Osman Ocalan, and Nizamettin Tas.

2. Quoted in Buldan, *PKK'de Kadin,* 89–90.

3. See VOA news reports for October 1999 on www.globalsecurity.org.

4. For an English-language review of Ocalan's views, see Michael Gunter's review of Ocalan's defense statement in the online Zagros magazine of the Washington Kurdish Institute at http://www.kurd.org/Zagros/Zagros8.html, February 2000 issue.

5. Quoted in Buldan, *PKK'de Kadin*, 91.

6. "PKK 7. Olaganustu Kongresi'ne," *Serxwebun*, January 2000.

7. Quoted in Buldan, *PKK'de Kadin*, 93.

8. For more details, see Sait Curukkaya's (Dr. Suleyman) report "Faşizmin olduğu yerde cinayetlerde vardır," on www.rizgari.com.

9. Elections were April 1999. See Jon Gorvett, "Turkey's Kurdish Workers' Party Rebels," Washington Report on Middle East Affairs, Oct./Nov. 1999, available at www.wrmea.com; also Nicole F. Watts, "Turkey's Tentative Opening to Kurdishness," MERIP, June 14, 2004, at www.merip.org; and the party's own website, www.dtpgm.org.tr.

10. Human Rights Watch, *World Report 2005* (Turkey section) http://hrw.org/english/docs/2005/01/13/turkey9882.htm; see also broadcast law at www.rtuk.gov.tr, the Turkish state's radio and television commission's site.

11. In 2002, at the PKK's 8th Congress, the name was changed to KADEK (Kurdistan Freedom and Democracy Congress); in 2003, this was changed to Kongra-Gel (Kurdistan People's Congress).

12. The TAK webpage, in which the group explains in detail how to make bombs, had been blocked as of August 2006; English-language information on the group's attacks can be found at www.Dozame.org.

13. See the report by the Council of Europe's European Committee for the Prevention of Torture and Inhuman or Degrading Treatment or Punishment (CPT), based on their 2003 visit to Imrali, and Turkey's formal response, at http://www.cpt.coe.int/documents/tur/2004-02-inf-eng.htm.

14. See compiled transcripts in Erdal Simsek, *Imrali PKK'nin Yeni Karargahi* (Istanbul: Neden Kitap, 2006); also www.welatparez.com.

Notes to the Conclusion

1. See, among other reports on www.kurdishmedia.com, "Trial of 7-men accused of assassination of Kamal Shahin adjourned," 9/5/2005.

Bibliography

Books and Articles

Ahmad, Feroz. *The Making of Modern Turkey.* London: Routledge, 1993.

Anter, Musa. *Hatiralarim.* Istanbul: Doz Yayinlari, 1990.

Aslan, Gunay. *Kurt Partilerinin Cozum Oneriler.* Koeln: Mezopotamya Yayinlari, August 1999.

Aslan, Yasathak. *Devrimci Yol.* Ankara: Arayis Yayinlari, 2005.

Baksi, Mahmut. *Her Kus Kendi Surusuyle Ucar.* Stockholm: Wesanen Rewsan, 2001.

Balikci, Faruk, and Namil Durukan. *Olumun Iki Yakasinda.* Istanbul: Berfin Yayinlari, May 2004.

Balli, Rafet. *Kurt Dosyasi.* Istanbul: Cem Yayinevi, 1993.

Barkey, Henri J. "Hemmed in by Circumstances: Turkey and Iraq since the Gulf War." *Middle East Policy Council Journal,* October 2000, Vol. 7, No. 4.

Barkey, Henri J., and Graham E. Fuller. *Turkey's Kurdish Question.* Lanham, Md.: Rowman & Littlefield, 1998.

Bila, Fikret. *Satranc Tahtasindaki Yeni Hamleler: Hangi PKK?* Ankara: Umit Yayincilik, 2004.

Birand, Mehmet Ali. *Apo ve PKK.* Istanbul: Milliyet Yayinlari, January 1993.

Birand, Mehmet Ali. *The Generals Coup in Turkey.* London: Brassey's Defense Publishers, 1987.

Birand, Mehmet Ali, and Soner Yalcin. *The Ozal: Bir Davanin Oykusu.* Istanbul: Dogan Kitapcilik, Sept. 2001.

Bolukbasi, Suha. "Ankara, Damascus, Baghdad, and the Regionalization of Turkey's Kurdish Secessionism." *Journal of South Asian and Middle Eastern Studies,* Summer 1991, Vol. 14, No. 4, 15–36.

van Bruinessen, Martin. "Between Guerrilla War and Political Murder: The Workers' Party of Kurdistan." *Middle East Report,* July-August 1988.

van Bruinessen, Martin. *Agha, Shaikh and State.* London: Zed Books, 1992.

van Bruinessen, Martin. "Transnational Aspects of the Kurdish Question." Working paper. Robert Schuman Centre for Advanced Studies, European University Institute, Florence, 2000. See http://www.let.uu.nl/~Martin .vanBruinessen/personal/publications.

Buldan, Nejdet. *Bitmeyen Yolculuk.* Istanbul: Pencere Yayinlari, 2000.

Buldan, Nejdet. *Savas'a Mektuplar.* Istanbul: Pencere Yayinlari, 2002.

Buldan, Nejdet. *PKK'de Kadin Olmak.* Istanbul: Doz Yayinlari, 2004.

Bulut, Faik. *Filistin Ruyasi: Israil Zindanlarinda 7 Yil.* Istanbul: Berfin Yayinlari, July 1998.

Burkay, Kemal. *Devrimcilik Mi Terorizm Mi? PKK Uzerine.* Ozgurluk Yolu Yayinlari 13, March 1983.

Cakir, Rusen. *Turkiye'nin Kurt Sorunu.* Istanbul: Metis Yayinlari, 2004.

Calislar, Oral. *Ocalan ve Burkay'la Kurt Sorunu.* Istanbul: Pencere Yayinlari, 1993.

Celik, Selahattin. *Agri Dagini Tasimak.* Frankfurt: Zambon Verlag, 2000.

Cemal, Hasan. *Kurtler.* Istanbul: Dogan Kitapcilik, April 2003.

Chubin, Shahram, and Charles Tripp. *Iran and Iraq at War.* London: I. B. Tauris, 1989.

Cobban, Helena. *The Palestinian Liberation Organisation: People, Power and Politics.* Cambridge: Cambridge University Press, 1990.

Cook, Helena. *The Safe Haven in Northern Iraq, International Responsibility for Iraqi Kurdistan.* University of Essex and London: Human Rights Centre and Kurdistan Human Rights Project, 1995.

Criss, Nur Bilge. "The Nature of PKK Terrorism in Turkey." *Studies in Conflict & Terrorism,* 1995, Vol. 18, No. 1.

Criss, Nur Bilge, and Yavuz Turan Cetiner. "Terrorism and the Issue of International Cooperation." *Journal of Conflict Studies,* Spring 2000, Vol. 20, No. 1.

Cubukcu, Aydin. *Bizim '68.* Istanbul: Evrensel Basim Yayin, July 1998.

Curukkaya, M. Selim. *Aponun Ayetleri.* Istanbul: Doz Yayinlari, 2005.

Dagli, Faysal. *Birakuji (Kurtlerin Ic Savasi).* Istanbul: Belge Yayinlari, 1994.

Dirilisin Oykusu (Yalcin Kucuk'un Abdullah Ocalan ile yaptigi roportaj). Wesanen Serxwebun: 59, Subat, 1993.

Dowd, Siobhan (ed.). *This Prison Where I Live: The PEN Anthology of Imprisoned Writers.* London: Cassell, 1996.

Entessar, Nader. *Kurdish Ethnonationalism.* Boulder, Colo.: Lynne Rienner, 1992.

Erdost, Muzaffer Ilhan. *Semdinli Roportaji.* Ankara: Onur Yayinlari, 1993.

Erserver, A. Cem. *Kurtler PKK ve A. Ocalan.* Ankara: Ocak Yayinlari, 1994.

Ersoz, Gurbetelli. *Gurbet'in Guncesi: Yuregimi Daglara Naksettim.* Istanbul: Aram Yayinlari, 2001.

Erzeren, Omer. *Septemberspuren.* Hamburg: Rowohlt, 1990.

Genc, Yuksel. *PKK'de Kadinin Donusum Anatomisi.* Wesanen Jina Serbilind-11, Nisan 2002.

Ghareeb, Edmund. *The Kurdish Question in Iraq.* Syracuse, N.Y.: Syracuse University Press, 1981.

Gunter, Michael M. *The Kurds of Iraq.* New York: St. Martin's Press, 1992.

Gunter, Michael M. *The Kurdish Predicament in Iraq.* New York: St. Martin's Press, 1999.

Gunter, Michael M. "Turkey and Iran Face Off in Kurdistan. *The Middle East Quarterly*, March 1998, Vol. 5, No. 1, at www.meforum.org.

Gurbey, Gulistan, and Ferhad Ibrahim (eds.), *The Kurdish Conflict in Turkey.* New York: St. Martin's Press, 2000.

Gursel, Kadri. *Dagdakiler: Bagok'tan Gabar'a 26 Gun.* Istanbul: Metis Yayinlari, 1996.

Halis, Mujgan. *Batman'da Kadinlar Oluyor.* Istanbul: Metis Yayinlari, 2002.

Harris, George S. *Turkey: Coping with Crisis.* Boulder, Colo.: Westview Press, 1985.

Heper, Metin, and Ahmet Evin (eds.). *State, Democracy and the Military.* Berlin / New York: Walter de Gruyter, 1988.

Iddianame DEP. Istanbul: Orman Yayincilik, 1994.

Il Gostergeleri, 1980–2003. Ankara: T. C. Basbakanlik Devlet Istatistik Enstitusu Yayinlari, 2004.

Imset, Ismet G. *the PKK: A Report on Separatist Violence in Turkey.* Ankara: Turkish Daily News Publications, 1992.

Imset, Ismet G. *PKK: Ayrilikci Siddetin 20 Yili (1973–1992).* Ankara: Turkish Daily News Yayinlari, 1993.

Imset, Ismet. "PKK 5th Congress Update." Available at http://www.etext.org/ Politics/Arm.The.Spirit/Kurdistan/PKK.ERNK.ARGK/pkk-5th-congress .txt.

Inanc, Unal, and Can Polat. *Imrali'da Neler Oluyor: Apo, PKK ve Saklanan Gercekler.* Ankara: Guvenlik ve Yargi Muhabirleri Dernegi, May 1999.

Info-Turk. *Black Book on the Militarist Democracy in Turkey.* Brussels, 1986.

Izady, Mehrdad R. *A Concise Handbook: The Kurds.* Washington, D.C.: Taylor & Francis, 1992.

Jongerden, Joost. *Settlement Wars: An Historical Analysis of Displacement and Return in the Kurdistan region of Turkey at the turn of the 21st century.* Wageningen University Thesis. 2006.

Kaya, Ayhan. *Mordem'in Guncesi.* Istanbul: Aram Yayincilik, 2004.

Kaya, Serafettin. *Diyarbakir'da Iskence.* Halk Yayinlari (no date).

Kaya, Yasar. *Gundem Yazilari.* Cologne: Kurt Demokrasi Vakfi Yayinlari / Belge Yayinlari, 2001.

Kaya, Yasar. *Ocalan'la Konusmalar.* Stockholm: Kurt Demokrasi Vakfi Yayinlari, August 2002.

Kirisci, Kemal, "Post Cold-War Turkish Security and the Middle East." *MERIA Journal*, July 1997, Vol. 1, No. 2.

Kirisci, Kemal, and Gareth M. Winrow. *The Kurdish Question and Turkey: An Example of a Trans-State Ethnic Conflict.* London / New York: RoutledgeCurzon, 2004.

Kizilyaprak, Zeynel Abidin (ed.). *1900'den 2000'e Kurtler.* Istanbul: Ozgur Bakis, January 2000.

Kocoglu, Yahya. *Kursunla Sansur: Gazeteci Cinayetleri.* Istanbul: Ozan Yayin-cilik, 1993.

Kotan, Mumtaz. *Yenilginin Izdusumleri.* Dortmund, Germany: Yunan Kurt Dostluk Dernegi Yayinlari, 2003.

Kucuk, Yalcin. *Dirilisin Oykusu.* Koeln: Wesanen Serxwebun 59, February 1993.

Kundakci, Hasan. *Guneydogu'da Unutulmayanlar.* Istanbul: Alfa Yayinlari, February 2005.

Kutschera, Chris. "Disarray inside PKK." *Current Affairs,* May 2000.

Kutschera, Chris. "Revelations on the PKK." www.chris-kutschera.com.

Kutschera, Chris. "Leyla Zana, the only Kurdish woman MP." www.chris-kutschera.com.

Laizer, Sheri. *Martyrs, Traitors and Patriots: Kurdistan after the Gulf War.* London: Zed Books, 1996.

Lipovsky, Igor P. *The Socialist Movement in Turkey, 1960–1980.* Leiden: E. J. Brill, 1992.

Lyon, Alynna J., and Emek M. Ucarer. "The Transnational Mobilization of Ethnic Conflict: Kurdish Separatism in Germany." Paper prepared for the March 1998 International Studies Association. Available at http://www2.hawaii.edu/~fredr/kurds.htm.

Makovsky, Alan. "Defusing the Turkish-Syrian Crisis: Whose Triumph?" *Middle East Insight,* Jan.-Feb. 1999, The Washington Institute for Near East Policy.

Maoz, Moshe. *Asad: The Sphinx of Damascus.* New York: Weidenfeld and Nicolson, 1988.

Mater, Nadire. *Voices from the Front.* New York: Palgrave Macmillan, 2005.

McDowall, David. *A Modern History of the Kurds.* London: I. B. Tauris, 1996.

McDowall, David. *The Kurds of Syria.* London: Kurdish Human Rights Project, 1998.

Metz, Helen Chapin (ed.). *Turkey: A Country Study.* Washington, D.C.: GPO for the Library of Congress, 1996.

Montgomery, Harriet. *The Kurds of Syria: An Existence Denied.* Berlin: Europaisches Zentrum fuer Kurdische Studien, 2005.

Mumcu, Ugur. *Kurt Dosyasi.* Ankara: Um: AG Vakfi Yayinlari, 1993.

Ocalan, Abdullah. *Ortadogu'nun Cehresini Degistirecegiz.* Secme Reportajlar, Cilt I. Wesanen Serxwebun 69, December 1994.

Ocalan, Abdullah. *Devrimin Dili ve Eylemi.* Wesanen Serxwebun, August 1996.

Ocalan, Abdullah. *Ilk Konusmalar,* Cilt II. Wesanen Serxwebun 91, January 1999.

Ocalan, Abdullah. *3. Kongre Konusmalari.* Koeln: Wesanen Serxwebun 61, 1993.

Ocalan, Abdullah. *PKK IV Ulusal Kongresi'ne sunulan Politik Rapor.* Koeln: Wesanen Serxwebun, March 1992.

Ocalan, Abdullah. *PKK 5. Kongresi'ne sunulan Politik Rapor.* Wesanen Serxwebun 73, June 1995.

Ocalan, Abdullah. *Ozgur Insan: Savunmasi.* Istanbul: Cetin Yayinlari, August 2003.

Ocalan, Abdullah. *PKK'ye Dayatilan Tasfiyecilik ve Tasfiyeciligin Tasfiyesi.* Koeln: Wesanen Serxwebun 60, August 1993.

Ocalan, Abdullah. *Bir Halki Savunmak.* Istanbul: Cetin Yayinlari, June 2004.

Odabasi, Yilmaz. *Eylul Defterleri.* Istanbul: Scala Yayincilik, 2000.

Olmez, A. Osman. *Turkiye Siyasetinde DEP Depremi.* Ankara: Doruk Yayinlari, 1995.

Olson, Robert. *The Emergence of Kurdish Nationalism and the Sheikh Said Rebellion, 1880–1925.* Austin: University of Texas Press, 1989.

Olson, Robert. *The Kurdish Question and Turkish-Iranian Relations from World War I to 1998.* Costa Mesa, Calif.: Mazda Publishers, 1998.

Olson, Robert. *Turkey's Relations with Iran, Syria, Israel, and Russia, 1991–2000: The Kurdish and Islamist Questions.* Costa Mesa, Calif.: Mazda Publishers, 2001.

Ozcan, Nihat Ali. *PKK (Kurdistan Isci Partisi), Tarihi, Ideolojisi ve Yontemi.* Ankara: ASAM Yayinlari, 1999.

Ozdag, Umit. *Turkiye Kuzey Iraq ve PKK.* Ankara: ASAM Yayinlari, 1999.

Ozkan, Tuncay. *Operasyon.* Istanbul: Dogan Kitapcilik, March 2000.

Pamukoglu, Osman. *Unutulanlar Disinda Yeni Bir Sey Yok.* Harmoni Yayincilik, 2004.

Polat, Edip. *Diyarbakir Gercegi.* Ankara: Basak Yayinlari, 1991.

Pope, Nicole, and Hugh Pope. *Turkey Unveiled: Ataturk and After.* London: John Murray, 1997.

Randal, Jonathan C. *After Such Knowledge What Forgiveness? My Encounters with Kurdistan.* New York: Farrar Straus and Giroux, 1997.

Rosenberg, Michael. "On the Road: Archaeological Adventures in Anatolia." *The Middle East Quarterly,* March 1994, Vol. 1, No. 1.

Sahan Timur, and Ugur Balik. *Itirafci: Bir Jitem'ci Anlatti. . . .* Istanbul: Aram Yayincilik, February 2005.

Sakik, Semdin. *Apo.* Sark Yayinlari, March 2005.

Seale, Patrick. *Abu Nidal: A Gun for Hire.* New York: Random House, 1992.

Seale, Patrick. *Asad: The Struggle for the Middle East.* Berkeley: University of California Press, 1990.

Sezal, Ihsan, and Ihsan Dagi. *Kim Bu Ozal? Siyaset, Iktisat, Zihniyet.* Istanbul: Boyut Kitaplari, November 2001.

T.B.M.M. Faili Mechul Cinayetler Arastirma Komisyonu Raporu (Taslak). Istanbul: Birlesik Sosyalist Parti Istanbul Il Orgutu Yayinlari, July 1995.

Tirman, John. *Spoils of War: The Human Cost of America's Arms Trade.* New York: The Free Press, 1997.

Uyan, Memduh Mahmut. *Gerilla Kartaldir.* Istanbul: Belge Yayinlari, 1993.

Wahlbeck, Osten. *Kurdish Diasporas: A Comparative Study of Kurdish Refugee Communities.* London: Macmillan, 1999.

Wallach, Janet, and John Wallach. *Arafat: In the Eyes of the Beholder.* Secaucus, N.J.: Carol Publishing Group, 1997.

White, Paul. *Primitive Rebels or Revolutionary Modernizers.* London: Zed Books, 2000.

Yasar, Hatice. "Stratejiye Donusen bir Siyasi Taktigin Iflasi," *Sterka Rizgari,* Mayis-Haziran 2002: 65–96.

Yuce, Mehmet Can. *Dogu'da Yukselen Gunes* (Cilt I, II). Istanbul: Zelal Yayinlari, April 1999.

Yuce, Mehmet Can. *Bildirgesi.* Cedex, France: Wesanen Sosyalisten Soresger, 2004.

Yuce, Mehmet Can. *Diyarbakir Zindan Direnisi.* Cologne: Wesanen Serxwebun 47, 1991.

Zana, Leyla. *Writings from Prison.* Watertown, Mass.: Blue Crane Books, 1999.

Zana, Mehdi. *Prison No 5.* Watertown, Mass.: Blue Crane Books, 1997.

Zana, Mehdi. *Bekle Diyarbakir.* Istanbul: Doz Yayinlari, 1991.

Zinarin'in Guncesi. Koeln: Mezopotamya Yayinlari, 1999.

Zurcher, Erik J. *Turkey: A Modern History.* London: I. B. Tauris, 1994.

PKK Organization Publications

ARGK Genel Yonetmeligi. Wesanen Serxwebun 75, August 1995.

Direnmek Yasamaktir. Koeln: Wesanen Serxwebun 22, December 1984 (originally released in 1981).

Ideoloji ve Politika Nedir Nasil Ortaya Cikmistir. Koeln: Wesanen Serxwebun 31, May 1986 (originally released in 1978).

Kongra-Gel: Kurdistan Halk Kongresi Demokratik Kurulus Belgeleri. Istanbul: Cetin Yayinlari, December 2003.

Parti Gercekligimizi Tum Yonleriyle Kavrayalim ve Uygulayalim. Koeln: Wesanen Serxwebun 21, July 1984.

"PKK II Kongresine Sunulan PKK-MK Calisma Raporu." Koeln: Wesanen Serxwebun 20, April 1984.

PKK 5. Kongre Kararlari. Koeln: Wesanen Serxwebun 72, 1995.

Serxwebun. "Haki Karer ve Halil Cavgun un Anisi Olumsuzdur." Ozel Sayi 1, May 1979.

Serxwebun. "Teslimiyet Ihanete Direnis Zafere Goturur." Ozel Sayi 4, September 1979.

Serxwebun. *Sehitlerimiz Kurdistan'dir.* 1994 Sehitler Albumu.

Media

Turkish-language: *Cumhuriyet* newspaper, *Hurriyet* newspaper (online), *Milliyet* newspaper, *Yeni Ulke / Ozgur Gundem* (European editions), *Serxwebun*.

English-language: *Kurdistan Report* (London), BBC reports (online), VOA reports (online), also news reports collected at www.globalsecurity.org and www.kurd.org.

Kurdish Websites

Dozame.org (sympathetic to the PKK)
Kurdmedia.com (independent)
PKK.org (PKK's official site)
Hpg-online.com (PKK's armed wing)
Serxwebun.com (PKK's party newspaper)
Rizgari.com (oppositionist)
Kurdistan-Post.com (nonoppositionist)
Firatnews.com (sympathetic to the PKK)
Welatparez.com (oppositionist)
Nasname.com (oppositionist)
Kurdishinfo.com (nonoppositionist)

Human Rights Reports

Amnesty International. *Turkey: No Security Without Human Rights.* New York: Amnesty International USA, 1996.

Council of Europe, Committee on Migration, Refugees, and Demography. "Humanitarian situation of the Kurdish refugees and displaced persons in South-East Turkey and North Iraq." June 3, 1998, Doc. 8131, http:// assembly.coe.int/Documents/WorkingDocs/doc98/edoc8131.htm.

Helsinki Watch. *Freedom and Fear: Human Rights in Turkey.* March 1986.

Helsinki Watch. *Human Rights in Turkey's 'Transition to Democracy.'* November 3, 1983.

Helsinki Watch. *Destroying Ethnic Identity: The Kurds of Turkey, an Update.* March 1988.

Helsinki Watch. *Destroying Ethnic Identity: The Kurds of Turkey, an Update.* September 1990.

Human Rights Watch. U.S. Cluster Bombs for Turkey? December 1994, Vol. 6, No. 19 (at http://www.hrw.org/reports/1994/turkey2/).

Human Rights Watch. *World Report* (Turkey section). 1993–2006 (at www.hrw .org).

IHD Sube ve Temsilciliklerinin. Olaganustu Hal Bolge Raporu 1992. Diyarbakir: IHD Diyarbakir Subesi Yayinlari.

Turkey Human Rights Report. 1991, 1992, 1993, 1994. Ankara: Human Rights Foundation of Turkey Publications.

U.S. State Department. Turkey Human Rights Practices (also called Turkey Country Report on Human Rights Practices). Annual reports, 1993–2005.

Index

About the Author

ALIZA MARCUS, a journalist for more than 15 years, began reporting on Turkey and the Kurdish guerrilla war in 1989. She worked for Reuters News Agency in New York for two years before being named Istanbul correspondent in 1994. In 1995, a Turkish state security court opened a case against her for a news article on the Turkish military's forced evacuation of Kurdish villages: The charge was "inciting racial hatred" under since-repealed Article 312. After being acquitted, she was transferred to the Reuters Middle East/Africa editing bureau in Cyprus. Between 1998 and 2000, she worked in Israel as a special correspondent for *The Boston Globe,* and between 2002 and 2006, she was based in Berlin. Currently, she lives in Washington, D.C.

This photo was taken at a tea house next to a military checkpoint between Sirnak and Cizre in southeast Turkey around 1992. The author is sitting between her driver on the left, and a Turkish military officer on the right. Photo provided by author.